Sexuality

A Reader

EDITED BY

feminist
Review

VIRAGO

Published by Virago Press Limited 1987
41 William IV Street, London WC2N 4DB

This collection copyright © *Feminist Review* 1987

Copyright © in each contribution held by the authors 1987

All rights reserved

British Library Cataloguing in Publication Data

Sexuality: a reader.
  1. Women—Sexual behaviour
  I. Feminist Review Collective
  612′.6′0088042   HQ29

  ISBN 0-86068-802-X

Photoset in North Wales by
Derek Doyle & Associates, Mold, Clwyd
Printed in Great Britain by
Cox & Wyman Ltd. of Reading, Berkshire

UNIVERSITY OF WALES SWANSEA
PRIFYSGOL CYMRU ABERTAWE
LIBRARY/LLYFRGELL

Classmark   HQ 21 547 1987.

Location   banwen

100576522X

Contents

Introduction   1

Feminism and the Politics of Sexuality

A Feminist Sexual Politics: Now You See It,
Now You Don't   19
Beatrix Campbell

Passionate Beginnings: Ideological
Politics 1969-72   40
Sue O'Sullivan

Talking Sex: A Conversation on Sexuality
and Feminism   63
*Deirdre English, Amber Hollibaugh and
Gayle Rubin*

Seeking Ecstasy on the Battlefield: Danger
and Pleasure in Nineteenth-Century
Feminist Sexual Thought   82
Linda Gordon and Ellen DuBois

Abortion: Individual Choice and Social
Control   98
Susan Himmelweit

The Construction of Sexual Difference

Slags or Drags   105
Celia Cowie and Sue Lees

'I Just Wanted to Kill a Woman' Why?
The Ripper and Male Sexuality   123
Wendy Hollway

Jealousy and Sexual Difference   134
Toril Moi

Sexuality and Psychoanalysis

Psychoanalysis: Psychic Law and Order?   157
Elizabeth Wilson

Femininity and its Discontents   177
Jacqueline Rose

Issues around Lesbianism

The Dyke, the Feminist and the Devil   201
Wendy Clark

Becoming Visible: Black Lesbian
Discussions   216
Carmen, Gail, Neena and Tamara

'Everybody's Views Were Just Broadened';
A Girls' Project and Some Responses
to Lesbianism   245
Mica Nava

Upsetting an Applecart: Difference,
Desire and Lesbian Sadomasochism   277
Susan Ardill and Sue O'Sullivan

Pornography and Representation

Sexual Violence and Sexuality   307
Rosalind Coward

The White Brothel: The Literary
Exoneration of the Pornographic   326
Susanne Kappeler

Anti-Porn: Soft Issue, Hard World   340
B. Ruby Rich

Notes on Contributors   355

References   358

Index   371

Introduction

In contemporary feminism the debate on sexuality has caused some of
the most productive and the most painful explorations of the meaning
of sexual difference in western society. This collection brings together
seventeen articles from seven years of writing on sexuality in *Feminist
Review*, centring on the contents of our special issue on sexuality (No.
11, 1982) now out of print. Most of the articles we have chosen also
include new introductions by their authors, especially written for this
volume. These set the pieces in their past and present contexts.

The making of that issue focused and clarified our perspective on
the debates as they stood at that time, and the editorial which we
wrote for it still provides a useful introduction to the political and
theoretical framework in which we have been considering questions of
sexuality:

To politicize sexuality has been one of the most important
achievements of the women's liberation movement. Whatever
differences of theoretical perspective there may be, feminists have
insisted on examining the role of sexuality in the construction of male
domination and female subordination, and this has at least created the
space in which women can refuse sexual exploitation and begin to
reflect on our own desires. Yet the space that ten years of feminist
activity has created remains a fragile one.

We believe that there are two major problems which we must

confront if we are both to widen our understanding and assert our right to an active and pleasurable sexuality of our own. The first problem is one that has always been with us – although its meaning and effects may have been changed to some extent by the past ten years: that is the very extent and power of what might be called the 'masculinization' of human sexuality. A major concern of feminists over the past decade has been to make *visible* the extent to which sexuality has been defined by men and is experienced by women as coercive and objectifying. (It is perhaps one of the most extreme forms of alienation when not even one's sexuality is one's own.) It is easy to forget how difficult it was at the beginning of the women's movement to challenge the male notions of sexual beauty and pleasure. Feminists were harangued and derided, and, unlike the suffragists, we had no male 'friends' to offer reassurance and strength. At the beginning the feminist protest survived only because the challenge was supported by the mass of women who for the first time could identify with other women, or with their own voices. This moment of mutual recognition, after years of self-distrust and isolation, was the material basis for the slogan of 'Sisterhood', a term that is now often derided as either sentimental or dogmatic.

But this suspicion of a slogan – sisterhood – that now seems, perhaps, too simple or too hopeful, also reflects a changing reality which has in part been created by the very success of the women's liberation movement in making at least some forms of sexual exploitation unacceptable (and in making it possible to grow up knowing that there is a women's movement). In this situation the earlier high of self-recognition in other women's voices is no longer possible in the same way. Simply because we have made advances, the old simple certainties have given place to an insistence on the complexity of our experience of sexuality, and the complexity of the construction of our gender.

The second major problem also arises out of advances that have been made rather than any failures of the movement. To acknowledge that we needed to develop both a theoretical understanding of sexuality, and a personal sexual life which supported and sustained us and simultaneously expressed the political objective of feminism, did not just make it happen – it quickly became apparent that the spontaneous will which had led thousands of women with no political experience to organize and speak out with some success could not easily be harnessed to change sexual desire; to practise non-monogamy or to live collectively did not automatically abolish jealousy and romantic longings. At that time there was no theoretical work which could explain the construction of 'femininity'. The very theories that purported to explain sexuality, that is, theories based on psychoanalysis, seemed the most insulting attempts to legitimate male power. We had all experienced the use of concepts such as 'penis envy' and 'castration' to explain and justify assertions that women are inferior. To be beaten around the head with a phallic symbol was supposed to bring us to a chastened acceptance of our inferior genital equipment – the ultimate reality principle. Many of us had grown up with the spectre of the woman who refused to 'accept her femininity'. At one level the women's movement was a collective refusal to accept the feminine role.

Inevitably we then fell back on what might be called commonsense sociology. Our sexuality was conditioned by a 'male' society even more deeply than we had at first realized. However, whilst such behaviouristic perspectives provided at least a way of describing our experience critically, they gave rise to various political as well as theoretical problems. Where was the personal space to fight back? What was the process of deconditioning or reconditioning? What was the basis on which we would attempt to create alternative 'feminist' structures? How can a society be created in which the conditions for sexual freedom exist when we are all so in thrall to our conditioning?

A more promising line of investigation seemed to lie in the work that socialist-feminists were beginning to do on the nature of ideology. Much of this work came originally out of the Marxist feminist study groups which flourished in the early mid seventies. These eventually led to the early socialist-feminist conferences. It is this period that Sue O'Sullivan discusses in her article ... not as an exercise in feminist nostalgia, but to reappraise the experiences of those years in the belief that we can still learn from them.

The discussion on ideology made it possible to form a critique of those political practices hitherto sacrosanct that were based on or influenced solely by 'the relations of production'. It thus became possible within the left to assert and insist on the importance, indeed the centrality, of the women's liberation movement. The notion of ideology as 'false consciousness' was held up for examination and rejected. Ideology was neither 'brain-washing' nor 'the natural'; but the lived reality of subjectivity was recognized, and once ideology was understood as centrally woven into one's identity it became possible to examine its social construction. This led on to the possibility of making an important new analysis of sexuality, by way of Louis

Althusser's Marxist appropriation of certain psychoanalytic concepts. This work made possible certain crucial advances. It has challenged the processes whereby the 'taken for granted' nature of sexual difference is created – that is, the processes whereby we come to believe that an amazingly complex developmental procedure, the creation of femininity and masculinity, comes to seem 'natural'; and a careful distinction has been made between 'gender differences' and 'sexual difference'. We have not solved, but are more aware of the problem of the relation between gender and sexuality. The recognition of fantasy and sexual desire as well as of hatred and jealousy has not only been a relief to many women, but has also allowed feminists to reclaim vital areas of experience which seemed at times to have been banished from the movement we ourselves had created. Our sexuality and gender are contradictory and not just a matter of rational political choice.

Some feminists, nonetheless, have felt that this work has had little influence on the politics of the women's movement (even, for example, on feminist therapy). One reason for this may be the relatively abstract level at which the debate has been conducted. A central disagreement concerning psychoanalysis is whether it accurately reflects a patriarchal world, or whether it reproduces as inevitable women's subordination.

Feminists using a psychoanalytic perspective have tended to focus on the creation and problems of heterosexuality, yet lesbianism has been a central concern of the women's movement almost since its beginnings. It is interesting that in some ways it has been easier for feminists to discuss lesbianism than female heterosexuality. Yet the heterosexual feminist voice and the lesbian feminist voice have often been saying rather different things. For example, when the demand on sexuality was added to the already existing demands of the women's movement at the 1974 National Women's Liberation Conference in Edinburgh, it was expressed as an end to discrimination against lesbians and a woman's right to determine her own sexuality and the issues were then expressed as different but related. The differences are complex and often difficult for feminists. On the one hand, lesbians have been seen as a paradigm of 'sisterhood', as the ultimate pro-woman position; on the other hand, lesbianism incarnates female sexual desire. The first view tends to asexualize lesbians, to emphasize the common oppression of women rather than genital sexuality; the second recognizes the significance of sexual desire but often equates the appearance of sexual desire with that of modes of male domination and female subordination. Wendy Clark takes up these issues in her article, as do Deirdre English, Amber Hollibaugh and Gayle Rubin in the discussion we have reprinted from *Socialist Review*. Although written from different experiences, both articles insist on the strength and importance and above all on the unorthodoxy of female sexual desire. In the United States this debate has tended to concentrate on the issue of sadomasochism, precisely because sadomasochistic desire does raise in an extreme form the question; can dominance and subjugation, to some extent at least, be chosen or created, or are they always determined by a gendered difference which prescribes women's subordination? So whilst sadomasochism might seem outlandish or extreme it does relate to problems that are central to feminism.

This is particularly apparent in the important work at present being produced on pornography and on sexual violence. Both in Britain and the United States campaigns against male violence are undoubtedly the most important and public campaigns being conducted by feminists at present. These campaigns have seen the reworking of the earlier objectives of the women's movement: that is, the exposure of the male control of female sexuality. However, this time what is being discussed is direct physical violence and coercion, and the explanations put forward describe a wholesale split between male and female which can only be resolved when women overthrow male tyranny. The distinction which many socialist-feminists have drawn between sex and gender has become irrelevant to discussions of male violence. Biological sex and political destiny are described as co-terminus – although this description of an eternal antagonism between man and woman does not amount to an explanation of it. ... Rosalind Coward ... attempts in her article on pornography to develop a different approach to the social construction of pornography and questions the political implications of campaigns that simply see pornography as an incitement to, if not a direct cause of, rape.

Her conclusions remain tentative – as do ours – for the attempt to create a materialist explanation of sexuality, and female sexuality in particular, is still at an early stage. Moreover, and rather strangely, it is being constructed in isolation from discussions of other forms of relations such as the family, which have received more attention from socialist-feminists. It remains to be seen whether the discussion of sexuality and gender difference can be advanced without a regeneration of socialist-feminism both at a political and at an analytical level.

Our editorial, and indeed most of the pieces in this anthology, relate issues of sexuality to wider issues within modern feminism, asking how it is possible to think about and live one's sexuality not only as a woman but also, and importantly, as a self-consciously feminist woman. The effect of those debates on issues in the wider political arena in Britain has been profound, but the main difference between 1982 and 1986 is the absence of a direct line between public discussions on sexual mores and the intervention of the women's movement. The ways in which these issues are now fielded is discussed below, but it is perhaps that overt and central connexion which above all characterizes feminist debates on sexuality from the early seventies through the early eighties. The fragmentation, both in Britain and elsewhere, of the women's movement as a broad-based social movement has certainly contributed to this shift in the style and politics of debates on sexuality, but the integration and appropriation of feminist argument into other agendas has also altered the character of the dialogue and changed its dynamic.

■ Current issues

In Britain at present two major issues around sexuality have come to prominence. The first is the question of male sexual violence, which women, collectively and individually, have dragged out of the cupboard of privacy and made a public issue. It started with the Women's Aid movement and its refuges for battered women which exposed the extent of domestic violence and revealed how the prevalent idea of the sanctity of the home left women at the mercy of their men, unprotected by their neighbours or the law. Then there was the network of Rape Crisis lines, giving evidence of the enormous extent of unreported rape and of the way in which women who did give evidence against their rapists in court were themselves treated as criminals. More recently, there has been the emergence of Incest Survivors' groups, revealing how commonly men sexually abuse children within the family and with what traumatic consequences for many of their victims.

These three movements have a number of elements in common. They are movements by and on behalf of women who are increasingly coming to see their experiences as frequent and shared, rather than rare and isolating; who insist on talking about what has happened to them, despite disbelief or a conspiracy of silence; who reject the usual myths that blame women for colluding in their own victimization – the seductive child, the woman who takes risks, the inadequate wife – and who are taking their fate into their own hands by seeing themselves as survivors rather than just victims. They have created a new climate in which it is possible for more women to come forward, so that police, social workers and the media have the impression of a great upsurge in male sexual violence.

The media, on the whole, have striven to accommodate this to the old image of 'sex fiend' versus normal man. Meanwhile, discussions among social workers and allied professionals have taken exactly the opposite direction, especially in the case of battering and incest, where male abuse is seen as part of a 'family pathology' and treatment is directed towards reconstituting family relationships so that the man no longer needs to abuse. Although this pro-family response is not what feminists have called for, at least it means that women and children can report violence and rape without feeling that they are summoning the blunt instrument of the criminal law to disrupt their entire lives and make them an even likelier target for abuse. The increased awareness of incest, and of child sexual abuse in general, has produced some very interesting propaganda directed at children, asserting their right to refuse any contacts they are not happy with, whoever the adult involved, and advising them to seek advice from other adults. If this sort of approach can really be effective it will greatly weaken men's sexual power over children.

This is an area in which campaigns originating in the women's liberation movement have taken off way beyond our sphere of influence. In some ways this is gratifying and a mark of our success; but it is also disturbing to see how little of an explicit feminist voice there is in debates about public policy on the problems we have exposed.

The other current issue is the question of pornography. When *Feminist Review* No. 11 appeared in 1982, pornography and violence against women were central concerns of radical and revolutionary feminists, who saw them not just as a reflection of women's subordination but as primary means of achieving and maintaining that subordination. Women Against Violence Against Women (WAVAW) especially had captured the political and emotional imagination of many, mainly white feminists. They sought to mobilize a wide spectrum of women against pornography, through demonstrations at porn shops and cinemas and through meetings at which the horrific effects of pornography on women were recounted in a highly charged, almost evangelistic atmosphere. The most extreme end of such activity at that time was the fire-bombing of porn shops by disparate autonomous groups known as 'Angry Women'.

Since then, in the United States, some feminists have moved on from the tactics of mobilization, demonstration and zapping towards legal measures against pornography. In 1983, two radical feminists, Andrea Dworkin and Catharine MacKinnon, drew up a model law for the city of Minneapolis. It was not a criminal law making certain forms of obscenity illegal, leading to arrest and imprisonment, but a civil law enabling individuals to sue makers and distributors of pornography, to be enforced by court injunctions. Its supporters claim, therefore, that it is not right-wing censorship but feminist enactment of women's rights. In Minneapolis, its impetus was largely feminist; it was passed by a progressive city council and vetoed by the mayor. But this law has been used as a model elsewhere, most notoriously in Indianapolis, where it was supported by extreme right-wing religious fundamentalists, while there was no local feminist support.

Socialist-feminists and others who have been anxious that anti-pornography campaigns might lead to censorship, implemented in the end by a male-dominated legal apparatus, feel like saying 'I told you so'. And many radical feminists are rethinking their position on legal measures. But does this mean that we should retreat from any politics of pornography and content ourselves with academic analyses of its methods and meanings? Clearly the political strategy will depend upon how we see the role of pornography – how it is related to male violence, whether it is a mechanism for oppressing women or a reflection of our oppression, whether it is part of a continuum of objectifying representations of women and of our sexuality or a distinct category. The articles in the final section of this book are concerned with these analytical questions and their political implications.

But meanwhile, in Britain, there have been a couple of interesting political initiatives which may suggest ways out of the censorship/anti-censorship impasse. One is within progressive organizations where feminists are beginning to find a voice and are persuading their colleagues to ban images that are offensive to women. Within some trade union branches women have tackled 'nudie' calendars and pictures in this way, arguing that an area of an office or factory that is so decorated is effectively a male zone. Within the Greater London Council, before its demise, feminists got adopted a policy banning from London Transport facilities advertisements that present women as sexual objects. Two things are important here: one is that feminists are claiming a relatively small sexism-free space, with the aid of relatively progressive men; the other is that they are attacking the supposedly harmless representations of women, the ones that the conservative anti-porn crusaders *do not* get steamed up about.

The distinction between the conservative and feminist position has come out very clearly in 1986 in the responses to MP Clare Short's initiatives in the House of Commons to ban the 'girlie' pictures commonly shown on Page Three of some popular newspapers. When she first presented her proposal as an amendment to a right-wing censorship Bill, it was greeted with sniggers and guffaws from the Tory back benchers, for whom it is sexual explicitness and not the objectification of women that is at issue. Her amendment was certainly worthwhile, if only for giving some feminist arguments a public airing and showing us how far we have to go before they are even understood, let alone treated as reasonable, in the national legislature. But there is more doubt among many feminists as to whether Clare Short should go forward with her independent Indecent Displays Bill. It is the first Bill here to be formulated with a feminist perspective and it purposely avoids the puritans' stamping ground; but it is still censorship. If it fails it may be the occasion for some telling propaganda; but if it succeeds ...

■ The contents

Such questions about the present moment remain unresolved, as are those discussed in the 1982 editorial. Different feminisms have produced very diverse takes on the politics of sexuality, and in an important sense that range and diversity of opinion and analysis has been one of the most generative and stimulating qualities of the debate – though it has at times, been both divisive and frustrating to any sense of an overarching coherence of feminist thought or an agreed agenda on sexuality for the women's liberation movement. The essays included in this book by no means represent that full range of discussion, nor do they provide a single socialist-feminist position on sexuality. Rather, they suggest that even within a materialist analysis very different theoretical perspectives and political strategies can be developed. The more recent articles in this collection which extend the discussion of psychoanalysis, pornography and particular issues in the politics of lesbianism cannot be unproblematically assimilated with a more general feminist politics. The very different paths followed here, once one has left behind the notion of a natural and naturally divided sexuality, should suggest not only the theoretical difficulty of the issues at stake, and their cultural complexity, but also the productive possibilities for change in thinking about them in various ways. Most of the articles argue against replacing dominant values with a narrowly held feminist moralism; equally, most of them are unwilling to consign sexuality to a social and psychic space untouched by the ethical and political. Instead they are concerned with clearing new ground for future debate and practice.

We have divided the articles in this book into five sections. 'Feminism and the Politics of Sexuality' examines some of the assumptions underpinning feminist sexual politics past and present. Beatrix Campbell's article, first published at a time when some women were castigating the women's movement for anti-lesbianism, caused controversy by arguing that the radical feminist position, in dismissing men as irredeemable and idealizing lesbianism as the appropriate feminist sexuality, simply obscured the problematic of female heterosexuality and hindered the formulation of a feminist sexual politics. She contrasted the current narrowness of focus on sexual questions with the more open and exploratory positions of earlier days, when consciousness-raising groups provided a forum in which women's sexual demands could begin to be formulated.

Sue O'Sullivan's 'Passionate Beginnings' also reflects approvingly on the legacy of the period 1969-72. She maintains that the twin practices of consciousness-raising and high-profile demonstrations for propaganda purposes (like those against the Miss World contests) were radical and widely influential ways of challenging women's internalized oppression and their acceptance of pre-given social and sexual roles. While critical of some aspects of that phase and appreciative of theoretical developments since, she argues for a return to radical activism as a means of taking feminist ideas to a wider audience of women.

In 'Talking Sex', a group of North American women, some of them associated with SAMOIS and well-known in the USA for their liberationist views, discuss the anti-pornography campaigns there as an example of feminist attitudes to sexuality. They suggest that women's legitimate fear of male violence and sexual abuse, which has coloured feminist attitudes towards sex since the nineteenth century, so influences current feminist sexual politics that anti-sexism is in danger of being confused with a rejection of sex. They would like to see some of the gains of the sexual liberation movement of the sixties extended to women, and for this to happen, they argue, there has to be freer discussion of sexual issues than is presently possible in the women's movement.

The legacy of earlier feminist approaches to sex is assessed by Linda Gordon and Ellen DuBois in 'Danger and Pleasure in Nineteenth-century Feminist Thought'. They discuss two conflicting traditions: the 'social purity' movement which emphasized the dangers of sex the better to organize resistance to sexual oppression; and another, always a minority tradition among feminists, stemming from the 'free love' and utopian movement of 1820-40 and represented in the early twentieth century by women like Emma Goldman and Margaret Sanger, which asserted women's right to be sexual. The latter current, they argue, was limited by its conception of female sexuality as exclusively heterosexual and by the distance it took from its feminist heritage.

In the closing article of this section, Susan Himmelweit reflects on her experience of helping to organize opposition to the Corrie Bill of 1980 which proposed restricting abortion rights, and comments on the wide popularity of the slogan 'a woman's right to choose'. She argues that this position, although important in building a broad defensive campaign, may be counter-productive for women in the long run: it accepts the popular notion of 'separate spheres', confining issues around reproduction to the realm of the private and individual, and denying the possibilities of struggle and change in that area.

The next section concentrates on the social construction of sexual difference. Celia Cowie and Sue Lees explore the 'slag/drag' opposition as this is understood by a group of North London schoolgirls, and so illuminate the ways in which young women learn to accept the idea that male sexuality is 'naturally' predatory, while they are condemned to negotiate the boundary between sexual unattractiveness and an active sexuality.

Wendy Hollway studies the press reports of the 'Yorkshire Ripper' trial of 1981 and shows how legal, psychiatric and journalistic discourses co-operated to mark the similarity between Peter Sutcliffe's sexuality and that of other men. In doing so, she argues, they place male sexuality – which, all agreed, contains an element of 'normal' aggression – beyond scrutiny.

Toril Moi's article attempts to explain the fact that women are more often jealous, but men more morbidly and violently so. She draws on psychoanalysis – one account of the construction of human sexuality – to reveal the differing constitution of male and female jealousy: women's containing a strong element of *loss*, leading to depression, men's of *rivalry*, leading to paranoia. However, she maintains, psychoanalytic explanations are not in themselves sufficient to explain this difference: we need social and historical explanations to account for the fact that, for example, women more often have cause to be jealous because men are more often unfaithful, and for the high incidence of male violence towards female sexual partners.

The question of the value of psychoanalysis for feminism has been the subject of lively, recurring debate within the women's movement. The section on psychoanalysis covers some of the ground of the debate. In 'Psychic Law and Order?', Elizabeth Wilson criticizes the psychoanalytic tradition for its account of women's sexual identities as fixed – in marked contrast, she suggests, to the uncertainty Freud himself showed towards the question of female psychic development. To show women as locked in a structure of psychic difference, as she claims Juliet Mitchell does, is as determinist as the more traditional biologism from which Mitchell attempts to rescue Freud. Psychoanalysis ignores changes in family forms and other material factors that might open up real possibilities for restructuring sexual identities, Wilson points out, and it also, notoriously, fails to account for lesbianism.

Jacqueline Rose, on the other hand, charges that Elizabeth Wilson and others who attack psychoanalysis are helping to prolong its marginalization in British culture, and so to block its radical insights. These, she argues, could make an important contribution to feminism. Freud's notion of the unconscious as disrupting the process of emergence of a coherent identity explains the failure, especially within women, of the process of sexual and gender differentiation. Lacan and Mitchell, both targets of Wilson's criticism, represent this radical moment within psychoanalysis. Rose concedes that the idea of a fractured self may not assist feminist efforts to organize around the commonality of women's interests, but she insists on the value of psychoanalysis as a theory which makes it possible to approach subjectivity as a political problem.

The articles gathered under the heading 'Issues around Lesbianism' are concerned less with lesbian sexual practices than with the question of lesbian identity. Wendy Clark in 'The Dyke, the Feminist and the

Devil' contrasts pre-feminist notions of lesbian identity with its new definition within feminism. Feminism has undoubtedly provided a much more positive image for lesbians; but this, she argues, has been at the cost of weakening the autonomy of lesbianism as a sexual preference. Very often lesbianism has been equated with feminism, when the more valuable course would be to re-examine the neglected heritage of lesbian identities in the light of the latter.

The discussion among Black lesbians (from No. 18, the Black feminist issue of *Feminist Review*) explores the interaction of lesbianism with other social and political identities: feminist, Black and socialist. The four participants propose that Black lesbians should work together to create a strong basis from which to make demands of the Black, feminist, gay and socialist movements. From this complex and often exposed position, they argue against the simplicities of regarding either patriarchy or capitalism as the only, or the primary, organizing structure of oppression.

Mica Nava, in 'Everyone's Views Were Just Broadened', shows how a small group of young women, lesbian and heterosexual, can overcome the limits described earlier by Cowie and Lees. Through a series of interviews, she traces how, by mutual support, they were able to challenge the sexist and heterosexist assumptions of at least a section of their local community, their parents and peers. This article stimulated a considerable response (part of it published in *Feminist Review* No. 14) from readers objecting to a discussion of lesbian issues by a heterosexual woman. *Feminist Review* did not consider the article anti-lesbian and still does not: one of our reasons for publishing it was our objection to the attempt to censor it (by exclusion from the book for which it was written) on these grounds.

Susan Ardill and Sue O'Sullivan's 'Upsetting an Applecart' is an account of a bitter struggle in the London Lesbian and Gay Centre over whether SM (sadomasochism) groups should be able to meet there. It illustrates vividly the quality of much of the internal politics of the women's movement over the past few years, where difference among women – often marked out by cross-cutting divides and claims to represent the most multiply oppressed category – has superceded sisterhood. It illustrates, too, the way in which British debates reflect and transform debates in the United States. And it highlights the central and curious position that questions of sexuality have come to occupy within feminism: the battle 'was ostensibly about sexuality and yet sexuality was hardly mentioned in detail'.

The articles in the last section offer differing, sometimes conflicting views of pornography and the appropriate feminist response to it. Rosalind Coward defines pornography as a system of representations of sex which make regular use of certain codes of meaning. It is not the representation of sex itself that is offensive, she argues, but the conventional messages of pornographic representation; and these are not peculiar to pornography. The representation of women as submissive and available to men is commonplace across the whole span of visual culture. Thus, Coward concludes, the attack on pornography is misconceived: what is required is opposition to sexist representations generally, on grounds independent of both permissive and anti-sex positions.

Susanne Kappeler takes D.M. Thomas's bestselling novel _The White Hotel_, and the critics' reaction to it, as a case of the interaction between the pornographic and the literary, showing how the one is redeemed by the other from 'culture's dustbin'. Pornography, she argues, is a vivid illustration of our generally sexist culture. The main elements of _The White Hotel_ – the masochistic sexuality of the central female character, the Nazi sadism at Babi Yar – are the ordinary ingredients of pornography, mystified and made respectable by the 'literary' bad faith of the novelist and his critics.

B. Ruby Rich's discussion of the much-screened Canadian anti-pornography film _Not a Love Story_ also rejects the simple distinction between pornography and eroticism. It enables an evasion of the hard issues that feminism has posed and a retreat into the relatively soft politics of legal restrictions and social hygiene. She argues that the film's narrative, its camera technique and its use of pornographic footage all potentially contradict its overt message, revealing the dangers of attempting to operate within the assumptions of middle-class heterosexual moralism.

The articles in this book do not constitute a coherent theory of sexuality, socialist-feminist or otherwise, but there are some common themes and concerns that run like a thread through many of them. There is an emphasis on the social construction of sexual identity – opposed equally to the perceived biologist elements in Freud, and the essentialism of some feminist theories of women's 'natural' sexuality. There are pleas for the recognition of both a separate lesbian identity (one not based on hatred of men) and the rights of heterosexual women to negotiate sexual relations with men on a more equal basis. There is an insistence that sexuality is constructed differently in different historical periods. (There is also a surprising lack of discussion around sexuality and class in most of the articles.) But above all, there is an optimistic belief that, though the sexual arena is indeed a battlefield, it can and could also be a site of pleasure. We still have a lot to learn about our desires and relationships – hence the need for broader-ranging and more open discussion of sexual issues in the women's movement than is the case at the moment.

FEMINISM AND THE POLITICS OF SEXUALITY

A Feminist Sexual Politics: Now You See It, Now You Don't

Beatrix Campbell

This was written in the late 1970s when sexual politics seemed to be the site of an implosion within the Women's Liberation Movement, which was no longer a safe and sisterly place. Almost more than class or nationality, sexual desire and orientation seemed to divide and disturb. So perhaps the objective of the piece was nostalgic: in backtracking across some of the sociological literature which predated women's liberation, it was searching for some common ground that both lesbians and heterosexual women could share. Its limited object was the myth of 'the sexual act', a myth whose history and function was the representation of patriarchal heterosexuality as inevitable, natural *and* complete. *From the very beginnings of women's liberation in the 1960s, the concept has been problematized, just as from its very beginnings the Women's Liberation Movement created the context in which both heterosexuality and lesbianism were possible. The critique of patriarchal heterosexuality was implicitly a critique of heterosexism too. So this politics implied the reconstruction of heterosexuality, and the embrace of lesbianism.*

The challenge of separatism on sexual politics, and particularly the 'political lesbianism' of the late 1970s, was met, however, by what seemed to be a defensive retreat. Lesbianism had always been represented by some heterosexual women as 'other', something with which they had nothing in common. Lesbianism was, and still is, blamed by some heterosexual feminists for the political pains of women's liberation, for detonating the sanctuary of sisterhood. On the other hand, while heterosexuality's retreat sometimes seemed to render it heterosexist too, separation sometimes seemed more concerned with the power of masculinity, or rather masculinity as power, than with desire for the 'feminine' – something which all too rarely determines the terms of discussion about lesbianism.

As a lesbian, I was opposing separatism's reduction of our political problematic to 'men are the enemy', because it stood in direct opposition to sisterhood, because it abandoned the development of strategic sexual politics for the real world in which women are never only powerless victims, and because it seemed to be about neither women nor the erotic. I was also opposing the heterosexism of some heterosexual feminism – the refusal to create alliances with lesbians, the construction of lesbians as the problem, and the reduction of political positions to sexual orientation. I, for one, am a lesbian who is fed up with my critique of masculine power within the labour movement being covertly judged with: 'Well, she hates men.'

The article does not deal with the emergence of psychoanalysis, and feminism's critical deployment of it, which has massively expanded the parameters of feminist sexual politics. Nor does it deal with the bold explorations within lesbian feminism of the relationship between power and desire.

There was a time when feminism was caricatured as being obsessed with orgasm and life's private parts. It couldn't and probably wouldn't be now, not least perhaps because of the demise of a *feminist sexual politics* as an optimistic feature of the women's liberation movement. The time is ripe to review our sexual politics, and I get the feeling anyway that there are the rumblings of an uprising in the mainstream of the movement. There is dissatisfaction among lesbian, celibate and heterosexual women certainly, but the greatest sense of grievance is among heterosexual feminists who've felt outcast – they're the Fifth Form Remove, the bad girls who smoke in the changing room and go with men.

Heterosexuality has to feature in our politics as more than a guilty secret; indeed, in order that women mobilize any political combativity around it, it must be restored as a legitimate part of feminism's concern. It is, after all, the primary sexual practice of most women. It also needs to be present to help clarify lesbianism's place within feminism. Lesbianism is a specific sexual practice between women, with its own history and culture; it is not *the same as* sexual expression between women, political rejection of men, or a historically specific sexual liberation movement.

It's a commonplace to say that feminism in part grew out of the sexual and student revolutions of the 1960s. What's less clear is why and how. Any account of that period is doomed to be selective and subjective. So, after owning up to both, I'd say that there were two important themes in women's response – an ambiguity about sexual freedom at the expense of sexual protection (actually it's probably doubtful whether the men ever thought that their sexual freedom meant we could have it too) and an incipient critique of patriarchal heterosexuality.

The sixties evoke a little less than nostalgia. It is not so much a remembered resistance to men's clamour for sex, but that it was more of a rather antique variety. No doubt there was, too, a certain lack of sympathy with an ideology of freedom that did not acknowledge the non-equivalence of men's and women's social and sexual position. For many women historically men's sexual freedom was associated with the loss of women's protection, albeit a protection associated with dependence. Having said that, the permissive era had some pay-off for women in so far as it opened up political-sexual space. It permitted sex for women too. What it did not do was defend women against the differential effects of permissiveness on men and women. It was a sexual revolution that implied the separation of sex from reproduction, but that remained implicit and besides, then as now, there was no *absolute* guarantee against the risk of pregnancy. But anyway, it was primarily a revolt of young *men*. It was about the affirmation of young men's masculinity and promiscuity; it was indiscriminate, and their sexual object was indeterminate (so long as she was a woman). The very affirmation of sexuality was a celebration of *masculine* sexuality.

By the onset of the women's liberation movement, women's critique of the sexual revolution was about the quality of the act. Having bounded into sex with considerable gusto, we were faced with rapid and relentless disillusion. Women were acknowledged to be sexual – the Kinsey Report and Masters and Johnson had shown that already. Men's duty was to satisfy women. That's what the books told us. They just had to be patient in the knowledge that we might be slow in coming, but with the right knack and a strong wrist come we would. It was a waiting game for us and a fitness test for them, where the climax deserved a Duke of Edinburgh award for heroic acts of endurance in deep and dark places. There was no disgrace worse than battle fatigue.

Women's nostalgia for pre-fucking sex rather than that

unmemorable first fuck seems to be for the rampant sensuality of those adolescent fumblings and gropings. When the agonized decision about whether to go the 'whole way' was resolved into 'doing it' the fun seemed to stop. It was down to a quick prelude, known in those days as 'foreplay' (which all the books said was very important to women), and then bang. The books seemed to pre-empt women's disappointment with 'it' when they counselled patience in the face of failure and frigidity. Frigidity, we knew, was a female condition, but having embraced sex nothing could be worse than having to own up to yourself being part of that female condition. In my school, whenever someone did actually 'do it' the collective curiosity about 'what is it like' was never met with celebration. At best it was 'all right'. I don't think that low-profile response, nor the fond memories of endless snogging at parties and bops speak of women's preference for the sensual rather than the sexual, but rather expressed a dumb critique of normative patriarchal fucking. The trouble was, it wasn't even a tentative critique that could be informed by a culture of masturbation equivalent to men's adolescent masturbatory culture, which at least might have given clues. Instead we lurched rather unselfconsciously into feminism either with a mysterious sense of sexual disappointment, or with a strong, yet untheorized sense of the mismatch between the natural order of heterosexual practice and the nature of women's desire.

Initially the women's liberation movement detonated the whole problematic, not least because through the medium of small, consciousness-raising groups women were beginning to organize their ideas about sexual practice together, without men. And this provided women with a political instrument with which to reorganize their sexual relation to men. But despite the affirmation of autonomy, that is, of women's right to organize separately from men, the politics of autonomy remained untheorized, and ultimately fell prey to paralysing confusion as the emergent radical feminist tendency in the movement equated autonomy with separatism. In effect two quite separate things were conflated – political separation for definite means and ends, and lived separation.

Separation as political autonomy has a political function, which is to provide a context in which women prepare their intervention in society; in social relations with both men and women, and in politics. It is a means of organizing that intervention. It is not sanctuary from society. By 1973 the confrontation between socialist-feminists and radical feminists had become chronic, and resulted in the hegemony of radical feminist rhetoric. The guilt and difficulty associated with heterosexual struggles were damned by a rhetoric which castigated it as 'sleeping with the enemy'. No doubt many heterosexual women talked to one another about what they were doing, but there was, and still is, no culture within the women's liberation movement that represented or legitimated their struggles. This had the effect of denying what has been precariously achieved. Heterosexuality as a political problematic was dismissed by radical feminism's dismissal of men. Problem solved.

It is from this perspective that the following notes consider the sexual reform movements that pre-dated contemporary feminism, and review the development of sexual politics within women's liberation.

■ Sexual reform in the twentieth century

A dominant feature of sexual reform movements in the twentieth century, apart from control of fertility, has been the recruitment of women into *active* participation in heterosexuality, in contrast to the fetishistic reticence which demobilized the sexuality of the feminine women in nineteenth-century ideology.

Woman as conundrum is the object of sexual discourse in the twentieth century. Woman as object, a problem for men and a problem for heterosexuality. Until the women's liberation movement, when women became the subject of sexual politics, the quest of sexual reform was, in a sense, to release the dumb insolence and resentful, thwarted immobility of many women's sexual relation to men.

Having constituted the feminine as sexless, the imperative became to reconstruct her, albeit modestly, as (in Simone de Beauvoir's phrase) man's sexual counterpart. The object was to mobilize women's active engagement in sex by disinterring her entombed organicity and restoring bits and pieces of her biology (generally the wrong bits, as it happened) to their 'natural' place and purpose.

Clearly the debates of the sexual reform movements should not be treated as reflecting reality. Their importance for us lies rather in the extent to which they were reference points for contemporary feminist sexual politics. The main preoccupations of these debates were virginity and extra-marital sex; reproduction, sex and political repression, and frigidity and the nature of orgasm.

■ Frigidity and orgasm – now you see it, now you don't

The problems of frigidity and fertility control were the key questions preoccupying the sex reform movements of the early twentieth century. Frigidity was held to be symptomatic of something approaching mass neurosis among women. Frigidity, you will remember, was the diagnosis offered by men to the women they'd failed to 'satisfy' – or rather women who'd failed to be satisfied. Feminine participation, it seemed, could not be guaranteed by spontaneous combustion; since femininity was constitutionally passive, woman had to be wooed and won, patiently. Woman wasn't only passive, however, she was enigmatic. Her engagement demanded virtuosity and depended on man's organizational flair. His failure was her frigidity. Thus feminine sexuality was rendered dependent upon masculine resourcefulness; indeed the masculine sexual project seemed to involve a delicate war against a tendentially frigid femininity.

R.L. Dickinson and L. Beam (Dickinson and Beam, 1932), in the first major medical analysis of marriage, revealed dreadful pain and maladjustment. Of the 1,000 cases they studied only 363 were 'adjusted' and without complaint. Some writers suggested – tentatively – that frigidity could be seen as covert rebellion. One survey of about 150 women said that some described the pain of sex not as frigidity 'but lack of consent'. 'It takes two persons to make one frigid woman', said the sympathetic Dickinson, a gynaecologist who had worked with women for forty years. 'Frigidity is best understood as a positive quality and cannot be translated into absence of sexual desire'. British sex reformers such as Dora Russell, Stella Browne and Marie Stopes strenuously affirmed women as sexual beings. They saw this as being confirmed by the evidence offered by women's freer lives during the First World War, the twenties and the thirties; and they rejected oft-repeated allegations of women's sexual apathy or anaesthesia. There is a tone in some of their work of resistance to, or impatience with, feminist antecedents who had advocated sexual restraint, and cold, sex-denying women. Stella Browne deplored this: 'Cold women', she declared, have 'a perfect mania for prohibition as a solution for all ills' (Browne, 1915.)

Dr Magnus Hirschfield, founder of the World League for Sexual Reform, which attracted participation from individuals such as Dora and Bertrand Russell, Bernard Shaw and Vera Brittain as well as from marriage and birth control counsellors operating in working-class districts, warned of the devastating effect on men of women's frigidity, and produced graphs to show the unfortunate effect of the different *pace* of arousal in men and in women. He attributed the problem to the 'divergence between the curve of sensual pleasure in the male and the female: the man has passed the peak point of sexual excitement while the woman is still getting there' (Hirschfield, 1953). Failure to reach orgasm, recorded explicitly or suggested implicitly, operated for anywhere between one-third and two-thirds of women in most of the case studies carried out in the first half of the twentieth century. Problems of pregnancy and the question of orgasm were the fundamental issues which emerged in the work of East London counsellor Janet Chance, who reported on her work with the Bow Marriage Education Centre to the 1929 Sexual Reform Congress; while according to Hannah and Abraham Stone, failure to reach orgasm 'is perhaps the most frequent sexual complaint among women who are otherwise entirely normal' (Stone and Stone, 1952).

But despite the good intentions of sexual reformers, their movement suffered from fatal flaws which derived from its location of woman as *the* problem for heterosexuality. This meant that although birth control was advocated alongside the positive affirmation of women's sexuality, there was no critique of 'normal' heterosexuality and its essentially (for women) procreative mode. Thus its form always put women at risk of pregnancy. Secondly, there was (and is) an assumption of necessary complementarity between men's and women's sexual (as against procreative) faculties, which meant that the clitoris was necessarily subsumed to the vagina as the throne of the women's sensuality.

Thus the radical implications of what Simone de Beauvoir later referred to as the independence of the clitoris for women's non-procreative pleasure were dissolved, which allowed the concept of the sex act to depend both on procreation and the penis. Dora Russell's views illustrate this difficulty and some of the social implications of women's independence. She welcomed disruption of enforced chastity and compulsive monogamy and encouraged a light-hearted treatment of sex-play (not least amongst the children in her school – she commented that the children still made jokes about sex). That was okay, she said – 'the sexual process is, after all, rather odd' – but she reprimanded those flighty feminists who were busy earning their own living and being sexually independent, since they were at the same time thwarting parenthood.

For women, she insisted, the sexual moment was but 'the merest incident in the satisfaction of the older impulse to gain power and abundant and eternal life by multiplying her own body' (Russell, 1927). For her, sexual freedom was not to be achieved at the expense of maternity – a dilemma many contemporary feminists share. And there were few in her time (but a few there were) who were not prepared to celebrate maternity.

A later sexual reformer, Dr Eustace Chesser, who wrote numerous sex handbooks and became momentarily notorious in Britain in the fifties on account of some of his views, adopted a similar position in opposing 'free love'. He polemicized against the work of individuals such as the American radical judge, Ben E. Lindsay, who became the object of a Ku Klux Klan witchhunt because he advocated 'companionate love', a variant on the trial marriage theme. Chesser alerted his many readers to the fate worse than death that awaited the 'free woman', who, he claimed, envied married women, since the sex act for women was only a prelude to satisfaction of the maternal instinct 'and finding joy in the life of the family'.

Even those sexual reformers who were feminist usually represented the subject of sexuality as male, which had the effect of blurring the distinction between women's reproductive and sexual faculties. It would be too simple to argue that in this schema the clitoris was banished. It was always there, sort of. Havelock Ellis claimed that its importance had been recognized only in the latter half of the nineteenth century (Ellis, 1928). So little had been known about it that in 1593 a man by the name of Columbus first claimed to have 'discovered' this organ, although it was later shown that other anatomists had discovered it before. Presumably its discovery was as much a surprise to its owners as the discovery of America was to its indigenous occupants.

It is not so much denial of the clitoris that is striking as its appearance and disappearance in theories of female sexuality and, where it is acknowledged, its displacement in favour of the mythologized vagina in defence of the penis as the organizing principle of the sexual act. This displacement allows the idealization of the simultaneous orgasm and a plethora of neurotic symptoms, notably premature ejaculation and frigidity. It has been common for frigidity to be blamed on premature ejaculation. Marie Stopes emphasized that 'mutual orgasm is extremely important'. Sadly, too often the man 'comes so swiftly that the woman's reactions are not really ready, and she is left without it'. She condemned *coitus interruptus*: 'while it may have saved the woman the anguish of bearing unwanted children yet it is very harmful to her, and is to be deprecated. It tends to leave the woman in "mid air" as it were; to leave her stimulated and unsatisfied.'

The Dutch gynaecologist, Thomas Van de Velde, typified the progressive view. He recognized the clitoris as 'an organ of voluptuous sensation exclusively' (Van de Velde, 1928) and acknowledged women's multi-orgasmic capacity, but still shifted that sensibility to the vagina by insisting that the final climax was realized on the signal either of the contractions of a man's penis during his orgasm, or by the impact on the vaginal walls of his ejaculation: 'It forms a fit and perfect line in the wonderful chain of love process.' The procedures envisaged bestowed the favours of loveplay on the clitoris until the lady was suitably aroused and the pair reached a 'crescendo of emotion' at which the penis penetrated and it all happened.

Following Havelock Ellis, Van de Velde asserted that in the sexual act man and woman exult in male dominance; the act expresses the 'essential force of maleness', for male eroticism 'belongs to the moment of coitus and not to its preliminaries. If the force fails to ignite the organ of voluptuous sensation then the man should manipulate her to "concert pitch" and if that, too, fails then the objections are far from trivial' (Van de Velde, 1928). Our man on sex, Chesser, followed this patriarchal model, though with rather less bravado, because women are slower than men they have to be stimulated by loveplay until 'union' is desired and (hopefully) mutual orgasm takes place.

The Stones in their classic and much-reprinted *A Marriage Manual* (1952) described the clitoris as 'perhaps the main seat of the woman's sensuous feelings'. Its stimulation is the prelude to the big moment. It induces a state of: 'readiness for entry and mutual orgasm'. However, they point out that many women never reach orgasm. This high rate of failure seemed inexplicable. Perhaps it was anatomical, they suggested. They acknowledged, too, that 'in many cases the sexual response can only be evoked by direct stimulation of the clitoris' and then slipped into a prescription for normative fucking which was supported by the commonly held faith that while the clitoris remained the erotic place *par excellence*, the vagina, if worked on, might become sensitized and even have primary erotic sensation transferred to it. The success rate was expressed in Chesser's calculation, based on American and European studies, that 70 per cent of women never achieved satisfaction.

Up to this point only a particular genre of sexual reform has been considered, which does not incorporate the impact of psychoanalysis. Without offering an account of this, it is important to note the consensus – within which sexual reform and psychoanalysis co-existed – about the subsidiary role, or immaturity, of clitoral orgasm. However, a crucial divergence erupted over precisely the role of the clitoris, and took a particularly acrimonious form in the fifties after the publication of the Kinsey Report in 1953.

Within the genre of sex counselling a poignant confrontation with the contradictions lurching around all this stuff is to be found in the work of Dr Helena Wright in Britain. Her book *More About the Sex Factor in Marriage* (1947) is a model: the sole purpose of the clitoris is pleasure; man has the joy of arousing woman and 'creating in her an ardour equal to his own' ... at the moment of sufficient excitement the woman is ready to receive the male, the mutual climax consummating the act is completed: 'thought is abandoned, a curious freeing of the spirit, very difficult to describe ... a pleasure of the soul ...' In this account, which typifies contemporary sentimentality, there are caveats, however, which are significant in her later revisions of this scheme. First she insists on two essential conditions for success; constant contact with the clitoris and free hip movement. Clitoral sensation seems natural in every woman, she observes. Vaginal excitement is more difficult. Although 'theoretically it might be said the ideal type of feminine sensation is concerned with the vagina alone ... that ideal is seldom realized'. In a classically suggestive phrase she declares; 'nearly all women find vaginal sensation through, as it were, the gateway of clitoris sensation ...'

More than twenty-five years later she criticized the naive view that the main problem of the day was ignorance, largely it seems because she had to face her readers' complaints that they'd rigorously followed her blueprint but it didn't work: 'Try as we may my wife can attain no orgasm from intercourse', complained a reader, one among many. Wright's attention was thus dramatically drawn back to the site of woman's pleasure, and she isolated three major misunderstandings. Firstly, there was a failure to grasp the difference between general sexual response and orgasm; secondly, there was a lack of understanding as to the unique role of the clitoris; and lastly there were preconceptions about women's feelings during intercourse, based on the male pattern. This last produced the belief that during penetration

> women will have an answering orgasm felt in the vagina induced by the movement of the penis ... so strongly held and widespread is this expectation that it can be said to amount to a penis-vagina fixation. (Wright, 1947)

Her autocritique, which pre-empted the findings of the 1953 Kinsey Report, reflected upon 'being confronted for many years by the complaints of patients'. In vain they had followed her advice and still failed to achieve vaginal orgasm. Thus,

> I began to criticize this universal demand ... as soon as I began
> to shake myself free of the current ideal and expectations, and to
> doubt the efficacy of the penis-vagina combination for
> producing an orgasm for a woman, the path was cleared and
> progress began to be made. (Wright, 1947)

Having snuffed out the vagina she then confronted the nature of
orgasm. Here, too, confusion was rampant among readers and
patients; it was clear that many had no idea what an orgasm was like.
So she told them. Firstly, anyone who only *thinks* they've had one
hasn't. Secondly it isn't a general sensation, but very specific; like a
sneeze it is preceded by tension, there's a short explosion, then relief,
and it happens in one place only – in the relevant organ.

However, the nub of Wright's self-criticism was bitterly contested in
sex literature. What is fascinating from our point of view is that what
the women's liberation movement may have thought it invented, in
Anne Koedt's essay 'The Myth of the Vaginal Orgasm', had a long
pre-feminist history.

Among the influential analysts, clinicians and counsellors, there had
long been little doubt as to the erotic significance of the clitoris.
During and after the Second World War empirical research confirmed
Wright's conclusions, and there is evidence among some sexologists of
growing confidence in challenging what Dickinson called 'phallic
fantasies'. However, their work was still treated as more or less
scandalous. Furthermore, the absence of a substantial feminist
movement after the First and still more after the Second World War
meant that the implications of such work could not readily be pursued
or generalized. It seems to have fallen on deaf ears. It is worth noting
that the very influential Chesser continued in the wake of Wright's
mea culpa to write mushy manuals which replicated the very
mystifications which Wright had tried to disentangle. Perhaps it is an
index of the political mood in Britain after 1945 that Chesser's own
sex report, modelled on Kinsey's, and which provoked something of a
scandal, aroused this response less because of its sexual than because
of its moral implications. Chesser later had an essay in a British
Medical Association handbook banned. Despite his rather devastating
findings on the lack of 'satisfaction' among women, Chesser went
down as the man who got banned for saying chastity was outmoded.

At the heart of the conundrum, which Wright was to spot and later
sexologists were to confront, too, was the problem of the absence of
any necessary correspondence between the reproductive act and the

orgasmic moment for women. A number of other myths came under attack in the Kinsey Report (Kinsey, 1953). Kinsey made the outrageous proposal that there was no essential difference between the infant and the adult orgasm – which was to prove one of its major points of contention for Freudian opponents. The Report also suggested a much more widespread engagement in the erotic than the moralists thought proper. Thirty per cent of those questioned by Kinsey recalled preadolescent heterosexual fun and games, and 33 per cent recalled homosexual practices, the latter being very important in teaching women how to masturbate successfully; indeed it seems to have been a more relevant pedagogical resource than heterosexual hanky-panky. Sixty-four per cent of married women had experienced orgasm before marriage, mostly through masturbation, half had had pre-marital coitus, and 71 per cent achieved orgasm in 'marital coitus'.

The Kinsey Report was a sociological survey which had enormous impact, both because of the scale of its sample (although this was predominantly middle class) and because of its committed findings which tended to challenge the penis-vagina fixation as well as myths about women's chastity. It became a major issue of public concern. Among Kinsey's most virulent antagonists were Freudian fundamentalists who not only challenged the basis of the study (which did not calculate for *unconscious* response) but also the criteria for frigidity. Edmund Bergler, who fiercely contested the Kinsey findings, insisted that 'under frigidity we understand the incapacity to have a vaginal orgasm during intercourse ... the sole criteria of frigidity is the absence of vaginal orgasm' (Bergler, 1954). Not surprisingly he claimed a frigidity rate of between 80 and 90 per cent. This kind of claim was to founder on the clinical evidence produced a decade later by William H. Masters and Virginia Johnson (1966). But even before this, Albert Ellis was to make an intervention in the Kinsey debate which anticipated modern feminism. He rejected the Freudian notion that clitorial orgasm was immature and confirmed that in most women it was the occasion of greatest intensity. It was 'clinically certain' that some women 'who experience the most intense kinds of orgasm imaginable, experience it only or mainly as a result of clitoral (or other non-coital) stimulation' (Ellis, 1953). There was no evidence, he said, that what was known as the vaginal orgasm came from that place, nor any that the clitoral orgasm didn't have a more general pelvic effect. Later he was to infer from the Kinsey Report a more general critique of the sex manuals' 'emphasis on coital techniques' and suggested attention to the labia and clitoris 'rather than concentration on coital positions'.

Masters and Johnson were to consummate this decades-long project. 'Phallic fantasy' had fostered the way that 'clinical error has dominated the assignment of the clitoral function ... The primary focus for sexual response in the human female's pelvis is the clitoral body' (Masters and Johnson, 1966). Marriage manuals concentrated on clitoral stimulation 'as the basis of adequate coital foreplay' when the 'infinitely more important question' was how to address the clitoris in its own right. Men didn't appreciate this, and vainly went for 'the deepest possible vaginal thrust' followed by 'spastic deep vaginal entrenchment' during ejaculation. Wrong! said Masters and Johnson. But despite these devastating insights they still baulked at the full separation of penetration from the independent interests of the clitoris, because, they argued, vaginal thrusting stimulated the clitoris by 'traction exerted on the wings of the minor labial hood' which enables them in turn to locate the vagina as the 'primary physical means for heterosexual expression for the human female'. Vaginal and clitoral orgasm, for them, became the same thing. (A quaint reminder of the heterosexist equation of penetration with the sex act came in the trial of Jeremy Thorpe, ex-leader of the British Liberal Party, who was accused of having had a homosexual relationship with Norman Scott and of having subsequently conspired to murder him when Scott threatened to make their relationship public, and did begin to make it public. During the trial, Thorpe's alleged involvement with Scott was not represented as 'buggery' but rather as 'the sexual act' or its synonym-penetration, proof that 'real sex' had taken place.)

Kinsey and these other writers fuelled the moral angst which surrounded the sexual debates of the fifties and sixties, and which particularly focused in Britain on homosexual law reform and pre-marital sex. Whatever the crisis in the moral climate, it was clear that people were 'doing it' and on a rather large scale, aided and abetted by an anti-censorship, anti-obscenity law lobby which if it didn't fully embrace any amount of any kind of sex as a good thing, affirmed it as possibly fun, as a sacrament and – when it was written about – as art. The political significance of sexual difference between men and women was increasingly blurred as the sexual revolution took sway, with women's resistance being represented as conservative diffidence. Lesbianism may have had more space to develop, simply as a function of liberalism, but the Permissive Era in the end consolidated the heterosexual imperative. Elizabeth Wilson (Campbell and Deer, 1979) has commented that lesbianism was equated with celibacy. The Permissive Era's object was consonant with the twentieth-century theme described earlier; to recruit women into an active engagement in heterosexuality. The chastity lobby didn't give in, of course, but there were certain facts which reinforced the liberationists, from Kinsey and, in Britain, from the Registrar General himself: in 1950 one quarter of mothers conceived their first child before their wedding day (Wimperis, 1960). But underneath the chastity debate, there remained the core theme – the mystery of women's sexuality, and the implications of women's sexual self-assertion, exemplified in a grumpy satire by Malcolm Muggeridge (before he became totally ridiculous) in which he lamented the substitution of sexual revolution for social revolution. He growled that 'to the self-evident rights in the Declaration of Independence must be added another – the right to orgasm' (Muggeridge, 1965). Writing of the Masters and Johnson study he wondered what could be more gross than the investigation of the female orgasm in a laboratory: 'this surely is the apogee of the sexual revolution, the ultimate expression of the cult of the orgasm'. What he *didn't* own up to was that the problem wasn't just any old orgasm, but *women's*. This dotty volley from Muggeridge is interesting nevertheless for its hostility to the central concern of sexual reform movements in this century – women's sexuality – even though that preoccupation was not necessarily disclosed in the rhetoric of the sexual revolution.

I've gone through all this to indicate some of the ideological conditions out of which a feminist sexual politics emerged, in particular to illustrate the instabilities inherent in the sexual reform movement's approach to heterosexuality. Firstly, it is clear that there was a relative decline of the vagina to a subsidiary role in the representation of women's physical sexuality. Secondly, however, there was still a continuing dependence on the vagina in concepts of heterosexuality. Even though the centre of gravity shifted to the clitoris, the quintessential moment of heterosexuality remained penetration, the sexual act. A feminist heterosexuality has not yet been fully and confidently elaborated that, by making woman subject, marginalizes penetration for women, and in so doing dissolves the notion of the sex act. The necessity of penetration for men had hitherto constructed the moment of penetration as *the* sexual moment. And while feminist heterosexual practice may not exclude penetration, it would seem that it renders it subsidiary for women. I suspect that while this may be the case in practice, indeed surely is the case, feminism's dissolution of the notion of penetration as the sexual act has not been fully brought to the movement's sense of a feminist sexual politics.

■ The women's liberation movement

The subsequent notes are intended to be a polemical review of contemporary British feminism's development of sexual politics.

The first thing that can be said is that feminism more fully politicized sexuality than the advocates of the Permissive Era ever did, both by establishing women as the subject of feminist sexual politics, and by proposing a politics of personal life. Women's liberation was initially concerned to make heterosexuality problematic. And secondly it established orgasm and women's pleasure as a stake in sexual struggle. This shifted the centre of gravity of permissive sexual politics in which women were simply objects of pleasure. Even though it may have been influenced by the permissive radicalism of left sexual politics of the sixties, it readily criticized the Marcusian or Reichian approach for failing to specify the contradiction between men and women and failing to address the patriarchal character of normative heterosexuality. Implicit, too, in the development of feminist sexual politics was a critique of the essentialism inherent in the Marcusian repression thesis, which envisaged liberation of erotic sensuality as a socio-political detonator (Marcuse, 1970). It is a critique that goes much further than latterday libertarian cynicism about the sexual revolution, which has simply expressed a weary disappointment at the ways in which capital, no longer needing compulsive monogamous marriage, has coralled and appropriated the supposedly disruptive impact of sexual liberation (Dahmer, 1978). Feminism was, then, initially concerned to scrutinize heterosexuality as a practice in which femininity itself was constructed. In that sense it went beyond the sixties pleasure programme, even though it may not yet have had available to it a vocabulary that enabled the theorization of sexuality as a site in which femininity is constructed, and is thus a site of combat. A theoretical idiom for this only began to emerge in the seventies, with the application of Althusserian Marxism and psychoanalysis. The typical preoccupations of feminist sexual politics (exemplified by say Whiting, 1972) were with women's active sexual engagement and an opposition to subordination/passivity, together with an insistence on the separation of sex from reproduction.

The political instrument by which sexuality was politicized was consciousness-raising, in which other women provided the means for collective self-recognition. It provided an alternative to the dispersal of women in male-dominated politics, by means of separation, distance, autonomous political space. It is worth recalling that all this was happening in the context of the dominance of heterosexuality as a practice. Most feminists were *in* heterosexuality, and through women's liberation were beginning to be able to *organize* their engagement in heterosexuality. At the very least it encouraged a culture in which a critique of heterosexuality was feasible – and I will argue later that, sadly, this process was thwarted by other political problems within feminism. The effect was to block the growth of confident feminist mobilization around heterosexuality, except insofar as autonomy was a condition of mobilizing *any* feminist critique of heterosexuality. Consciousness-raising was also a provisional means of constructing alternative representations of women, because within that process women were able to make problematic the category 'woman'. Consciousness-raising was a means of opposing habitual ways of being feminine. It also served as a place of resource – one of the functions outlined by the Italian Marxist, Gramsci (Gramsci, 1971) – for the political forms of subordinate social classes or groups (Campbell, 1978). However, the full political potential suggested by this development was not realized – largely because of divisions within the movement from about 1973. But a feminist sexual politics was also thwarted by feminism's approach to sex itself. It would seem that an essential component of feminist sexual politics should be a feminist erotica. But with a few exceptions there's been little enough of that. There has been little space for a feminist erotica which could represent heterosexuality as both erotic and as an arena of contradiction and contestation. There's some contemporary lesbian erotica, though much of it, in my view, tends to be maudlin, complacent or didactic rather than erotic. It still seems difficult to produce an erotica that isn't easily happy or halcyon.

The struggle is undoubtedly not helped by men. Few seem worth wooing. And just as women's relationship to femininity remains problematic, so does our response to masculinity. A simple inversion won't do – the feminization of masculinity, the enervation of men and a celebration of passivity and lack of energy in men, rendering soft sex the 'sound' mode. Then there are those men who assume that feminism produces a simple transition in women from passivity to activity – their dream come true, access to the pyrotechnical lady lover. And of course feminism can be used to beat her over the head if she remains passive.

■ Crisis of sisterhood

Apart from the conflict between socialist-feminism and radical feminism within women's liberation, confidence in the autonomy of the movement cracked also because of the experience of the limits of consciousness-raising on the one hand, and the sense of marginality in relation to political forces outside the movement on the other hand. Furthermore, the movement's internal practice celebrated a form of sisterhood, again through the medium of consciousness-raising, which depended on common identification as the source of collective self-knowledge and the condition of collaboration – it didn't easily accommodate difference. Sisterhood became transposed in some variants of feminism into a cult of woman. It took many forms, from resurrection of the matriarchy, through Earth-Motherhood to bovver-girl with a bottle of Newcastle Brown. What was common to all these modes was a sentimentalization of femaleness and an essentialism based on a cult of women-are-wonderful, or rather women-without-men-are-wonderful, in their natural state, free of men's rude interruptions. Through sisterhood some women searched for authenticity, a female essence, which could be achieved by a voluntaristic choice – to become woman through being with women. The woman cult depoliticized women's sexuality, firstly by romanticizing it and secondly by abstracting it from gendered social relations and practices. This produced a new femininity – it didn't matter that it mirrored entrenched stereotypes, what mattered more was that these modes fetishized women-togetherness. And all this coincided with the increasingly antagonistic contradiction between radical feminism and socialist-feminism. A feminist sexual politics was defeated indirectly by the hegemony of radical feminism. That's not to say that only socialist-feminism could have produced a feminist sexual politics. Socialists in the movement were probably still too tentative about the status of personal life at that time. But rather, it is to say that the conditions for its construction were wiped out by the bust-up between the two major tendencies. Heterosexuality was banished to the swamp. Those women unfortunate enough to remain unreconstructed, languishing in the het. jungle were, in effect, accused not only of allowing themselves to be cosseted and corrupted by men – cowards who chose to sink with the men rather than swim with the ladies – but also of failing politically to prioritize women.

The political sectarianism was armed by radical feminist

appropriation of lesbianism, and now 'political lesbianism', tuned in less to erotic affirmation of women − if nothing else, that's what lesbianism is about − than to a polemical inquisition against women who fuck men. So in that sense it's more about men than about women.

Lesbianism first emerged as a hot issue at the national conference of the women's liberation movement at Skegness in 1971, when a couple of small but powerful Maoist groups fell in round one in their attempts to isolate lesbianism as a bourgeois deviation. That was not only a specific campaign against lesbianism, but also against *any* sexual politics, and reflected their belief that the capital-labour contradiction was sufficient to account for the sexual antagonism. Lesbianism became an issue in its own right, just about, at the movement's national conference in Edinburgh in 1974 with the adoption of the Sixth Demand, which coupled an end to discrimination against lesbians with a general demand for women's right to be sexually self-determining (an unhelpful coupling which still needs to be parted). But it was during 1974-5 that the combat between the two major tendencies assumed a particularly destructive force, over arguments about the nature of the Women's Liberation Workshop in London, and over the presence of men on the International Women's Day marches. The effect was to dismember the Workshop as a centre for the whole movement in London, and to disperse the many groups previously associated with it. Many women in the movement retreated in hurt confusion, and there's a feeling of alienation that still prevails today among many activists − they feel it doesn't belong to them. What was left took on all the characteristics of an exclusive and marginal culture. This was compounded in the autumn of 1974 by the approving serialization over ten issues of the Women's Liberation Workshop Newsletter of a toxic diatribe which had first appeared in the New York radical feminist publication, *Off Our Backs*: 'straight women think, talk, cross their legs, dress, come on like male transvestite femme drag queens. Bisexuality maintains the patriarchy. Lesbianism understood is a revolt against the patriarchy ... Everybody knows from the first minute the Women's Liberation Movement hit that feminism means lesbianism ...' (CLIT, 1974) Half a dozen issues on, the next instalment declared: 'The danger of straight women is their disguise, they look like women ... they are men in disguise.' There we had it. Heterosexual women were dangerous. They weren't even women. There were rather timorous complaints in the Newsletter, but the diatribe went on and on. And just when it seemed to wane there would be a new wave. Radical feminism regrouped, appropriated and inverted Marxist theory and ultimately came up with a novel but strategically inept formulation, ' "workers" control of reproduction'; the novelty wore off, things quietened down, only to erupt at the 1978 Women's Liberation Movement national conference in Birmingham, and then towards the end of 1979 we were gonged into the next round with the emergence of 'political lesbianism' in a debate in the national Newsletter, *Wires*.

To some extent this culture was armed with the vocabulary of the movement's tentative explorations of sexuality, which drew on a perfectly honourable tradition, not least *The Second Sex* by Simone de Beauvoir (1953), which represented penetration as trespass and invasion, and as the moment of women's subordination. Of course it had a certain strength as a critique of patriarchal fucking. It was supported by the argument that penetration was fairly insignificant to women except insofar as it brought pleasure to men and only incidental pleasure to women; and also that penetration was a practice involving risk to women insofar as it was coupled with ejaculation, leaving women with the penalty of pregnancy and total responsibility for contraception. However, the representation of penetration by feminists as *the* moment of heterosexuality's subordination ignored its place as an arena of struggle between men and women, both to transform its meaning for both sexes, and to displace it as the sexual act. Radical feminism drew on a vocabulary of visceral colonialism – we had a plethora of phallic imperialisms, penile tyrannies and so on enumerated in the Newsletter, for example, which in effect rendered the act of penetration and the possession of a penis as, of themselves, constituting domination. And it still goes on. 'Only in the system that is male supremacy does the oppressor actually invade and colonize the interior of the oppressed', writes Leeds Revolutionary Feminist Group in *Wires* (No. 81, December 1979). All this rhetoric flourished in the absence of a feminist erotica and despite the development of theoretical work on ideological practices. The effect was to reduce the mainstream of the movement to dumb insubordination in the sex war, leaving heterosexual struggle to the individual initiatives of women more or less on their own. The representation of penetration as necessarily colonialistic foreclosed any programme of struggle in heterosexual practice.

In the end feminist sexual politics has become an analogue of lesbian politics. This has been primarily expressed in two ways. Firstly it emerges in the slogan 'Any woman can (be a lesbian)'. While no doubt, in a certain sense, true, this denies the specific autonomy of lesbianism within feminism, and it also denies the specific sexual circumstances of most women. Secondly, there has been the equation of lesbianism with prioritization of women and not wasting time on men. Strategically this approach offers only flight from heterosexuality which is represented as sex collaboration equivalent to class collaboration – fraternizing with the enemy. Far from proposing lesbianism as a *possible* practice, with all its important implications of non-dependence on men, within a pluralism of practices in feminism including heterosexuality and celibacy, lesbianism is represented as the *only* possible practice. The new 'political lesbianism' confounds the development of a *sexual* politics by suggesting that a political lesbian 'is a woman-identified woman who does not fuck men. It does not mean compulsory sexual activity with women.' So it isn't even about sex.

These approaches have to be rejected not only because they are undemocratic, but also because they deny any political practice within heterosexuality and they don't safeguard specifically lesbian culture and sex. They *prohibit* the formulation of a feminist sexual politics. What would the conditions for the latter be?

First, pluralism in the movement; second, heterosexuality would have to be legitimated as a field for feminist presence and, third, recognition of feminism's impact on sexual relations with men. Feminist intervention in heterosexuality proposes its reorganization. Radical feminist lesbianism has to deny the possibility of any change in heterosexuality, of course, and its prophecy has been self-fulfilling – we've little idea how women have been able to intervene in heterosexuality; but it also has to deny possible change because its advocacy of lesbianism depends on a failure of heterosexuality – and that, to me as a lesbian, smacks of the familiar slur that lesbians only do it with women because they can't get it together with men. Thirdly, rather than proposing lesbianism as the only possible feminist sexual practice, it seems to me that the autonomy of a lesbian presence as such has to be defended in the women's liberation movement.

Fourthly, it is clear that feminism has enabled both the beginnings of a transformation of heterosexuality and the possibility of a politically supported sexual practice which engages both men and women, and which is neither categorically heterosexual or lesbian; furthermore this can't be represented as the closet gayness which could have been asserted politically by Gay Liberation. Part of the problem here is that on the one hand gayness can't be denied its cultural concomitants, which I think is an effect of so-called political lesbianism, but equally while bisexual practice in the context of feminist politics can't be tarred with the closet brush, it doesn't yet have a political agreement, for which (contrary to how things might seem) common ground exists – it is a shared critique of sexist heterosexuality. But that needs to be armed by a political alliance engaged in diverse and shifting practices.

An essential condition for this must be an organizational form within which the politics of personal life can be developed. That we lack at the moment, because of the demise of consciousness-raising, but without suggesting a nostalgic and uncritical rehabilitation of the movement's early forms it does seem that we need to review that experience with a view to constructing a new political space for personal life.

Passionate Beginnings: Ideological Politics 1969-72

Sue O'Sullivan

Apart from a slight unease on re-reading words written five years ago, my responses to this article are mixed. At the beginning I set a tone I'm now critical of. I said, '... other people's revolutions and struggles moved us' (my emphasis). Although five years ago I was careful to note class and race divisions between women, I still wrote the 'us' inclusively, when in fact I was speaking exclusively of a primarily (never totally) white-dominated experience.

For me, the five years since have been filled with confrontation, erratic change, sporadic 'homework', particularly around racism, anti-semitism and sexuality. Today I would construct a different framework for my recollections – one which I hope would be both more solid and subtle.

The article was purposely specific; it did not describe all women's experiences in consciousness-raising groups in those early years or explore the breadth of influences on different groups of women. I wanted to be very careful in how I situated myself – neither individualizing myself into a corner nor claiming that my experience represented a common one. I wanted to be careful not to misrepresent feminist political positions which were not my own. It always irked me to see radical feminist politics crudely and incorrectly described. In fact, the most useful and interesting feedback I had when Feminist Review *No. 11 came out was from radical feminist friends.*

So much has changed in the last five years. The harshness and danger of Britain in 1987 is more than I think I imagined it might be in 1982. I don't have any certainty about what one can extract from the early years of the women's liberation movement. I'm a harsher person today but not without hope for tomorrow and for the possibility of more passionate politics.

These days, in different circles of feminists and in feminist publications and conferences, there are various assertions about the ideas and actions from the beginning years of the women's liberation movement. Many of these assertions have taken on the air of received 'truths'. 'Socialist-feminists never paid any attention to sexuality.' 'Radical feminists don't take class into account.' 'Lesbian feminists forced heterosexual feminists to accept the necessity of an autonomous movement.' And so on. None of these statements (I've actually heard them all at one time or another) take into account the vast differences which existed (and still exist) between women identifying as socialist-feminists, radical feminists and lesbian feminists, nor any of the other political groupings of feminists. Instead they have seized upon statements of one group or individual and produced an all-time label. Non-aligned socialist-feminists have been continuously branded with the economism of some of their aligned sisters' political positions – from the absurdity of the early Maoist groups to the more complex opportunism of some Trotskyist women's single-issue campaigning.

Radical feminists, because they proclaimed the primacy of sex-class oppression of women, were assumed to have no position on class divisions and no matter how often they rebelled against this label (Feminist Practice, 1979), it stuck. And the false assumption that heterosexual feminists were not active in the early days in creating and defending an autonomous women's liberation movement helps to obscure the more substantial questions of heterosexual privilege and anti-lesbianism which were (and are) dividing women.

Another problem is that some feminist intellectuals appear to have cornered areas which have long been concerns of the women's liberation movement and have, by dint of the obscure way in which these issues are now presented, temporarily scared many women off the areas they pronounce so seriously on. I recognize that theories cannot always in themselves be 'easy' to understand, but surely it is necessary to re-assert the earlier emphasis feminists put on the link between theory and practice and to remember how deeply rooted early discussions and actions were in questions of ideology. What is the point of developing sophisticated feminist theories of ideology if these appear as incomprehensible and irrelevant to many and also end up fuelling a general anti-intellectualism which feminists are not immune from.

I want to recall that the concerns of the early women's liberation movement were grounded in issues of ideology: in questions about the construction of femininity, motherhood and sexuality, in grappling with internalized inferiority, and a ghettoized 'private life'. Many of the actions taken by women in those years were around those areas. 'Consciousness raising' was, after all, about consciousness and change: about collective exploration of personal experiences and emotions, in turn leading to the necessity of struggle for personal and social change. Whether or not consciousness raising took place in a small group or in a larger meeting, at a national conference or in action, it represented part of a unique politics and one which we forget – to our disadvantage – today.

Although the tendency to label was there from the beginning it was more or less irrelevant for the first few years. Our early discoveries and ventures into action were intuitively and spontaneously imbued with and fired by ideas and issues which came from our own specific experiences as women as well as from a large and eclectic melting pot of 1960s radical politics. Of course there were different ideas, different analyses, but they were not yet exclusive. Women belonging to sects or parties were often viewed with suspicion by the non-aligned, exactly because they were assumed to have worked-out 'lines'.

By recalling where some of our ideas came from, I'd like to pull out the way in which other people's revolutions and struggles moved us, whether it be the Chinese revolution or Frantz Fanon's observations on colonialism in Algeria. And I want to think about some of our early concerns and actions – from leafleting the Ideal Home Exhibition to the Miss World demonstration. Why? Partly because many feminists now weren't around then; partly to identify times and places I think were influential; partly to start at the beginning and see what relevance, if any, those beginnings have to our politics today. In light of an economic crisis, a crisis in politics, and the various voices from within our movement which are telling us what we must do, think, experience, I think it will help to reflect on our emergence as a movement which significantly broke with previous ways of defining politics, allowed women to speak for themselves from their own experience, and, in doing so, reached thousands of women.

The early collective uncovering of women's oppression – the *necessity* and commitment to changing and challenging the world –

bound feminists together in sisterhood. Throughout history movements for social change have given their members a world view which made sense of life and created solidarity in struggle. The women's liberation movement did this. The difference was our focus on the divisions between men and women in all areas of life, and our insistence on the political nature of the family, 'private' and personal life, and sexuality.

My personal evocation of the early years runs the risk of appearing nostalgic. That I do not want to be. Feminism changed my life in a way nothing else ever has. But if some of the strengths of the early years have been lost, there is much to be critical of in a retrospective look as well.

In this article I am being selective in my attempts to explain and describe aspects of the early women's liberation movement. I am *not* trying for a comprehensive overview. I've chosen to focus on the years between 1969 and 1972 and to relate them to today because I feel, more than I can prove, that that was a relatively cohesive time. Nothing changed suddenly in 1972. Much of what happened came out of the necessity feminists felt by then to try to move beyond spontaneity to a more sophisticated level of analysis and long-range strategy. I know there are traceable, although complex, interactions and tensions which led to the muting of early insistence on the interdependence of theory and practice. After all, we didn't have a lot of theory and we certainly wanted to reach more women with our practice. But that must be the work of another article.

Looking back to 1969, 1970, 1971, 1972; remembering those early years. Many of us, in London at any rate, didn't even call ourselves feminists. We had responded to women's liberation on the basis of our own contradictory experiences of the world and with men in that particular historical period. Our knowledge of the long history of women's oppression and struggles against it, our own recognition of ourselves as feminists, came later. At that point it was the desire for liberation for all oppressed women which overwhelmed us. We righteously proclaimed our disdain of the possibility of being equal with unfree men. We wanted much more than that.

> This is what is so exciting about the ideas generated by this movement ... it leads you on to question everything ... all our social institutions, the whole way our society is structured. (Camden Women's Liberation Open Meeting. Hampstead Town Hall, 7 July 1971)

We don't want to demand an equally bad education as men –
we want equal resources, not equal repression. We want to fight
for real education, to make our own jobs and opportunities
(Women's Newspaper No 1, 6 March 1971).

I do not intend to justify my struggles for liberation. I am
oppressed and that is sufficient. I do not intend to ask
permission from Pekin before proceeding, I do not intend to
neurotically consult Marxengelslenin before baring my teeth or
my teats. I do not intend to give ladylike (read suckass)
reassurance to male radical chauvinists during the course of this
struggle; even if it means losing their friendship (i.e. patronage!)
('The Female Separatist', *Shrew*, July 1969).

Looking back ... those early years are vivid and alive. I imagine the
spinning feeling that we had stepped into something which had to
change history, but brought with it frightening doubts that we'd
personally be able to change as much as our ideals demanded. But
today how and what do I recall so vividly from yesterday? All these
years later, how do I filter and translate, magnify and minimize what I
lived through? The tension between my objectivity and subjectivity
makes *me* tense; this article is no listing of truths, although I have
gone through my rat-pack bags of early newsletters and magazines to
try to check and match my memories with the memorabilia. I am
wary of pronouncements on the way things were. Still ...

At the beginning of the women's liberation movement, we faced
problems about our identity as an oppressed group – especially when
we tried to go beyond the deeply felt gut knowledge that it was true. If
women were oppressed because of their sex, why was there, in
comparison with other oppressed groups, so little history of collective
rebellion? Feminist history came later and most of us weren't
academics. The history of struggles around class and race formed,
however erratically or with whatever mystification, part of those
groups' identities – general strikes, revolutions, slave revolts,
anti-imperialist struggles.

The way in which many women came to articulate their oppression
as women, to perceive their subordination in the world of men, was
partly through empathy with others' struggles. By the late 1960s the
politics coming out of such struggles included observations, analysis
and practice which women in turn seized hold of to help them define
themselves ... Mao, black power, Fanon, Vietnam, Reich,
libertarianism, sexual liberation. All this was double-edged, for

although complacencies of the old left and the establishments were being shaken up around issues such as leadership, democracy and sex, women and 'private life' were left out. Not only were they left out, women were oppressed. So we were using the male-dominated politics of revolution to help us define our own politics of revolution but these same events, texts, ideas, with their overall negation of women, propelled us towards the formation of the women's liberation movement itself.

Some of these diverse influences came via the United States. There, by the late 1960s, many women were familiar with the politics of liberation from the Black movement, the new left and the anti-Vietnam movement. These three areas expressed, within male domination, questions of consciousness – 'Black is beautiful', opposition to hierarchy and dogma, and challenges to imperialism from 'within the belly of the monster' itself. These three movements (never totally separate) in turn had their influence on politics in Britain. The experiences of American women active in these movements played a significant part in the formation of women's liberation groups and influenced us in Britain. But this was always in play with our own history – the long struggle for equal pay within the labour movement, and a Marxist intellectual tradition which had already produced feminist writings by the mid-1960s. None of this is to imply that white British feminists had transcended racism or a middle-class bias.

At around the same time, the brief and dramatic risings in France of 1968 brought forward some specifically European left-wing but 'alternative' politics which drew our eyes towards China of the Cultural Revolution. Also we were aware, within the European/Third World tension again, of the work of Frantz Fanon, who raised issues of consciousness, oppression and liberation within the framework of the Algerian revolution. Even considering his stunning lack of recognition about the oppression of women, these issues reverberated in the small groups of women I knew. We were devouring any literature we could find if it helped us to understand and name our own oppression and the contradictions our new consciousness brought to light in our own lives.

Finally, the libertarians and the 'situationists' of the 1960s and the 1930s 'sexual politics' of Reich, all found a place in our armoury of books and ideas. Looking back, it's all too easy to see the faults, the gaps and the false pictures we sometimes took from what we read in our rush to find explanations, descriptions, which made us say 'Ah yes! That's it. That's true for women too.'

Our growing collective recognition that all men of all classes and races oppressed at least some women, plus our appropriation of the descriptions and analyses of oppression from male writers and participants who totally ignored or put down women may appear now as a contortionist's act. It led, in some cases, to an appreciation (sometimes ironic) of the contradictions inherent in liberation struggles, without necessarily writing them off, and to an empathy (sometimes simplistic), usually open-eyed, with the struggles waged around imperialism and class. But all along we insisted, 'no revolution without women's liberation'. Feminists held up the essential nature of *women's* liberation ... no more taking the back row. And as we sharpened our understanding of the depths of women's oppression, some women despaired and rejected any of the male-dominated politics which were initially compelling.

At that point we found in Mao and Fanon ideas about consciousness and change which related to our practice of consciousness raising. Women took note when Frantz Fanon described how even in situations of overt repression in Algeria the people could internalize their oppression and believe they deserved it.

> For unconsciously I distrust what is black in me, that is, the whole of my being. (Fanon, 1967)

> ... that the total result looked for by colonial domination was indeed to convince the natives that colonialism came to lighten their darkness. (Fanon, 1965)

Couldn't we say that women had been colonized by men and through that and their isolation within the family came to identify with their oppressors?

> One has to deal, for example with the uneasiness that comes with a shift in loyalties from one's husband or lover, maybe, to the group. The safety and reflected power that makes it comfortable to identify with one's oppressor has to be given up and strength found to identify with one's oppressed group and other oppressed groups. The group itself should provide this strength. (Shrew, 1971)

It was the difficulty of explaining why women participated at all in their own oppression at whatever level which led to descriptions of marriage as a 'gilded cage', to discussions of 'the man in our head', to debunking for ourselves as well as others the accepted 'truths' of human nature. We explored and rejected traditional and deeply ingrained beliefs, particularly as they applied to motherhood and sexuality ... the myths of the vaginal orgasm and female passivity and of 'natural' fulfilment through maternity and childcare. Fanon in Algeria and Black power groups in the USA expressed the necessity of oppressed people turning over their consciousness in order to struggle effectively. Women understood that they too had to struggle against guilt, conditioning and internalized self-hatred as women in order to begin new definitions of being women ... new definitions of liberation.

In the late sixties and early seventies, when looking at China, it was clear that the gap between the feudal patriarchal life of Chinese women in pre-evolutionary China and the relatively privileged lives of British women was vast. However the overt, totally accepted subservience and inferiority of most women in traditional Chinese society, which was reflected and recognized in poetry and literature, struck chords with western women who had no such totally clear cultural history of their own oppression to refer to. When we read books like *Fanshen* in our small women's group, it was *not* identification we experienced as the story of one Chinese village's passage from bondage to revolutionary beginnings unrolled. It was more a sense of connexion and a thrill of admiration that the unambiguous oppression of women in China was being shaken. We felt a connexion across thousands of miles and years of different histories:

> Women said 'Our husbands regard us as some sort of dogs who keep the house ... After we get our share we will be masters of our own fate.'

And:

> By 'speaking pains to recall pains', the women found that they had as many if not more grievances than the men and that once given a chance to speak in public they were as good at it as their fathers and husbands ... (Hinton, 1966)

We took inspiration from the fact that even the most intense material deprivation interwoven with the most deeply ingrained beliefs about women could, by dint of enormous effort, passion and upheaval united in revolution, be shifted. Cracks existed and could be widened – change was possible.

Some of us went on to find out more about the Chinese revolution and to be inspired by it, but even women who did not take a special interest in China were curious (and a little dubious) about it and about the subsequent Cultural Revolution in the 1960s. The cultural revolution, as we understood it, spoke volumes to feminist insistence that the seizure of economic power was not enough; that women had been badly served after the revolution in the Soviet Union and that prolonged and intense struggle would be necessary to change what went on (and on) in people's heads after any revolution.

One chapter of the 1949 classic, *China Shakes the World* (Belden, 1970) made the rounds of feminists as a little pamphlet called *Gold Flower's Story*. On her wedding night when she was fifteen, her husband

> ... almost tore her head off with a blow of his fist. Blood ran down Gold Flower's face. She lay back exhausted and in a quick fit of passion he raped her.

At eighteen, when the revolutionary Eighth Route Army entered her village and cadres came to organize, things began to change for Gold Flower. She heard women talking of struggling against their enslavement as women.

> 'That's right. Ah, that's right!' Gold Flower said to herself over and over again, as she listened to this woman who seemed to be speaking directly to her heart.

At a meeting of the village women Chang (Gold Flower's husband) was asked if he was ready to bow to women. His answer was not sincere.

> As if by a signal, all the women pushed forward at once. Gold Flower quickly went in back of her husband. The crowd fell on him, howling, knocked him to the ground, then jumped on him with their feet. Several women fell with him, their hands thrashing wildly. Those in the rear leaped in, tore at his clothing, then seized his bare flesh in their hands and began twisting and squeezing till his blood flowed from many scratches. Those who could not get close, dove under the rest and seized Chang's legs, sinking their teeth in his flesh.
>
> Chang let out an anguished howl. 'Don't beat me! Don't beat me!' he bleated in terror. 'I'll reform. Don't hurt me any more!'

But it was clear that Chang had not really changed.

> The chairwoman went up to the roof of her house and called through a megaphone. 'Comrade women! Come at once! Something of importance!' Out from nearly every clay hut in the village tumbled a woman. Rushing toward the Women's Association Building, they heard the chairwoman explain: 'Gold Flower's husband is bad again! Get ropes and catch him!'
>
> With Gold Flower in the lead, forty howling women ran through the village. But her husband had already fled.

Gold Flower's Story was both audacious and moving and also more extreme than most of us would have ever dared to imagine. I remember feeling a mixture of real malicious pleasure at the descriptions of man-beating but also feeling a bit guilty and voyeuristic. As she 'stood up', Gold Flower confronted her oppressors and most directly that meant her husband. However, her actions were only possible in the context of monumental social upheaval. In my 'small group' many of the women were aware of the contradictory nature for women of life 'in and against' advanced capitalism and male domination. A monumental social upheaval was not around the corner in England, and many women in purely material terms were not desperate. It was in exploring those contradictions as women that we began to develop our own political confidence.

Gold Flower was part of a movement against overt terror and repression. While stunned by her courage (the courage of the Chinese masses) we realized we had to break through an ideological stranglehold within a very different economic situation. Confronting the man in the house who was 'sympathetic' was not easy. In a March 1971 issue of the London Women's Liberation magazine, *Shrew*, an article described a 'confrontation'.

> Her husband was sympathetic on the theoretical level to the general tenets of Women's Lib but these views were not from the woman's point of view, being translated into reality in their home and particularly in the care of the small children.
>
> ... it was clear that both she and her husband were not alone in their failure to work out together the tensions and practical aspects which arose from childcare and housework and also out of her struggle to begin to define herself and her needs. These problems were made more acute and pressing for all the women in the group because of their involvement in Women's Lib.

After discussing the problem and considering a number of possibilities, the women decided to ask all the men they were in relationships with to attend an 'emergency' meeting. The meeting was held and was an anticlimax ... 'puzzled' sympathetic men and nervous evading talk. I am not guessing about any of this because it was my 'small group' which called the meeting and wrote the article afterwards.[1] 'We were feeling our way in fits and starts towards being a 'person in my own right'.

> I challenged him on the hypocrisy of his political attitudes. Wasn't I oppressed too? He hadn't even come to terms with this fact, let alone the fact that he was my oppressor. I looked after the home and kids so that he could be free to do what he liked. (*Shrew*, March 1971)

Being aware personally of one's desire and need for liberation was seen as a collective process. In the *Women's Liberation Workshop Manifesto* which was pulled together at a meeting of fifty to sixty women before the first women's liberation conference at Ruskin College in February 1970, the emphasis was on the necessity for social change:

> Each small group is autonomous, holding different positions and engaging in different types of activity. As a federation of a number of different groups, the Women's Liberation Workshop is essentially heterogeneous, incorporating within it a wide range of opinions and plans for action. We come together as groups and individuals to further our part in the struggle for social changes and the transformation of society.

Women were in the process of defining their own political perspectives and entering into actions which helped them define aims. Between early 1969 and 1972 in London small groups spread, growing in number from two to over eighty. We continued to express the contradictions and anger of our daily lives in our rotating monthly magazine, *Shrew*. We got into the straight press through our actions and 'outrageous' views.

> We decided to have a sticker campaign which would be concentrated in the Underground and would among other things, publicize the Equal Pay rally to take place in May. Our first batch of stickers were made by the Poster Workshop but were so huge that it was impossible to strike quickly and run.

The next batch was much smaller and had already sticky backs. Each set was aimed at exploitative and/or blatantly anti-woman or women-as-object advertisements. One was designed to be placed specifically on the Temp ads in the trains. For one week we saturated the escalators, station and train ads. And we did get publicity but not one paper mentioned the sticker which had all the details for the Equal Pay rally and most articles made a joke out of the attacks. Also some people were misreading the stickers. My baby-sitter, a Catholic school girl, thought they were the work of puritanical, crazed nuns racing through the subways in outrage at the display of nudity in the posters. (From a paper of my own, written in December 1970)

We continued to explore how we saw ourselves, how others saw us. What sort of actions should we undertake? What was our attitude to the media?

The nature of the politics we were developing was bound to stir up contradictory emotions and situations. It was generally agreed that society had to change in order for women to be free. But we were very confrontational about men. We weren't going to wait for a revolution before we tried to change our lives. We said it could begin now ... that the more we could transform ourselves, our relationships, our consciousness, the more we would move towards a possibility for fundamental change. The back and forth tension between our consciousness and our actions arising out of that consciousness elevated our perception of the necessity for women and ultimately men of breaking through the stranglehold of male-dominated bourgeois ideology. We were impatient with suggestions that we work within existing power structures, although not averse to exploiting contradictions in order to get money, for instance to set up an alternative childcare project. We were saying that women's struggles *now* were essentially revolutionizing – without struggle now we'd be sold-out and co-opted and anyway we felt we had no real choice; we could not wait.

We were becoming clearer, though, about what a long, uneven process gaining a new consciousness was: overthrowing the old system would not simply be a matter of taking up the new. The contradictions in the process, the revelations of reactionary and progressive ideas and impulses in each individual as well as in all social relations, made us in turns pessimistic and optimistic. From *Bird* in 1969:

They talked at length of women being second class people, questioned our every belief about the family and children by questioning the organization of society in general, tackling the whole thing with honesty and thoroughness. Afterwards we were split. For some of us Hilary and Juliet had shown up our middle-class meanderings for what they really were – rubbish leading to a dead-end. For others they were branded as dangerous militants ... But all in some way felt that they didn't really feel second class in every cell of their bodies, and refused themselves any real feeling of fervour, possibly because in some way it might mean betraying their men.

Later:

Gradually, through minor actions, through more group discussions, through more reading and learning we are all becoming militant. The skin over our eyes is peeling back, and people are trying to emerge out of passive female shells.

We'd read about Chinese women 'speaking bitterness' and thought that as part of raising political consciousness, this served a similar function for western women even in our very different circumstances. The insistence on focusing on our own experiences and on our 'private' lives was one of the most important forms of women's politics to come out of the movement. It created solidarity and sisterhood between women.

By the present separation between private life and social life, women are persistently thrown back into individual conflicts requiring solution in the private sector. Women are still being educated for private life, for the family, which, for its part, is dependent on the conditions of production against which we are struggling. Education for a specific role, the inculcated feeling of inferiority, the contradiction between their own expectations and the demands of society, all generate a constant feeling of guilt prompted by an inability to do justice to the many demands, for having to choose between alternatives which in each case involve the renunciation of vital needs.

Women can

only emancipate themselves if their own conflicts, which are suppressed into private life, are articulated. (Helke Sanders, SDS

Conference Frankfurt Sept 1968. Translated and distributed here 1969)

Ironically this new form of politics was most despised by the various British Maoist sects who had picked up very quickly on the woman question, only to lambast the new movement (which they tried to control) as totally reformist. In the *News of the World* on 15 November 1970 members of the Women's Liberation Front (a mixed Maoist sect) were quoted as saying

> To me [The Workshop] seems just a group of people so hung up on sex that they just use their sessions as group therapy. They spend all their time sitting around contemplating their bodies. We don't want to be associated with their ideas. They're just man-haters, and that we certainly are not. Their magazine *Shrew* some months is full of dirty jokes and four-letter words – totally irrelevant to any issue of inequality. Their meetings are barred to men, while we welcome men at ours. I mean, if you want to change things then you've got to educate men to accept things too, haven't you? At the conference we had in Sheffield, they would not allow any men to be present and when they didn't agree with one of the speakers they barracked her with yells of 'Man – you're a Man!' They were so ridiculous and childish it wasn't true.

In a letter to the Women's Liberation Front from the London Workshop came the following response:

> It seems to us, from reading other material put out by the WLF, that you do not really understand either the politics of the workshop or the importance which we attach to aspects of women's oppression like sexuality and the family.

At the national women's liberation conference at Skegness in 1971, which was organized primarily by the Women's Liberation Front and the Union of Women for Liberation (another Maoist group), the differences between 'feminists' and the Maoists erupted into plenary violence. From my own notes made at the time:

> Too much! My god. We lost the vote to exclude men from first session in *order* to get the creche and literature stalls 'manned'. So now pleas for women to come to 'man' these things. The Front and Union *much* in evidence *but* since vote went to them guess IS [International Socialists, now SWP] Socialist Women

[IMG], other city's groups must be weak on this point or are afraid of 'feminism' – Maysal, from the Union, does her best to put across the view that feminists are stupid.

But later at the conference women, many of them lesbians, attempted to get rid of the men who continued to operate from the stage ... mayhem ...

Maysal grabbing mike from women – women grabbing it back. Brar (a man) rushing in to really be a shit – kicking and shouting. The whole session shouting 'out', 'out' and voting almost unanimously to have him leave and him REFUSING – Union women really fighting to keep him in. So sick – hysteria and screaming was incredible. He was finally ejected by a combination of women, the management and one Maoist man.

All this at a trade union conference centre where IS was also having a national conference and a strip show was being put on in the evening.

In December 1971 the Union made its position clear on at least one area of feminist concern:

In this class society which maintains the basic inequality of the bourgeoisie and the working class many groups of people are *victims* (sic) of injustice, moral hypocrisy, social ostracism, etc. These groups which form the lumpen-proletariat may be thieves, prostitutes, the 'mentally ill', tramps, beggars, homosexuals, etc. But each of these groups is not maintained directly to serve the ruling class; they are merely the by-products of bourgeois rule. (Concerning the Gay Liberation Front and the Women's Liberation Movement, 7 December 1971)

At that point, most left groups had no time for the direction the women's liberation movement was heading. Going to the Ideal Home Exhibition in 1969 with leaflets and trying to interview women we could persuade to stop and talk to us was not quite what they had in mind as 'real' political activity. Our leaflet said:

Properly manipulated ('if you're not afraid of that word') housewives can be given the sense of identity, purpose, creativity, the self-realization, even the sexual joy they lack – by the buying of things. (From an interview with Ernest Dichter, head of multi-million pound motivation research firm. Issued by Women's Liberation Workshop, 31 Dartmouth Park Hill, NW5)

Our questions asked, 'Do you think Ideal Homes is aimed specifically at women? Why?' 'Do women control much money?' 'Do you think you could trade places with your husband, boyfriend, if you had equal training? Would you want to? Why? Why not?' 'Do you feel men and women should be equal? Why? Why not?' We weren't really clear about what we were doing at the Ideal Homes, but obviously felt it was a public manifestation of women's oppression. However, there were doubts: 'How liberated are we from advertising and other influences? We may have rejected the cruder forms of acquisition but are we really free of it?' (my own notes for discussion in the Tufnell Park small group).

The very fact that we believed out of our own experience that women could be reached politically in their roles as housewives, consumers and mothers, and at the same time emphasized the way in which those roles captured women and slowly and steadily sucked their identity away, went against any frozen notions of the proletariat and/or point-of-production politics.

When women demonstrated outside the Miss World contest in November 1969, they wore sashes printed with the following slogans:

MIS-FIT REFUSES TO CONFORM
MIS-CONCEPTION DEMANDS FREE ABORTION FOR ALL WOMEN
MIS-FORTUNE DEMANDS EQUAL PAY FOR ALL WOMEN
MIS-JUDGED DEMANDS AN END TO BEAUTY CON-TESTS
MIS-DIRECTED DEMANDS EQUAL OPPORTUNITY
MIS-LAID DEMANDS FREE CONTRACEPTION
MIS-GOVERNED DEMANDS LIBERATION
MIS-USED DEMANDS   24   HOUR   CHILDCARE CENTRES
MIS-PLACED DEMANDS A CHANCE TO GET OUT OF THE HOUSE
MIS-TREATED DEMANDS SHARED HOUSEWORK
MIS-NOMER DEMANDS A NAME OF HER OWN
MIS-QUOTED DEMANDS AN UNBIASED PRESS

Although the demonstrators were not aiming their protest at the contestants ('whoever becomes Miss World is more than just a trade mark. She is a woman. She is a person. She has a mind.' From a leaflet *What Price Miss World?* put out by the Women's Liberation

Workshop), they did not take enough care to ensure that this was completely clear in their publicity. The impact on the media was unexpected and women were not prepared for it: 'To everybody's astonishment the TV and Press turned up in numbers, with much snapping, popping and aggressive interview technique' (*Shrew* Nov/Dec 1969).

The next year events were better planned and publicity expected, although the explosion of a bomb under a BBC Outside Broadcast van parked outside the Albert Hall early on the day of the contest was a shock. 'MISS WORLD SABOTAGE BID' was the full top-page headline in the *Evening Standard* of 21 November 1970, and the day after the contest *The Times* said, 'Police, who had been ringing the Albert Hall from before the contest began, joined security guards and stewards to remove the demonstrators, most of them girls. Mr Hope returned on stage to say: "This was good conditioning for Vietnam".' *The Times'* leader that day said, 'And a powerful antidote to women's liberation lies in the plain fact of biological function, with all the deep differences in the behaviour and life-experiences which this entails. Perhaps the real criticism of the Miss World competition should also be applied to the Women's Liberation movement: that they both exalt an essentially functionless feminism.'

Five women were arrested during the evening's events and four went on to stand trial. Three of them defended themselves, all received fines, and in the long process the trial received an enormous amount of publicity. The women produced their own pamphlet, *Why Miss World*, a fascinating document which integrated the history of businessman Morley's Miss World competition, the demonstrators' feelings and preparations before the event, the evening itself and finally the trial and the participants' final assessments of the venture:

> THE COMPETITION WILL SOON BE OVER ... WE HAVE BEEN IN THE MISS WORLD CONTEST ALL OUR LIVES ... JUDGING OURSELVES AS THE JUDGES JUDGE US – LIVING TO PLEASE MEN – DIVIDING OTHER WOMEN UP INTO SAFE FRIENDS AND ATTRACTIVE RIVALS – GRADED, DEGRADED, HUMILIATED ... WE'VE SEEN THROUGH IT.
>
> MECCA ARE SUPERPIMPS SELLING WOMEN'S BODIES TO FRUSTRATED VOYEURS UNTIL AGEING BUSINESSMEN JUMP YOUNG GIRLS IN DARK ALLEYS – BUT THEY'RE ONLY SMALL-TIME PIMPS IN

OUR EVERYDAY PROSTITUTION: WOMEN'S BODIES USED BY BUSINESSMEN TO SELL THEIR GARBAGE – LEGS SELLING STOCKINGS, CORSETS SELLING WAISTS, CUNTS SELLING DEODORANTS, MARY QUANT SELLING SEX ... OUR SEXUALITY HAS BEEN TAKEN AWAY FROM US, TURNED INTO MONEY FOR SOMEONE ELSE, THEN RETURNED DEADENED BY ANXIETY. WOMEN WATCHING ... WHY ARE YOU HERE?

THE MAN'S MAKING MONEY OUT OF US.

WE'RE NOT BEAUTIFUL OR UGLY WE'RE ANGRY.

The women writing said, 'We were dominated while preparing for the demonstration by terror at what we were about to do. To take violent action, interrupting a carefully ordered spectacle, drawing attention to ourselves, inviting the hostility of thousands of people was something that we had all previously thought to be personally impossible for us, inhibited both by our conditioning as women, and our acceptance of bourgeois norms of correct behaviour.' They too made it clear that they were not opposed to the women in the competition: 'The pre-contest planning meeting had unanimously rejected the use of any slogan or action that could possibly be construed as an attack on the contestants, or that might lead us to any violent confrontation.' But even though there was much more thought and political sophistication involved in the 1970 Miss World demonstration, those involved could see weaknesses and problems afterwards.

This lack of positive strategy towards the media revealed the confusion and ambiguity that surrounded the Miss World Action. There was an irresolvable contradiction in its conception. On the one hand because the contest was an Ideological target, the intention of the demonstration was propaganda by deed, ie, we were not deliberately recruiting, but we were attempting to make our politics and ideas accessible to other women. On the other hand we were firmly against any co-operation with the bourgeois media. There is something self-defeating in the politics of a movement which is prepared to burst onto the screen of 7 million viewers one minute, but withdraw the next into a jealously guarded privacy.

And the 'big-splash' politics of the demonstration was finally criticized as the basis for sustained politics:

We've worked more in the communities we live in – fighting for nurseries, playhouses for our kids, working with unsupported mothers in the Claimants Union, meeting in small groups. Some of us have tried to live in collectives, some have worked with GLF. Most of it has been slow, painstaking organizing compared with the Miss World demonstration – but it's in the home around kids, sexuality, that our oppression bites deepest, holds hardest. The 'left' have always said the economy – our exploitation has to be changed *first* before our lives, our oppression. We say both have to be changed at once – the struggle against internalized oppression, against how we live our lives, is where we begin, is where we've been put. But we can't end there – it's through that initial struggle that we understand that we can't live as we want to until the power structures of society have been broken. (*Why Miss World*)

By the next year, the inevitable demonstration at Miss World was assured publicity and on 10 November 1971 *The Times* carried a little news item 'Police with a search warrant issued under the Explosives Act search the "Women's Lib" headquarters in Little Newport Street, Soho, yesterday. The search was made a few hours after threats of disruption at today's Miss World contest by militant women.' The bourgeois press went to town; the radical and semi-radical press covered the event. In fact it was the last big Miss World demonstration. This was not because, as one radical feminist wrote in 1972, '... we must realize that women (we) act in our own self-interest within the meagre choices offered us. No blame attaches to self-interest, or why did we want a movement of our own? Miss World actually offers the competitors a chance of limited self-expression – *very* limited admittedly ...' (*Why Not Miss World*, 1972) but more because it was becoming a predictable ritual which actually appeared to add a bit of spice to an occasion the media had a taste for anyway.

In the first years, though, angry women, women in small local groups, women tentatively and unevenly trying to come to grips with the intertwined social relations of class and sex, quickly understood how political their voices and actions were, if only because of the force of reaction from left to right. It was understood that 'We have no line. As of yet we have no heavy theory. We are a beginning and a tremendously exciting one' (Sue O'Sullivan to meeting of 'housewives', 1971). The women's liberation movement needed to go somewhere, develop out of its early years ... I'm not saying we should have remained where we were – at an only partially conceptualized state of theory and practice. An indication of how much women felt the need to make more sense of it all was the proliferation of women's study groups from about 1972. No intellectual baddies zoomed into the field and left us 'ordinary' small group 'real' feminists gasping at their 'heavy' theories. The growing awareness of the complexity of women's oppression, our own contradictory reactions to change, and the deep entrenchment of women's inferiority made many of us feel the need to understand more clearly how it all arose, and what long-term strategies and tactics might best be developed to move towards liberation ...

But somehow between then and now the theories did become 'heavy' enough to lose contact with many women and with their basic impulse of political engagement at every level: that basic feeling that we could connect, through all the contradictions, with all women's lives. This belief got blurred. Theories and analyses began to explain the differences between women, which increasingly we had been experiencing, but instead of leading to more fruitful connexions with women where their lives *did* or could intersect (and with an awareness and commitment to act against the different oppressions which many women experience) they seemed to separate us more. To many women sisterhood became an empty slogan.

Obviously all was not lost ... feminism is here and alive and in many ways kicking. It seems to me that now, more than ever before, we have to make that personal, political connexion with women not yet convinced or touched directly by feminism; yet we flounder, and doubt ourselves. The 'new' angry women of 1981-82 who may or may not be connected in some way with WAVAW: the women espousing political lesbianism; women involved in anti-Tory or single-issue campaigns; those involved in women's studies or other feminist 'jobs for the girls' – none of these necessarily share the premise that the personal is political in the same way that early feminists did. Consciousness raising is something which perhaps the majority of feminists around now have not gone through, and although CR and sisterhood are certainly not magic formulae, they do appear to lead towards a confidence to engage with contradictions instead of assertions. Assertion politics (you must, you should, it *all* boils down to ...) too often ignores the rich history of work on the ideological level which did (with many faults and failures) break through the stranglehold of bourgeois/male dominated ideology. Newer concerns of feminism such as heterosexism and male violence are important to feminism, as is the present economic crisis which hits women so hard. But any feminist politics or theories which even vaguely mimic tired-out forms are not using to best advantage our history and knowledge. The economism of Wages for Housework is simply more crude than that of groups who maintain that a lack of waged work makes women concerned with issues of sexuality. The reformism of concentrating primarily on parliamentary struggles, the way in which the Labour Party features as a political priority for so many feminists, tends to side-step revolutionary feminist politics. And the ultra-leftism of being told to will yourself into an 'advanced' position – be that political lesbianism, or telling women that all men are rapists thereby lifting the clouds from their eyes so they 'see' the truth and repudiate all men as the agents of their oppression – doesn't *use* what we've learned through the last ten or more years about the way struggle and contradiction can move us in fits and starts forwards.

Yet, the time is as ripe as ever – only the veneer has been reinforced. Happiness with our 'lot' is not running at a high tide any more than it was in the late sixties. Women are still exploited. The confusion and anger are there – even if in economic crisis women themselves try to shove their unhappiness into second place. We know that male-dominated fucking, whether it's a *Cosmo* variety or the old thrusting and banging, makes many women miserable; that kids and isolated housing drive women mad; that combining shitty capitalist waged work, with unwaged work in the home, with caring for and being responsible for raising children, with all the assumptions of heterosexuality, drives many women crazy. Even as they try harder to cope! And it should all be in the *frontline* ... surely we know that! Shouldn't we attempt to reach that point in the majority of women where contradictions reside and help them to develop; help develop a wider and wider feminist world view and a sharper and sharper courage to believe and act on the possibility of change?

What is worth recapturing from our early years is exactly how profoundly ideological the original tenets of our movement were and how profoundly they led to political engagement and action. Can we afford to let Erin Pizzey declare in a *Sunday Times* article (13 December 1981): 'Why is it that there is no effective broad-based women's movement in Britain – a movement which could be a huge and effective force in engineering social change for women, yet not be hostile to men?' Can we afford to let her put forward such a 'heart-felt' plea and at the same time, after having been 'accused' of being a lesbian, report that 'My first feeling was of unbearably painful hurt. I heard my voice calmly telling anyone who was listening that I wasn't a lesbian: I was a happily married woman with children and grandchildren ... I felt myself cringe with shame and embarrassment as I babbled inanely. I put down the phone and went to our room and was unable to cry.'

Women like Erin Pizzey, who represents herself as a 'real' feminist; women like Shirley Williams, who comes across as a reasonable, working woman; women the media see as charmingly eccentric and hard working but certainly not loony feminists, are often as effective in undermining the women's liberation movement as denouncements from the hard right. There is nothing intrinsically revolutionary about advocating equal pay, childcare facilities, or abortion rights, especially when the institutions, power imbalances and social relations of class, sex, race remain unchallenged. Our task is surely to advocate rights, *and* struggle to build and maintain a revolutionary vision with many political offensives. Part of that is what we started off with. 'Such consciousness changing is as absolutely fundamental a form of progress toward a better society as any material or organizational gains – in fact, probably more fundamental, *since* consciousness must be the basis of political struggle' (Gordon, 1981).

I'm *not* advocating a return to the late 1960s, nor nostalgic evocations; we were confused if energetic beginners at politics – but driven by what felt like absolute necessity, we cut through some of the encrusted bullshit of traditional and/or male dominated forms of politics. In our exploration of our own experiences, how we were socialized, and formed, of all oppressed people's struggles, we found a way of talking about consciousness which led to a collective appreciation of women's oppression and the need for revolutionary change and action.

■ Notes

In this article I quoted from some of the earliest publications of the London women's liberation movement. These include pamphlets and magazines – *Harpies Bizarre, Bird*, and the long-running *Shrew*. The London newsletter, begun in 1969, is now published weekly from A Woman's Place. I have not quoted from internal newsletters and where possible I have tried to check the quotations here with the women concerned.

1   We were, at that time, all heterosexual in my small group. Well, as far as
    I know we were. None of us articulated anti-lesbianism in the group ...
    we didn't need to as we kept the issue collectively locked away. Who
    knows what we thought about individually. My imagination was hooked,
    although it was years before ...

Talking Sex:
A Conversation on
Sexuality and
Feminism

Deirdre English, Amber Hollibaugh
and Gayle Rubin

Deirdre: Feminist discussions of sex seem to take place in a vacuum. We often ignore some of the extreme changes going on in society as people react to the ideas of sexual freedom and of equality of the sexes. Those reactions are highly charged, whether positive or negative, and their intensity has often intimidated us. I would go as far as to say that on the whole the women's movement is not as farsighted as some of the more progressive areas in the field of sex research, where psychologists have really come to grips with people's emotions and behaviour. They have learned through their practices not be threatened by the sexual realm; they have developed an acceptance of fantasy, an acceptance of women's sexuality and of diverse forms of sexual expression.

Gayle: You're right. There is certainly a branch of the sex field that is progressive. Many women, even feminists, even dykes, work in that field. Instead of assuming that sex is guilty until proven innocent, these people assume that sex is fundamentally okay until proven bad. And that idea has not penetrated the women's movement or the left.

Some feminists cannot digest the concept of benign sexual variation. Instead of realizing that human beings are not all the same, that variation is okay, the women's movement has created a new standard. This is like the old psychiatric concept, that dictates a 'normal' way to do it. Male-female, heterosexual, married, man on top, reproductive sex was okay. But all other behaviour was measured against that standard and found wanting.

Deirdre: The old idea of malignant variation was in the service of a particular kind of social structure, the patriarchal heterosexual structure. But I think that some feminists also have a concept of sexuality in service to society.

Amber: The notion that sex has no right to exist for itself – that sex is good or bad only in terms of the social relations.

Deirdre: Right. And at worst, this feminist vision would bar some forms of sexual expression. One of the first things it would probably get rid of is heterosexuality. The man on top, heterosexual, reproductive.

Gayle: That for sure will not be permitted after the revolution.

Amber: No one will want it, you see! These things are all imposed by sexist male domination and patriarchy which has brainwashed us from childhood into believing that our bodies are driven to this, in spite of the terrifically healthy erotic desires which would bloom in a new, revolutionary society. That's hogwash. My fantasy life has been *constructed* in a great variety of ways. My sexual desire has been channelled. But what that view takes from me is my right to genuinely feel, in my body, what I want.

What it says is that I have no notion of healthy sexuality, and that anything sexual now is unhealthy and contaminated because of the culture I live in. So the notion of pleasure in sex is now a forbidden one – it's a contradiction in terms. The theory is that lesbianism comes the closest to being a pro-female sexuality, because it's two women together. However, when you acknowledge power between women – that you would like to be dominated or dominate another woman in a sexual exchange rather than Cinderella, lesbian Cinderella-ism, you are told that you have a heterosexual model for your lesbian sexuality, you have left over penetration fantasies you really should re-examine. There's never been anything in that rap about sex that has much joy, pleasure, power or lustiness.

Gayle: I don't think there has been a feminist discussion of sex. And that's not just the fault of the women's movement. People don't utilize the best analysis of progressive sex research because they don't really know about it.

I firmly believe that sexuality is not natural, not an unchanging, ahistorical item in the human repertoire of behaviour. Which means that 'after the revolution', in utopia, it would obviously be different. However, that idea, that sex will change if society changes, is confused in a peculiar and perhaps fundamentally Christian way. The idea of sex after the revolution is so removed from anything that we do now that it transcends the flesh itself. It becomes an *absence* of anything that we do now, all of which is contaminated by this earthly, fleshy existence. So 'sex after the revolution' becomes a transcendent image of celestial delight.

When we talk about how work will change, we don't say work will disappear. We talk about how what people do will be different, how social relations will be different, but we don't therefore condemn what everybody does now and say that they are bad people for doing it. We treat sex as a special case at almost every point. And we use different standards to judge it.

The late sixties and the early seventies saw the so-called sexual revolution. Women like me felt that it hadn't worked because it was male-dominated but we still wanted it in a non-sexist way. Other women said, it's male-dominated, it hasn't worked for women, and it won't. And we don't want anything to do with it. So basically the people who don't want anything to do with a sexual revolution are now defining the discourse around sex, rather than those of us who want to have some kind of sexual liberation that is not sexist.

Yet this sexual revolution was only a liberalization so of course it didn't do what we wanted. People's standards for what should have happened are based on the assumption that this *was* the revolution. It's like saying that socialism will never work, look at the Soviet Union.

Deirdre: It's very popular now to say that the sexual revolution of the sixties was incredibly oppressive to women, that it was just a male-dominated thing. That's too simple – my recollection of it is that it was not an unmitigated disaster. The sexism was there, but women were actually having more sexual experience of different kinds and enjoying it. Women were having more sex that was not procreational, and claiming the right to it as well by paying a lower social and emotional cost. There were obstacles, and many women were disappointed. They were often disappointed by the nature of the sexuality that they found with men. That's not too surprising, historically. But the raised sexual expectations created enormous social and sexual gains for women. There was a fresh, post-Victorian discovery of the female orgasm. Many women were actually able to change the way that men made love with them as well as the way they made love with men. Not enough, but there were dramatic changes. Women were fighting for rights and often getting them.

Amber: We forget that ten or twelve years ago, you were a strident ballbuster if you were a woman who was sexually self-defined, who said what she wanted and sought her own partners, who perhaps was not heterosexual. It was not very long ago that the notion of being sexual *and* being female was outrageous. Part of my attraction to feminism involved that right to be a sexual person. I'm not sure where that history got lost.

Deirdre: We didn't win. We made great gains, but we had enormous losses. Now we're in a period in which a lot of women are looking only at the losses and are saying give up, back to square one, better sexual expression. But can't we have a non-sexist sexual liberation? Can't we still go for that?

Amber: Marxism hasn't taken sexuality very seriously. It's not only that feminism doesn't take it very seriously, but most progressive movements have been very unprogressive about sexuality, and we've inherited that tradition. When we analysed sexism, we found it hard to separate sex and pleasure from sexism, and didn't realize until fairly recently how to use Marxist tools to help look at sexuality in a historical perspective. The left shares responsibility for the vacuum in sexual theory that the feminist movement has a need to fill. Sexuality has not been thought of as a central part of human life. It has even been thought to be frivolous. Or that the left's been sexually repressive. Lenin said that if women were not monogamous, for the man it was like drinking out of someone else's glass.

Gayle: I thought all of the questions that weren't answered for me in the left would be answered in the women's movement. In 1968, compared to the left, the women's movement had everything to say about sex. Not just about gender, but about sex. It's only become clear more recently that feminist theory, although it talks about sex, mostly talks in terms of gender and gender hierarchy and the relationships between men and women. It doesn't really have a language for sexual desire and wants. Feminist concepts and Marxist concepts are indispensable for dealing with sex. But you have to deal with sex, and not assume that if you're talking about class or gender or romance, you're talking about sex.

■ Lesbianism and heterosexuality

Deirdre: What you're saying might not be true if the movement had not been willing to make women feel guilty about heterosexuality.

Gayle: What happened around lesbianism is interesting and complicated. Suddenly some of us could go out and be sexual without dealing with sexism and men. And that changed the issues we faced. Many of us became lesbians in a quest for greater and better sexual experience. And other people became lesbians to get away from sex. Both a seeking of sex and a running away from it got involved in early lesbian theory and practice.

Amber: Are you thinking about 'The Woman-Identified Woman'?

Gayle: Yes, around 1970, the 'Woman-Identified Woman' paper basically argued, in the popular phraseology, that feminism was the theory and lesbianism the practice ...

Amber: That all women were lesbians or potential lesbians.

Gayle: And that to be a lesbian was to revolt against patriarchy. All of which made sense ...

Deirdre: Therefore heterosexuals are what? Deviants?

Amber: Heterosexuality was an imposed system that women suffered from. But all women – if they only knew it – were woman-identified. The lesbian in all of us was closer to the surface in some of us and bubbled forth, while in other people it was silent.

Gayle: Lesbianism at that time was presented as the oppressed getting together, as if women were the proletariat getting together to relate to each other instead of to the oppressor. At the time it seemed to justify the lesbian experience pretty well. Though it didn't account for male homosexuals.

Yet it made heterosexual feminists into second-class citizens and created a decade of problems for heterosexual women in the radical women's movement. In retrospect, I also think it abused lesbians. By conflating lesbianism (which I think of as a sexual and erotic experience) with feminism – a political philosophy – the ability to justify lesbianism on grounds other than feminism dropped out of the discourse. If you recognized it was okay to be a dyke whether or not it was politically correct, that the basic lust itself was legitimate – then at some level you had to recognize that other people's basic lust, no matter how it looked in an oppressive time, was also legitimate. And people didn't want to do that. In defining both heterosexuality and lesbianism in terms of one's relationships to patriarchy, the erotic experience dropped out. Definitions of sexual orientation became completely unsexual. And so no one has really had to think explicitly about the erotic components of anybody's sexual orientation for ten years. And this has led to a new hierarchy of what's okay. First, it was that lesbians were better than straight women. And now it turns out that some lesbians are better than other lesbians, and some straight women can be permitted to be political lesbians, but not others. We have now replaced the old psychiatric view of what's permissible and non-permissible in sexual behaviour with a new hierarchy based on the notion that lesbianism somehow is exempt from the patriarchy.

What angers me most about this is the assumption that lesbianism is not a social construct. The fact that lesbianism is as much a social construct of the current system as anyone else's sexuality. It has a different, specific relationship to the system as a whole. Everything does. But lesbianism relies on aspects of the system as it is. For instance, the sense of lesbianism being a rebellious sexuality is predicated on male supremacy. If men did not oppress women, that valence would presumably be gone from lesbianism.

Amber: Parts of the feminist movement basically said that sexuality really wasn't very important, and other kinds of relationships had to take priority. Lusting in whatever form was unacceptable. The lesbian was not supposed to be any lustier than the heterosexual woman, and the heterosexual woman was not to be sexual at all. As a lesbian who was a lesbian before the feminist movement, with a lover in the closet, I was told that we couldn't go to women's conferences and stay in the same bedroom, that we were not allowed to show physical desire for each other in public, and we were not to dance together in any particularly heavy sexual way. We were asked to leave some parts of the women's movement if we were sexual with each other, because women had been terrorized by sexuality and were sick of it. Our dirty sex lives were no better than anybody else's, especially since there was no way to keep us out.

Deirdre: Let's talk about heterosexual women and their acceptance of this theory. I find it fascinating and almost funny that so many heterosexual feminists, especially in the socialist movement, seemed to accept the idea that heterosexuality meant co-operating in their own oppression and there was something wrong with being sexually turned on to men. How many times have I heard this? 'Well, unfortunately, I'm not a lesbian ... but I wish I was, maybe I will be.'

Amber: 'I'm a lesbian in my mind. But I'm still a heterosexual in my body.'

Gayle: The mind is willing but the flesh is weak.

Deirdre: 'And so for reasons I cannot explain, unfortunately, except from my patriarchal conditioning, I have sex with this man every night.'

Amber: In the dark though, in the dark.

Deirdre: 'But never mind, I'll never discuss the pleasure I get from it. I'll never raise that, I'll never ask for that to be legitimate. I know it's illegitimate and I'm guilty!'

How did it serve heterosexual feminists to adopt a theory that was – on the surface – so self-denying? Partly it was a relief to be able to consider themselves deviant.

With heterosexual desire itself, I can see no criticism. But heterosexuality does give you access to privileges that lesbian women or women not associated with men do not have. The feminist understanding of how women are protected by their alliance with men is valid.

I think it was convenient for heterosexuals to be able to feel guilty for this trait, which was advantageous to them and allied them with powerful men, while still being considered a deviant – and not having to change anything. That much is perhaps ironically amusing. But it doesn't advance our thinking, and it doesn't provide honest emotional support to anyone – female, male, straight or gay. And for some women guilt over heterosexual relations sometimes also fed a sad and bitter sexual self-denial.

Amber: Maybe some of the confusion about lesbianism and sexuality occurred when lesbianism began to be the model for describing good sex. Everybody, heterosexual or homosexual, used it to describe non-genitally organized sexual experience. That was a way to reject men fucking for a minute and a half and pulling out, a way to talk about nonmissionary-position sexuality, foreplay as all-play. The description of lesbian feminist sexuality actually resembles a feminist description of what good sex is supposed to be more than a description of lesbian sex. And all women in the feminist movement were trying to make love the way dykes were supposed to.

Gayle: But it's turned the other way now, now sex has to occur in a certain way for it to be good. And the only legitimate sex is very limited. It's not focused on orgasms, it's very gentle and it takes place in the context of a long-term, caring relationship. It's the missionary position of the women's movement.

■ Violence against women

Amber: Categories like that need careful exploration – romance, long-term relationships, sex, sexism, a whole variety of things all got thrown into the same washing machine, and this very odd-coloured garment came out. If you combine incorrectly then you can't do anything within that discussion. That's what I feel about the way questions get raised by the anti-porn movement. I don't even want to try and answer those wrong questions, even though the issue is crucial. The issue is taken from us if we question any of the objects of struggle. For instance, if you question pornography's ability to turn out masses of rapists, it is assumed that you are encouraging rape. You have no right to make sexual violence against women your issue. To people like Susan Brownmiller and Andrea Dworkin, pornography and violence against women are seen as absolutely, intimately linked.

Deirdre: I find myself wondering what the purpose of the anti-porn movement is in its own terms. Of course, I'm against violence against women, because the only form in which a politics opposed to violence against women is being expressed is anti-sexual. I'd like to take back the night, and I like to go on those marches, and if it's a march through dark and dangerous areas of town, then I find that easy to do. But if it's a march through the porn district, then I experience it very much as being directed against the women who work in those districts, and as an unnecessary attack on a small zone of some sexual freedom. One thing that became clear to me working on the porn issue at *Mother Jones* is that the issue pushes people's buttons.[1] They polarize and go to their corners very fast. They're scared of each other, and scared of what's being said. If you criticize the feminist anti-porn movement, you very quickly get accused of calling those women prudes. Or you get accused of defending pornography or getting off on pornography, and therefore there's something wrong with you. It's difficult even to create a clearing in which we can have a conversation. I think women are almost at panic point about violence all the time, and are in a place where we are willing to make terrible bargains. We will do anything to be rid of that terror.

Amber: When I heard Andrea Dworkin speak, she named my relationship to porn as a form of being raped. I wanted to say, 'Do anything to me but still let me be alive at the end.' I had to smash pornography because if I didn't, it would take my life. It was not one more position I should understand and debate as a feminist, but a life and death issue.

I went to an anti-porn conference, because I was very confused about my own positions. At the workshops I heard some of the most reactionary politics I've ever heard about how we had to smash pornography and save the family. In fact, it was a radical right critique, much more so than a left critique.

Gayle: We're all terrorized about a range of possible ways that violence is done to us, whether it's rape or being beat up on the streets or whatever. We're all in the state of severe intimidation, and that's a very powerful and strong feeling. The other strong feeling that is involved is disgust and horror at explicit images of sex. Those images can call up disgust and repulsion in people – especially women – who are not familiar with them. What the anti-porn movement has done is to take those very powerful feelings around sex and link them to very powerful feelings around violence and sexual abuse, and say it's all the same subject.

We all agree about the problem. We don't agree on the solution – would ending porn have an appreciable effect on rape and violence and abuse? But these connexions have been foisted upon the movement in a really unprecedented way. I have never seen a position become dogma with so little debate, with so little examination of its possible ramifications or of other perspectives. One reason is that anyone who has tried to raise other issues and who has questioned this analysis has been trashed very quickly as anti-feminist or personally attacked. This has also affected the better parts of the left that of course want to be pro-feminist.

Deirdre: One of the things women have been taught to help repress us sexually is that if you begin to deal with sexuality at all, if you begin to become explicit, then you will pay the price of unleashing and stimulating male violence. Once you permit yourself to be perceived as a sexual creature, then you become open territory, open prey. Actual sexual violence oppresses us. But the climate of fear we live in also oppresses us horribly and makes us feel that we cannot afford to take any risks to discover our own sexuality and be experimental in any way.

Gayle: Let's look back at what we thought that threat was when we were growing up. Part of the problem is that sex itself is seen as dangerous and violent. It is predicated on a Victorian model of distribution of libido in terms of male and female. There was the good woman who was not sexual. There is the man who is sexual. So whenever sex happens between a good woman and a man, it's a kind of violation of her. It's something she doesn't want. The good woman, you know, doesn't move. Her husband, of course, is more of an animal, so he gets off. If you were a good woman and had sex, terrible things might happen to you; good women who had sex out of wedlock became bad women. They fell, and became prostitutes and they were excluded from the comforts of family and home.

This model imposes a moral discourse over a class analysis of who is really doing what sexually. Because the women who were by and large hooking in Victorian England were poor women. And the women who were able to maintain their purity were middle-class women or well-to-do women. And this model scares women into being sexually repressed, and gives women the idea (especially respectable women) that sex itself is violence.

Amber: It was terrifying that there was so little birth control, which added another element of fear to sex.

Gayle: I'm not denying that there was a semi-rational basis for these views. But I am saying that the notion that sex itself is violent is very much with us. The woman who raised me was raised by a Victorian. We're not that far from that system and you have to remember that in the nineteenth century, great social resources were expended trying to eliminate masturbation under the theory that masturbation caused insanity, disease and degeneration.

Deirdre: We live in such a strange transitional time that we bear the marks – we women – of extreme sexual repression, total lack of images being motivated by sexual desire. Even predatory women in the movies are motivated by romance, or romantic pathology. But there are few images of healthy, assertive sexuality. Or lust. Yet at the same time we no longer want to be sexually repressed.

Gayle: There's a geography of access to certain kinds of sexual and erotic experience. I wouldn't call them liberated zones, because they're not. But there really are zones of more and less freedom. For instance, there is the gay community. There are the porn districts, which provide people with a range of experiences they can't get in a suburban family.

Part of what the politics of sex is about is respectable society trying to keep those other sectors at bay, keeping them impoverished, keeping the people in them harassed, not letting people know they are there, and generally making sure that they are marginal. That permits an enormous amount of exploitation of the people in them. One of the reasons why women in the sex industry are exploited is because of the police and social pressures on the industry. It means the people in the industry do not have unions, they do not have police protection, and they can't organize to improve the conditions of their work.

Part of the problem is that we use different standards when we talk about sex than for almost any other aspect of life. Whatever your analysis of commodities, people are not upset that we have to go and get food. People are upset at the structure of the organizations that provide and produce the food, but the food itself is okay. We don't feel that way about sex. We also feel that it's okay to exchange food for some other service. But when we think about sex, we think that any social exchange of sex is bad other than a romantic one. I don't think this is either a socialist or feminist idea. I think it's either a Christian or a Victorian one.

Amber: There's an assumption that pornography is only for men, and there is no female counterpart. But that's not true. A recent article argues that there is a female counterpart, in Harlequin Romances.[2] This is my experience. I grew up reading those books, I still read them. These were acceptable for women – romance books where it took 89 pages for a reluctant first kiss and another 120 to get married and a fade out. The endless pages of tingling skins and the desire to bruise the mouth have never been described as porn. But that's really what they are.

Gayle: Well, they are and they aren't. They're turn-on literature for women, but there's no explicit sex in them. They are not literally pornographic in that sense.

Amber: But they are a sexual literature.

Gayle: Yes, and one of the interesting things about them in terms of the anti-porn analysis is that the social relations in the Harlequin and gothic novels always display a basic sexism unparalleled in the culture. There's always a very strong man who sweeps this woman off her feet, and through romance the gender hierarchy is reproduced. Yet I have seen no one marching in the streets to ban the neo-gothic novel.

Deirdre: I think that the anti-porn movement would say that that's okay because they're harmless, that feminists only oppose materials that provoke violence against women.

Amber: I could make a strong argument for the potential violence of Harlequin romances around gender and roles.

Gayle: I think those novels help teach women a structure of fantasy that enables them to participate in unequal social relationships. One response might be then, well, those novels have to be changed, too. What's interesting is that the question of the social reproduction of the emotional and erotic components of gender hierarchy is reduced to the question of sexual materials. Much of the argument about porn says that what's wrong with it is the bad social relations in it. But since there are equally bad social relations in a whole range of other forms, what distinguishes porn from the other media is that it is the explicit sexual medium.

Amber: Absolutely. In the history of women's sexual experiences from the Victorian era, love has been women's sphere, and men's has been sex. So I don't think that it's an accident that Harlequin romances are not sexual explicit but create a romantic fantasy life for women, while *Hustler* and *Penthouse* purport to be for men. Women also read them so I don't want to argue that they are only for men. But the industry at least initially was based on a male market and male fantasies.

Gayle: The industry of sexual fantasy has been sex segregated. The romances are basically oriented towards women and porn is basically oriented towards men. Having access to sexually explicit material has by and large been a male privilege. Yet rather than wanting to get rid of it, since women haven't been able to get it, I want women to be able to get it.

Amber: Deirdre said something in her article that I agree with. 'There's still a long way to go to uncover the feminist or pro-women or equal love life. To get there we need non-sexist sexual images. A lot more of them. In short, perhaps what we need even more than Women Against Pornography are women pornographers, or eroticists, if that sounds better.'

Deirdre: But that doesn't mean that women will want to create and consume the same sexual imagery that we currently see in the domain of pornography. They might. But they might create something completely different.

Gayle: Well, we might. And we probably will. But some of the first and major victims of the anti-porn sentiment have been indigenous female eroticists. And it's gotten to the point now in the women's movement that if anything is sexual, it's immediately considered to be violent. The porn that's available now is not so wonderful or gratifying. I mean I go to a porn show now and there's almost nothing about my fantasies. I see very few women in blue jeans, very few women with broad shoulders and muscles, standing next to motorcycles, and a whole range of other things I find a turn on. The fact is that there's not a lot of porn oriented towards minorities of any sort. Gay men probably have the best-produced porn. And one reason gay male porn is better is that a lot of it is produced by gay men and for gay men.

■ What is pornography?

Amber: What is pornography? What do we define as pornography?

Gayle: I have a three-part definition. One, the legal definition, is that it's sexually explicit material designed to arouse prurient interest. I think that definition, at least for this historical time and place, is the most useful one. We should remember that porn is not legal, by this definition material that has no focus but to arouse is not legal. In other words, a sexual aim is not considered legitimate in this culture. But we also need a historical definition, i.e. porn as we know it is widely available commercial erotica, as opposed to the older erotica that was hand-produced and was mostly something that rich people collected. In the middle of the last century, mass production of erotic materials started to take place, resulting in the cheap, printed dirty book. Thirdly, I have a sociological definition: pornography is a particular industry located in certain places, with certain kinds of shops which tend to put out a product with certain conventions. One convention, for example, is that a man's orgasm never happens inside the woman. Pornography has a concrete existence that you can define sociologically. But that's not the current, so-called feminist definition of porn.

Amber: What's that – 'what we don't like is pornographic'?

Gayle: The definition used in the anti-porn movement is that pornography is violence against women, and that violence against women is pornography. There are several problems with this. One is a replacement of the institutional forms of violence with representations of violence. That is to say, there's been a conflating of images with the thing itself. People don't really talk about the institutions, they talk about the images; images are important, but they're not the whole thing.

Actually, if you walk into an adult bookstore, 90 per cent of the material you will see is frontal nudity, intercourse and oral sex, with no hint of violence or coercion. There are speciality porns. There's gay male porn, that's a big sub-genre. There used to be a genre of porn that featured young people, although that's now so illegal that you don't see it any more. And there is a genre of porn that caters to sadomasochists, which is the porn that they focus on when you see a WAVPM or a WAP[3] slide show. They show the worst possible porn, and claim that it's representative of all of it. The two images that they show most are sadomasochistic porn, and images of violence that contain sex. For instance, the infamous *Hustler* cover with the woman being shoved through a meat grinder. An awful picture, but by no means a common image in pornography.

Deirdre: It was self-parody. It was gross but it was actually satirical, a self-critical joke, which a lot of people didn't get.

Gayle: They include images that are not pornographic, that you cannot find in an adult bookstore. For instance, the stuff on billboards, the stuff on record covers, the stuff in *Vogue*. None of it has explicit sexual content. At most, it's covert. And what they do is draw in images that they consider to be violent, or coercive, or demeaning, and call that pornography. That definition enables them to avoid the empirical question of how much porn really is really violent. Their analysis is that the violent images come out of porn and into the culture at large, that sexism comes from porn into the culture. Whereas it seems to me that pornography only *reflects* as much sexism as is in the culture.

The existence of S/M porn enabled this whole analysis to proceed. It's very disturbing to most people, and contains scenes that most people don't even want to encounter in their lives. They don't realize that S/M porn is about fantasy. What most people do with it is take it home and masturbate. Those people who do S/M are consensually acting out fantasies. The category of people who read and use S/M porn and the category of violent rapists is not the same. We used to talk about how religion and the state and the family create sexism and promote rape. No one talks about any of these institutions any more. They've become good guys!

Amber: And now pornography creates sexism and violence against women.

Deirdre: One of the things that has amazed me, and I don't know what to make of it, is that many anti-porn activists see red if they hear you say that the violent porn is a minority within the whole industry. They would just not agree with you. Now, when I went into those bookstores, I saw basically what you see. And I agree with your description.

Gayle: When I went on the WAVPM tour, everybody went and stood in front of the bondage material. It was like they had on blinkers. And I said, look, there's oral sex over there! Why don't you look at that? And they were glued to the bondage rack. I started pulling out female dominance magazines, and saying, look, here's a woman dominating a man. What about that? Here's a woman who's tied up a man. What about that? It was like I wasn't there. People said, look at this picture of a woman being tied up!

Amber: Another example in the WAVPM slide show, there will be an image from a porn magazine of a woman tied up, beaten, right? And they'll say, *Hustler* magazine, 1976, and you're struck dumb by it, horrified! The next slide will be a picture of a woman with a police file, badly beaten by her husband. And the rap that connects these two is that the image of the woman tied and bruised in the pornographic magazine *caused* the beating that she suffered. The talk implies that her husband went and saw that picture, then came home and tried to recreate it in their bedroom. That is the guilt by association theory of pornography and violence. And I remember sitting and watching this slide show and being freaked out about both of those images. And having nowhere to react to the analysis and say, what the hell is going on? I found it incredibly manipulative.

Gayle: Some of the anti-porn people are looking at material that is used in a particular subculture with a particular meaning and a particular set of conventions and saying, it doesn't mean what it means to the people who are using it, it means what we see! They're assuming that they know better than the people who are familiar with it. They're assuming, for example, that S/M is violent, and that analysis leads to the view that S/M people can't be the victims of violence.

Amber: It also discourages anyone from making explicit any sexual fantasy which seems risky to them or from exploring a sexual terrain that's not familiar. It ignores the fact that you learn what you like and what you don't through trying things out. What it says is that these forbidden desires are not ours but imposed on you. You never experiment sexually.

Yet most people know goddamn well that their sex lives are wider than those standard notions let them play in. They may feel guilty about it but they know it. So they don't need one more movement to tell them that they can't play.

Gayle: Anal sex is a real good example, I think, of some of the way that this all works. It can seem like the most appalling thing in the world, so unpleasant that your idea is that no one else would find it pleasant unless they were coerced into it. And therefore all anal sex is a form of coercion or rape. And the truth is that anal sex for some people is pleasurable, and is not always done under duress. That's true of almost all of the sexual variations. What is one person's horror show is another person's delight.

■ The politics of pornography

Amber: In fact, some women working in the anti-porn movement would agree with us about opening up sexual possibilities for women but still believe that pornography is the link with violence against women.

Gayle: Sure, there are differences in that movement. I just think that they have to be held accountable for the social impact of the politics they're promulgating. I think that to focus on porn as a solution to the problem of violence is wrong. It won't substantially reduce the amount of violence against women. Porn may not be the most edifying form of sexual material that we can imagine, but it is the most available sexual material. To attack that is ultimately going to reduce the amount of social space available to talk about sex in an explicit way.

Deirdre: I think we're being too uncritical of porn. Your definition of porn is probably more positive than the way pornography functions for a lot of people. It's important to point out that a great deal of pornography is deeply sexist. And that it contains a hideous and misogynistic view of women.

Gayle: It also contains a hideous view of sexual minorities, including the people who do all the stuff the anti-porn movement is so upset by, including S/M.

Deirdre: And the constant repetition of those sexist images of women does validate the sexism of sexist people who buy and consume it.

Gayle: So does the TV they watch.

Deirdre: Yes.

Gayle: And the novels they read.

Deirdre: Yes, and everything else. But there may be nothing in their lives that ever says to consumers of pornography that shows violence against women, this is a fantasy, women don't really want to be raped or brutalized. They may never get the message that porn depicts behaviour that is in fact not acceptable to women. And that is a serious problem.

Gayle: I disagree. I think there is a serious problem with pornography when it does not challenge sexism or racism or homophobia or anti-variation bigotry. But again, while there is sexism in all porn and there are violent images from a variety of media sources, there is not a whole lot of violent porn *per se*.

Amber: Then let's really talk about sexist porn.

Gayle: Okay. I have no objection to being critical of the content of porn, recreating non-sexist porn, and having better sex education and talking to men about what women really want sexually. But that has not been the agenda of the anti-porn movement.

Deirdre: All right. But I want to stress that we are strongly speaking for an anti-sexist movement in every domain of society.

Amber: Pornography is not the first thing to worry about in trying to go to the root of things that destroy, brutalize and murder women.

Deirdre: Right. I don't think I'd try to change pornography first. What I'm trying to say is that what's very important is that there be a strong anti-sexist movement as a point of reference. For example, women should be able to enjoy, say, masochistic pornography or dominance and submission fantasies in a safe context. But there should also be a source of support, a movement saying that that does not mean women want to be beat up.

Gayle: Absolutely. But the fact that we have a movement against sexism does not mean that the movement is always wise or alert to the real sources of distress that people feel. For two or three years now, ever since Anita Bryant, there has been an enormous increase in police activity and state repression against all of those parts of the sexual world that are not mainstream. The cost to the people who've been beaten up and who've gone to jail and lost their livelihood is immense. There is an insidious moral blindness to this reality in the women's movement, one encouraged by the anti-porn line. Two resolutions that were recently passed disturb me. One is a resolution passed by the National Organization for Women in 1980 that reaffirms NOW's support for lesbian rights, but specifically says that public sex, pederasty, S/M and pornography are issues of violence and not of sexual preference. These are specifically excluded from the definition of a lesbian or gay group that NOW would work with. The second resolution was passed by the National Lawyers Guild, a resolution against porn based on all of the analyses we've been talking about, saying that it is violence against women. It encourages the members of the Guild not to defend people who are arrested on porn charges, and to defend people who are arrested doing anti-porn work. This isolates the victims of repression and delivers them up to the state.

Amber: These resolutions close off the only areas in which some of these victims of repression could hope to find support. They need to be placed in a context, which is reification of the nuclear family and re-emphasis on male-dominated, heterosexual marriage as the only sexual model. And when the feminist movement focuses on pornography rather than the violence of institutions like marriage and enforced heterosexuality and a variety of other things, it endangers its own future.

Deirdre: But I think that it's very important for us to have a critique of sexist pornography as well as a critique of the anti-porn movements.

Gayle: But issues that are very important to me have been compromised by bad politics. I would love to go, as you were saying earlier, Deirdre, on a march to take back the night, and demonstrate against violence. But I would not like to go on an anti-porn march. I would love to talk more about the whole issue of the way that the media are involved in the social reproduction of sexism. There are things being promoted in the name of feminist ideology that are destructive. I don't want a viable and powerful women's movement to create social havoc rather than create social good. Many social movements have had wonderful intentions but left a dreadful legacy. And we're not magically an exception to that.

Amber: What we began talking about and what hopefully we end on is that this is an opening up of the discussion that will allow us to figure out what these questions are. We're not really arguing that everything we're saying is correct, but the feminist movement has got to allow a wider discussion of all sorts of sexual issues and what they are and how they combine.

■ Notes

This conversation was first published in the American magazine *Socialist Review* (No. 58; Vol. 11 No. 4, 1984). *Feminist Review* thanks the three women who had the conversation and *Socialist Review* for permission to reprint it.

1 See English (1980).
2 See Snitow (1979:141-61).
3 Women Against Violence in Pornography and the Media, and Women Against Pornography.

Seeking Ecstacy on the Battlefield: Danger and Pleasure in Nineteenth-Century Feminist Sexual Thought

Linda Gordon and Ellen DuBois

It is often alleged that female sexuality is a more complex matter than male, and if so, a major reason is that sex spells potential danger as well as pleasure for women.[1] A feminist politics about sex, therefore, if it is to be credible as well as hopeful, must seek both to protect women from sexual danger and to encourage their pursuit of sexual pleasure.

This complex understanding of female sexuality has not always characterized the feminist movement. In general we inherit two conflicting traditions in the feminist approach to sex. The strongest, virtually unchallenged in the mainstream women's rights movement of the nineteenth century, addressed primarily the danger and few of the possibilities of sex. Another perspective, much less developed but with some eloquent spokeswomen by the early twentieth century, encouraged women to leap, adventurous and carefree, into sexual liaisons, but failed to offer a critique of the male construction of the sexual experience available to most women. It is no use labelling one side feminist and the other anti, to argue by name-calling. We cannot move ahead unless we grasp that both traditions are part of our feminism.

Neither feminist tradition is adequate to our needs today. Both were thoroughly heterosexist in their assumptions of what sex is. Even the nineteenth-century women who experienced intense emotional and physical relationships with each other did not incorporate these into their definition of what was sexual. Certainly women had relationships with other women that included powerful sexual components, but the feminists who are the subjects of this paper did not theorize these relationships as sexual (Smith Rosenberg, 1975; Cook, 1977; Faderman, 1981).[2]

Furthermore, both feminist lines of thought – that emphasizing danger and that emphasizing pleasure – were often moralistic. They condemned those whose sexual behaviour deviated from their standards, not only sexually exploitive men, but also sexually non-conforming women.

Still, without an appreciation of these legacies and the processes of thought and experience that produced them, we cannot have much historical insight into our own concerns. Without a history, political movements like ours swing back and forth endlessly, reacting to earlier mistakes and overreacting in compensation, unable to incorporate previous insights and transcend previous limitations. Today we observe some of that pendulum-like motion. In reaction to the profound disappointments of what has passed for 'sexual liberation', some feminists are replicating an earlier tradition, focusing exclusively on danger and advocating what we believe to be a conservative sexual politics.

We use a label like 'conservative' cautiously. Such terms, like 'left' and 'right', come to us from class politics. When applied to sex and gender, they fit less comfortably. The oppressions of women, the repressions of sex, are so many and so complex, by virtue of their location in the most intimate corners of life, co-existing even with love, that it is not always obvious in which direction a better world lies. We use the term 'conservatism' to characterize strategies which accept existing power relations. We are suggesting that even feminist reform programmes can be conservative in some respects if they accept male dominance while trying to elevate women's status within it. In this case, we believe that the nineteenth-century feminist mainstream accepted women's sexual powerlessness with men as inevitable, even as they sought to protect women from its worst consequences. Their appraisal of women's sexual victimization was not, on balance, offset by recognition of women's potential for sexual activity and enjoyment.

We think our judgement will be justified by the historical description which follows. Through that description we hope to show, too, that despite the stubborn continuities of women's sexual oppression, there have also been momentous changes in the last 150 years, changes which require different strategies today.

The feminist movement has played an important role in organizing and even creating women's sense of sexual danger in the last 150 years. In that movement, two themes more than others have encapsulated and symbolized women's fears: prostitution and rape. There is a certain parallel construction between the nineteenth-century focus on prostitution and the modern emphasis on rape as the quintessential sexual terror. It is remarkable, in fact, how little emphasis nineteenth-century feminists placed on rape *per se*. It is as if the norms of legal sexual intercourse were in themselves so objectionable, rape did not seem that much worse! Instead feminists used prostitution as the leading symbol of male sexual coercion. While rape is an episode, prostitution suggests a condition which takes hold of a woman for a long time, possibly for life, difficult to escape from. The symbolic emphasis in prostitution is on ownership, possession, purchase by men, while in rape it is on pure violence. Finally, while rape can happen to any woman, prostitution involves the separation of women into the good and the bad, a division with class implications as we shall see, even when the division is blamed on men.

Lest it seem trivializing to the real sufferings of women as prostitutes or rape victims to treat these experiences as symbols or metaphors, let us emphasize again our subject: we are looking at how feminists conceptualized different sexual dangers, as a means of organizing *resistance* to sexual oppression. We want to look at how these feminist strategies changed, so that we can examine historically how we conduct feminist campaigns around sexual issues today.

In different periods, feminists emphasized different aspects of prostitution. In the 1860s and 1870s, for example, they focused on the economic pressures forcing women into sexual commerce, while in the early Progressive period their primary theme was 'white slavery', the physical coercion of women into the trade. Despite these shifts, however, aspects of their approach to prostitution were consistent. First, they exaggerated its magnitude.[3] They did so because their definition of prostitute included virtually all women who engaged in casual sex, whether or not they were paid. Second, feminists consistently exaggerated the coerciveness of prostitution. In their eagerness to identify the social structural forces encouraging prostitution, they denied the prostitute any role other than that of passive victim. They insisted that the women involved were sexual innocents, helpless young women who 'fell' into illicit sex. They assumed that prostitution was so degrading that no woman could freely choose it, even with the relative degree of freedom with which she could choose to be a wife or a wage-earner. Thus the 'fallen woman' was always viewed as a direct victim, not only of male dominance in general, but of kidnapping, sexual imprisonment, starvation and/or seduction in particular (Connelly, 1980; Walkowitz, 1980). These attitudes towards prostitution were not exclusive to feminists, but were also part of the ideological outlook of many male reformers, including some anti-feminists. Our point here, however, is that feminists not only failed to challenge this oversimplified and condescending explanation of prostitution, but also made it central to their understanding of women's oppression.

The feminists' exclusive emphasis on the victimization of the prostitute ultimately prevented their transcending a sexual morality dividing women into the good and the bad (Jameson, 1977; Goldman, 1981). They wanted to rescue women from prostitution, and to admit prostitution's victims into the salvation of good womanhood; but they clung fast to the idea that some kinds of sex were inherently criminal, and they were confounded by the existence of unrepentant whores.

Their equation of prostitution with any illicit sex indicates that a crucial element of their fear was loss of respectability. The power of prostitution rested on the common understanding that once a woman had sex outside marriage she was 'ruined', and would become a prostitute sooner or later. Nor was this loss of respectability imaginary. It was a real, material process with sanctions that varied by culture and class. For middle-class and many white working-class women, the loss of purity – we would call it, getting a bad reputation – damaged prospects for marriage. It led to a total loss of control over one's own sexuality, as once 'used' by a man women became free game for that entire sex.

Maintaining respectability was an especially severe problem for Black women, fighting to free their entire race from a slave heritage which tended to place them at the disposal of white men's sexual demands. Thus the Black women's movement conducted a particularly militant campaign for respectability, often making Black feminists spokespeople for prudery in their communities (Lerner, 1972; Neverdon-Morton, 1978). White feminists assimilated the horror of Black slavery to their fears of prostitution. They understood the sexual tyranny of slavery as central, and as a form of prostitution; among their most powerful anti-slavery writings were images of beautiful, pure Black womanhood defiled; and white feminist abolitionists found it difficult to accept the possibility of willing sex between Black women and white men (Child, 1833; Stanton, 1860).

The fear of prostitution represented also a fear of direct physical violence, but in a displaced manner. In the nineteenth century, as today, women encountered sexual and non-sexual violence most often at home. Rape in marriage was no crime, not even generally disapproved; wife-beating was only marginally criminal. Incest was common enough to require scepticism about the idea that it was tabooed. Although feminists occasionally organized against domestic violence, they did not make it the object of a sustained campaign, largely because they were unable to challenge the family politically (Gordon, 1976; O'Neill, 1971). The focus on prostitution was a focus on extra-familial violence. They came closer to intra-family matters in the temperance campaign. Their criticisms of drinking were laced through with imagery of the bestial, violent quality of male sexuality, but blaming alcohol also allowed a displacement of focus to avoid criticizing men and marriage directly (Epstein, 1981; Bordin, 1981).

Certain dangers in marriage had to be faced. One was venereal disease, and this too was assimilated to the central imagery of prostitution, for men who patronized prostitutes could then transmit disease to their wives. In keeping with the division of women between good and bad, feminists implicitly considered prostitution as the source of VD. The communicability and incurability of these diseases proved to them that absolute monogamy was women's only source of safety amid the sexual dangers (Sigsworth and Wyke, 1972; Walkowitz, 1980; Connelly, 1980; Gordon, 1976). Feminists also opposed the sexual demands of self-centred husbands on their wives, which law and convention obliged women to meet. But instead of protesting 'marital rape', as we do, they criticized what they called 'legalized prostitution' in marriage (Stanton, 1869; Chandler, 1888).

Sex posed another serious danger in marriage – unwanted conception. Given the equation of sex with intercourse, and the lack of access to reliable contraception, desire to control conceptions often led women to antisexual attitudes (Gordon, 1976). Despite a great reverence for motherhood, an unexpected pregnancy was often threatening. For poor women, for virtually all Black women, having children meant introducing them into social and economic circumstances where their safety and well-being could not be guaranteed. Even for prosperous women, mothers' economic dependence on men was extreme. Single motherhood was an extremely difficult situation in the absence of any regular welfare or childcare provisions. Mothers were frequently forced to remain with abusive men for fear of losing their children. Indeed, prostitution was sometimes seen as an option for a single mother, for at least she could do it while she remained at home with her children![4] A bitter irony surrounds the place of motherhood in the sexual system of nineteenth-century feminism. Clearly it was women's greatest joy and source of dignity; for many women it was what made intercourse acceptable. But at the same time motherhood was the last straw in enforcing women's subordination to men, the factor that finally prevented many from seeking independence. What was conceived as women's greatest virtue, their passionate and self-sacrificing commitment to their children, their capacity for love itself, was a leading factor in their victimization.

Of the many factors constructing the feminist fear of prostitution perhaps none is so hard for contemporary feminists to understand as religion. But we would miss the dilemma that these women faced in dealing with sex if we did not thoroughly appreciate their religious culture. Those actively rebelling against established religion were as influenced by it as the dutiful church members or Christian reform activists. All had been raised on the concept of sin, especially sexual sin. They all shared the view that there could be high and low pleasures, and the guilt they felt about indulging in the low was not just psychological self-doubt. It was a sense of self-violation, of violation of the source of their dignity (Sklar, 1973; DuBois, 1981).

We are arguing here that the feminist understanding of sexual danger, expressed so poignantly in the fear of prostitution, must be seen as part of a sexual system in which they were participants, sometimes willing and sometimes unwilling, sometimes conscious and sometimes unaware.[5] Their very resistance often drew them into accommodation with aspects of this oppressive system. What is surprising is the extent of resistance that actually challenged this sexual system. Some women labelled 'loose', who might or might not have been prostitutes, rejected the notion that their disreputable sexual behaviour was something to be ashamed of or something that had been forced upon them (Rosen, 1977). There were young sexual 'delinquents' who took pleasure and pride in their rebellion (Freedman, 1981; Rosenberg, 1982; Glueck, 1934; Fernald, 1920). There were women who passed as men in order to seize male sexual (and other) prerogatives, and to take other women as wives (Katz, 1976). Even respectable, middle-class married women had orgasms more than they were supposed to. One survey had 40 per cent of women reporting orgasms occasionally, 20 per cent frequently, and 40 per cent never, proportions which may not be so different than those among women today (Degler, 1980; Campbell, 1981; Hite, 1976).

About the present, it is angering that so many women do not experience orgasm; about the past, it is impressive – and analytically important – that so many women did. In other words, our nineteenth-century legacy is one of resistance to sexual repression as well as victimization by it.

Despite resistance, the weight of the nineteenth-century feminist concern was with protection from danger. This approach, usually known as 'social purity', reflected an experienced reality and was overwhelmingly protectionist in its emphasis.

The major target of the feminist social purity advocates was the double standard. Their attack on it had, in turn, two aspects: seeking greater safety for women and more penalties for men. Their object was to achieve a set of controls over sexuality, structured through the family, enforced through law and/or social morality, which would render sex, if not safe, at least a decent, calculable risk for women. Social purity feminists railed against male sexual privileges, against the vileness of male drunkenness and lust, and they sought with every means at their disposal to increase the costs attached to such indulgences (Pivar, 1973; Degler, 1980; Gordon, 1976; Walkowitz, 1980).

The most positive achievements of social purity feminism were in the homes and communities of the middle-class women most likely to be its advocates. Here, efforts to make marriage laws more egalitarian, upgrade women's property rights, and improve women's educational and professional opportunities altered the balance of power between husband and wife. Social purity thought emphasized the importance of consensual sex for women, and insisted that even married women should not be coerced into any sexual activities they did not choose freely; inasmuch as they believed that sexual drive and initiative were primarily male, they understood this as women's right to say no. Through organizations like the Women's Christian Temperance Union, feminists propagandized for these standards, with tirades against the threat to civilization caused by immorality, and energetic moral and sex education programmes (Epstein, 1981; Bordin, 1981). And they succeeded in changing culture and consciousness. Without knowing precisely how much people's lives conformed to this standard, we can say that the ideals of marital mutuality and a woman's right to say no were absorbed into middle-class culture by the turn of the century. There is mounting evidence that, for reasons not yet clear, immigrant and poor women did not establish the same standards of marital mutuality, but fought for power within their families differently, by accepting certain patriarchal prerogatives while asserting their power as mothers and housewives (Degler, 1980; Zaretsky, 1980; Hall, 1978).[6]

The negative consequences of social purity's single-minded concentration on sexual danger come into focus when we look at their vigorous campaign against prostitution. Over time the repressive tendencies of this campaign overwhelmed its liberatory ones and threw a pall over feminism's whole approach to sexuality. The beginning of women's reform work on prostitution in the early nineteenth century was a big step forward in the development of feminism. That 'respectable' women took the risk of reaching out, across a veritable gulf of sexual sin, to women stigmatized as whores, was a declaration of female collectivity that transcended class and moralistic divisions. The reformers visited and talked with prostitutes, conducted public discussions of the issue, and established homes into which prostitutes could 'escape'. In doing so they were opening a crack in the wall of sexual 'innocence' that would eventually widen into an escape route for women of their class as well. The attitudes that we today perceive as a patronizing desire to 'help' were initially a challenge to the punitive and woman-hating morality that made sexual 'ruin' a permanent and unredeemable condition for women (Smith Rosenberg, 1971; Ryan, 1979; Berg, 1978).

In the 1860s and 1870s feminists reactivated themselves into a militant and successful campaign to halt government regulation of prostitution. The system of regulation, already in existence in France and parts of England, forced women alleged to be prostitutes to submit to vaginal examinations and licensing; its purpose was to allow men to have sex with prostitutes without the risk of VD. Feminist opposition drew not only from their anger at men who bought female flesh, but also reaffirmed their identification with prostitutes' victimization. Feminists asserted that all women, even prostitutes, had a right to the integrity of their own bodies (Walkowitz, 1980; Pivar, 1973; Burnham, 1971).

But, after a relatively easy victory over government regulation, social purity feminists began to press for the abolition of prostitution itself. They sponsored legislation to increase the criminal penalties for men clients, while continuing to express sympathy with the 'victimized' women. The catch was that the prostitutes had to agree that they were victims. The 'white-slavery' interpretation of prostitution – that prostitutes had been forced into the business – allowed feminists to see themselves as rescuers of slaves (Connelly, 1980; Pivar, 1973; Walkowitz, 1980; Buhle, 1981; Gorham, 1978). But if the prostitutes were not contrite, or denied the immorality of their actions, they lost their claim to the aid and sympathy of the reformers. 'The big sisters of the world [want the] chance to protect the little and weaker sisters, by surrounding them with the right laws for them to obey for their own good,' one feminist explained, unwittingly capturing the repressive character of this 'sisterhood' (Norton, 1913). The class nature of American society encouraged these middle-class feminists to conduct their challenge to the double standard through other women's lives, and to focus their anger on men other than their own husbands and fathers.

Another attack on prostitution which sometimes turned into an attack on women was the campaign to raise the age of sexual consent (Pearson, 1972; Pivar, 1973; Degler, 1980; Gorham, 1978). In many states in the nineteenth century this had been as low as nine or ten years for girls. The feminist goals were to deny the white slavers their younger victims, to extend sexual protection to girls, and to provide punishments for male assailants. Like most of these feminist sexual causes this one had in it a radical moment: it communicated an accurate critique of the limitations of 'consent' by women in a male-dominated society. Yet by late in the century, when urban life and the presence of millions of young working girls changed the shape of family and generational relations, age-of-consent legislation explicitly denied women the right to heterosexual activity until they were adults, or – and note that this qualification applied at any age – married. In fostering this hostility to girls' sexual activity, the feminists colluded in the labelling of a new class of female offenders: teenage sex delinquents. Sex delinquency was soon the largest category within which young women were sent to reformatories (Schlossman, 1977; Thomas, 1923). These moralistic reformers, some of them feminists, allowed the criminal justice system to take over the task of disciplining teenage girls into respectable morality.

This inability to see anything in prostitution but male tyranny and/or economic oppression affected not only 'bad' women, but the 'good' ones as well. Feminists' refusal to engage in a concrete examination of the actuality of prostitution was of a piece with their inability to look without panic at any form of sexual nonconformity (Fishbein, 1980). We do not suggest that prostitutes were necessarily freer than other women sexually. Our point is that feminists remained committed to the containment of female sexuality within heterosexual marriage, despite the relative sexual repressiveness which marriage meant for women at that time. 'Are our girls to be [as] free to please themselves in indulging in the loveless gratification of every instinct ...

and passion as our boys?' the social purity feminist Frances Willard asked her audience in 1891; and we can imagine that they answered with a resounding 'No' (quoted in Pivar, 1973).

Feminist politics about sex became more conservative in the pre-World War I period because women's aspirations and possibilities outstripped the feminist orthodoxy. Growing feminist organizational strength, and the ability to influence legislation, combined with the class and racial elitism of the world in which the feminists moved, further strengthened their conservative political tendencies. Social purity feminists not only accepted a confining sexual morality for women, but excluded from their sisterhood women who did not or could not go along. The prostitute remained, for all their sympathy for her, the leading symbol of the woman excluded, not only from male-bestowed privilege, but also from the women's community (Rosen, 1977).

Yet, just as there was behavioural resistance to the sexually repressive culture of the nineteenth century, so too there was political resistance within the women's movement. Although a decidedly minority viewpoint, a thin but continuous stream of feminists insisted that more (heterosexual) sex was not incompatible with women's dignity and might even be in women's interests. We refer to this as the pro-sex tendency within the feminist tradition. It began with the free love and utopian movements of the 1820s-1840s. These radicals challenged the identification of sexual desire as masculine; and even though they remained for the most part advocates of the strictest monogamy, they challenged the coercive family and legal marriage as the channels for sexuality (Stoehr, 1979; Sears, 1977; Gordon, 1976; Marsh, 1981; Leach, 1981). In the 1870s the free lover Victoria Woodhull appeared as a spokesperson from within the women's movement, idealizing as 'true love' sex which involved mutual desire and orgasms for both parties (Woodhull, 1874). At the same time Elizabeth Cady Stanton, a revered if maverick heroine, also asserted women's sexual desires (DuBois, 1981). In the 1880s and 1890s a few extremely visionary free love feminists began to formulate the outlines of a sexuality not organized around the male orgasm. Alice Stockham, a physician and suffragist, condemned the 'ordinary, hasty and spasmodic mode of cohabitation ... in which the wife is a passive party' and envisioned instead a union in which 'the desires and pleasure of the wife calls forth the desire and pleasure of the husband' (Stockham, 1897). Still, on the whole these nineteenth-century feminists were only *relatively* pro-sex, and most of them shared with social purity advocates a belief in the need to control, contain and harness physiological sex expression to 'higher' ends. Furthermore, even this limited sex-radical tradition was so marginal to American feminism that when the twentieth-century feminist Margaret Sanger searched for a more positive attitude to sex for women, she had to go to Europe to find it.

The only issue within mainstream nineteenth-century feminism where pro-sex ideas had a significant impact was divorce. Led by Elizabeth Cady Stanton, some feminists argued that the right to divorce and *then to remarry* – for that was the crucial element, the right to another sexual relationship after leaving a first – was a freedom important enough to women to risk granting it to men as well. Still, most feminists took a strict social purity line and opposed divorce for fear it would weaken marriage and expose women to even greater sexual danger (O'Neill, 1973; DuBois, 1981; Leach, 1981).

Ironically, one sexual reform strongly supported by social purity advocates became the vehicle by which a new generation of feminists began to break with the social purity tradition. This was birth control (Gordon, 1976; Reed, 1978). Nineteenth-century feminists had argued this as 'voluntary motherhood', the right of women to refuse intercourse with their husbands if they did not want to conceive. Voluntary motherhood was a brilliant tactic because it insinuated rejection of men's sexual domination into a politics of defending and improving motherhood. Consistent with its social purity orientation, voluntary motherhood advocates rejected contraception as a form of birth control for fear it would allow men to force even more sex upon their wives and to indulge in extra-marital sex with even greater impunity. In the early twentieth century, by contrast, an insurgent feminist support for contraception arose, insisting that sexual abstinence was an unnecessary price for women to pay for reproductive self-determination, and that sexual indulgence in the pursuit of pleasure was good for women.

That this new generation of feminists could break with social purity was possible in part because they were no longer controlled by their fear of becoming, or being labelled, prostitutes. They no longer saw the prostitute as only a victim; they began to break the association between sexual desire and prostitution. Indeed they embraced and romanticized sexual daring of all sorts (Ware, 1935; Dorr, 1924; Dell, 1926; Buhle, 1981; Gordon, 1976; Schwarz, 1982). The spectre of the white slaver no longer haunted them and they were willing to take risks. They ventured unchaperoned into theatres and bars, lived without families in big cities, and moved about the city to discover the lives of those across class and race boundaries where their mothers would not have gone. Some of their names you recognize – Emma Goldman, Margaret Sanger, Crystal Eastman, Elizabeth Gurley Flynn, even Louise Bryant – but there were many, many more. Above all they asserted a woman's right to be sexual. They slept with men without marrying. They took multiple lovers. They became single mothers. Some of them had explicitly sexual relationships with other women, although a subsequent repression of evidence, along with their own silences about homosexuality, make it hard for us to uncover this aspect of their sexual lives (Schwartz, 1982; Sanders, 1973; Katz, 1976; Cook, 1977).[7]

In many ways these women were beginning to explore a sexual world which we are determined to occupy. But as pioneers they could explore only part of it and they did not imagine changing its overall boundaries. Even when it contradicted their own experience, they continued to accept a male and heterosexual definition of the 'sex act'. They were, so to speak, upwardly mobile, and they wanted integration into the sexual world as defined by men. The man's orgasm remained the central event, although now it was preferable if a woman had one at the same time; stimulation other than intercourse was considered foreplay; masturbation was unhealthy. And sex, all the more desirable now because of the transcendent possibilities they attributed to it, remained bound up with the structure of gender: it could only happen between a man and a woman (Gordon, 1976).[8] These feminists criticized male dominance in the labour force and in the public arena, but they did not seem to notice how it shaped sex. They fought for women's freedom but they rarely criticized men.

Once the organized women's rights movement began to fade, women who advocated this pro-sex politics were more and more alienated from a larger community of women; they seemed to feel that to enter the world of sex, they had to travel alone and leave other women behind. This rejection of women occurred both because the dominant tradition of feminism was so antisexual, and because their own understanding of sex was so heterosexual. They were part of a generation that branded intense female friendships as adolescent (Sahli, 1979; Simmons, 1979; Faderman, 1980). The tragedy was that in rejecting a community of women which they experienced as constricting and repressive, they left behind their feminist heritage.

At the same time these pioneering sex radicals offer us a positive legacy in their willingness to take risks. It would be easier if we could progress towards sexual liberation without sufferings, if we could resolve the tension between seeking pleasure and avoiding danger by some simple policy; but we cannot. We must conduct our sexual politics in the real world. For women this is like advancing across a mine field. Looking only to your feet to avoid the mines means missing the horizon, and the vision of why the advance is worthwhile; but if you only see the future possibilities you may blow yourself up.

If this is warlike imagery, it is not bravado. The dangers are substantial, women are assaulted and killed. But each act of violence against women would be multiplied in its effect, if it prevented us from seeing where we have won victories, and induced us to resign ourselves to restriction of our sexual lives and constriction of our public activities.

Seen in this light, the contemporary focus on rape and other sexual violence against women represents an advance over the earlier campaign against prostitution. Through our new conceptualization of the problem of sexual danger, feminists have rejected the victim-blaming that was inherent in the notion of the 'fallen woman'; we know that any of us can be raped. Our critique of sexual violence is an institutional analysis of the whole system of male supremacy which attempts to show the commonalities of women, as potential agents as well as victims. Thus the campaign against rape comes out of our strength as well as our victimization. Whether the actual incidence of rape has increased or decreased, the feminist offensive against it represents an escalation of our demands for freedom. We have redefined rape to include many sexual encounters that nineteenth-century feminists would have considered mere seduction, and for which they might have held the woman responsible; we have included in our definition of rape what was once normal marital intercourse. We have denied impunity to any men: we will bring charges against boyfriends, fathers and teachers; we will label as sexual harassment what was once the ordinary banter of males asserting their dominance. We declare our right – still contested, viciously – to safety not only in our homes but in the streets. We *all* intend to be street-walkers!

It is vital to strategy-building to know when we are winning and when losing, and where. Failing to claim and take pride in our victories leads to the false conclusion that nothing has changed. When the campaign against rape is fought as if we were the eternal, unchanged victims of male sexuality, we run the risk of re-entering the kind of social purity worldview that so limited the nineteenth-century feminist vision (Brownmiller, 1975). It is important to offer our comprehensive critique of misogyny, violence and male dominance without ceding the arena of sexuality itself to the men, as the nineteenth-century feminists did.

We have tried to show that social purity politics, although an understandable reaction to women's nineteenth-century experience, was a limited and limiting vision for women. Thus we called it conservative. Today, there seems to be a revival of social purity politics within feminism and it is concern about this tendency that motivates us in recalling its history. Like its nineteenth-century predecessor, the contemporary feminist attack on pornography and sexual 'perversion' fails to distinguish its politics from a conservative and anti-feminist version of social purity, the moral majority and pro-family movements of the new right. The increasing tendency to focus almost exclusively on sex as the primary arena of women's exploitation, and to attribute women's sexual victimization to some violent essence labelled 'male sexuality' is even more conservative today, because our situation as women has changed so radically. Modern social purists point to one set of changes. The rise of sexual consumerism and the growing power of the mass media to enforce conformity to sexual norms are debilitating for women's sexual freedom. As feminists, we are learning to be suspicious of a sexual politics that simply calls for 'doing your own thing', and to ask whether women's desires are represented in visions of sexual freedom. We must not make the same mistake as early twentieth-century sexual libertarians, who believed that ending sexual inhibition in itself could save women. Instead, we have to continue to analyse how male supremacy and other forms of domination shape what we think of as 'free' sexuality.

But there have been liberatory developments as well that we can ill afford to ignore. Women have possibilities for sexual subjectivity and self-creation today that did not exist in the past. We have a vision of sexuality that is not exclusively heterosexual, nor tied to reproduction. We have a much better physiological understanding of sexual feeling, and a vision of ungendered parenting. We have several strong intellectual traditions for understanding the psychological and social formation of sexuality. Perhaps most important, we have today at least a chance of economic independence, the necessary material condition for women's sexual liberation. Finally we have something women have never enjoyed before – a feminist past, a history of 150 years of feminist theory and praxis in the area of sexuality. This is a resource too precious to squander, by not learning it, in all its complexity.

■ Notes

1   Since this paper grew out of work we have been thinking about for years, our intellectual debts are literally innumerable. For specific critical comments on this paper we want to thank Ann Ferguson, Vivian Gornick, Amber Hollibaugh, Jill Lewis, Cora Kaplan, Esther Newton, Ann Snitow, Judith R. Walkowitz, Carol Vance and Marilyn B. Young. About this paper we need to add, more than ever, that we alone are responsible for our conclusions!

2   We distinguish here between behaviour recognized as sexual by its actors and behaviour not so recognized, aware that some historians will not agree. Furthermore, we are also emphasizing the importance of conscious sexual thought, theorizing and politicizing for the feminist effort to transform women's sexual experience. We do so aware that, in the past decade, in an exciting renaissance of feminist historical scholarship, women's historians have chosen to focus more on behaviour and culture than on political ideology. In the history of American feminism, for reasons that are undoubtedly important to explore, the initial focus for explicitly sexual politics was on the relations between women and men. The history and chronology of the feminist conceptualization of what we today call lesbianism is different and we do not address it here, but Carroll Smith-Rosenberg and Esther Newton do so in their unpublished paper, 'The Mythic Lesbian and the New Woman: Power, Sexuality and Legitimacy,' delivered at the 1981 Berkshires Conference on Women's History.

3   For instance, in 1913, a suffrage newspaper estimated that there were 15,000-20,000 prostitutes in New York City, who serviced 150,000-225,000 male customers daily; this would work out to roughly one out of every 100 female persons in all five boroughs and one out of every ten male persons (*Women's Political World*, 2 June 1913, p.7). Using a more precise definition of prostitution, e.g. women who supported themselves solely by commercial sex, a member of New York City's Vice Commission estimated less than half that number (Frederick Whitten to Mary Sumner Boyd, 17 March 1916, NAWSA Collection, New York Public Library).

4   Evidence of these problems abounds in case records of social-service agencies used by Linda Gordon in her research on family violence, and in her unpublished paper, 'Single Mothers and Child Neglect, 1880-1920', *American Quarterly* 37 #2, summer 1985.

5   In taking this approach, we are drawing on two recent schools of historical interpretation: feminist historians, for instance Nancy Cott, Gerda Lerner and Ann Douglas, who emphasize the role of women as

active agents of cultural change, but who have concentrated on domesticity rather than sexuality; and male theorists of sexuality, notably Michel Foucault, who regard sexuality as a socially constructed, historically specific cultural system, but leave women out of their accounts.

6   We deliberately avoid expressing this difference as a contrast between middle- and working-class families. We suspect that greater male sexual dominance is not so much a matter of proletarian experience as it is of peasant authoritarian background and women's extreme economic dependence.

7   Elizabeth Gurley Flynn's long relationship with the pioneering lesbian, Marie Equi, is traced by Rosalyn Baxandall in her forthcoming collection of Flynn's writings on women (New Brunswick, N.J.: Rutgers University Press, 1987). There is also some suggestion that Elizabeth Gurley Flynn gave lesbianism a positive treatment in her original version of *The Alderson Story: My Life as a Political Prisoner* but that Communist Party officials insisted that she rewrite the material and make her portrait more judgemental and negative (Rosalyn Baxandall, private communication to authors, 1982). The largest issue of repression of evidence in lesbianism is considered in Cook (1979: 55-60).

8   Note the *new* insistence on the importance of the vagina, replacing an older recognition of the role of the clitoris in women's experience of orgasm.

Abortion: Individual
Choice and Social
Control

Susan Himmelweit

This article was written at the height of the campaign against the Corrie Bill, which attempted to restrict the grounds under which women could get an abortion. Its defeat remains one of the few victories for women since 1979, despite the effects of changes in the wording of doctors' consent forms and cuts in the National Health Service on the availability of abortion since then.

In 1980, defending the right of women not to have to bear unwanted children was the central focus of campaigns around reproductive rights in this country, at least for white women. Since then new reproductive technologies have raised some of the issues confronted in the article in a different form. In-vitro fertilization, because it requires the intervention of expensive technology, which is not under a woman's own control, begs the question of which women, among those otherwise infertile, are to be allowed to be given a chance to bear children. Pre-natal diagnosis of foetal sex and disabilities raises the question of whether abortion should be made available to women who want to bear a child but do not like certain characteristics of their potential offspring. These reproductive issues not only have to be looked at at the level of individual rights, as the right of an individual woman not *to bear a child could be, but require that feminists also give thought to the way in which we want reproduction to be socially organized and the effects this will have on society as a whole. For barring total transformation of the means of reproduction, large numbers of women* will *continue to bear children and the conditions under which they do so will be a fundamental determinant of the female condition.*

This article attempted to put the recognition of that necessity on the socialist-feminist agenda. It has to be there even more crucially today. What is needed, however, is to give it content: to envisage what might be meant by a society in which production and reproduction were more integrated, and what concrete moves could be made to lessen the burden of their current separation on women today, whether they be mothers or those who decide not to bear children.

Collecting signatures for the petition against the Corrie Bill in Parliament has been a very instructive and encouraging process. Popular support for 'A Woman's Right to Choose' is clearly enormous. Nearly all women and many men are prepared to sign the petition and often express their horror most colourfully at the very idea that anyone but the woman concerned should have any part in the decision. Suggestions as to what might be done to Corrie's genitals have not been infrequent. Even anti-abortionists have signed on the grounds that while they themselves would never have an abortion they do not see why they should prevent others coming to their own decisions.

Why is it that this issue has such support? Why has the abortion issue won such rapid acceptance over the past few years? When campaigning against James White's similar Bill years ago, I often got involved in technical and moral disputes with people before they would sign; now I get interrupted half-way through my explanation with 'Oh, you mean women's right to choose, yes I believe in that.' Thinking about these questions has led me to a few wider, somewhat disturbing ones. I would like to know what other women think about them.

One of the most important ways in which women are oppressed in our society is through the social separation of production and reproduction. Production (or much of it anyway) is a social activity, under the control of capital, socially valued and distributed through the price of its products and for which workers are paid a wage. Reproduction (in the sense of having babies) is a private activity with no direct control by capital, no social mechanism for its recognition and co-ordination, and for which no recompense is paid to women. Women as, at least, the biological reproducers of our society are identified with the second activity. One of our fights is against that necessary identification of all women some of the time and some women all of the time.

But we are also fighting against that separation itself both in practice and in theory. We have to change society in such a way that the processes of production and reproduction are both recognized as social activities equally necessary to the existence and reproduction (in its more general sense) of society. We have to insist that theory recognizes reproduction and the struggles set up over it as a material force, as part of the material base whose social forms are crucial to the characterization and explanation of oppression. But, if we are socialist-feminists, we have to do so in such a way that production and reproduction are not posed as two competing material bases, one appropriate to the analysis of class oppression, one to women's oppression, with all the problems of ordering the importance of those oppressions that this separation poses. Otherwise we would just be both socialists and feminists.

Instead we have to build a theory in which the material base includes both those activities and explain why *in current society* there is such a separation made between the two. If we cannot do this, then we will have to fall back on some sort of biological argument, and concede that the socialist and feminist struggles are separable. For if the separation of reproduction from production is seen as natural, not social, and if women are oppressed because of their role in reproduction now, that potential for oppression will always be there. If on the other hand we can show how that separation is socially constructed, the possibility of its removal is posed and the potential unity of struggles against oppression in each of the two currently divided spheres is given. This, it seems to me, is what a socialist-feminist programme is all about.

If that is the case, then the popularity of the idea of private choice in reproduction is a reflection and acceptance of the existing division. Capital and the state have no right to interfere in what they *themselves* have designated as the private arena not subject to social control. One does not have to step outside capitalist morality at all to support 'A Woman's Right to Choose'. Those who try to prevent abortion by law are going against capital's own logic. It is they who have to produce the specific arguments, not us. That is why they always have to invoke things from outside the social system: mystical conceptions of when life begins or a morality based on the teaching of some God. That is why the horror stories of specific cases have to be fabricated and made so much of. The anti-abortionist argument actually goes against the existing division in our society that leaves questions of reproduction as private and therefore, implicitly, subject only to individual decision. Indeed, things may well have been made easier for us by the current stress on the ideology of individual responsibility that has been encouraged in the attempt to justify cuts in social services.

But what if we had gone out campaigning for 'A Woman's Right to Choose' whether to be a producer or not (rather than whether to be a reproducer). How much support would we have got then? We might have got some misplaced support from people who thought a woman's place was in the home, but once we explained that that was not exactly what we meant, that we did not mean that a woman should have the choice whether to get a paid job or whether to work in the home but, that 'A Woman's Right to Choose' meant the right to choose whether or not to work *at all*, those supporters would quickly dwindle.

And when we then explained that we were also demanding the economic circumstances in which we could freely make that choice, they would just think we were faintly barmy. And that clearly is not what we are demanding (except perhaps some women who have followed 'Wages for Housework' to one of its many political dead ends). We are not after all demanding the right for women to be parasitical but for women to have the right to a full, equal and valued role in society and in its transformation.

So are we implicitly accepting that separation of production and reproduction into the social and the private? Are we accepting that under socialism, or whatever name we give the society we are working for, production will be planned, ever so democratically but still planned for the benefit of all, but reproduction will remain a private, individual decision and right? If we do, do we not cut out from under ourselves the basis for demanding true equality and an end to the segregation of women into the private sphere? If not, what happens to 'A Woman's Right to Choose'?

I raise these questions not because I believe that in the present climate and under the present threats we have any choice but to wage a defensive struggle to claim the little areas of freedom that the present system has partially granted us and now threatens to take away. Indeed the very reasons why it may be ideologically problematic for the state to attempt to control our fertility are precisely why it is so important for it to do so.

Capitalists and workers are also supposed to be free to make

UNIVERSITY OF WALES
L.I.S.
SWANSEA

choices, to produce or not to produce, to sell their labour-power or not to sell it. But behind that freedom lies the control of the law of value, by which individual decisions are constrained by the needs of the system as a whole, the needs of the system of production for profit. If something cannot be produced profitably it will not be produced. So the right that individuals have to make their own choices is actually out of a very limited range of alternatives and the outcome of these decisions is predictably safe (under normal circumstances) for the system as a whole.

But under capitalism for decisions about reproduction there is no such social mechanism to regulate the outcome of a mass of individual decisions. When we make the demand for 'A Woman's Right to Choose' we are demanding no more than that individual right, but in an area in which there is no form of social control once the direct control of our own bodies has been won. Capital's ideology may well support a demand which, if genuinely realized, could undermine capital's own basis and control.

THE CONSTRUCTION
OF SEXUAL
DIFFERENCE

Slags or Drags

Celia Cowie and Sue Lees

We would like to present this as a working paper for discussion rather than as a finished product. We have only started to explore some of the questions that it raises. It is based on a pilot study involving group discussions and in-depth interviews with thirty-two adolescent girls aged fourteen and a half to nearly sixteen, at two Islington comprehensive schools. This part of the project was carried out in the summer of 1980. We are grateful for the co-operation of the ILEA, the schools and the willing participation of the girls themselves. Clearly our sample is very small and quite unrepresentative of a normal population. Most of the girls would be considered 'working class' according to the Registrar General's Classification though many of them considered themselves 'middle class'; the sample was multi-racial and came from one specific inner-London area. Thus we make no claims that our findings are generalizable to other girls, though we suspect that there would be more similarities than differences.

Very few comparable studies of girls are available. Of these the most significant is probably that conducted in a Birmingham youth club by Angela McRobbie (1976). Researchers have met with some difficulties in talking to girls, leading McRobbie to conclude that:

> *Girl culture ... is so well insulated as to operate to effectively exclude not only other undesirable girls but also boys, adult teachers and researchers. (McRobbie, 1976)*

By conducting our interviews and discussions during school time rather than the girls' own leisure time we avoided encroaching on their own time and provided a welcome diversion from classes. We found them not only willing to talk but prepared to discuss intimate questions about their lives with verve and humour. This is not to say that the girls did not view us as different from themselves and that this might have affected their response. Several commented on our clothes and some of them were perplexed by our marital status or lack of it. It was clearly more acceptable to be separated with children than never to have married. It is impossible to know how far such factors influenced the course of the interviews but we did gain the impression that the group discussions 'took off' to render those factors relatively unimportant. We used unstructured interviews as a means of probing the meanings the girls attached to four aspects of their lives – school, friendships, sexuality and their views of the future. By using this method of non-directive questioning we tried to avoid structuring their responses through the imposition of preconceptions; instead we always tried to follow up what they themselves contributed.

We have not systematically gathered and ordered facts about girls which we present as the object of analysis. Instead our paper is an organized collection of quotes, and so we must raise the question of what status these quotes have as data. Their use as evidence in support of arguments would not be justified if those arguments were not wholly an attempt to make sense of what the girls have said. However, we at no point wish to imply that what the girls say can be taken as a simple reflection of reality or even of their experience of reality. But rather that what they say has a shared though hidden organization that structures, indeed produces those cultural meanings through which they relate to the world. Our analysis is, therefore, concerned with penetrating that hidden organization by placing question marks over the contradictions, the gaps and the often taken-for-granted terms which the girls commonly use.

The initial focus of this paper is on one such term, 'slag', which arose spontaneously and vividly in all the groups, taking us by surprise since it has been almost entirely neglected in the literature. In looking at it we found that many questions were raised about the construction of sexuality (on this point we wish to be clear that we take sexuality to have no essential quality but are concerned with the social construction of the individual as a sexed and gender specific being); the place of marriage in the girls' lives and the social organization of gender relations.

■ The category 'slag'

The term slag or its equivalents – slut, scrubber, old dog, easy lay – is so familiar, so taken for granted, that it has rarely received serious analysis as a cultural form:

> Certainly reputations for 'easiness' – deserved or not – spread very quickly. The 'lads' are after the 'easy' lay at dances, though they think twice about being seen to 'go out' with them. (Willis, 1977: 44)

From a first reading of this quote from Willis it would seem that the term slag or easy lay simply stands for certain identifiable girls. But as soon as you raise doubts about the deservedness of the reputation 'easy' and more especially when you ask girls to whom and how is the term applied, then it becomes clear that you have only begun to scratch the surface of a very complex phenomenon. Whilst everyone apparently knows one and stereotypically depicts her as thick, poor, untidy, untastefully dressed and made-up, loud-mouthed and, of course, she sleeps around, it seems to us that such a stereotype bears no relation to the girls (virtually any girl) to whom the term is applied.

One difficulty is the constant sliding that occurs between the use of the term as friendly joking, as bitchy abuse, as a threat or as a label. What is more, and what makes it unique, in our view, as a deviant category, is that it is always being shifted elsewhere, from one group to another, and that shift is invariably socially downwards. This seems to be borne out by Smith's study (1978) of delinquent girls, who are the ones typically ostracized as slags; but they too reject the label and react aggressively against the accusation of 'easiness' contained in it. What sense can be made of such labelling if the category is constantly being shifted across a wide range of girls amongst whom it is always another who embodies the term? It strikes us that it is the 'presence' of the category which is important, not the identification of certain girls. Indeed the notion of 'a small core of promiscuous girls' (Nicholson, 1980), evidenced by the apparent fact that boys have more sexual partners than girls, remains more of an assumption than an established fact. For the purpose of our analysis it becomes irrelevant to look for actual girls. Instead, it seems more important to explore how the term is used. The following quotes should indicate some of the complexity of the term:

> At least the girls we go with ain't second-hand. (Conversation between boys baiting another boy – overheard by two girls in our study)

> When there's boys talking and you've been out with more than two, you're known as the crisp that they're passing round ... The boy's alright but the girl's a bit of scum. (Fifteen-year-old girl)

> After you've been with one like, after you've done it like, well they're scrubbers afterwards, they'll go with anyone. I think it's that once they've had it, they want it all the time, no matter who it's with. (Willis, 1977:44)

Willis, whilst allocating little enough space for an analysis of the term as used by his 'lads', does perhaps go the furthest in reading the term as a representation: 'woman' who as a sexual object is a commodity that becomes worthless with consumption and yet who as a sexual being, once sexually experienced, becomes promiscuous. But this reading falls short precisely because it fails to take up the significance of the term as the location of both worthlessness and sexuality. By locating the site of female sexuality in the 'slag' is both to remove it from would-be non-slags and to ensure it is deemed bad, since the term represents 'a dirty person' unclean both literally and sexually and is akin to the term 'whore', thereby carrying all the connotations that surround it.

Willis recognizes the suppression of explicit sexuality in women and attributes 'a half recognition' of this to the 'lads' who, he argues, fear that the opening of the floodgates of female desire will lead to promiscuity. Why is only one of the questions this raises about the construction of masculine desire around a sexual object that is attractive because it is untouched; discardable once consumed; then re-sought having become generally 'available' but denigrated?

But what of the girls? In what ways is this split between decency and sexuality effected? It is certainly not a question of a straightforward fall from grace by the act of intercourse. Any girl (except perhaps middle-class girls who may have some protection by their class position) is *always available* to the designation slag in any number of ways. Appearance is crucial: by wearing too much make-up (how do you know how much is too much); by having your slit skirt too slit; by not combing your hair, wearing jeans to dances or high heels to school; having your trousers too tight or tops too low. As one girl said – 'sexual clothes'. Is it any wonder that if girls have to learn to make such fine discriminations about appearances they may spend so much time deciding what to wear – although this is not necessarily the only reason for such activity.

But behaviour in relation to boys is perhaps the riskiest terrain: hanging around too much waiting for boys to come out (yet all girls must hang around sufficiently); talking or being friendly with too many boys; or the wrong boy; or someone else's boy; or too many too quickly; or even more than one boy in a group; or just by being ditched.

In other words a vast range of activities and ways of appearing are 'sexualized' and so deemed 'bad'. It is clearly a very narrow tightrope to walk to achieve sexual attractiveness without the taint of sexuality. How the criteria for such discriminations are generated remains obscure. What is certain, from our own sample and others, is that the criteria shift from group to group:

> The boys had, of course, classified all the girls into the familiar two categories: the slags who'd go with anyone and everyone (they were all right for a quick screw, but you'd never get serious about it) and the drags who didn't but whom you might one day think about going steady with. Needless to say, different cliques of boys put different girls in each of the two categories, and there was often a good deal of argument about the status to be accorded to particular girls. (Robins and Cohen, 1978: 58)

We would argue that despite the *apparent* connexion between the designation 'slag' and sexual promiscuity, the term has probably very little to do with actual sexual behaviour, as the following quote, perhaps more than any other, indicates:

> Like this girl that I know, this boy that she used to go out with right, he started calling her names and so all his friends started calling her names.
> *Q. What sort of names?*
> Like slag, prostitute, whore, all these things.
> *Q. While she was going out with him?*
> No, after she had finished with him. He went round saying that she couldn't kiss, see, cos she sorts of gets embarrassed, she's like that with me even, and she can't help it or anything, she gets very embarrassed over the slightest thing, he stayed with her for

four months and then he goes round saying she couldn't kiss. I admit she only kissed him once but he knows that is why she wouldn't because she was embarrassed and that and he went round saying that she couldn't kiss and yet he's saying she's a slag and all. So I thought to myself how could he stay with her for four months and go round saying that. He really liked her, he would have bought her anything. It's too bad.

There is nothing romantic in the girl's stark, indeed grim appreciation of the state of gender relations and it is here that the term 'slag' is always pivoted:

As soon as he's got it he'll drop you and if you take too long to give it then he drops you anyway.
Q. What do you think about sex?
Oh I agree with it if you want it, I dunno, I'd hate to be pestered into it.
Q. How do you think boys are about it?
I dunno, the girl's always got fears about the boy going behind their backs and saying 'Oh you know, had it with her' – they've always got that sort of thing.
Q. What's the fear about?
I dunno, being called an old dog or something I suppose.
Q. By other girls or everybody?
Everyone, but the girls are just as bad. You say to someone 'how far did you get?' and she'd tell you and then you can always go to someone else and say 'Oh she did you know'.

And from another girl:

My friend knows this girl and she's a bit of a tart and she invites boys to her house and once these skinheads came along and she started taking her clothes off and everything and these boys said they didn't have any girlfriends but the girls were waiting outside and they brought the girlfriends in and beat her up and everything and she was in hospital, so now no one takes any notice of her or anything, they just leave her to herself.
Q. The girls beat her up?
Yes, the boys as well, kicked her about and everything.
Q. What do you think about that?
It was her own fault. She shouldn't do it – it's horrible. Mind you two wrongs don't make a right.

What is of particular interest here is the operation of an ideology that transforms the experience of very unfair relations between the sexes into an acceptance of those relations as *natural*. It is somehow wrong and horrible for a girl to invite sexual activity but somehow natural for the boy to be after it, to attempt to pester you into it, to tell if you do and to fabricate its occurrence if you don't.

A feminist analysis of this 'law of nature' is required. All we can do here is to speculate on this ideological transformation of unfair relations into sexual differences as inherently given.

The construction of female sexuality seems to involve the construction of a difference between slags and drags: a certain kind of sexuality – essentially promiscuous/dirty in nature – is not 'natural' for all girls/women but only resides in the slag. Yet non-slags are always viewed as possibly available, potential slags, until tried and found to be drags or possible wives. In other words there is always a blurring of the two categories. It is not easy to make the distinction, despite the apparent essential differences, since the status is always disputable, the gossip always unreliable, the criteria always obscure. So what marks the difference? What functions as the location of a sexuality appropriate for nice girls? *Love*.

> The fundamental rule governing sexual behaviour was the existence of affection in the form of romantic love before any sexual commitment. For most of the girls, love existed before sex and it was never a consequence of sexual involvement. (Wilson, 1978: 70-1)

Deirdre Wilson goes on to note, however, that

> given this threat of rejection (for sex without love) it was difficult to discover just how many girls *actually* believed in the primacy of love, and how many simply paid lip service to the ideal. Nevertheless the fact that the girls found it necessary to support this convention, whether they believed in it or not, was an important fact in itself. (Wilson, 1978)

Nice girls cannot have sexual desire outside of love. For them sexuality is something that just happens if you are in love, or, if you are unlucky, when you are drunk:

> They reckon that if you are in love and you get carried away it is alright – but if you are on the pill then you planned it. (McRobbie, 1978:99)

McRobbie argues that if you took contraceptive precautions on a casual date you would be laying yourself open to savage criticism because it is premeditated sex which contravenes the 'dominant code of romance'. It is not so much a code of romance as a complex intermeshing of ideological relations. What is at risk for the girl is her reputation. What is not clear, even to her, is quite what might lead to her downfall:

> I wouldn't go on it [the pill], don't think it right really because I know if you go on the pill you're going to lose will power in the end and just let yourself go.

Interestingly, the phrase 'letting yourself go' has connexions with both sexual excitement and becoming sluttish. Love seems to play an important ideological role in permitting the former whilst offering some protection from the latter. Love or 'falling in love' is therefore both a denial and an expression of sexuality:

> I used to fall in love with pop stars, now I fall in love with people. When you're in love you ain't got no problems.

The upsurge of excitement at the sight of the object of love/desire is surely sexual but, significantly, is not recognized as such by the girls:

> Within these groups of girls, expressions of sexuality could only receive support or be condoned when they maintained the triangular relationship of love, sexuality and marriage (Wilson, 1978:71).

Even though love may make sexuality more of a possibility it does not necessarily protect the girl from the designation slag, especially once that relationship has finished. Engagement offers additional protection for the girl as a boy is considered somewhat blameworthy for having sexual relations and then ditching a girl, if he is engaged to her. Marriage is the only safe place for the expression of female sexuality. Yet even here the slag categorization operates where 'sluttishness' refers to both extra-marital sexual relations and failure to fulfil the expected marital role.

■ Marriage

It is not surprising, then, that almost all our girls took for granted that they would get married and also clearly wanted this. Yet when you look at the various kinds of comments they make, what emerges is not so much a romantic as a realistic view of the grimmer aspects of women's lot in marriage:

> I think that once you get married you lose pride in yourself, really.
> *Q. What about boys, do they lose pride in themselves?*
> The ones I know they don't really lose pride because they sort of go out, they don't have to wear a ring or anything do they? They still go around free as though they weren't married.

They saw marriage for women involving shouldering a domestic burden that carries little in the way of status and rewards:

> My dad won't do anything, he won't make a cup of tea, he says he does the work for the money and the rest is up to my mum — she does part-time work.

Another girl said:

> The wife has to stay at home and do the shopping and things, she has got more responsibility in life and they haven't got much to look forward to ... We've got to work at home and look after the children till they grow up, you've got to go out shopping, do the housework and try to have a career. Then the man comes in and says 'where's my dinner?', when we've been to work. They say 'you don't work'. It's because boys are brought up expecting us girls to do all the work. They expect their mums to do it and when they get married they expect their wives to do it. They are just lazy.

And financial dependency that was both a constriction on mum and a bone of contention between mum and dad:

> My dad won't give in like. My mum she sort of goes short, now and again, and she asks him for extra money and he just won't give it her and I think other families are like that. If you don't have to rely on a man they don't feel so tight with their money.

What was mentioned most of all was the isolation of being at home, such comments as:

> If you stay at home you get bored and lonely.

or

> My mum hates being at home you know but she has to stop

working because she's going into hospital and she's going to hate that – she's going to be so bored.

Q. Is that why she goes to work?

Yes, she just don't like being at home.

Work often envisaged as a career rather than just a job was seen as some kind of salve to these grimmer aspects:

I want to get married, I don't want to stay single but I also want a career. If you marry and it's just the man who goes out to work ... I would want to go out to work, I wouldn't want to be stuck in the house because then that's just – that's just like the woman's job, really being stuck in the house.

or as another said:

I'd like to work as well cos I'm used to being on my feet. I can't stay at home in the house. I mean I could cook and that lot – I would be glad to do it, cooking and that lot, but not stay at home all day, like looking after kids – I couldn't do something like that.

The most extreme aspects mentioned were beatings and cruelty, to be avoided by being careful whom one married:

I will get someone who doesn't like drinking a lot and just has a little coke or something.

Q. Is it common for men to come home drunk?

Yes, it's like this lady round our flats, she gets beaten every night because her husband goes drinking, comes home about twelve, starts beating her you know for nothing, saying she's been out with this man, she's done this and done that, he just makes it up, any lies, and starts trouble.

Overall the girls' view of marriage was not romantic but seemed to be realistically based on their observations of their own parents, relatives or acquaintances. What then needs explaining is why the girls we interviewed wanted to get married. Perhaps it is worth bearing in mind that marriage is now more prevalent than ever – 90 per cent of the population marrying at least once – and until recently has been occurring at a younger age than at any period for which there are reliable records. At one level this can be seen as a reflection of a strong cultural expectation affecting both sexes. For working-class boys and girls there is little alternative way of leaving home. Diana Leonard's research in Cardiff (1980) indicates that it is unusual for either a boy or a girl to move away from home before marriage. She points out that a home is seen as something developed by the married couple and there is no real notion or real possibility of an alternative kind of domestic unit. To live away from home in the same town would be seen as a real slight on one's parents.

Though little research has focused on why boys want to get married we would argue that marriage offers material advantages in terms of what the 'lads' in Willis's study describe as a 'missus' – a wife who will run the house and look after them. Nor does marriage involve a disruption of other important areas of life such as friendships and work, as it usually does for girls. As Spike in Willis's study says:

> I've got the right bird. I've been going with her for eighteen months now. Her's as good as gold. She's fucking done well, she's clean. She loves doing fucking housework. Trousers I bought yesterday. I took 'em up last night, and her turned them up for me. She's as good as gold and I wanna get married as soon as I can. (Willis, 1977)

In contrast girls do not describe marriage as offering such material advantages. Yet any relationship without marriage is unimaginable. When Diana Leonard asked the girls in Cardiff when they had decided to get married they could not remember a time when it was not a consideration. As one girl put it – rather than choosing not to get married they fail to get married. Why then is a relationship without marriage in mind unimaginable? We would argue that in such a relationship the girls fear being ditched and fear becoming open to the 'slag' categorization.

This puts marriage in a new light as something almost inevitable. As one girl put it: 'The girls who didn't want to get married are lezzies and the boys who didn't are queer.' Another girl, when asked why she thought girls were concerned with how other people thought they looked, replied:

> This idea of love and marriage. I think you're all broken down into thinking you're eventually gonna get married and have kids, you know. If you're really ugly or in a right state or something then you're not going to – you're not going to go out and meet a bloke – it's like that.

The choice of getting married then becomes a negative one – of avoiding being left on the shelf, with all the opprobrium attached to the spinster. A whole battery of neglect, suspicion and derision is directed at the non-married and the childless and they are stereotyped as shirking their duty, selfish, immature, lonely, bitter, abnormal and unattractive or pathetic (Comer, 1974).

In this context it is perhaps less relevant that most girls saw themselves as getting married than that most of them wanted to put it off for some time, usually for about ten years. It is important to bear in mind that ten years, when one is fifteen, seems a lifetime away. As one girl put it:

> I don't think about the future at all until it happens. I don't think – oh what am I going to do in ten years time for a start. I never think that. I've never thought that in my life. I think what am I going to be doing tomorrow.

By delaying marriage many girls thought they would be able to have some fun, often to travel and see the world. Marriage was something you ended up with after you had lived:

> I don't really want to get married cos I want to go round the world first like me dad did ... they got married when they were thirty years old, they just sort of had their life first and then they got married and had us, but when you're an air hostess you don't start the job until you're twenty so I want to work until I'm thirty-five.

Many realized that relationships with boys might upset these intentions and steered clear of them:

> If a boy does ask us out we say no, don't want to know because we want a career and go round the world and all that lot. So we just leave them alone ... we talk to some boys and they always go around with girls, so if they [the girls] see us they start calling us names and it will aggravate us and we would not be able to get on with our work, so we just tell them [the boys] to go away.

Or, as another put it:

> I don't really bother about boys now – just get on with my homework. I go out with my friend and then go back home. I was brought up not to like boys really cos I've heard so much

about what they do, robberies, rapes and all that, so I keep away from them.

Q. What do you mean – brought up not to like them?
Well my mum told me never to go with them because they're bad and they damage your health and things like that, don't know what she meant but she says they ruin your life if they get you pregnant, she said it's best to keep away from them, so I do.

Or another:

I think there's a lot of decisions to make which I really don't want to make at the moment so I'd rather act childish so I don't have to make the decisions.

In her study of fifty-six working-class girls aged fourteen to sixteen from a council estate in Birmingham, Angela McRobbie (1976) found that there was wholesale endorsement of the traditional female role and of femininity simply because these seemed to be perfectly natural to the girls. McRobbie argues that two factors saved the girls from what they otherwise envisaged as an unexciting future; first, their solidarity with each other, their best-friend relationship; and secondly, their immersion in the ideology of romance. Our findings confirm the importance of friendships and it is these that are the girls' major source of fun. It is not romance that saves them from an unexciting future but having fun now before you get married. Our girls did not talk in romantic terms. They did, however, talk about love but only in relation to finding a man who will understand them, share things with them and protect them from the loneliness that they see around them. What they seem to be expressing is the hope that love will save them from the grim reality of most of the marriages they observe. This may well be a romantic hope. It certainly stands in marked opposition to marriage as realistically observed, as illustrated in the following quote:

Quite a few girls say I'm going to marry for money. I say if I had a man it's going to be for true love. Other people think I am stupid but I don't think it's stupid. If you marry for money you like half the person.

Q. What do you think true love is?
I think when you agree on most things and you're both the same in your ways. I don't see it very often but it's important to know that you are going to agree cos if you disagree then there'll be rows and arguments. When I think of some boys they're going to boss the girls around and they'll swing in circles.

Q. What about working? Do you think you will be working?
Oh yes. I would hate to rely on a husband. I see how my mum
depends on my dad and it's turned her against him. I'm not
going to marry a husband like my mum did. My dad he doesn't
help at all. I don't know what they see in each other. They must
love each other.

Here she starts by saying she is going to marry for love rather than
simply for money – otherwise marriage will be full of arguments. She
is not being romantic about marriage, she sees the risks involved. The
only thing you can hope for is to find someone who will understand
you and share things with you. This can be seen as setting up a sort of
myth that attempts to counteract the reality around. She is under no
illusion that marriage is paradise. She ends up noting that love has not
saved her mother – he does not help, it turned her against him – yet
they must love each other. She articulates the contradiction though
she is unable to grasp it.

When talking about marriage these girls describe a bourgeois
pattern of married life emphasizing privacy and isolation from the
wider community and intense relationships between parents and
children. Recent research into inner-city areas in places as diverse as
London, Liverpool, Wolverhampton and Bristol compared with
studies carried out in the 1950s indicates that there has been a decline
in community and a move away from traditional ideas about the role
of the extended family, brought about by drastic housing
redevelopment and incentives for the more skilled to move out of inner
areas. (Between 1966 and 1972 22 per cent of the total number of jobs
in manufacturing in London disappeared.) For married women in
Bethnal Green in the 1950s, according to Wilmott and Young (1976)
for example, the bond with mum was almost as important as the bond
with a husband. Now living close to kin is no longer common. There is
some evidence that living in flats decreases social life, as this quote
clearly implies:

I don't like London myself, all these high-rise flats and things.
Down in Worthing it's all little houses. People pop in to talk to
you now and again and you feel as if you are a family even
though you're not – with the neighbours and that. They all pop
in and say 'Can I come in for a cup of tea, you must come round
to my house.' Here they couldn't care less if you dropped dead.
Most people couldn't care really. In our flats if anything

happened to us there's only the people upstairs that would really worry out of 140 flats.

Almost all the girls mentioned the boredom and loneliness of being at home that could only be relieved by the possibility of working. These perceptions are borne out by research which has indicated that working-class women with young children experience isolation from the wider community and dissatisfaction with their marriage. Brown and Harris in their study of the social origins of depression (1978) found that working-class women were at a higher risk of depression when they had children at home. They found that two in three working-class women with a child at home were suffering from clinical depression or were borderline cases, compared with 17 per cent of a cross sample of all women in the study. Working-class husbands were likely to fail to recognize the difficulties of childcare, which they saw as a cushy job; this trivialized the women's work and lowered their self-esteem. What Brown and Harris did not emphasize or analyse are the structural factors that led to the experience of isolation and powerlessness.

Finally there is some evidence that it is particularly difficult for working-class women to pursue outside interests. Our questionnaires indicated that whilst dads had a variety of interests and activities, mothers had few, if any, and rarely went out. This does not merely reflect structural factors such as their family responsibilities and lack of community facilities, but may be due to the tendency for any activity they engage in to be sexualized or trivialized. Diana Leonard describes the way teenage girls tend to drop interests once they started courting. She found that they rejected earlier activities such as riding, judo, playing the piano, dancing (other than disco dancing) as childish and unfeminine. One girl who continued dancing while courting dropped it because her boyfriend characterized the dance hall as a knocking shop.

It appears that recent changes in the pattern of married life have had severe effects on working-class women which are likely to be exacerbated by the rise in unemployment in the public sector where many women are employed. Brown and Harris found that having a job was a protective factor against depression – perhaps not surprising when seen as the only legitimate way of spending much time outside the home. This kind of change was graphically perceived by our girls for whom marriage was nevertheless the only alternative to being left on the shelf or on the slag-heap.

■ Some theoretical considerations

Given this kind of material, and there is much more on what the girls do and think together which we have had to leave out for the purposes of this paper, the question arises as to how and where to situate work on adolescent girls. And more specifically, how to theorize gender relations within current debates on capitalism and patriarchy? To attempt to address ourselves to this requires a short digression into subcultural theory, since this is the main perspective which recent studies are drawing on. We wish both to raise as problematic the insertion of girls into a subcultural framework and to question the consequent attempt to produce a specifically female subculture – namely a bedroom culture and a lavatory culture. Such an attempt is not as useful as it seems because it seeks to contain work on adolescent girls within subcultural theory, or at least hinge such work on to a body of theoretical perspectives which cannot or have persistently failed to analyse gender relations.

McRobbie (1976) has done the major work of drawing attention to the virtually total omission of girls from subcultural literature and has usefully asked why, to conclude that girls are excluded because the terms as defined in the literature are entirely masculine – as expressed subsequently by Brake (1980): 'if subcultures are solutions to collectively experienced problems, then youth culture is highly concerned with the problem of masculinity'. Finding that girls are invisible in the literature, McRobbie then asks how absent or present are they in male subcultures – in reality. She concludes that they are only marginally present and that their marginal presence is simply a reproduction of their 'cultural subordination'.

Yet girls participate in drugs, drink, sex, fighting and crime (Wilson, 1978; Smith, 1978). Girls are on the street:

> I reckon we fight as seriously as the boys. You know, if anybody comes up to us we'll smack a bottle in their faces ... any Greasers or Hairies come in [our territory] and there's trouble ... I always carry a knife or dog chain when I go down there. (Skinhead girl quoted in Smith, 1978)

There can be little doubt about the seriousness of their group involvement. However, the extent of girls' participation or exclusion on the street would seem to be less than boys', but remains to be fully investigated. The more important question of the *terms* of their participation or exclusion as laid down in the street has been neglected. Instead, McRobbie has asked whether there are 'complementary ways in which girls interact among themselves and with each other to form a distinctive culture of their own', and suggests that:

> When the dimension of sexuality is included in the study of youth subcultures, girls can be seen to be negotiating a different space, offering a different type of resistance to what can at least in part be viewed as their sexual subordination.

By focusing on sexuality through the term 'slag', rather than simply inserting sexuality as a dimension, we hope we have begun to show that there can be no 'different space' that is not always and already the product of gender relations. Surely, to look for a 'cult of femininity', a specifically female cultural product, without locating that product within the actual gender relations that obtain, is to fail to see those phenomena as an articulation of those relations not a resolution or resistance.

Indeed, this very tendency in subcultural theory to argue that subcultural groups exist in a space that marks a temporary escape from the pressures and demands of society and that youth's response to its situation, where it takes a distinctive form, marks a kind of resolution or resistance to that situation cannot be sustained in work on sexuality. Subcultural theory is fundamentally based on a class analysis that cannot be simply appropriated to a gender analysis.

This raises the whole problematic of the relation of patriarchy to capitalism. With regard to this we can only indicate our line of thinking which follows the useful clarification of some of the issues that Cousins (1978) and Adlam (1979) have made.

Questions about sexual division cannot be inserted into a Marxist analysis where the material base for that analysis lies in specific economic relations and their effects, unless gender relations are reducible to economic relations. But there is no requirement in the concept of mode of production for the social division of labour to be realized as a sexual division. So there is no possible basis for a specific analysis of gender relations. In contrast, patriarchy asserts the primary of sexual divisions but in seeking a material origin to what is assumed to be *a specific* subordination of women to men, is open to the danger of seeking a 'universal cause' as origin, that logically must reside in some essential antagonism between the sexes.

Not only are the two clearly incompatible:

Insofar as they locate a different material base and do so through a different conception of determination, they cannot be sustained as being complementary. (Cousins, 1978: 65)

But neither is adequate, the former in its indifference to sexual divisions and the latter in its reduction of problems of sexual difference to 'an always already antagonistic relation between two social groups ...' (Adams, 1979:57).

To return to the street – McRobbie argues that one reason the street remains taboo to women is made clear by the disparaging term 'street walker'. We would add, however, that the term 'street walker' does not necessarily ban them from the street but pronounces the terms on which they can be seen on the street, i.e. as girlfriend or slag. In other words the girls' appearance on the street is always constrained by their subordination. The term 'slag' is, we think, one of the ways through which their subordination is effected. The general use of the term, or its equivalents, requires analysis as a *practice* within which and through which the category itself is produced.

'I Just Wanted to Kill a Woman' Why? The Ripper and Male Sexuality

Wendy Hollway

I re-read this article worried that it would come across as saying that all men are violent towards women, which is a position I am critical of now, just as I was when the article was written. I was relieved to find it avoided that position, but nonetheless it could be read as reducing to that claim by virtue of the fact that it gives no explanation of differences in sexual violence towards women among men. Since advertising, pornography, and so on are, as I argued, addressing all men, what makes some men less violent, less threatened, more able to handle the contradictions which construct women? I don't think feminist theory has got much further on this question. It has asserted for a long time that male sexuality and power are inextricably linked, but how? A further understanding of that relationship will have to shift the focus from male sexuality to masculinity; that is, from sexuality to gender. I have argued elsewhere that gender is a relation of difference based on power (Henriques et al, 1984) and that an analysis of women's power should not be excluded (Hollway, 1984: 63-8). These emphases help us to see male sexuality and masculinity as a social and psychic construction and not as something monolithic and predetermined or natural. In summary, then, I am saying that an important line of inquiry is to understand the differences within gender.

The trial in 1981 of Peter Sutcliffe, the 'Yorkshire Ripper', was dominated by attempted explanations of his motives. Through an examination of newspaper reports[1] of the trial, I want to try to uncover the assumptions made about Sutcliffe's sexuality and its relation to the women who were his victims. I want to show how the discourses – the frameworks within which explanations are sought – have the effect of distorting systematically (though not necessarily intentionally) the understanding of men's masculinity and its expression through their sexuality.

Sutcliffe's trial demonstrated men's collaboration with other men in the oppression of women. As the mouthpieces for legal, psychiatric and journalistic discourses, men collaborated in reproducing a view of the world which masks men's violence against women. This position will certainly be objected to on the grounds that Peter Sutcliffe was punished; that the law has done its duty. But women are not safe from men's violence just because one 'Ripper' has been locked up. The trial refused to recognize the way in which Sutcliffe's acts were an expression – albeit an extreme one – of the construction of an aggressive masculine sexuality and of women as its objects. This 'cover up' exonerates men in general even when one man is found guilty. It is not necessary to argue that the men whose accounts I cite were doing this consciously or intentionally. The power of a discourse resides in its hegemony, in the way it passes as truth, and in the way its premises and logic are taken for granted. Yet, despite this there were many indications of the explanations for Sutcliffe's actions, pointers which could not be grasped by the men involved. Maybe they were suppressed precisely because:

> We love the criminal and take a burning interest in him, because the Devil makes us forget the beam in our own eye when observing the mote in our brother's, and in that way outwits us. (*Observer*, 24 May 1981)[2]

As women we are not blinded by that particular beam. Because of the enormity of Sutcliffe's acts, we should not hesitate in using the trial to point to the potentially horrific consequences of contemporary masculinity. Men deal with the requirements of their gender in diverse ways. Most do behave differently from Sutcliffe and the discourses exemplified here help them to feel far removed from the Ripper. But if similarities were recognized between the construction of Sutcliffe's sexuality and that of other men, it would be clearer to men that the reproduction of patriarchal discourses on masculinity not only promotes women's oppression but is also against their own interests.

Because Sutcliffe admitted performing the killings, but entered a plea of guilty of manslaughter on the grounds of diminished responsibility, the trial took the relatively unusual form of turning on 'the state of the accused's mind at the time of the killings' (1 May 1981).[3] The way the question was represented to the jury by Sir Michael Havers, QC (prosecuting), was as follows:

> He had committed crimes which were beyond ordinary comprehension, but 'does it mean he must be mad – or just plain evil, plain bad?' (20 May 1981)

Therefore, 'we are really dealing here with motives, reasons, motivations. They are often very difficult to discern', the judge told the jury before they were sent out to consider their verdict (21 May 1981). The jury's job – and consequently the job of the prosecution, defence, expert witnesses and reporters – was therefore to understand the reasons for, and causes of, Sutcliffe's action. Seventeen days later the jury, by a majority of ten to two, came to a verdict of guilty of the murder of thirteen women. (Sutcliffe had already pleaded guilty to the attempted murder of another seven.) It is because of this feature that the trial offers such powerful evidence of the patriarchal discourses on sexuality. They are to be found in Sutcliffe's own testimony, and other lay accounts; in the psychiatric evidence through which his so-called 'paranoid schizophrenia' is explored; through the arguments of prosecution and defence in explaining his actions as bad or mad. Then there is the influential way that the judge presents the issue to the jury. For example, he advised them that if they believed that Sutcliffe

> was deluded into believing that he had a divine mission to kill prostitutes and that at the time of each killing, that his victim was a prostitute then the correct verdict was probably manslaughter. (21 May 1981)

These proceedings are only relayed to us women readers after journalists – again exclusively men – have turned it into a newsworthy story.

■ Men's 'natural' sexuality

The lay, legal, psychiatric and journalistic discourses all shared an assumption about what is normal masculine sexuality. Mostly this remained implicit, although deducible from the lines of questioning used. However one journalist Piers Paul Read made the assumption explicit, backing it up by 'scientific expertise':

> As Anthony Storr says in his book *Human Aggression*, 'male sexuality, because of the primitive necessity of pursuit and penetration, does contain an important element of aggressiveness; an element which is both recognized and responded to by the female who yields and submits.' (*Observer*, 24 May 1981)

To the extent that this assumption is never challenged, the patriarchal discourse is reproduced and strengthened by such an event as this trial. To the extent that explanations of Sutcliffe's actions can depend on people's acceptance of this 'truth', sexual violence, a most significant and deep-rooted form of men's oppression of women, goes unchallenged. One effect of the proceedings was to single out the Ripper as an abnormal phenomenon, explicable only by the difference between him and other men, thus reproducing the sexuality and relations of 'normal' men as unproblematic. It has been possible to achieve this with such consensus because of the scale of the murders. In one sense, any man who murders, or attempts to murder, a total of twenty women is different from the norm. The attempts to explain the aberration are therefore geared to accounting for that difference. If he was 'mad' this makes him quantitatively different from other men. If he was 'bad' it is more difficult to exonerate others: what made him qualitatively different?[4] Able to provide no satisfactory explanation, the press split off his bad/mad side from the normal man offered to the public in such press comments as 'everyone who knew Sutcliffe thought he would have made an ideal father' (23 May 1981).

■ Mad?

There is one significant difference in the choice of 'mad' rather than 'bad' as an explanation of Sutcliffe's killings. Whereas 'bad' is a label which requires an understanding of the moral, that is social, content of the acts, 'mad' is a label which is used as if it were a self-sufficient explanation: it is a form of diagnosis which avoids considering the content of the acts and thus avoids seeing the link between individual and society. Instead, psychiatry looks to biology for causes. Dr MacCulloch said in his report: 'I suspect there is a link [between the motorcycle crash and his madness] and that there is some organic impairment' (19 May 1981). However it was Sutcliffe's representation of the 'divine mission' which psychiatrists relied on for an explanation.

Mr Chadwin (for the defence) told the jury that 'he had to persuade them that Sutcliffe had, at the time of the killings, believed he had been receiving instructions' (20 May 1981). This would count as evidence that he was deluded, and be a major contributor to a diagnosis of 'paranoid schizophrenia'.[5] No one seemed to point out what to me was the obvious loophole in the psychiatric argument: the explanation that it was a delusion does not show *why* the voice told Sutcliffe to kill women. Whether it was God's voice, the Devil's, or the projected voice of Sutcliffe's own hatred makes no difference: the content derives from a generalized, taken-for-granted misogyny. The psychiatric discourse was one means whereby the legal process could avoid asking uncomfortable questions about male violence.[6] For example, when Dr MacCulloch was asked what he thought caused Sutcliffe to kill women he replied 'I think it was the divine mission.' When pushed further, he explained: 'It is well known that in schizophrenia killings take place – and bizarre killings at that – and it is not possible to offer any logical explanation for the killings because of the nature of schizophrenia' (19 May 1981).

■ Bad?

The case for Sutcliffe being 'bad' rested, for the prosecution, on trying to prove that there was a 'sexual component' in Sutcliffe's attacks. This and the 'divine mission' were contested as if they were mutually exclusive. Yet in the face of evidence of Sutcliffe's brutal attacks, only on women, a feminist analysis sees no incompatibility between a mission to kill women and this man's sexuality. Nonetheless, the 'logic' of their argument powerfully illustrates the assumptions made about male sexuality. Dr Milne's position that there was 'no underlying sexual component to his attacks' was challenged by Mr Ognall (prosecuting) in the following terms:

> Mr Ognall held up a seven inch screwdriver which, he said, Sutcliffe had stabbed three times into the vagina of Josephine Whitaker. 'That indicates the most fiendish cruelty, deliberately done for sexual satisfaction?'. (15 May 1981)

Despite the recognition of the act's 'most fiendish cruelty', a sexual component can only – to these men – mean 'sexual satisfaction'. Men's sexual desire is seen as an untainted urge, product of nature not society. So because 'There was no suggestion that he derived sexual pleasure from the killings', there was no sexual component. Sir Michael Havers thus draws distorted conclusions:

> Why had he stabbed one of his victims in the vagina? Why had he so often stabbed his victims' breasts? ... Was he getting sexual gratification from these injuries? ... If it was true that he felt repulsed by prostitutes and if he truly was seething with hatred for them, how was it that he had sex with one of his victims? ... 'You talk about your mission. And then surprise, surprise, here's pretty little Helen Rytka and you have sex with her'. (7 May 1981)

His reasoning goes that the woman's attractiveness (as sex-object) produces the man's sexual arousal and desire for gratification (as is so commonly argued in rape cases to absolve the man of responsibility). He cannot recognize the social meanings expressed through sexuality. But Sutcliffe's reply acknowledges those social meanings: 'To be honest I pulled up her clothing to satisfy some sort of sexual revenge on her'. (7 May 1981)

■ Sexual revenge

What was Sutcliffe revenging, and on whom? There are no isolated causes of feelings which are the product of patriarchal relations and which lead to violence against women – least of all a knock on the head or a divine voice. In fact Sutcliffe's history in relation to sex and prostitutes seems fairly typical. He was given to boasting with his friends about sex with prostitutes, on one occasion telling a friend 'that two girls had followed him back to the car the previous night. He said he had one of them in the back and one over the bonnet' (8 May 1981). Men's acceptance of masculine sexual violence was shown in the testimony of another friend with whom Sutcliffe went on 'red light jaunts'. This man told the court that 'He said he'd followed a woman to a house somewhere. I think he said he'd hit her ... He pulled a sock from his pocket and there was a small brick or stone in it' (8 May 1981).

He must have accepted this as fairly normal since, despite seeing the evidence, he did not pursue the matter. The patriarchal discourse sees as quite 'natural' a bit of aggression in men's sexuality (witness Storr's account cited above). To this extent Sutcliffe is normal. But what made him kill? Male sexual violence must be seen as a way of asserting 'masculinity' by exercising power over a woman. Sutcliffe's first murder came after a prostitute had accused him of being 'fucking useless' when he was slow to get an erection (7 May 1981), after which he said he felt a 'seething rage', and attacked and killed her. Clearly his masculinity was threatened by his impotence in the face of this woman's sexuality and her taunt. This is a matter which some of the men involved in the trial are quick to seize upon sympathetically:

> It is not hard to see how this cocktail of frustration, guilt and humiliation could lead to fury, and the fury to an urge not just for revenge but for the satisfaction in spirit if not in body of his sexual urge. (*Observer*, 7 May 1981)

Sir Michael Havers, commenting in similar terms on the event, says of the prostitute's behaviour 'Was this not a classic example of provocation?' (20 May 1981). By blaming the victim, Havers colludes in avoiding the threatening recognition that a man will kill when mocked about his sexual potency. Thus he avoids asking the question why – why did Sutcliffe kill women – the answer to which would demand that he and other men faced the problem of masculinity. The ability to get an erection is the symbol of a man's masculinity, and it signifies his power. It is no coincidence that there is a common etymology for the words 'potency' and 'power'. When Sutcliffe had got his sexual revenge, he said he had a feeling of 'satisfaction and justification' (7 May 1981). But he went on to kill other women. Did they 'provoke' him?

■ Women blamed

Prostitutes, the main victims, were blamed for provocation. But it is on the generalized victim, woman, that the blame is laid. The search for a sexual component led straight to Sutcliffe's wife. If men's natural sexual urges were taken care of by the women whose duty it is to respond in a yielding manner, they would have no problems.[7] Hence Dr Milne could report

> that he had been particularly careful to look for a sexual component in the killings. He was satisfied that neither Mr nor Mrs Sutcliffe was sexually deviant. (7 May 1981)

Having accepted Sutcliffe's claim that he was not violent towards his wife, the psychiatrist appeared not to pursue questions concerning the quality of his relationship to this woman. Sonia Sutcliffe gets no such gentle treatment. After stating that she had been mentally ill, the report continues:

She had shown no signs of a recurrence of her illness, but in interviews with Dr Milne 'she readily admits that she had been at times temperamental and difficult and freely admits that she has frequently teased and provoked her husband. (7 May 1981)

Note how the sentence construction 'although ... she *admits*...' imputes blame. Often the conclusion which we are supposed to draw remains implicit, but Havers actually specified it:

Or is [Sutcliffe's behaviour] because he was having a rough time after his marriage? Was his wife, also because of her own illness, behaving impossibly so that he dreaded going home? (20 May 1981)

A great fuss was made in the news of evidence from a prison officer (which the judge did not see fit to exclude as irrelevant) that 'Mrs Sutcliffe used to run the visits, she used to take the lead' on the basis of which he concluded 'she completely overwhelms and dominates him in the situation' (20 May 1981). Sutcliffe is presented as the henpecked husband who was driven to commit terrible acts because his wife dominated him.[8]

Peter Sutcliffe's behaviour to Sonia was worth consideration. He was obsessively jealous and on several occasions had fantasies that Sonia was a prostitute. But rather than blame Sutcliffe, the psychiatrist referred to it as a delusion, thus incorporating it into the category of phenomena that have no explanation.

■ Women's sexuality

Sutcliffe's claim that 'God encouraged me to kill people called scum who cannot justify themselves to society' was eagerly seized upon by the press who failed to point out the inconsistency of the fact that for Sutcliffe only prostitutes fell into this category (and not for example the men who, like him, used and abused them). As prostitutes and feminists have pointed out,[9] the distinction between prostitutes and 'totally respectable' women victims clearly testified to a value that the lives of prostitutes were worth less and that Sutcliffe's mission in wiping them out was somehow more justifiable. Thus Sir Michael Havers said of Sutcliffe's victims 'some were prostitutes, but perhaps the saddest part of this case is that some were not' (*West Indian World*, 6 June 1981).

Whether Sutcliffe believed that all his victims were prostitutes became crucial to the verdict. Sir Michael Havers told him 'Your story would have gone straight down the drain if you had to say to the doctors that six of them were not prostitutes' (13 May 1981). This can only be because the dominant discourse regards prostitutes as not 'innocent' (blaming the victim again), and indeed this is how Sutcliffe represents it:

> Sometimes after killing women who were not prostitutes he had worried that it might be the voice of the devil. But he was able to tell that they were prostitutes by the way they walked. He knew they were not innocent (7 May 1981).

In fact there was no distinction between his feelings about his victims: 'I realized Josephine was not a prostitute but at the time I wasn't bothered. I just wanted to kill a woman', and 'I realized now I had an urge to kill any woman' (7 May 1981). Not 'scum of the earth', just 'any woman'. Why was any woman in this category? The link is women's sexuality. 'By the way they walked' he could tell a woman was not innocent. Guilty of sexuality. In this society prostitutes symbolize sexuality. Images of women are split into the innocent and guilty: the virgin and the whore; Mary and Eve; the wife and the mistress.[10] Only the latter are meant to be 'guilty' of sexuality. The religious myth of the Virgin Mary represents the wife/mother as asexual, achieving what is impossible in reality by denying her sexuality while claiming her reproductivity. Sutcliffe had trouble maintaining this separation with respect to Sonia. He constantly imagined that she was having sexual relationships with other men and had fantasies that she was a prostitute. But from the 'voice' 'I had reassurance that she was a good girl and that the prostitutes were responsible for all the trouble' (12 May 1981).

Sutcliffe hated women for their sexuality, which he split off into prostitutes rather than acknowledge in his wife. Yet he was also obsessed by them. For it is against women's sexuality that men are motivated to measure their masculinity and because they must prove this at each encounter, their masculinity never rests assured. Sutcliffe's desire for 'sexual revenge' was not satisfied by one murder.

The discourses representing women as sex-objects to be dominated pervade the culture: in sexist jokes; pornography depicting violence; and men's boasts. They not only address us women as sex-objects from the advertising hoardings, but often present the predatory man for the male public to identify with. The hoardings are beckoning men to live up to their masculinity by preying on women as sex-objects. It is through their sexuality that men are expected to prove themselves. As I stated above woman-as-sex-object is not the only image which is reproduced. Men are torn between reverence, need and hatred of women and deal with these contradictions in diverse ways. But the threats represented by women as a result of these contradictions can contribute – as they did in Sutcliffe's case – to an extreme desire to punish women for their sexuality. That desire is legitimized by the patriarchal discourse which sees men's aggressive sexuality as natural. The lawyers, psychiatrists and journalists involved in the trial used and reproduced this discourse. But the 'voice' that Sutcliffe obeyed was the voice, not of God or delusion, but of the hoardings on the streets, of newspaper stands, of porn displays and of films. It is the voice which addresses every man in our society and to that extent, as the feminist slogan claims, 'all men are potential rapists'.

■ Notes

1   I have made no attempt to cover the reporting of the trial in all Britain's newspapers. The coverage in 'quality' newspapers such as the *Guardian* is a good deal less sensational, and often less blatantly sexist in its lines of reasoning. If the case I am making stands up from these reports, it would thus go for any reports – save feminist ones – of the trial.

2   The quotation is from Jung, but the *Observer* article ended with it. Maybe it was a covert recognition of the responsibility of men as a group for recognizing the problem as one of contemporary masculinity and ceasing to blame the victim.

3   Unless otherwise stated, dates in brackets refer to articles in the *Guardian*.

4   After the trial, questions were asked why the Attorney General, Sir Michael Havers, had been prepared to accept a manslaughter plea because 'it would spare the families of the victims' (5 June 1981). As the families had expressed a wish to see 'justice done', and felt that this would not have been so had Sutcliffe got away with a manslaughter verdict, Havers must have had other motives. I can only speculate, but from my arguments here, it seems likely that men would have felt much more comfortable if there was never any doubt as to Sutcliffe's insanity. Why else would four psychiatrists unanimously find him mad on the basis of evidence that turned out, in the process of the trial and the eventual verdict, to be incomplete, partial and distorted?

5   The other symptoms cited by Dr Milne sound uncannily similar to normal masculinity:

> There were his preoccupation with prostitutes, his over-controlled behaviour, his illogical thinking, his lack of insight into the reasons

for his actions, his feeling that his mind was being controlled, his distortions of thought and perception. (He goes on to mention Sutcliffe's jealousy concerning Sonia.) (20 May 1981)

6   This discourse has a long history. In the case of Pierre Rivière, Foucault (1975) documents its use in 1835 in rather similar circumstances.
7   After the trial, Sutcliffe's father commented that it would never have happened if his son had married a different girl.
8   When Sutcliffe's upbringing was considered, blame was sought in his mother. When it became apparent that 'he was much fonder of his mother than he was of his father' (7 May 1981) the matter was dropped.
9   The fact that prostitutes and feminists demonstrated outside the court in order to make this point received almost no press coverage.
10 Read (*Observer*, 24 May 1981) refers to this dichotomy in images of women but relates it specifically to Sutcliffe's Catholic background:

There is undoubtedly a tendency among Catholics to be confused by this contradiction, and to solve it by dividing women into two – the pure and the Wanton ... loving one and desiring the other.

While this may be true of Catholic men, it functions here to mask the generality of the phenomenon in patriarchal discourses on sexuality.

Jealousy and Sexual Difference

Toril Moi

This article was written in the autumn of 1980 when I was a visiting student at Cornell University. At the time my intention was to go on to study representations of jealousy in French fiction from different periods in order to re-evaluate the purely psychological theories of this essay when confronted with specific historical contexts. For various reasons that project never materialized, and I then decided to publish the piece on its own. By the time it appeared in Feminist Review *in 1982, however, my own theoretical interests had changed. Influenced by poststructuralism, and particularly by French feminist theory, I felt the need to examine the political consequences of the often unacknowledged assumptions at work in feminist literary criticism in some depth before producing any critical work of my own. My work in this area eventually led to the publication of my book* Sexual/Textual Politics *(Methuen, 1985). Looking back on the essay today, I feel that it still contains much valuable research, but also that the whole theoretical basis of my arguments would need re-examination. I would particularly want to reassess the question of sexual difference in jealousy in the light of Lacanian and Kristevan psychoanalysis, and also to question the stability of the so-called jealous triangle. Is it always as easy as I seem to think to distinguish jealous subject from victimized object? Or rival from lover? Would lesbian or gay relationships be any different in this respect? Although the way in which I try to relate questions of psychology to social relations of power now strikes me as somewhat too simplistic, it is nevertheless precisely this effort which gives the essay its feminist profile and still, I hope, makes it worthwhile reading for other women.*

Jealousy is one of those affective states, like grief, that may be described as normal. If anyone appears to be without it, the inference is justified that it has undergone severe repression and consequently plays all the greater part in his unconscious mental life. (Freud 1922:223)

Jealousy is a notoriously dangerous passion and constitutes a well-recognized motive for crimes of violence, particularly of a gynocidal nature. (Shepherd, 1961)

Jealousy, then, is perfectly normal, and murder and madness follow in its wake. It is striking that such a fascinating phenomenon has not given rise to a plethora of learned investigations. During the past few decades, jealous feelings have become hopelessly unfashionable, and this is probably the reason for the conspicuous absence of recent research on the subject. But even earlier generations of theorists, less hostile to the idea of being jealous, did not explore the subject to any great extent.

■ Which is the jealous sex?

Most authors who have written on jealousy are extremely interested in the question of sexual difference. They declare either that women are more jealous than men, or that men are more jealous, or manage to suggest that both sexes are more jealous. An example of the latter, somewhat contradictory, position can be found in Arnold L. Gesell's still relevant 1906 article on jealousy. He starts by tracing jealousy back to the instinct for possession in animals, and emphasizes, with Darwin, that in sexual rivalry jealousy 'is largely confined to the male' (1906:449). This male instinct is still the basis for human jealousy:

However complex, in its higher states, human jealousy may be, it will always be found to bear the 'stamp of its lowly origin' and will become more comprehensible in the light of its pedigree. (1906:452)

But when actually discussing sexual difference in human jealousy, Gesell states rather lamely that

> ... the question of *sex difference* in criminal and normal jealousy is very complex and delicate. The weight of quotable (male) authority is to the effect that women are more susceptible to jealousy. (1906:483)

I take it that the brackets around 'male' indicate Gesell's own uneasiness with this conclusion.

Most authors are not quite as confused as Gesell. If we ask them which sex they think is the more jealous, they will give a clear answer. It is however striking that the answer seems to be directly related to the professional interests of the author. Sociologists and social anthropologists tend to believe that jealousy is a male passion, but they vary in their reasons for this belief. Their earliest representative is Darwin, who thought that jealousy, being an inborn instinct, prevented promiscuous intercourse in primitive tribes. This prompted him to draw the following picture of life in primitive society:

> Therefore, looking far back in the stream of time, and judging from the social habits of man as he now exists, the most probable view is that he aboriginally lived in small communities, each with a single wife, or if powerful with several, whom he jealously guarded against all other men. (Quoted in Westermarck, 1901:117)

For Darwin, wives obviously do not belong to the race of 'man', and therefore only men are jealous.

Edward Westermarck, who shows clear Darwinian leanings in his study of marriage practices in a great number of human societies, concludes that 'jealousy is not exclusively a masculine passion, although it is generally more powerful in men than in women' (1901: 496). Westermarck notes that wives are generally considered the husband's property, and sees male jealousy as the normal expression of the instinct for possession. Since women (wives) cannot own their husband, they cannot be jealous either. In most societies, adultery is seen as a violation of the husband's property rights, and the punishment for such a crime is severe: 'Most commonly, among uncivilized nations, the seducer is killed, adultery on the woman's side being considered a heinous crime, for which nothing but death can atone' (1901: 121).

Westermarck also studies the fate of widows in this context, and states: 'And so strong is the idea of a wife being the exclusive property of her husband, that, among several peoples, she may not even survive him' (1901: 125). The plight of widows in Fiji is particularly instructive. According to Westermarck,

> ... they were either buried alive or strangled, often at their own desire, because they believed that in this way alone could they reach the realms of bliss, and that she who met her death with the greatest devotedness, would become the favourite wife in the abode of spirits. On the other hand, a widow who did not permit herself to be killed, was considered an adulteress. (1901: 125-6)

Westermarck does not tell his readers what the punishment for adultery was in Fiji, but among such jealous men one fears the worst for them.

The American sociologist Kingsley Davis believes that only men can own sexual property and therefore that only men are jealous. Davis sees jealous behaviour as conditioned by the rules for ownership of sexual property in a given society. Jealousy will then only be expressed when a 'Rival/Trespasser' breaks these rules by trying to take away from the 'Ego' property acquired in a legitimate way. If we want to study all the aspects of jealousy, we must therefore study the attitude of the 'Ego', the 'Trespasser' and the 'Woman', Davis tells us (1959: 181).

For Davis, jealousy is highly functional: 'The social function of jealousy against a trespasser is therefore the extirpation of any obstacle to the smooth running of the institutional machinery.' This functionalism constitutes the clearest flaw in Davis's analysis of jealousy. He fails to see that his analysis is relevant only for patriarchy, and would probably reject the notion of change, since this would inevitably upset 'the smooth running of the institutional machinery'. He states, for instance, that the absence of jealousy would lead to promiscuity, which for him means anarchy. Promiscuity, he writes, can only take place 'in so far as society has broken down and reached a state of anomie' (1959: 189).

The sociologists argue the case for jealousy as a male phenomenon convincingly, but most psychiatrists would disagree with them. The Norwegian psychiatrist Gabriel Langfeldt, for instance, in his study of erotic jealousy, refuses to believe that men are more frequently jealous – in spite of the fact that male patients actually made up the majority of his material. Langfeldt thinks that this may be due to a higher frequency of alcoholism in men than in women, 'since a *normal* tendency to jealousy is, as we know, more frequent in women' (Langfeldt, 1961: 55).[1]

Kauko Vauhkonen, a Finnish psychiatrist who has written the most exhaustive study of jealousy to date,[2] shows that 'morbid jealousy occurs more frequently in men than in women', but also maintains that 'both everyday experience and certain studies ... suggest that in our culture the inclination to jealousy reactions is more frequent in women than in men' (1968: 171).

Both Vauhkonen and Langfeldt, like Gesell earlier, seem to accept some kind of 'popular wisdom' as proof when it comes to deciding which sex is the more jealous. But this kind of 'proof' relies heavily on ideological assumptions about the nature of the sexes, and therefore cannot be taken seriously in patriarchal society.

These assumptions, however, completely dominate the work of the third group of writers we are dealing with. The writers of popular books of jealousy positively revel in commonplaces and spicy erotic anecdotes. In his *La jalousie passionelle*, written in pre-'68 France, Noël Lamare states flatly that

> so-called passionate jealousy ... is notably more common in the fair sex ... The jealousy of woman is, if not always, at least generally more serious and also more pronounced in its features than the jealousy of man ... This is because affective and emotional life – 'nerves' – have a much more important place and role in woman than in man. (Lamare, 1967: 13-14)

Lamare's account of jealousy is, predictably enough after this introduction, flagrantly sexist. His main theme seems to be the ghastly sufferings of innocent men caught in the clutches of jealous women.[3]

Which *is* the jealous sex then? One must admit that so far the picture is inconclusive. Sociologists tend to think that men are jealous in order to protect their property (that is, women). Clinical psychiatrists believe that women are more frequently jealous but that men are more likely to become morbidly jealous. The popular writers on the theme are convinced that women are indeed the jealous sex, deploring their possessiveness and piously hoping for a freer sex-life for modern man.

If we want an answer to our question, we need to examine some new source of information. If neither anthropology, nor sociology nor psychiatry can help us, it seems to be time to turn to psychoanalysis.[4]

■ Freud's theory of jealousy

As a rule, psychoanalysts are not particularly interested in the question of sexual difference in jealousy, but they do provide valuable insights into the nature of jealousy. Our strategy, then, must be first to listen to the relevant psychoanalytic theories, and then to use their insights to find an answer to our own question.

The obvious starting point for our investigations is Freud's theory of jealousy. Freud distinguishes between what he calls three layers of jealousy: 1) competitive or normal, 2) projected and 3) delusional jealousy. *Normal* jealousy, according to Freud, is

> ... compounded of grief, the pain caused by the thought of losing the loved object, and of the narcissistic wound; further, of feelings of enmity against the successful rival, and of a greater or lesser amount of self-criticism which tries to hold the subject's own ego accountable for his loss. (Freud 1922: 223)

'Normal' jealousy is, however, far from rational. Even in this layer of jealousy, Freud claims, we will find traces of the oedipal conflict with ensuing homosexual or bisexual fantasies.

Projected jealousy is derived 'either from [the jealous person's] own actual unfaithfulness in real life or from impulses towards it which have succumbed to repression' (1922: 224). Freud stresses that *everybody* experiences some temptation to unfaithfulness. These tendencies must nevertheless be denied, and the subject will then 'make use of an unconscious mechanism of alleviation':

> He can obtain this alleviation – and, indeed, acquittal by his conscience – if he projects his own impulses to faithlessness on to the partner to whom he owes faith. (1922: 224)

The partner's own unconscious tendencies to unfaithfulness facilitate this projection. The jealous subject is, paradoxically, often not as wrong as he may think he is.

The third layer is the *delusional* type of jealousy. Freud states:

> It too has its origin in repressed impulses towards unfaithfulness; but the object in these cases is of the same sex as the subject. Delusional jealousy is what is left of a homosexuality that has run its course, and it rightly takes its position among the classical forms of paranoia. (1922: 225)

The formula for this kind of jealousy is (in a man): '*I* do not love him, *she* loves him!' In a delusional case, one will always find all three layers of jealousy present, never only the third alone.

A husband suffering from paranoia of jealousy accused his 'impeccably faithful wife' of infidelity. Freud points out that this man was

> ... extraordinarily observant of all [the] manifestations of her unconscious, and always knew how to interpret them correctly, so that he really was always in the right about it ... His abnormality really reduced itself to this, that he watched his wife's unconscious mind much more closely and then regarded it as far more important than anyone else would have thought of doing. (1922: 226)

This conclusion may seem astonishing, but we must recall that, according to Freud, desire is endless. When forced to live in monogamy, everybody will harbour desires to be unfaithful. In cases of delusional jealousy, then, it is not so much the symptoms that the paranoiac perceives, but the exaggerated interpretations he places on them that constitute the delusions. Freud states that in cases of paranoia, it is not the presence of certain persecutory ideas that matters, but the 'quantitative factor', that is 'the degree of attention, or more correctly, the amount of cathexis that these structures are able to attract to themselves' (1922: 228).

Delusional (or paranoid) jealousy therefore occurs when the subject employs an exceptional amount of libidinal energy in order to repress his homosexuality, and not only, as in the case of projected jealousy, to repress his tendencies to infidelity.

Freud's article is still the most important work in this field. It has nevertheless a fundamental flaw; its case material is all male. At this point we do not even know if the process of jealousy is the same for both sexes. It is clearly important to try to discover whether it is, and the solution may perhaps be found in psychoanalytic theory of sexual difference. Two problem areas are in this context immediately relevant: the child's relationship to the preoedipal mother and its experience of the oedipal stage.

■ The child and the preoedipal mother

Melanie Klein has, more than any other psychoanalyst, stressed the importance of the baby's relationship to its mother during the first months of life. For Klein, the mother is the baby's first object of love and hate: she is 'both loved and hated with all the intensity and strength that is characteristic of the early urges of the baby' (Klein, 1975: 306). Klein emphasizes the lasting effects of this early mother-child relationship:

> Because our mother first satisfied all our self-preservative needs and sensual desires and gave us security, the part she plays in our minds is a lasting one, although the various ways in which this influence is effected and the forms it takes may not be at all obvious in later life (1975: 307).

In her article 'A Contribution to the Psychogenesis of Manic-Depressive States' from 1935 (1975: 262-89), she develops her theory of the early stages of infant development. In these stages, Klein also finds the origins of adult paranoia and depression.

According to Klein, the baby already has sadistic impulses against the mother in the very first months of its existence: it wants to devour and destroy the breast and the threatening insides of her body. In this very early stage of development, the early oral phase, the baby is governed by two psychological mechanisms: introjection and projection. It also has some notions of 'good' and 'bad' objects – an object is 'bad' when the baby projects its own aggressions on to it, and not only because it frustrates the baby's desires. The breast is thus seen to be both 'good' and 'bad', and the baby introjects both aspects without being able to make any separation between them. The child sees the 'bad' objects not only as 'bad', but as actively dangerous – as

> ... persecutors who it fears will devour it, scoop out the inside of its body, cut it to pieces, poison it – in short compassing its destruction by all the means which sadism can devise ... Hence, quite little children pass through anxiety-situations (and react to them with defence-mechanisms), the content of which is comparable to that of the psychoses of adults. (1975: 262)

One of the earliest defence-mechanisms is projection and/or expulsion. The baby tries to defend itself against internalized persecutors by projecting or expelling them. But the dread and anxiety of these internalized objects persist even after they have been projected, and Klein states that 'These anxiety-contents and defence-mechanisms form the basis of *paranoia*' (1975: 263; my emphasis). Klein therefore calls this position the paranoid position, which lasts until the child is about four or five months old.

After the paranoid position follows the depressive position. But since Klein's account of this position is closely related to Freud's description of adult depression, it is worthwhile to examine Freud's point of view before we continue.

According to Freud, depression (or melancholia) is a reaction to the loss of a loved object. The libido that cathected the loved object is not displaced on to another object, but withdrawn into the ego. Here it serves to establish an identification of the ego with the abandoned object. Due to the repressed ambivalence towards the object, the introjected (devoured) object becomes the target for strong aggressive impulses. But because of the identification of the ego with the introjected object, this aggression turns back on the ego, and now the ego itself is treated as a hated object. Freud writes that 'no neurotic harbours thoughts of suicide which he has not turned back upon himself from murderous impulses against others' (Freud 1917: 252). Freud gives the following description of the typical symptoms of depression.

> ... a profoundly painful dejection, cessation of interest in the outside world, loss of the capacity to love, inhibition of all activity, and a lowering of the self-regarding feelings to a degree that finds utterance in self-reproaches and self-revilings, and culminates in a delusional expectation of punishment. (1917: 244)

These symptoms must be seen as the expression of the hitherto repressed hatred against the loved object, a hatred which now is turned back on to the ego itself. The desire for suicide, which often accompanies the extreme loss of self-regard that Freud mentions, is then nothing but the heavily repressed desire to murder the loved object.

This urge to destroy the internalized loved object is also of prime importance in Klein's description of the depressive position. The transition from the paranoid position to the depressive position is marked by an important change in the child's perceptions. In the paranoid position it perceived only part-objects, whereas in the depressive position it becomes able to perceive whole objects. The feeling of *loss*, so characteristic of the depressive position, is related to this change: 'Not until the object is loved *as a whole*', Klein states, 'can its loss be felt as a whole' (1975: 264). The child now identifies with the whole, good object (the good mother), and internalizes (devours) it. This, however, generates deep anxiety in the child: it now dreads that it has destroyed the good object by its cannibalism.

Since it also fears that it may destroy the good object along with the bad, it can no longer use the 'old' mechanism of expulsion and projection. The child still does not distinguish very well between 'reality' and itself, and therefore also fears that its aggression and hate have destroyed not only the internalized object, but the real object, the real mother, as well.

This fear of having destroyed the loved object leads to strong feelings of guilt, anxiety and remorse, and the child will try to restore the loved object to its former perfection (to make reparation) by reconstructing it in its fantasies. If the feelings of guilt and anxiety are too intense, this will inhibit the drive and capacity to make reparation. Klein argues that this early anxiety is at the root of all later inhibition to work and/or create, and of all later depression.

In summary, we may say that the baby in the paranoid position seeks to defend itself by expelling and projecting the persecutors, whereas its main concern in the depressive position is to preserve and protect the internalized good object with which the ego is identified. This leads to the marked loss of self-esteem and feelings of guilt and anxiety characteristic of this position. One might add that paranoid suspicions and fears may be reinforced by the child as a defence against the anxieties awakened by the depressive position. The depressive position is always derived from the paranoid position, says Klein; it does not cancel it out, but integrates it.

■ Sexual differentiation and the oedipus complex

The preoedipal development is, generally speaking, similar for boys and girls. Sexual differentiation is achieved in the oedipal stage. So far, the main love-object for both sexes has been the mother. Now the little girl is required to change her object-choice: she must take the father as her love-object. Little boys maintain the mother as their love-object, but have to face the anxiety-provoking fear of punishment, of castration if they continue to desire her genitally.

The little boy has to identify with the father and with the father's penis at the same time as he has to cope with his deep feelings of aggression towards him. There is thus a conflict between his identification-love for his father and his rivalry with him. The normal solution of the oedipus complex is the renunciation of the oedipal love for the mother and adoption of full identification-love for the father, based on the formula: 'I would like to be as big as he is and be allowed and able to do all that he does' (Fenichel, 1945:88).

This development leaves the boy with a strong impression of the suffering and anxiety experienced in the rivalry with the powerful, adult father. This, then, is the oedipal background for masculine jealousy. We may also note that the oedipal situation forces the boy to abandon all identification with the mother, since continuing identification with her might lead to homosexuality. The taboo on homosexuality is for the little boy reinforced by the fact that, in our civilization he is normally not encouraged to develop close, physical ties with his father or other men. In the normal boy, one must therefore assume that tendencies to a homosexual object choice are thoroughly repressed.

The little girl then, has to change her choice of object. This is achieved by activating hostile feelings towards the mother, who is accused of having deprived the daughter of something (the penis), of having frustrated her in some way. It is obvious that this change of love object is not easy to carry out; Otto Fenichel states that

> ... conflicts about preoedipal love for the mother play an important role in the neuroses of women. In normal development, too, the relationship of women to their mothers is more frequently ambivalent than is that of most men to their father. Some remnants of preoedipal mother fixation are always found in women. (1945: 90)

This implies that the tendency to homosexuality is stronger and less repressed in women, and moreover that women's later experiences, including jealousy, will be influenced by their ambivalent, preoedipal relationship to their mother. This is culturally reinforced by the encouragement of physical contact between the girl and her mother and among girls in general. The dominant, dynamic force in woman's psyche is not castration anxiety but the fear of loss of love (see 1945:99).

■ Jealousy and sexual difference

Now that we have examined the basic outlines of infantile psycho-sexual development, it is time to ask how all of this influences the expression of adult sexual jealousy. The problem seems to be feminine jealousy, since there is no reason to assume that Freud was wrong in his outline of masculine jealousy. Masculine jealousy is probably predominantly oedipal[5] as Freud says, because boys are more completely oedipalized than girls. It seems reasonable to assume that feminine jealousy then will be more markedly preoedipal. Joan Rivière's Kleinian views on feminine jealousy bear this out:

> ... jealousy and infidelity may have their foundation in the pre-genital levels of oral-erotic and oral-sadistic impulse. In persons whose psychical composition includes either jealousy or infidelity as a major pattern, my conclusion is that the 'loss of love' or the 'search for love' in question refers ultimately to something deeper than a genital relation to the desired parent ... The 'search' or the 'loss' in such cases can be traced back to *oral envy*, and to the deprivation of the breast or father's penis (as an oral object) – the objects with which the parents in coitus are felt to be gratifying each other. This and only this experience furnishes a rational basis for the acute and desperate sense of lack and loss, of dire need, of emptiness and desolation felt by the jealous one of a triangle and reversed by the unfaithful. The oral basis of jealous impulses may explain the greater incidence of jealousy in women, whose psychosexual development is more closely linked with the oral libido-organization than that of men. (1932: 420-1)

Rivière emphasizes the feeling of *loss* as fundamental in jealousy, and points out that this experience of oral deprivation is more dominant in women than in men. In the case of masculine jealousy it is reasonable to assume that feelings of loss and deprivation often will be masked by the stronger oedipalization of the masculine psyche. This means that women may experience jealousy predominantly as a terrible feeling of loss, men predominantly as intense anger against the rival, who stands in for the castrating father. This means in turn that jealousy will provoke a depressive reaction in women, and an aggressive or even paranoid reaction in men. This hypothesis is supported by the findings of the Finnish psychiatrist Vauhkonen, who writes that

> ... frustrations in infantile longings for love and disappointed narcissistic expectations appeared to make for the development of jealousy in female patients more often than in male patients (1968: 198).

If I am right in assuming that the normal reaction of a jealous woman will be predominantly depressive, this also explains why psychiatrists find that women are more jealous *in general*, but less prone to become *morbidly* jealous. Women in patriarchal society must learn how to live with feelings of loss and lack of self-esteem, since women are constantly devaluated and depreciated in most social contexts. In patriarchal society, a depressed woman is a normal woman, and as such is not likely to be hospitalized, unless her depression reaches quite excessive proportions. On the other hand, a man with delusions will automatically be considered in need of professional care.

Feelings of loss and wounded self-esteem are conducive to depression. In order to be respected and esteemed, women in patriarchal society must demonstrate that they can catch and keep a man. To lose one's lover/husband is interpreted as a blow to the woman's worth as a human being. It is then easy to understand why depression should be a widespread reaction in women who discover that they have a rival.

The fact that more men than women are defined as morbidly jealous is, however, also a result of the way psychiatrists define the word 'morbid' in relation to jealousy. Vauhkonen writes that in his material

> ... the jealousy of female patients was more frequently neurotic and less frequently psychotic than that of male patients. In other words, there is a greater tendency for male patients to fall ill with a grave, delusional type of jealousy as compared with female patients ... Thus, men seem to become morbidly jealous more frequently, more gravely and more rapidly than women. (1968: 171)

Elsewhere he gives a more precise definition of 'pathological jealousy':

> Jealousy was regarded as pathological in cases where the suspicious partner had no conclusive evidence of the other partner's infidelity, or, when such evidence was present, where the jealous reaction was so strong or prolonged as to necessitate psychiatric care (1968: 172).

This definition is highly representative – and highly revealing. Most authors on the subject consider jealousy to be morbid when it has no function in reality – that is when it is delusional. Depression does not normally produce delusions. And even if we admit that depression may start as a result of an *imagined* loss, it is far more frequently a result of a *real* loss of love.[6]

The lower frequency of delusional jealousy in women can also be explained by the consequences women's links with the preoedipal mother have for feminine homosexuality. Dorothy Dinnerstein believes that women's strong identification with the preoedipal mother makes them more consciously aware of their homosexual tendencies.[7] We remember that Freud stressed the homosexual component particularly strongly in cases of delusional jealousy, where the man has to employ a considerable amount of libidinal energy in order to maintain defence-mechanisms against his repressed homosexual tendencies. These defence-mechanisms consist in paranoid delusions, where, typically the other man, the rival, is seen as the persecutor. For Freud, paranoia always has a repressed homosexual component; the persecutor is always of the same sex as the paranoiac.[8] If it is true that women repress their homosexual tendencies to a much lesser extent, it is also less likely that they will develop paranoid (delusional) jealousy, since they will not need to maintain elaborate defence-mechanisms against such tendencies.

I have argued that women may well be more jealous than men in general, but that their jealousy often passes unnoticed since it is rarely accompanied by spectacular delusions. But there is another, very simple reason for this belief: in patriarchal society, the actual frequency of male infidelity is probably higher than the frequency of female infidelity, due to the differing moral standards of the two sexes. It is therefore logical to assume that women may well be the jealous sex – they simply have much more reason to be so.

In patriarchal society women are considered men's property. This gives men a strong motive for jealousy, but they will be jealous only in so far as they feel that their property is threatened. Traditionally women have been totally dependent on men. A woman without a man has been a social anomaly, a destiny to be shunned at all costs. It therefore seems likely that women have been the jealous sex, in the sense that they have been jealous more frequently than men. This is mainly due to two factors: their total dependency on male protection and the frequency of male infidelity. Men seem able to rest secure in the knowledge of their total possession of the woman; but if they start to doubt this, their jealousy is more likely to become pathological and/or delusional.

■ Who kills whom? Jealousy and aggression

Jealous aggression provides the most striking manifestation of sexual difference in jealousy. The most extreme expression of jealous aggression is the *crime passionnel*. And here the authorities agree: the jealous man kills much more frequently than the jealous woman. The passage quoted as an epigraph to this article continues in this way:

> While detailed statistics are difficult to obtain it has been established that the majority of murders in this country are committed by men and that their victims are mostly women (Shepherd, 1961: 699).

Men are notoriously more aggressive and violent than women, whether they are jealous or not.

More puzzling is the fact that when jealous women do express their aggression, they tend to attack their rival, whereas men are inclined to kill the unfaithful partner. In other words, in the jealous triangle, it is always the woman who gets killed. This astonishing fact has been observed by several authors. Daniel Lagache, who has produced a monumental two-volume study of jealousy, finds that jealous aggression (*la lutte jalouse*) is expressed differently in men and women:

> ... in the man, jealous aggression tends to concentrate on the partner. The woman more frequently extends the aggression to the rival and third parties. (Lagache, 1947, Vol.2: 138)

Lagache goes on to comment:

> ... in our limited material, the murderously jealous men had only attacked their partner, and the jealous women mainly their rival. (1947, Vol.2: 321)

Lagache stresses that his material is limited, and is reluctant to draw conclusions from this observation. His findings are borne out, however, by the German psychoanalyst M. Marcuse, who according to Vauhkonen maintains that

> ... the main object of jealous aggression is invariably the woman, irrespective of whether she is the partner causing a disappointment or the rival. Thus, a jealous woman will always find extenuating factors responsible for her partner's conduct, whereas a man will not find any excuses for his wife's infidelity (1968: 47).

Arnold L. Gesell also remarks on this phenomenon, stating that 'a man does not abhor his rival as much as a woman does hers' (1906: 483).

Here we are really confronted with two problems: 1) Why do men kill their partner? and 2) Why do women kill their rival? Let us start with the first question.

Killing the woman one loves would seem counterproductive. This has led various writers to suggest that jealousy has nothing to do with love.[9] Boris Sokoloff, for instance, writes that 'It is only in the absence of love that insane jealousy may progress to such an extent that murder or suicide are the only logical ends of this emotion' (1947: 8). The relationship between love and suicide is extremely complex, and it is impossible to discuss it fully in this context. Lagache's typology of love has, however, a direct bearing on the problem of the murderous lover.

Lagache distinguishes between *l'amour captatif* and *l'amour oblatif*. *L'amour captatif* is a feeling which is characterized by the subject's desire to possess the object totally and exclusively. In this case the loved object is seen as a thing, not as an independent consciousness: the possessive lover refuses to acknowledge the alterity of the Other, of the beloved. For Lagache, jealousy can only exist within the limits of the *amour captatif*, and therefore the death of the beloved is the extreme but logical outcome of this kind of love: 'the jealous man's murder of his partner is an extreme act of sadistic domination, of narcissistic self-affirmation and correspondingly, a negation of the other and of reality' (1947, Vol.2: 320).

For the jealous man, the crime of the woman consists not so much in infidelity (the murderous jealousy may well be delusional) as in the fact that she is irredeemably Other, whether she asserts that alterity or not. Men kill the unfaithful woman in order to claim their complete ownership of her. Lagache then suggests that adoption of *l'amour oblatif* may put an end to excessive jealousy. *L'amour oblatif* is defined as a situation where the loving subject effaces itself completely, ascribing Godlike supremacy to the loved object. This kind of lover can never be jealous, states Lagache, and he may well be right, for who would dare to question God's actions? But one seriously doubts that a jealous man would be capable of suddenly changing from the one to the other. And even if he could, it seems to me that the sadistic desire for mastery characteristic of the *amour captatif* is no worse than the masochistic drive towards self-annihilation in the *amour oblatif*.

But male aggression toward the beloved woman can also be seen as an outlet for the aggression felt against the frustrating preoedipal mother. Vauhkonen found that in his case material both male and female patients had shown a clear mother fixation in the choice of spouse (1968: 182). A mother fixated man is more likely to have homosexual tendencies (see Fenichel, 1945: 331f), and if he represses these is also more likely to develop delusional jealousy.

In the oedipal triangle, the little boy has to repress his aggression against the father (the rival) for fear of castration, but if he transfers this aggression on to the mother (the beloved but unfaithful woman) he can give it outlet and still avoid castration. The paranoid structure of masculine jealousy will also lead to stronger feelings of aggression in general than the depressive feminine form. The paranoiac has projected the erstwhile introjected 'bad' and dangerous objects on to the outside world. The projection of the persecutors permits the ego to protect itself by unleashing its aggression on an external persecutor, whereas, in the depressive position, the ego itself becomes the target for this aggressive energy.

One of the main reasons for the more frequent male feelings of aggression against the partner is not, however, psychoanalytical, but social, linked to the fact that women are considered the property of men. The interaction in the triangle formed by the jealous man, the woman and the male rival certainly corresponds closely to Luce Irigaray's (1977) contention that all sexual relationships are homosexual, in that they take place among men only ('des marchandises entre elles'). Irigaray describes women as pieces of merchandise circulated among men, who by giving (and selling) women to each other express their mutual love. In the case of the 'male' jealous triangle, she certainly seems to be right. The description of masculine jealousy in Fay Weldon's *Female Friends* illustrates this point perfectly. In this novel, each of the husbands (Christie and Oliver) hands over his wife to a man he admires, but when the wife succumbs to the temptation and actually commits adultery, strongly influenced by the feeling that her husband must want her to do this, she is in her turn duly punished by the husband, who puts all the blame on the unfortunate wife.

As for women's hatred of their rival, it is important to remember that women always seem to be fascinated by their rival, whether they love her or hate her. We have already seen that women may have quite conscious homosexual desires for their rival. Women's incomplete oedipalization may also diminish their aggression towards the 'other woman': the little girl may not have felt the mother to be a particularly threatening and castrating rival in the conflict over the father's love. According to Fenichel,

> There are many more women who all their life long remain bound to their father or to father figures, or in some way betray

the relationship of their love object to their father, than there are men who have not overcome their mother fixation. (1945: 99)

The ambivalent relationship to the preoedipal mother seems to be recreated in the jealous woman's relationship to her rival. If the dominant feeling towards the mother was hatred, the woman will hate her rival. This seems to be borne out by a case of jealous paranoia in a woman referred to by Fenichel, where

... the conflict in regard to homosexuality followed the same lines as those outlined by Freud for men. The patient was an infantile personality whose conflicts centered around her preoedipal relationship to her mother and who never had achieved a normal Oedipus complex. (1945: 435).

As we have seen already, most women never relinquish their ambivalent feelings towards the preoedipal mother. Both the intense love and the incandescent hate they felt for the mother continue to influence them throughout adult life.

It is interesting to note that Lagache's explanation of the masculine *crime passionnel* sheds no light on the feminine equivalent. If the woman does not kill her lover, it must be because patriarchal society has taught her to concede that the man is an independent consciousness, not an extended part of her self. The feminine tendency to forgive the man is probably motivated by her social dependency on him, but it may also be rooted in her desire to punish the frustrating mother by turning her love on to the father. Instead of expressing her hatred against the loved object, the jealous woman turns her aggression towards her own ego, and this, of course, leads to depression. The jealous woman may thus at the same time forgive and love the unfaithful lover (and to this extent she may not seem to be 'jealous' at all) and hate and despise her rival.

■ Conclusion

I have established that women seem to be more frequently jealous than men. There is a reason: women's social dependence on men in patriarchal society. The experience of jealousy is not the same in the two sexes. Masculine jealousy is predominantly oedipal, and shows a greater frequency of aggressive and paranoid reactions. The jealous man directs his aggression towards the beloved woman, and in extreme cases (*crime passionnel*) he may kill her. Feminine jealousy is predominantly preoedipal. The jealous woman's reactions are strongly influenced by her ambivalent relationship with the preoedipal mother. Feminine jealousy tends to be depressive rather than aggressive. If the jealous woman exteriorizes her aggression, she tends to direct it against her rival and not towards her lover.

No purely psychoanalytic explanation of jealousy will suffice: it is always vital to place it in its social and historical context. Psychology becomes relevant only when jealousy has occurred; when and why somebody becomes jealous, and whether that jealousy is considered abnormal, are socially determined. Jealousy is not a stable, unchanging phenomenon; it changes with society. On this point at least one can agree with Kingsley Davis who writes:

> ... for a full understanding of jealousy the sociological approach is indispensable because it addresses itself to a real and important aspect of jealous behaviour – the social aspect (1959: 192).

Outbursts of jealousy are determined not only by psychology, but also by existing social codes, standards for behaviour in men and women, dominant sexual ideologies, and the power-balance between the sexes. For any full understanding of jealousy, it is these changing social and historical contexts which must be examined. I hope to develop these social aspects of jealousy, largely absent in this essay, in another context.

■ Notes

1 The theory that alcoholism causes morbid jealousy goes back to Kraft-Ebbing (1891) who stated that alcohol was the most important triggering factor for jealousy, and therefore also thought that only men were prone to jealousy, since they make up most of the heavy drinkers.

2 Gordon Clanton and Lynn G. Smith (1977) is more recent, but this is a popular collection of essays which does not pretend to be exhaustive and which does not provide much new or interesting information.

3 Philip M. Kalavros (1963) gives a remarkable insight into the workings of an obsessive and misogynist mind – that of the author.

4 Certain works set out to deal with jealousy from a psychoanalytic angle but do not in fact deal with sexual jealousy. M. and W. Beecher (1971) discuss, very superficially, rivalry and competition in general. Edmund Ziman (1949) is a good example of the numerous handbooks giving practical advice to parents, but it does not contain any new theoretical insights.

5 This is indeed borne out by the fact that several articles on the subject are

written as if the masculine oedipus complex was the only decisive factor in the development of jealousy. Ernest Jones starts his article 'La jalousie' (1929:228-42) by asking why women are more often jealous than men, but continues by analysing specifically male oedipal conflicts as the basis for jealousy. Jones does not refer to women again, except to ask how the beloved woman best can help her morbidly jealous lover.

Melitta Schmideberg (1953:1-16) states that jealousy 'often is an indication of impotence, or of doubts about potency' (p.8) and although this is doubtless true, there is no reference to any specifically feminine problem like frigidity, for example, in her article.

Robert Seidenberg (1952:345-53) adds a new point to Freud's theory about jealousy by elaborating on the male oedipal situation. He shows through two (male) case studies that the jealous man sometimes is repressing a wish that his own mother should be sexually unfaithful to his father – with the son himself.

6   Cf. Freud's 'Mourning and Melancholia' (1917).
7   Dinnerstein stresses only the positive feelings (love) towards the pre-oedipal mother, and leaves out the tremendous aggression the child also feels towards her, a point I will discuss later.
8   See Freud's 'Psychoanalytic Notes on an Autobiographical Account of a Case of Paranoia (Dementia Paranoides)' (1911), the famous Schreber case, and 'A Case of Paranoia Running Counter to the Psychoanalytic Theory of the Disease' (1915), the case of a woman who thought she was being persecuted by a man, who turned out to be a manifestation of her mother.
9   Ernest Jones (1929:242) states that 'jealousy signifies a weakness in the capacity to love, a lack of self confidence'.

SEXUALITY AND
PSYCHOANALYSIS

Psychoanalysis: Psychic Law and Order?

Elizabeth Wilson

Because of my sexual orientation, predominantly lesbian, and my training as a psychiatric social worker in the early 1960s (Wilson, 1982) – an experience of the psychoanalytic movement at its most conservative – I can never feel entirely unambivalent about psychoanalysis. Those conservative views are still all too influential in the 'caring professions' today, so I cannot accept the view that psychoanalysis is a marginalized discourse ever in danger of suppression.

Some feminists who regard psychoanalysis as the theory of the construction of gender difference argue that feminist objections to psychoanalysis (for example, that it is phallocentric) are out of date, either because it merely describes the unconscious as it is, or because psychoanalysis has begun to take feminism on board. To say (see Rose, 1983; this volume) that because there are and have been many women psychoanalysts this proves that psychoanalysis is progressive is as ridiculous as saying that because Mrs Thatcher is Prime Minister it proves that the Tory Party has the interests of women at heart. Such an argument, moreover, goes against Rose's own position insofar as it assumes that the category 'woman' is non-problematic.

I am, however, in agreement with much of Jacqueline Rose's eloquent defence of psychoanalysis, particularly with her account of the ego as 'necessarily non-coherent'. Nonetheless, it still seems legitimate to ask what are the consequences of such a notion for a feminist political project predicated on the notion of woman's identity.

My article should not, therefore, be taken as a wholesale rejection of psychoanalysis. Nor should it be labelled as a specifically Marxist rejection of Freud and psychoanalysis. In no way did it arise out of some ultra-orthodox notion of 'the political' – as if I rejected the very idea of 'the personal is political'. It arose out of my personal experience in the 1960s, and it traduces the spirit of feminism to imply that my doubts and criticisms can all be explained away by the label of 'Marxist'.

Too much in any case is made of Marxism as a seamless and total view of the world. For example, Anne Phillips (see Barrett et al, 1986) states that 'Marxism is a totalizing explanation of the world. If you drop from that to the idea that Marxism is a good explanation of certain things in the world, then it seems to me that that is not being a Marxist.' I deeply disagree with this definition, which necessarily reduces Marxism to a 'Stalinist' caricature. If psychoanalysis may be defended on the grounds that Freud's own work was an unfinished, 'fractured' body of thought, then the same may be said of Marx. It is mistaken to look to Marx for an explanation of subjectivity, sexuality or gender and then to reject his theory wholesale because he is not a twentieth-century feminist.

I find particularly bizarre the suggestion (Mitchell and Rose, 1983) that my 'Marxism ignores sexuality because it supposes sexuality is trivial', since my most serious doubts about psychoanalysis centre around the place it assigns to lesbianism and homosexuality. I am critical of the most influential feminist writers on psychoanalysis, who have remained largely silent on this issue, or have equivocated.

Of course both Marxism and psychoanalysis have been widely used as theoretical justifications for the marginalization of women and as instruments of male domination. Both are also incomplete projects which pose inescapable questions for women in our time. Rather than setting one against the other, therefore, it would seem more useful to recognize both as necessary tools in the elucidation of women's experience, even though their articulation with each other is problematic.

What are the political implications of psychoanalysis for feminists? What follows is an attempt to explore some of my own doubts whether the psychoanalytic path taken by many feminists and Marxists in recent years is really as fruitful as is claimed. Nor am I convinced that the *politics* of this theoretical position have really been thought through in any coherent way.

I am aware that I am taking up an unpopular position in questioning this new orthodoxy, and that my criticisms will be open to the charge that my stance is purely negative – the implication being that there is no point, or one is not justified, in criticizing the use of psychoanalysis unless one has something better to offer in its place. But although I, on the whole, think that a positive view is preferable, this cannot always be the only or the overriding imperative. In any case the debate around ideas should not be seen as negative, and I see this piece as inviting a debate that I hope will be taken up in the pages of *Feminist Review* and perhaps elsewhere.

■ Freud

Although I would agree that all accounts of 'what Freud really said' are themselves interpretations – because of the contradictions and gaps in his own writings – I shall begin with a brief outline of some aspects of Freudian theory in order to point up what I see as certain ambiguities. A fuller and far more adequate (although rather densely written) account of the theoretical controversies surrounding Freud and Lacan may be found in 'Psychoanalysis and the *Cultural Acquisition of Sexuality and Subjectivity'* by Steve Burniston, Frank Mort and Christine Weedon (1978).

Freud's work offers an explanation of the creation of individual identity based on the child's changing relationship to its own body (and particularly its sexual impulses, or drives), the early discovery of the boundary between 'self' and 'not self', and the limitations imposed on desire by reality. For Freud, the individual is socially constructed, albeit on a biological basis. At the beginning of its life the infant is dominated by the 'pleasure principle' and has virtually no Ego or conscious self as we understand it. This initial state is constantly modified by the incessant demands of reality, and it is this that creates what Freud came to call the Ego.

Although the Ego is the organizing and rationalizing part of the psyche, and although it is the most integrated part of the 'self' it remains the site of struggle between the pleasure demands of the Id or unconscious and the reality demands of the external world. It remains defensive, fluctuating and contradictory, and parts of it also remain cut off from consciousness; so that in the adult there is an Ego that has in many ways mastered or come to terms with reality, yet this adult psyche still consists also of an Id of which a large part consists of childish, repressed desires. These remain infantile because they have not been modified by the demands of reality, but have been dealt with in early life by being repressed – made unconscious – and thus placed beyond the reach of reality. Parts of the unconscious may however 'return' in certain circumstances. This notion of an unconscious hinterland to the 'personality' (for want of a better word), that somehow contains unresolved conflicts and wishes, explains our often irrational behaviour as adults, our own internal sense of conflict and contradiction, inappropriate feeling states, and indeed neurotic symptoms and dreams.

In his discussion of the development of identity Freud placed primary emphasis on the body and the role played in particular by the child's biological sex. For Freud the Ego was a bodily Ego; and since the infant was for Freud essentially a pleasure seeker, and since the child's bodily and soon enough specifically genital sensations provide him with his greatest sources of pleasure, sexuality and Ego must be complexly bound together. In the satisfaction of his needs the child is dependent upon others, usually primarily his mother, and a need for what the mother can give him eventually develops into a feeling with a momentum of its own: love. The relationship between the satisfaction of sensual needs and this love for another being leads directly in Freud's view to that love being eroticized. Indeed it is *because* of this that the child's sexual feelings can be directed towards another human being; otherwise he would remain locked within masturbatory auto-eroticism.

The infant initially loves his mother in a dual and symbiotic relationship. His feeding relationship with her breast was described by Freud as the prototype of all erotic satisfactions, and the bliss of the hunger-satisfied child asleep at the breast is reminiscent of the bliss of the satisfied lover asleep on the breast of his beloved. The crisis of the child's infant erotic life comes later with the Oedipus complex. By the age of three or four the child has realized that he does not have his mother all to himself, but shares her with another, his father, who has more comprehensive and explicitly sexual access to her. Thus he is caught in the most painful of love triangles, since he also loves his father.

Threats of castration as a punishment for masturbation take on a new and terrifying meaning. Not only has he by this time seen the female genital, and thus realized that some individuals *are* 'castrated', but the castration threat is interpreted as an expression of the father's jealousy. The little boy has both a narcissistic *and* a realistic attachment to his genital, so in order to preserve it he renounces his sexual love for his mother and instead he *identifies* with his father:

> the authority of the father ... is introjected into the ego, and there it forms the nucleus of the super-ego which takes over the severity of the father and perpetuates the prohibition against incest. (Freud, 1977: 319)

So far, it is the development of the little boy that has been discussed. Freud at first described the Oedipus complex in terms of the little boy and assumed that the little girl's development was the same in reverse. Later he recognized that the development of the little girl is both more complicated and more obscure. The little boy retains the same love object − a woman − throughout his life; his primary sexual organ is and remains the penis. The little girl, on the other hand, has to achieve a change of both organ and object. She, like the baby boy, begins life with an attachment to the breast and hence to the mother; yet she must transfer her affections to her father/men.[1] The only sexual organ of which she is aware (according to Freud, although here he was challenged by other psychoanalysts in the 1920s) is the clitoris: 'the little girl is a little man': yet she must transfer her sexual excitability from clitoris to vagina.

So Freud was forced to the conclusion that the Oedipus complex in girls is different from the boy's experience. The little boy's Oedipus complex is dissolved or 'smashed' when he gives up his love for his mother and identifies with paternal authority in order to avoid the dreaded retaliation of castration. But the little girl does not fear castration because she *is* castrated; this recognition for her initiates rather than demolishes the Oedipus complex. Only then can she move from the dual relationship with her mother into the triangular relationship in which she takes her father as the object of her desire, giving up her wish for the penis and replacing it by a wish for the baby the father could give her.

Three important consequences of this are that the little girl and the woman is dominated by penis-envy; that the female's super-ego is not so developed as the male's because she has not had to internalize the father; and:

> a third consequence of penis-envy seems to be a loosening of the girl's affectionate relation with her maternal object. The situation as a whole is not very clear, but it can be seen that in the end the girl's mother, who sent her into the world so

insufficiently equipped, is almost always held responsible for her lack of a penis. (Freud, 1977: 338)

Freud was always careful to insist on the fragmentary, indeterminate and unsatisfactory nature of his conclusions:

It must be admitted ... that in general our insight into these developmental processes in girls is unsatisfactory, incomplete and vague. (1977: 321)

At the same time, and this is presumably where Freud's own ambivalence emerges, he often slips into vulgar stereotypic generalizations. He allows himself to talk of woman as Enigma (as in his famous question: 'Was will das Weib?' – 'What does Woman want?'). He sees women as a problem because they deviate from the male model. For him, women *are* more vain and narcissistic than men; have less super-ego or 'conscience'; less sense of justice; less sexual libido; and less capacity to love another human being.

Yet there is more to Freud's account of women than this. His notorious statement 'anatomy is destiny', which even Juliet Mitchell describes as 'disastrous' is by no means as downright as most feminists have supposed. He was discussing the differences between the Oedipus complex in the little girl and little boy and all he said was:

the feminist demand for equal rights for the sexes does not take us far, for the morphological distinction is bound to find expression in differences of psychical development. (1977: 320)

To say that anatomical differences between the sexes are 'bound to' have some echo in psychological differences does not in itself seem an objectionable statement. Where there is disagreement is when psychological attributes of narcissism, stupidity, frivolousness and the rest are taken as inexorably and inevitably 'feminine'.

Freud was perfectly clear that to be anatomically 'male' or 'female' was no simple matter. Bisexuality was central to his theory, and moreover he realized that there was no one-to-one correspondence between anatomical maleness and 'masculinity' on the one hand, and anatomical femaleness and 'femininity' on the other. Although the male alone produces semen and the female alone ova (except in very rare cases):

Science ... draws your attention to the fact that portions of the male sexual apparatus also appear in women's bodies, though in an atrophied state, and vice versa in the alternative case. It regards their occurrence as indicators of *bisexuality*, as though an individual is not a man or a woman but always both – merely a certain amount more the one than the other. (1973: 147)

So bisexuality itself had an anatomical basis. It was also, for Freud, a part of mental or psychical life. He argues that really, when we speak of 'masculine' or 'feminine' behaviour, we are usually merely making a distinction between 'active' and 'passive'. He goes on to say that this analogy does have a biological basis since:

> The male sex-cell is actively mobile and searches out the female one, and the latter, the ovum, is immobile and waits passively. This behaviour of the elementary sexual organisms is indeed a model for the conduct of sexual individuals during intercourse. The male pursues the female for the purpose of sexual union, seizes hold of her, and penetrates her. (1973: 48)

We might quarrel with this description, and it has been pointed out that the ovum is just as active as the sperm in biological fact. Yet Freud himself goes on to point out that in some species this active/passive distinction is not assigned according to the male/female division in the expected way, but is reversed, so that the male cares for the young, in others the female pursues the male sexually, and so on. And Freud says:

> I shall conclude that you have decided in your own minds to make 'active' coincide with 'masculine' and 'passive' with 'feminine'. But I advise you against it. It seems to me to serve no useful purpose and adds nothing to our knowledge. (1973: 148)

Yet he often slips back into this terminology himself. He did believe that women must give preference to 'passive aims', and in the very paper in which he argues for bisexuality one of his not infrequent digs at 'feminists' reveals how his own thinking remained stamped with the very usages of which he seemed so critical:

> For the ladies, whenever some comparison seemed to turn out unfavourable to their sex, were able to utter a suspicion that we, the male analysts, had been unable to overcome certain deeply-rooted prejudices against what was feminine, and that this was being paid for in the partiality of our researches. We, on the other hand, had no difficulty in avoiding impoliteness. We had only to say: 'This doesn't apply to *you*. You're the

exception; on this point you're more masculine than feminine'. (1973: 150)

A final, and interesting point about Freud's theory of sexuality is his conviction, (of which he spoke in one of his last papers, and which applied equally to men and women, although it had different consequences for each) of the existence at the core of the individual of a 'bedrock' that rendered sexual satisfaction and the reconciliation of both men and women to their bisexuality virtually impossible. It is as if men are condemned to protest forever against any kind of passivity, particularly in relation to men, while women must mourn forever the penis they cannot have.

Freud's work is shot through with the consciousness of biology and its importance. This gives his work at times a contradictory and ambiguous character. Sometimes he seems to be addressing the problem of the psychological consequences of biology and how the psyche of the individual is built on a biological base; at others he seems rather to use biological analogies and metaphors. The difficulties that arise sometimes have to do with the absence of an adequate recognized language, and Freud himself refers to the problems of conceptualizing his thought within the then existing scientific language. Richard Wollheim (1971) has suggested that Freud's theory is built around a 'form of biological learning, in which unpleasure is the teacher'. Frank Sulloway (1979), another recent interpreter of Freud, has emphasized Freud's Darwinian and evolutionist legacy. In Darwinian vein Freud was highly teleological (that is he saw processes in terms of their ends or purposes), and he was constantly mindful of the fact that although sexuality is for the individual simply a source of personal pleasure and the satisfaction or relief of desire, it also serves a racial purpose, the continuation of the species:

> Since the penis ... owes its extraordinarily high narcissistic cathexis[1] to its organic significance for the propagation of the species, the catastrophe of the Oedipus complex (the abandonment of incest and the institution of conscience and morality) may be regarded as a victory of the race over the individual. (1977: 331)

Of course this means that the clitoris becomes a total mystery:

> The clitoris, with its virile character, continues to function in later female sexual life in a manner which is very variable and

which is certainly not yet satisfactorily understood. We do not, of course, know the biological basis of these peculiarities in women; and still less are we able to assign to them any teleological purpose. (1977: 374)

So part of Freud's attitude to the clitoris may be because for him it served no 'racial' purpose; although it is doubtful whether this kind of socio-biological argument may legitimately be used to explain the development of the individual psyche.

■ Juliet Mitchell

I hope that the above section will have indicated the kinds of ambiguity that arise in Freud's work around the issue of the relationship between the biological and the psychic. Burniston, Mort and Weedon have gone further than I have done in insisting that in Freud's own work 'the structuring of the Oedipal triangle is ... based on anatomical rather than social privilege' (1978: 111). Richard Wollheim (1971) and Frank Sulloway (1979) have based their readings on the more biologistic side of Freud's work. Juliet Mitchell in *Psychoanalysis and Feminism* (1974) on the other hand sought to retrieve Freud from biologism by using the structuralism of Louis Althusser and the work of Jacques Lacan, a French psychoanalyst who emphasized the importance of language and of the symbolic in his approach to Freud.

Why was it important for her as a Marxist and a feminist, to move away from a biologistic interpretation of Freud? 'Biologism' must be unacceptable to the progressively minded because it denies, or is usually used as an argument to deny, the possibility of change. Women, or the Black races, or the Jews are said to possess certain characteristics that derive from their biology. So, for example, women were said to be prone to hysteria *because* they have wombs. Juliet Mitchell effected the rehabilitation of Freud by presenting him as the theorist of the way in which the infant, 'a small human animal', achieves the entry into *culture*. A *social* not a biological process occurs. This process is the social construction of gender, whereby the infant internalizes the characteristics of 'masculinity' or 'femininity'. This gender identity has no one-to-one relation to biological sex differences, and so – to take an extreme example – it is possible for transsexual men to experience a fundamental conviction of their 'femininity'.

But, whereas there are many passages in Freud's work that are hard to read as anything other than assertions that the actual little boy is threatened with an actual loss of a real penis, and that the little girl is objectively inferior because her clitoris is actually an inferior penis, for Louis Althusser (following Lacan) and for Juliet Mitchell (following them both) the penis is not a penis but is the symbolic Phallus: 'the very mark of human desire', a phallus that 'represents the very notion of exchange itself' (Mitchell, 1974: 395). In this way she appears to transform Freud's theory from a theory about how things are biologically *and* socially, into a theory of the way things are in 'patriarchal society'. Yet since she also accepts the view of both Freud and Engels that equates human civilization with the same patriarchy, she does in effect universalize both the theory and women's oppression. Forever and a day the Phallus is and must be the dominating *symbol of power* around which the creation of sexual difference is organized.

This is perhaps a difficult concept that deserves further attention. Juliet Mitchell argues that the 'anatomical distinction' between the sexes is not biologically significant. But

> to Freud society demands of the psychological bisexuality of both sexes that one sex attain a preponderance of femininity, the other of masculinity: man and woman are made in culture. (1974: 131)

Juliet Mitchell has developed this line of argument in a recent book review (Mitchell, 1980) and to me it seems a strange one. Firstly it is *assumed* as something that need not be proven or argued that the biological differences (which do exist) between women and men are somehow insufficient to ensure the reproduction of the species. Secondly, '*masculinity and femininity only exist by virtue of their difference from one another*' (Mitchell, 1980). This statement translates the linguistic theory which Lacan imports into Freud very directly into the realm of the psychic. To see a system (of whatever kind) as a structure is to emphasize the relationship of one part to another. Structural linguistics stresses also the *arbitrary* nature of the linguistic sign. (A word – for example the name for a quality such as 'red' – is arbitrary. Moreover, just as the colour 'red' can be defined only in relation to other colours, yellow, orange, brown, so words have meaning only in relation to other words.) When Juliet Mitchell translates this arbitrary nature of the sign from the sphere of linguistics to that of psychology, the differences between men and women completely float away from biology and become purely social constructs. This happens because society 'needs' it to (a trace of Juliet Mitchell's functionalism here):

> So long as we reproduce ourselves as social beings *through a heterosexual relationship*, human society must distinguish between the sexes. It is because of this fundamental social situation that we need to feel ourselves as predominantly men or women … *for human society to exist at all*, men and women must be marked as different from each other [my italics]. (Mitchell, 1980: 234-5)

Yet the logic of this locks us as securely within the structures of phallic power as does 'biologism'. Instead of simply accepting certain biological distinctions between the sexes, of which the psychological and cultural consequences are not necessarily very great (we do not really know how important they are) we appear condemned perpetually and for all time to recreate – or to *create* – the distinction *culturally* because otherwise we could not survive *biologically*, or could not survive at least as distinctively human. Thus the touchstone of human culture itself becomes the difference between 'masculine' and 'feminine'. Strangely, this is both wholly arbitrary and absolutely inevitable. It seems odd to demolish the tyranny of biology only to put in its place an imperative equally tyrannical and unalterable. And I question whether the whole of human culture should necessarily be seen as resting primarily and predominantly on the creation of heterosexuality in this way.

Psychoanalysis and Feminism is both a polemic and a theoretical work. Just as Freud deceivingly slips from detailed theoretical investigation to speculative generalization, so Juliet Mitchell fluctuates between polemic and theory in a fashion that masks some of the weaknesses in her arguments. There is a slippage, for example, from her account of the Oedipus complex to a contentious ideological statement when she writes:

> The woman's task is to *reproduce* society, the man's to go out and *produce* new developments. There is an obvious link between the security of Oedipal father-love (the girl's destiny) and the happy hearth and home of later years. (1974: 118)

To say this is to argue that the sexual division of labour as we know it in an industrial capitalist society has some *permanent* correspondence with the creation of 'masculinity' and 'femininity'.

Both Burniston, Mort and Weedon (1978) and Cora Kaplan in her brilliant article on Kate Millett (Kaplan, 1979) criticize *Psychoanalysis and Feminism* on two major points. On the one hand there is Juliet Mitchell's determinism:

> Freudian theory, with its emphasis on repetition and reproduction of ideological positions, emphasizes, perhaps too heavily, the unalterable distance between gender positions so that they remain rather like Marvell's 'Definition of Love' stuck at distant poles, 'begotten by Despair/Upon Impossibility'. (Kaplan, 1979: 9)

Secondly, ideology and the economy are radically separated; the feminist struggle is against ideology, the socialist struggle against the capitalist infrastructure. There is a further point to be made about the political conclusions to *Psychoanalysis and Feminism*: that is, that they are characterized by voluntarism. Juliet Mitchell wrenches an optimistic, 'revolutionary' conclusion from her arguments when they do not support it. She asserts that a cultural revolution is just around the corner – patriarchy like capitalism is in its death-throes. The arguments to support this prediction appear to run as follows. In capitalism the patriarchy is mediated through the nuclear family, which is all that remains of the formerly elaborate kinship structures (in this respect she follows Talcott Parsons and other mainstream – and right-wing – functionalist sociologists). Yet capitalism also hastens the disintegration of the nuclear family. This in turn implies that patriarchy itself is disintegrating since it cannot survive without the structural support of the nuclear family. (This last assumption is never argued through and Mitchell does not explain why patriarchy could not be mediated through other institutions such as schools and the law.) She argues that patriarchy is disintegrating because the exchange of women and the old kinship relations are no longer *needed* and her political conclusion is that therefore the time is ripe for their overthrow in an autonomous struggle of women against ideology.

Yet Juliet Mitchell recognizes that the arrival of socialism does not necessarily ensure the demise of patriarchy; hence her insistence on the autonomy of the struggle against ideology. At the same time this recognition weakens the logic of the earlier part of her argument which suggested that capitalism and the patriarchy were so intertwined that they would fall together. And this optimistic scenario is supported by 'evidence' from the experience of the Second World War in Britain, which, she asserts, saw the virtual (temporary) cessation of the nuclear family with the socialization of the means of survival. This is just wrong historically. Whatever the heightening of neighbourliness and communal living amongst evacuated work-mates, in the army, and so on, I know of no evidence that family ties were correspondingly weakened. On the contrary, family support (for instance, grandmothers looking after children for mothers who went out to work) was often of vital importance, while the *idea* of family life as something the British were fighting to preserve was a very important one – hence the popularity of the Beveridge Report (Wilson, 1980).

■ The political consequences of psychoanalysis

The underlying assumption never really questioned by feminists who have followed Juliet Mitchell in exploring the relevance of psychoanalysis for feminist theory has been this: since the subordination of women is so heavily mediated through and in the private realm of marriage and other sexual relationships, in the family, in the reduction of women to sexual stereotypes, and in the threat of rape and generalized sexual violence, the overriding political imperative for feminists must be the immediate struggle against these practices.[2] Part of the Marxist heritage is the belief that political struggles have to be informed by a theory that will enable us to understand the nature of our exploitation/oppression/subordination. It is argued by feminists sympathetic to psychoanalysis that psychoanalysis is *the* theory of the construction of the sexual identity and gender relations; since it emphasizes the social construction of gender it must be the theory feminists need.

It is implied that psychoanalysis enables us to understand how we internalize an oppressive ideology. This in turn assumes (and Juliet Mitchell certainly *does* seem to assume) that women are in general *successfully* constructed as 'feminine' in our society. Women, according to her, *do* end up narcissistic, masochistic and the rest. This is rather curious since Freud himself laid great stress on the difficulty of this process and its incomplete success in many women.

This appears to me an unproven, certainly an under-researched area. Feminists who have talked with young teenage working-class girls appear to reach contradictory conclusions (McRobbie, 1978; Cowie and Lees, 1981 and this volume) but it does seem as if girls experience heterosexuality and marriage as inevitable rather than desirable. Social pressures of a direct kind as much as the internalization emphasized by psychoanalysis seem to ensure heterosexuality,[3] as well as a desire to be 'normal' which is not quite the same as 'feeling' feminine. But I hesitate to interpret the small amount of evidence available, and would simply suggest that it is a more unknown quantity than psychoanalytic theorists allow.

Even to the extent that women *do* internalize 'femininity', psychoanalysis, while of some use in explaining how this comes about, certainly does not give us much idea how we might escape. In this respect, psychoanalytic theory is odd in its mingling of the highly particular (the details of an individual's biography to elucidate an individual's current psychological state) with the universal and general (the general 'law' of the Phallus, and the necessity for the individual – and for all individuals – of entering culture via the Oedipus complex enacted in the nuclear family). At both these levels it misses the historically specific; that is, it can be 'true' of one individual and of all human history; it has little to say about one particular historical period. This makes it especially difficult to integrate with Marxism, since Marxism precisely deals with what is socially particular at a given historical period (Burniston, Mort and Weedon, 1978: 127). Although many such attempts at integration have been made, this latest feminist one seems, like the rest, destined to failure. The result has often been in recent years an effective withdrawal from or abandonment of Marxism. (I am not making a value judgement on this score; simply suggesting that it has happened.)

Lacanian theory does not confront the problem of what happens to the individual psyche when family patterns change. Freud's work was at least solidly based on clinical studies of the then contemporary nineteenth-century bourgeois nuclear family. But the family changes constantly. The generalizing abstractions of Lacan simply do not help us to understand these profound changes which must surely have some significance for the social construction of the individual. This appears to me another fascinating area unexplored by psychoanalysis. May we not be living in a period in which the construction of sexed identity is altering in important ways?

More generally feminist interest in psychoanalysis has not in practice led to a sharpening of feminist political struggle. On the contrary it has validated reactionary positions amongst feminists. I've already given an example of how these surface in *Psychoanalysis and Feminism*. It also appears to me that psychoanalysis has been the justification for some feminists to assert anew that the sexual division of labour presents no problems for feminists; that what is needed is to reassert the value of women's work (i.e. domestic labour) rather than seeking to socialize it; that careers for women may be irrelevant to feminism, even a result of penis-envy. I cannot cite written evidence for this. The statement may therefore be open to the criticism that it is unfair, contentious, distorted, or reliant on a kind of gossip of the women's movement to which only some are privy and that it is therefore elitist. But I am anxious to share with others my fear that such positions are returning; to me they seem to mark a return to constricting images of women accepted by feminists and non-feminists alike after 1945 and before women's liberation (Wilson, 1980). If my fears are unfounded, I hope that women will refute them. If they are justified I hope that women who hold such views will commit them to paper and argue them out in open debate. So far they have surfaced only as a kind of unease; for example, in discussions of divisions between mothers and non-mothers. Liz Heron in a succinct and wholly sisterly discussion of her similar worries on this score writes:

> In the early days of the [women's] movement, feminists with children discovered their oppression and had the support of their sisters in throwing off guilt and finding independence. Those founding mothers were striving to challenge the mystique – and the material realities – that made them prisoners, to live like those of us who weren't hemmed in by maternity. But their counterparts of today appear to be reversing the process, moving away from us and melting back into motherhood ... Will we move motherhood back to centre-stage? Bathe it in a glow of that old insidious prestige, that status of 'real womanhood'? Will we again pick up the ideological baggage we've fought for the last decade to discard? (Heron, 1980: 5)

Another rather different yet related problem about the appropriation by feminists of psychoanalytic theory is that it is used to close up further investigation into the construction of gender:

> From a feminist reading of anthropology we learned that the social meaning of maleness and femaleness is constructed through kinship rules which prescribe patterns of sexual dominance and subordination. From psychoanalysis we learned how these kinship rules become inscribed on the unconscious psyche of the female child via the traumatic re-orientation of sexual desire within the Oedipal phase away from the mother

and towards the father ('the law of the father'). (Alexander and Taylor, 1980:161)

If we have really 'learned' this with such finality, there seems nothing more to be done about it, and further theoretical discussion seems pointless. I, though, hope I have demonstrated that we cannot really give psychoanalysis this doctrinal status. I would also argue that this kind of determinism can only have pessimistic implications for feminism, suggesting as it does unchanging, static patterns of human psychic development.

I suggest that a more interesting point to discuss might be how we *are* to engage in struggle around issues to do with consciousness and its formation. Feminists drawing on a psychoanalytic perspective have had little to say about this. But what forms of political struggle does psychoanalysis suggest for feminism?

Another point, and an important one for feminists, is that feminist theoretical writings drawing on psychoanalysis have had remarkably little to say about homosexuality and lesbianism. If anything, psychoanalysis seems to have been used implicitly to justify heterosexual relationships at a period in the women's movement when women who wanted to relate to men sexually felt under pressure from feminists who were lesbians. It is of interest in this context that Juliet Mitchell fudges the issue of Freud's attitude to homosexuality. In seeking to reassure feminists that Freud's attitude was not one of hostility, she quotes his famous letter to the mother of a homosexual son. This is certainly a very kind and sensible letter, in which Freud tries to comfort the unhappy mother.

> Homosexuality is assuredly no advantage, but it is nothing to be ashamed of, no vice, no degradation; it cannot be classified as an illness; we consider it to be a variation of the sexual function, *produced by a certain arrest of the sexual development* ... [my italics]. (Freud, 1961: 277)

But in omitting the significant last phrase Juliet Mitchell might be taxed with evasion of an admittedly difficult issue.[4]

Another important question not being asked by Lacanian feminists is, what is the role of the orthodox institutions of psychoanalysis; and what is the role of the psychoanalytic therapy, and can it be changed? Another point of interest: there is a strong interest among feminists today in 'radical' and 'feminist' therapy, but this interest and the ongoing work of, for example, the Women's Therapy Centre, has remained apart from the body of theory I have been discussing; indeed the very concept of feminist therapy has been severely criticized by at least one Freudian feminist (Lipschitz, 1978; and in reply, Women's Therapy Centre Study Group, 1979). Yet after all, the issue of therapy is an important one. As Rosalind Delmar wrote:

> The prevalence of psychic distress in our society, which reproduces neurosis on a mass scale – the figures speak for themselves, represent ... what could be interpreted as a massive 'flight into illness'. Any political movement struggling to change society has to confront this striking phenomenon (Delmar, 1975: 21).

■ Can the iron law of the Phallus be overthrown?

Even the most meticulous critics of Freud within the contemporary debate (for example, Burniston, Mort and Weedon) usually back off at the last moment from a wholesale dismissal of Freud. I too believe, following Michèle Barrett (1980: 58), that since Freud's work is not internally consistent or coherent, but is, as some would say, a very 'fractured' body of work, we can if we wish retain some of his insights without buying the whole package, although I do feel there are dangers in this eclecticism. I accept the psychoanalytic account of the way in which sexual identity gets constructed – haltingly and with difficulty – and that, as we know it, it is constructed in the context of male power. Freud often describes very accurately the construction of that male power at the psychic level. But in the Freudian, and even more fatally in the Lacanian account, the organization of difference not only does but *must* occur around the dominant symbol of the Phallus, which also represents male power; although in many of these discussions, the Phallus becomes no more than a metaphor, be it for male power or for desire. Yet it is possible to imagine that personal identity could be, in a society in which male power did not dominate, organized around some other principle. There could be an adult sexual identity that was constructed around a different symbolic differentiator.

In conclusion, I wish to look again at some of the weaknesses of recent feminist psychoanalytic perspectives in a general way, and to suggest some possible political directions the debate might more usefully take.

I suggested earlier that because the subordination of women occurs in a privatized way it has often been assumed that the struggle against it necessarily consists of for the most part private struggles – to change men, to change relationships with men, or (an entirely different but equally problematic solution) to abandon all relationships with men and sexualize relationships with other women. Or else, individual children should be reared differently. And/or collective living relationships should be set up. Such attempts represent an important part of the feminist struggle. They will nonetheless remain privatized themselves unless the women's movement as a political movement socializes and collectivizes this struggle. This would mean a return to the largely abandoned arena of the family and the construction of campaigns to change the family at different levels and in different ways; social policy, income maintenance, childcare provision, obstetric practices are areas in which such a campaign could operate (and campaigns do flourish in these areas, although they are not ideologically linked to the extent that they might be).

The experience of Woman's Aid suggests that social provision may often come before individual change, or that certainly the two go together. It's hard even to say it in the current economic climate, but today we need more than ever non-sexist social provision for many needs currently catered for by the family. Unless the family *is* radically changed (not abolished) I do not see how we can develop different child-rearing practices in which a sexual identity is constructed that gives more conscious and creative control to the child than s/he currently enjoys, and which is not so hysterically obsessed with one particular form of difference – an unstable form, moreover, since the cultural construction of 'masculine' and 'feminine' is a massive edifice elevated on an arguably insignificant base. In other words, I am arguing for social solutions to the oppression we experience as private.

This does not mean that I reject in individual given circumstances the individual solution of psychoanalysis or therapy. Mental disorder is a serious problem. Even those of us who have no crippling 'symptoms' must often experience a loss of energy, a paralysis of the will and an apathy generated by the kind of society in which we live. But feminists who take psychoanalysis seriously will have at some stage to confront the sexism of the psychoanalytic movement and its institutional practices far more radically than has yet been done, just as feminist doctors have had to confront the medical hierarchy, and feminist social workers the social services hierarchy. One of the most serious weaknesses of the contemporary feminist psychoanalytic debate has been its failure for the most part (so far as I know) to engage in therapeutic practice.

Perhaps precisely the attraction of Lacan's 'law of the father' has been the sense that it *is* inescapable.[5] It has seemed that only through the gate of the Oedipal trauma could we become adult women and men and save ourselves either from a perpetuation of 'polymorph perverse' infantile sexuality; or from the psychotic symbiosis of the pre-Oedipal mother-infant relationship, at best a narcissistic mirroring. There is a sinister ring to the language used by Althusser to discuss this point:

> [the little girl] doubly accepts that she has not the same right [phallus] as her father, since her mother has not this right [no phallus] ... But she gains ... the promise of a large right, the full right of a woman when she grows up, if she will grow up accepting the Law of Human Order. (Althusser, 1971: 197)

There are similarities here to the language used in political debate since time immemorial, whereby anarchy on the one hand and law and order on the other are posed as antagonistic opposites in order to discredit anarchy, i.e. chaos. Feminists should know better than to be taken in by this kind of language which constantly seeks to mask the progressive or revolutionary implications of rebellion; rebellion is always stigmatized as flouting law and order and producing chaos.

The last thing feminists need is a theory that teaches them only to marvel anew at the constant recreation of the subjective reality of subordination and which reasserts male domination more securely than ever within theoretical discourse. Psychoanalysis is of interest in its account of sexual identity and its construction – indeed, in many ways it is fascinating. More useful to contemporary feminists may be theories of social change that speak to aspects of the self not harnessed to the Phallic taskmaster. To change the conditions of work – in the world and in the home – might do more for our psyches as well as for our pockets than an endless contemplation of how we came to be chained.

■ Notes

Thanks to those who read and commented on this article for me when it was in draft form: Angie Mason, Julia Naish, Marie Zaphiriou, Maxine Molyneux, Michèle Barrett, Victoria Greenwood and Wendy Hollway.

1 Freud nowhere gave a rigorous theoretical definition of 'cathexis' (Laplanche and Pontalis, 1973:63). Broadly speaking, it means the loading with nervous energy of an idea, symbol or event. We may say that the infant 'cathects' the mother when he invests her with the eroticized love arising out of his sensual satisfaction at the breast. A foot fetishist 'cathects' feet, or shoes. Or we may say that cathexis is the disposition of energy, or its distribution, in relationships with objects and with the self.

2 Parveen Adams, Beverley Brown and Elizabeth Cowie appear to be raising a rather similar question (1981: 3).

3 See Mary McIntosh (1981), who makes a similar point in relation to income maintenance.

4 It is noteworthy that Paul Hirst uses the same quotation in a recent article, perpetuating the crucial omission (1981: 112).

5 I am indebted to Angie Mason in this section.

Femininity and its
Discontents

Jacqueline Rose

This article was originally requested by the editors of *Feminist Review* to counter the largely negative representation of psychoanalysis which had appeared in the journal, and as a specific response to Elizabeth Wilson's 'Psychoanalysis: Psychic Law and Order' (*Feminist Review* No.8, 1981, and this volume. See also Janet Sayers, 'Psychoanalysis and Personal Politics: A Response to Elizabeth Wilson', *Feminist Review* No.10, 1982). As I was writing the piece, it soon became clear however that Elizabeth Wilson's article and the question of *Feminist Review*'s own relationship to psychoanalysis could not be understood independently of what has been – outside the work of Juliet Mitchell for feminism – a fairly consistent repudiation of Freud within the British left. In this context, the feminist debate over Freud becomes part of a larger question about the importance of subjectivity to our understanding of political and social life. That this was in fact the issue became even clearer when Elizabeth Wilson and Angie Weir published an article 'The British Women's Movement' in *New Left Review*, No. 148, November-December 1984, which, ignoring this reply, dismissed the whole area of subjectivity and psychoanalysis from feminist politics together with any work by feminists (historians and writers on contemporary politics) who, while defining themselves as socialist-feminists, nonetheless query the traditional terms of an exclusively class-based analysis of power (see Barbara Taylor, 1983, and Beatrix Campbell, 1984). I discuss these issues in greater detail in the

Introduction to *Sexuality in the Field of Vision*, London, Verso, 1986.

Is psychoanalysis a 'new orthodoxy' for feminism? Or does it rather represent the surfacing of something difficult and exceptional but important for feminism, which is on the verge (once again) of being lost? I will argue that the second is the case, and that the present discarding of psychoanalysis in favour of forms of analysis felt as more material in their substance and immediately political in their effects (Wilson, 1981, 1982a; Barrett, 1980; Sayers, 1982) is a *return* to positions whose sensed inadequacy for feminism produced a gap in which psychoanalysis could − fleetingly − find a place. What psychoanalysis offered up in that moment was by no means wholly satisfactory and it left many problems unanswered or inadequately addressed, but the questions which it raised for feminism are crucial and cannot, I believe, be approached in the same way, or even posed, from anywhere else. To ask what are the political implications of psychoanalysis for feminism seems to me, therefore, to pose the problem the wrong way round. Psychoanalysis is already political for feminism − political in the more obvious sense that it came into the arena of discussion in response to the internal needs of feminist debate, and political again in the wider sense that the repudiation of psychoanalysis for feminism can be seen as linking up with the repeated marginalization of psychoanalysis within our general culture, a culture whose oppressiveness for women is recognized by us all.

Before going into this in more detail, a separate but related point needs to be made, and that is the peculiarity of the psychoanalytic object with which feminism engages. Thus to ask for effects from psychoanalysis in the arena of political practice (Wilson, 1981) is already to assume that psychoanalytic practice is a-political. Recent feminist debate has tended to concentrate on theory (Freud's theory of femininity whether or not psychoanalysis can provide an account of women's subordination). This was as true of Juliet Mitchell's defence of Freud (Mitchell, 1974) as it has been of many of the more recent replies. The result has been that psychoanalysis has been pulled away from its own practice. Here the challenge to psychoanalysis by feminists has come from alternative forms of therapy (feminist therapy and co-counselling). But it is worth noting that the way psychoanalysis is engaged with in much recent criticism already divests it of its practical effects at this level, or rather takes this question as settled in advance (the passing reference to the chauvinism of the psychoanalytic institution, the assumption that psychoanalysis depoliticizes the woman analysand). In this context, therefore, the common theory/practice dichotomy has a very specific meaning in that psychoanalysis can only be held accountable to 'practice' if it is assumed not to be one, or if the form of its practice is taken to have no purchase on political life. This assumes, for example, that there is no politics of the psychoanalytic institution itself, something to which I will return.

Both these points – the wider history of how psychoanalysis has been placed or discarded by our dominant culture, and the detaching of psychoanalysis from its practical and institutional base – are related, inasmuch as they bring into focus the decisions and selections which have already been made about psychoanalysis before the debate even begins. Some of these decisions I would want to argue are simply wrong; such as the broad accusation of chauvinism levelled against the psychoanalytic institution as a whole. In this country at least, the significant impetus after Freud passed to two women – Anna Freud and Melanie Klein. Psychoanalysis in fact continues to be one of the few of our cultural institutions which does not professionally discriminate against women, and in which they could even be said to predominate. This is not of course to imply that the presence of women inside an institution is necessarily feminist, but women have historically held positions of influence inside psychoanalysis which they have been mostly denied in other institutions where their perceived role as 'carers' has relegated them to a subordinate position (e.g. nursing), and it is the case that the first criticisms of Freud made by Melanie Klein can be seen to have strong affinities with later feminist repudiation of his theories.

For those who are hesitating over what appears as the present 'impasse' between feminism and psychoanalysis, the more important point, however, is to stress the way that psychoanalysis is being presented for debate, that is, the decisions which have already been made before we are asked to decide. Much will depend, I suspect, on whether one sees psychoanalysis as a new form of hegemony on the part of the feminist intelligentsia, or whether it is seen as a theory and practice which has constantly been relegated to the outside of dominant institutions and mainstream radical debate alike – an 'outside' with which feminism, in its challenge to both these traditions, has its own important forms of allegiance.

■ Components of the culture

In England, the relationship between the institution of psychoanalysis and its more general reception has always been complex, if not fraught. Thus in 1968, Perry Anderson could argue (Anderson, 1968) that major therapeutic and theoretical advances inside the psychoanalytic institutions (chiefly in the work of Melanie Klein) had gone hand in hand with, and possibly even been the cause of, the isolation of psychoanalysis from the general culture, the slowness of its dissemination (until the Pelican Freud started to appear in 1974, you effectively had to join a club to read the *Standard Edition* of Freud's work), and the failure of psychoanalysis to effect a decisive break with traditions of empiricist philosophy, reactionary ethics, and an elevation of literary 'values', which he saw as the predominant features of our cultural life. Whether or not one accepts the general 'sweep' of his argument, two points from that earlier polemic seem relevant here.

Firstly, the link between empiricist traditions of thought and the resistance to the psychoanalytic concept of the unconscious. Thus psychoanalysis, through its attention to symptoms, slips of the tongue and dreams (that is, to what *insists* on being spoken against what is *allowed* to be said) appears above all as a challenge to the self-evidence and banality of everyday life and language, which have also, importantly, constituted the specific targets of feminism. If we use the (fairly loose) definition which Anderson provided for empiricism as the unsystematic registration of things as they are and the refusal of forms of analysis which penetrate beneath the surface of observable social phenomena, the link to feminism can be made (Anderson, 1966). For feminism has always challenged the observable 'givens' of women's presumed natural qualities and their present social position alike (especially when the second is justified in terms of the first). How often has the 'cult of common sense', the notion of what is obviously the case or in the nature of things, been used in reactionary arguments against feminist attempts to demand social change? For Anderson in his article of 1968, this espousal of empiricist thinking provided one of the chief forms of resistance to Freud, so deeply committed is psychoanalysis to penetrating behind the surface and conscious manifestations of everyday experience.

Secondly, the relationship between this rejection of psychoanalysis and a *dearth* within British intellectual culture of a Marxism which could both theorize and criticize capitalism as a social totality. This second point received the strongest criticism from within British Marxism itself, but what matters here is the fact that both Marxism *and* psychoanalysis were identified as forms of radical enquiry which were unassimilable to bourgeois norms. In the recent feminist discussion, however – notably in the pages of *Feminist Review* – Marxism and psychoanalysis tend to be posited as antagonistic; Marxism arrogating to itself the concept of political practice and social change, psychoanalysis being accused of inherent conservatism which rationalizes and perpetuates the subordination of women under capitalism, or else fails to engage with that subordination at the level of material life.

In order to understand this, I think we have to go back to the earlier moment. For while the argument that Marxism was marginal or even alien to British thought was strongly repudiated, the equivalent observation about psychoanalysis seems to have been accepted and was more or less allowed to stand. This was perhaps largely because no one on the left rushed forward to claim a radicalism committed to psychoanalytic thought. *New Left Review* had itself been involved in psychoanalysis in the early sixties, publishing a number of articles by Cooper and Laing (Cooper, 1963, 1965; Laing, 1962, 1964); and there is also a strong tradition, which goes back through Christopher Caudwell in the 1930s, of Marxist discussion of Freud. But the main controversy unleashed by Anderson's remarks centred around Marxism; Anderson himself in an earlier article had restricted his own critique to the lack of Marxism and classical sociology in British culture making no reference to psychoanalysis at all (Anderson, 1964; see also Thompson, 1965). After 1968, *New Left Review* published Althusser's famous article on Lacan (Althusser, 1969, 1971; see below) and one article by Lacan (Lacan, 1968), but for the most part the commitment to psychoanalysis was not sustained even by that section of the British left which had originally argued for its importance.

Paradoxically, therefore, the idea that psychoanalysis was isolated or cut off from the general culture could be accepted to the extent that this very marginalization was being *reproduced* in the response to the diagnosis itself. Thus the link between Marxism and Freudian psychoanalysis, as the twin poles of a failed radicalism at the heart of British culture, was broken. Freud was cast aside at the very moment when resistance to his thought had been identified as symptomatic of the restrictiveness of bourgeois culture. Juliet Mitchell was the exception. Her defence of Freud in 1970 and 1974 (Mitchell, 1970, 1974) needs, I think, to be placed first in this context, as a claim for the fundamentally anti-empiricist and radical nature of Freudian thought. That this claim was made via feminism (could perhaps *only* be made via feminism) says something about the ability of feminism to challenge the orthodoxies of both left and right.

Thus the now familiar duo of 'psychoanalysis and feminism' has an additional and crucial political meaning. Not just psychoanalysis *for* feminism or feminism *against* psychoanalysis, but Freudian psychoanalysis and feminism *together* as two forms of thought which relentlessly undermine the turgid resistance of commonsense language to all forms of conflict and political change. For me this specific sequence has been ironically or negatively confirmed (that is, it has been gone over again backwards) by one of the most recent attempts to relate psychoanalysis to socialism (Rustin, 1982) through a combination of F.R. Leavis and Melanie Klein – the very figures whose standing had been taken as symptomatic of that earlier resistance to the most radical aspects of Freudian thought (Klein because of the confinement of her often challenging ideas to the psychoanalytic institution itself, Leavis because of the inappropriate centrality which he claimed for the ethics of literary form and taste). I cannot go into the details of Rustin's argument here, but its ultimate conservatism for feminism is at least clear: the advancement of 'mothering' and by implication of the role of women as mothers, as the psychic basis on which socialism can be built (the idea that psychoanalysis can *engender* socialism seems to be merely the flip side of the argument which accuses psychoanalysis of producing social conformity).

This history may appear obscure to many feminists who have not necessarily followed the different stages of these debates. But the diversion through this cultural map is, I think, important insofar as it can illustrate the ramifications of feminist discussion over a wider political spectrum, and also show how this discussion – the terms of the argument, the specific oppositions proposed – have in turn been determined by that wider spectrum itself.

Thus it will have crucial effects, for instance, whether psychoanalysis is discussed as an addition or supplement to Marxism (in relation to which it is then found *wanting*), or whether emphasis is laid on the concept of the unconscious. For while it is indeed correct that psychoanalysis was introduced into feminism as a theory which could rectify the inability of Marxism to address questions of sexuality, and that this move was complementary to the demand within certain areas of Marxism for increasing attention to the ideological determinants of our social being, it is also true that undue concentration on this aspect of the theory has served to cut off the concept of the unconscious, or at least to displace it from the centre of the debate. (This is graphically illustrated in Michèle Barrett's book, *Women's Oppression Today*, in which the main discussion of psychoanalysis revolves around the concept of ideology, and that of the unconscious is left to a note appended at the end of the chapter (Barrett, 1980).)

■ Femininity and its discontents

One result of this emphasis is that psychoanalysis is accused of 'functionalism'; that is, it is accepted as a theory of how women are psychically 'induced' into femininity by a patriarchal culture, and is then accused of perpetuating that process, either through a practice assumed to be *prescriptive* about women's role (this is what women *should* do), or because the very effectiveness of the account as a *description* (this is what is demanded of women, what they are *expected* to do) leaves no possibility of change.

It is this aspect of Juliet Mitchell's book which seems to have been taken up most strongly by feminists who have attempted to follow through the political implications of psychoanalysis as a critique of patriarchy or, by extension, as a means of explaining how women internalize their role. Thus Gayle Rubin, following Mitchell, uses psychoanalysis for a general critique of a patriarchal culture which is predicated on the exchange of women by men (Rubin, 1975; for criticisms of the use of Levi-Strauss on which this reading is based see Cowie, 1978 and MacCormack and Strathern, 1980). Nancy Chodorow shifts from Freud to later object relations theory to explain how women's childcaring role is perpetuated through the earliest relationship between a mother and her child, which leads in her case to a demand for a fundamental change in how childcare is organized between women and men in our culture (Chodorow, 1978). Although there are obvious differences between these two readings of psychoanalysis, they nonetheless share an emphasis on the social exchange of women, or the distribution of roles for women, across cultures: 'Women's mothering is one of the few universal and enduring elements of the sexual division of labour' (Chodorow, 1978:3).

The force of psychoanalysis is therefore (as Janet Sayers points out;

Sayers, 1982) precisely that it gives an account of patriarchal culture as a trans-historical and cross-cultural force. It therefore conforms to the feminist demand for a theory which can explain women's subordination across specific cultures and different historical moments. Summing this up crudely, we could say that psychoanalysis adds sexuality to Marxism, where sexuality is felt to be lacking and extends beyond Marxism where the attention to specific historical instances, changes in modes of production etc., is felt to leave something unexplained.

But all this happens at a cost, and that cost is the concept of the unconscious. What distinguishes psychoanalysis from sociological accounts of gender (hence for me the fundamental impasse of Nancy Chodorow's work) is that whereas for the latter, the internalization of norms is assumed roughly to work, the basic premise and indeed starting point of psychoanalysis is that it does not. The unconscious constantly reveals the 'failure' of identity. Because there is no continuity of psychic life, so there is no stability of sexual identity, no position for women (or for men) which is ever simply achieved. Nor does psychoanalysis see such 'failure' as a special-case inability or an individual deviancy from the norm. 'Failure' is not a moment to be regretted in a process of adaptation, or development into normality, which ideally takes its course (some of the earliest critics of Freud, such as Ernest Jones, did, however, give an account of development in just these terms). Instead 'failure' is something endlessly repeated and relived moment by moment throughout our individual histories. It appears not only in the symptom, but also in dreams, in slips of the tongue and in forms of sexual pleasure which are pushed to the sidelines of the norm. Feminism's affinity with psychoanalysis rests above all, I would argue, with this recognition that there is a resistance to identity which lies at the very heart of psychic life. Viewed in this way, psychoanalysis is no longer best understood as an account of how women are fitted into place (even this, note, is the charitable reading of Freud). Instead psychoanalysis becomes one of the few places in our culture where it is recognized as more than a fact of individual pathology that most women do not painlessly slip into their roles as women, if indeed they do at all. Freud himself recognized this increasingly in his work. In the articles which run from 1924 ('The Dissolution of the Oedipus Complex', Freud, 1924) to 1931 ('Female Sexuality', Freud, 1931), he moves from that famous, or rather infamous, description of the little girl struck with her 'inferiority' or 'injury' in the face of the anatomy of the little boy and wisely accepting her fate ('injury' as the *fact* of being feminine), to an account which quite explicitly describes the process of becoming 'feminine' as, 'injury' or 'catastrophe' for the complexity of her earlier psychic and sexual life ('injury' as its *price*).

Elizabeth Wilson (1981) and Janet Sayers (1982) are, therefore, in a sense correct to criticize psychoanalysis when it is taken as a general theory of patriarchy or of gender identity, that is, as a theory which explains how women wholly internalize the very mode of being which is feminism's specific target of attack; but they have missed out half the (psychoanalytic) story. In fact the argument seems to be circular. Psychoanalysis is drawn in the direction of a general theory of culture or a sociological account of gender because these seem to lay greater emphasis on the pressures of the 'outside' world, but it is this very pulling away from the psychoanalytic stress on the 'internal' complexity and difficulty of psychic life which produces the functionalism which is then criticized.

The argument about whether Freud is being 'prescriptive' or 'descriptive' about women (with its associated stress on the motives and morals of Freud himself) is fated to the extent that it is locked into this model. Many of us will be familiar with Freud's famous pronouncement that a woman who does not succeed in transforming activity to passivity, clitoris to vagina, mother for father, will fall ill. Yet psychoanalysis testifies to the fact that psychic illness or distress is in no sense the prerogative of women who 'fail' in this task. One of my students recently made the obvious but important point that we would be foolish to deduce from the external trappings of normality or conformity in a woman that all is in fact well. And Freud himself always stressed the psychic cost of the civilizing process for all (we can presumably include women in that 'all' even if at times he did not seem to do so).

All these aspects of Freud's work are subject to varying interpretation by analysts themselves. The first criticism of Freud's 'phallocentrism' came from inside psychoanalysis, from analysts such as Melanie Klein, Ernest Jones and Karen Horney who felt, contrary to Freud, that 'femininity' was a quality with its own impetus, subject to checks and internal conflict, but tending ultimately to fulfilment. For Jones, the little girl was 'typically receptive and acquisitive' from the outset (Jones, 1933:265); for Horney, there was from the beginning a 'wholly womanly' attachment to the father (Horney, 1924, 1967:53).[1] For these analysts, this development might come to grief, but for the most part a gradual strengthening of the child's ego and her increasing adaptation to reality, should guarantee its course. Aspects of the little girl's psychic life which were resistant to this process (the famous 'active' or 'masculine' drives) were defensive. The importance of concepts such as the 'phallic phase' in Freud's description of infantile sexuality is not, therefore, that such concepts can be taken as the point of insertion of patriarchy (assimilation to the norm). Rather their importance lies in the way that they indicate, through their very artificiality, that something was being *forced*, and in the concept of psychic life with which they were accompanied. In Freud's work they went hand in hand with an increasing awareness of the difficulty, not to say impossibility, of the path to normality for the girl, and an increasing stress on the fundamental divisions, or splitting, of psychic life. It was those who challenged these concepts in the 1920s and thirties who introduced the more normative stress on a sequence of development, and a coherent ego, back into the account.

I think we go wrong again, therefore, if we conduct the debate about whether Freud's account was developmental or not entirely in terms of his own writing. Certainly the idea of development is present at moments in his work. But it was not present *enough* for many of his contemporaries, who took up the issue and reinstated the idea of development precisely in relation to the sexual progress of the girl (her passage into womanhood).

'Psychoanalysis' is not, therefore, a single entity. Institutional divisions within psychoanalysis have turned on the very questions about the phallocentrism of analysts, the meaning of femininity, the sequence of psychic development and its norms, which have been the concern of feminists. The accusations came from analysts themselves. In the earlier debates, however, the reproach against Freud produced an account of femininity which was more, rather than less, normative than his own.

The politics of Lacanian psychoanalysis begins here. From the 1930s, Lacan saw his intervention as a return to the concepts of psychic division, splitting of the ego, and an endless (he called it 'insistent') pressure of the unconscious against any individual's pretension to a smooth and coherent psychic and sexual identity. Lacan's specific target was 'ego-psychology' in America, and what he saw as the dilution of psychoanalysis into a tool of social adaptation and control (hence the central emphasis on the concepts of the ego and identification which are often overlooked in discussions of his ideas). For Lacan, psychoanalysis does not offer an account of a developing ego which is 'not *necessarily* coherent' (Wilson, 1982), but of an ego which is 'necessarily *not* coherent', that is, which is always and persistently divided against itself.

Lacan could therefore be picked up by a Marxist like Althusser not because he offered a theory of adaptation to reality or of the individual's insertion into culture (Althusser added a note to the English translation of his paper on Lacan criticizing it for having implied such a reading; Althusser, 1969, 1971), but·because the force of the unconscious in Lacan's interpretation of Freud was felt to undermine the mystifications of a bourgeois culture proclaiming its identity, and that of its subjects, to the world. The political use of Lacan's theory therefore stemmed from its assault on what English Marxists would call bourgeois 'individualism'. What the theory offered was a divided subject out of 'synch' with bourgeois myth. Feminists could legitimately object that the notion of psychic fragmentation was of little immediate political advantage to women struggling for the first time to find a voice, and trying to bring together the dissociated components of their life into a political programme. But this is a very different criticism of the political implications of psychoanalysis than the one which accuses it of forcing women into bland conformity with their expected role.

■ Psychoanalysis and history/the history of psychoanalysis

What, therefore, is the political purchase of the concept of the unconscious on women's lived experience and what can it say to the specific histories of which we form a part?

One of the objections which is often made against psychoanalysis is that it has no sense of history, and an inadequate grasp of its relationship to the concrete institutions which frame and determine our lives. For even if we allow for a moment the radical force of the psychoanalytic insight, the exclusiveness or limited availability of that insight tends to be turned, not against the culture or state which mostly resists its general (and publicly funded) dissemination,[2] but against psychoanalysis itself. The 'privatization' of psychoanalysis comes to mean that it only refers to the individual as private, and the concentration on the individual as private is then seen as reinforcing a theory which places itself above history and change.

Again I think that this question is posed back to front, and that we need to ask, not what psychoanalysis has to say about history, but rather what is the history of psychoanalysis; that is, what was the intervention of psychoanalysis into the institutions which, at the time of its emergence, were controlling women's lives? And what was the place of the unconscious, historically, in that? Paradoxically, the claim that psychoanalysis is a-historical dehistoricizes it. If we go back to the beginnings of psychoanalysis, it is clear that the concept of the unconscious was radical at exactly that level of social 'reality' with which it is so often assumed to have nothing whatsoever to do.

Recent work by feminist historians is of particular importance in this context. Judith Walkowitz, in her study of the Contagious Diseases Acts of the 1860s (Walkowitz, 1980) shows how state policy on public hygiene and the state's increasing control over casual labour relied on a category of women as diseased (the suspected prostitute subjected to forcible examination and internment in response to the spread of venereal disease in the port towns). Carol Dyhouse has described how debates about educational opportunity for women constantly returned to their evidence of the female body (either the energy expended in their development towards sexual reproduction meant that women could not be educated, or education and the overtaxing of the brain would damage their reproductive capacity (Dyhouse, 1981)). In the birth control controversy, the Malthusian idea of controlling the reproduction, and by implication the sexuality, of the working class served to counter the idea that poverty could be reduced by the redistribution of wealth (MacLaren, 1978). Recurrently in the second half of the nineteenth century, in the period immediately prior to Freud, female sexuality became the focus of a panic about the effects of industrialization on the cohesion of the social body and its ability comfortably to reproduce itself. The importance of all this work (Judith Walkowitz makes this quite explicit) is that 'attitudes' towards women cannot be consigned to the sphere of ideology, assumed to have no purchase on material life, so deeply implicated was the concept of female sexuality in the legislative advancement of the state (Walkowitz, 1980).

Central to all of this was the idea that the woman was wholly responsible for the social well-being of the nation (questions of social division transmuted directly into the moral and sexual responsibility of subjects), or where she failed in this task, that she was disordered or diseased. The hysteric was either the over-educated woman, or else the woman indulging in non-procreative or uncontrolled sexuality (conjugal onanism), or again the woman in the lock hospitals which, since the eighteenth century, had been receiving categories refused by the general hospitals ('infectious diseases, fevers, children, maternity cases, mental disorders, venereal diseases', Walkowitz, 1980:56). It was these hospitals which, at the time of the Contagious Diseases Acts, became the place of confinement for the diseased prostitute in a new form of collaborative relationship with the state.

This is where psychoanalysis begins. Although the situation was not identical in France, there are important links. Freud's earliest work was under Charcot at the Salpetrière Clinic in Paris, a hospital for women: 'five thousand neurotic indigents, epileptics, and insane patients, many of whom were deemed incurable' (Veith, 1965, 1970:229). The 'dregs' of society comprised the inmates of Salpetrière. (Psychoanalysis does not start in the Viennese parlour.) Freud was working under Charcot whose first contribution to the study of hysteria was to move it out of the category of sexual malingering and into that of a specific and accredited neurological disease. The problem with Charcot's work is that while he was constructing the symptomatology of the disease (turning it into a respected object of the medical institution), he was reinforcing it as a special category of behaviour, visible to the eye, and the result of a degenerate hereditary disposition.

Freud's intervention here was two-fold. Firstly, he questioned the visible evidence of the disease – the idea that you could know a hysteric by looking at her body, that is, by reading off the symptoms of nervous disability or susceptibility to trauma. Secondly (and this second move depended on the first), he rejected the idea that hysteria was an 'independent' clinical entity, by using what he uncovered in the treatment of the hysterical patient as the basis of his account of the unconscious and its universal presence in adult life.

The 'universalism' of Freud was not, therefore, an attempt to remove the subject from history; it stemmed from his challenge to the category of hysteria as a principle of classification for certain socially isolated and confined individuals, and his shifting of this category into the centre of everybody's psychic experience: 'Her hysteria can therefore be described as an acquired one, and it presupposed nothing more than the possession of what is probably a very widespread proclivity – the proclivity to acquire hysteria' (Freud, 1893-95:121, 187).[3] The reason why the two moves are interdependent is because it was only by penetrating behind the visible symptoms of disorder and asking what it was that the symptom was trying to *say*, that Freud could uncover those unconscious desires and motives which he went on to expose in the slips, dreams and jokes of individuals paraded as normal. Thus the challenge to the entity 'hysteria', that is, to hysteria *as* an entity available for quite specific forms of social control, relies

These are disturbing images of women. We are aware that they go against the policy of *Feminist Review* which has been to publish generally positive images of women. They have been chosen to illustrate and make available a moment of history in which the subordination of women can be seen as so closely tied to the use of the visual image itself and its history. All the images are from *Nouvelle Iconographie photographique de la Salpetrière*.

Tongue contractions produced by direct stimulus of an hysteric in a waking state.

Hysteric yawning.

Contractions produced by visual stimuli.

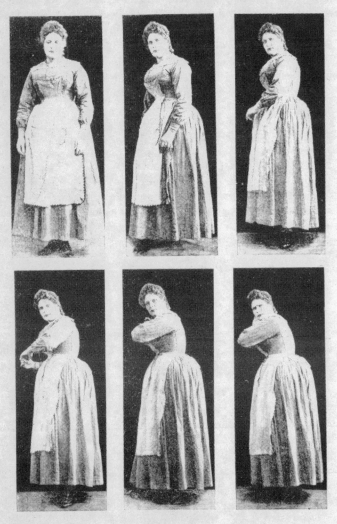

Gradual faradization of hysteric with catalepsy.

on the concept of the unconscious. 'I have attempted', wrote Freud, 'to meet the problem of hysterical attacks along a line other than *descriptive*' (my emphasis) (Freud, 1892-94:137). Hence Freud's challenge to the visible, to the empirically self-evident, to the 'blindness of the seeing eye' (Freud, 1893-95:117, *181*). (Compare this with Charcot's photographs offered as the evidence of the disease, some of which are reprinted here.) It is perhaps this early and now mostly forgotten moment which can give us the strongest sense of the force of the unconscious as a concept against a fully social classification relying on empirical evidence as its rationale.

The challenge of psychoanalysis to empiricist forms of reasoning was therefore the very axis on which the fully historical intervention of psychoanalysis into late nineteenth century medicine turned. The theories of sexuality came after this first intervention (in *Studies on Hysteria*, Freud's remarks on sexuality are mostly given in awkward footnotes suggesting the importance of sexual abstinence for women as a causal factor in the aetiology of hysteria). But when Freud did start to investigate the complexity of sexual life in response to what he uncovered in hysterical patients, his first step was a similar questioning of social definitions, this time of sexual perversion as 'innate' or 'degenerate', that is, as the special property of a malfunctioning type (Freud 1905). In fact if we take dreams and slips of the tongue (both considered before Freud to result from lowered mental capacity), sexuality and hysteria, the same movement operates each time. A discredited, pathological, or irrational form of behaviour is given by psychoanalysis its psychic value. What this meant for the hysterical woman is that instead of just being looked at or examined, she was allowed to *speak*.

Some of the criticisms which are made by feminists of Freudian psychoanalysis especially when it is filtered through the work of Lacan, can perhaps be answered with reference to this moment. Most often the emphasis is laid either on Lacan's statement that 'the unconscious is structured like a language', or on his concentration of mental representation and the ideational contents of the mind. The feeling seems to be that the stress on ideas and languages cuts psychoanalysis off from the materiality of being, whether that materiality is defined as the biological aspects of our subjectivity, or as the economic factors determining our lives (one or the other and at times both).

Once it is put like this, the argument becomes a version of the debate within Marxism over the different instances of social determination and their hierarchy ('ideology' versus the 'economic') or else it becomes an accusation of idealism (Lacan) against materialism (Marx). I think this argument completely misses the importance of the emphasis on language in Lacan and of mental representation in Freud. The statement that 'the unconscious is structured like a language' was above all part of Lacan's attempt to establish a continuity between the seeming disorder of the symptom or dream and the normal language through which we recognize each other and speak. And the importance of the linguistic sign (Saussure's distinction between the signifier and the signified; Saussure, 1915, 1974) was that it provided a model internal to language itself of that form of indirect representation (the body speaking because there is something which cannot be said) which psychoanalysis uncovered in the symptomatology of its patients. Only if one thing can stand for another is the hysterical symptom something more than the logical and direct manifestation of physical or psychic (and social) degeneracy.

This is why the concept of the unconscious as indicating an irreducible discontinuity of psychic life is so important. Recognition of that discontinuity in us all is in a sense the price we have to pay for that earlier historical displacement.

■ Feminism and the unconscious

It is, however, this concept which seems to be lost whenever Freud has been challenged on those ideas which have been most problematic for feminism, insofar as the critique of Freudian phallocentrism so often relies on a return to empiricism, on an appeal to 'what actually happens' or what can be *seen* to be the case. Much of Ernest Jones' criticism of Freud, for example, stemmed from his conviction that girls and boys could not conceivably be ignorant of so elementary a fact as that of sexual difference and procreation (Jones, 1933:15). And Karen Horney, in her similar but distinct critique, referred to 'the manifestations of so elementary a principle of nature as that of the mutual attraction of the sexes' (Horney, 1926, 1967:68). We can compare this with Freud: 'from the point of view of psycho-analysis the exclusive sexual interest felt by men for women is also a problem that needs elucidating and is not a self-evident fact based upon an attraction that is ultimately of a chemical nature' (Freud, 1905:146 n, 57 n). The point is not that one side is appealing to 'biology' (or 'nature') and the other to 'ideas', but that Freud's opening premise is to challenge the self-evidence of both.

The feminist criticism of Freud has of course been very different since it has specifically involved a rejection of the evidence of this particular norm: the normal femininity which, in the earlier quarrel, Freud himself was considered to have questioned. But at this one crucial level – in the idea of an unconscious which points to a fundamental division of psychic life and which therefore challenges any form of empiricism based on what is there to be observed (even when scientifically tested and tried) – the very different critiques are related. Juliet Mitchell based at least half her argument on this point in *Psychoanalysis and Feminism*, but it has been lost. Thus Shulamith Firestone in *The Dialectic of Sex* (1970, 1979), arguing that the girl's alleged sense of inferiority in relation to the boy was the logical outcome of the observable facts of the child's experience, had to assume an unproblematic and one-to-one causality between psychic life and social reality with no possibility of dislocation or error. The result is that the concept of the unconscious is lost (the little girl rationally recognizes and decides her fate) and mothering is deprived of its active components (the mother is seen to be only subordinate and in no sense powerful for the child; see Mitchell, 1974, 2, II, 5). For all its more obvious political appeal, the idea that psychic life is the unmediated reflection of social relations locks the mother and child into a closed subordination which can then only be broken by the advances of empiricism itself:

> Full mastery of the reproductive process is in sight, and there has been significant advance in understanding the basic life and death process. The nature of ageing and growth, sleep and hibernation, the chemical functioning of the brain and the development of consciousness and memory are all beginning to be understood in their entirety. This acceleration promises to continue for another century, or however long it takes to achieve the goal of Empiricism: total understanding of the laws of nature. (Firestone, 1970, 1979:170)

Shulamith Firestone's argument has been criticized by feminists (Delmar, Introduction to Firestone, 1979) who would not wish to question, any more than I would, the importance of her intervention for feminism. But I think it is important that the part of her programme which is now criticized (the idea that women must rely on scientific progress to achieve any change) is so directly related to the empiricist concept of social reality (what can be *seen* to happen) which she offers. The empiricism of the goal is the outcome of the empiricism at the level of social reality and psychic life. I have gone back to this moment because, even though it is posed in different terms, something similar seems to be going on in the recent Marxist repudiation of Freud. Janet Sayers' critique of Juliet Mitchell, for example, is quite explicitly based itself on the concept of 'what actually and specifically happens' ('in the child's environment' and 'in the child's physical and biological development') (Sayers in Wilson, 1982a).

■ Utopianism of the psyche

Something else happens in all of this which is probably the most central issue for me: the discarding of the concept of the unconscious seems to leave us with a type of utopianism of psychic life. In this context it is interesting to note just how close the appeal to biology and the appeal to culture as the determinants of psychic experience can be. Karen Horney switched from one to the other, moving from the idea that femininity was a natural quality, subject to checks, but tending in its course, to the idea that these same checks, and indeed most forms of psychic conflict were the outcome of an oppressive social world. The second position is closer to that of feminism, but something is nonetheless missing from both sides of the divide. For what has happened to the unconscious, to that divided and disordered subjectivity which, I have argued, had to be recognized in us all if the category of hysteria as a peculiar property of one class of women was to be disbanded? Do not both of these movements make psychic conflict either an accident or an obstacle on the path to psychic and sexual continuity – a continuity which, as feminists, we recognize as a myth of our culture only to reinscribe it in a different form on the agenda for a future (post-revolutionary) date?

Every time Freud is challenged, this concept of psychic cohesion as the ultimate object of our political desires seems to return. Thus the French feminist and analyst, Luce Irigaray, challenges Lacan not just for the phallocentrism of his arguments, but because the Freudian account is seen to cut women off from an early and untroubled psychic unity (the primordial state of fusion with the mother) which feminists should seek to restore (Irigaray, 1978). Irigaray calls this the 'imaginary' of women (a reference to Lacan's idea of a primitive narcissism which was for him only ever a fantasy). In a world felt to be especially alienating for women, this idea of psychic oneness or primary narcissism has its own peculiar force. It appears in a different form in Michèle Barrett's and Mary McIntosh's excellent reply to Christopher Lasch's thesis that we are witnessing a regrettable decline in the patriarchal family (Barrett and McIntosh, 1982). Responding to his accusation that culture is losing its super-ego edge and descending into narcissism, they offer the particularly female qualities of mothering (Chodorow) and a defence of this very 'primary narcissism' in the name of women against Lasch's undoubtedly reactionary lament. The problem remains, however, that whenever the 'feminine' comes into the argument as a quality in this way we seem to lose the basic insight of psychoanalysis – the failure or difficulty of femininity for women, and that fundamental psychic division which in Freud's work was its accompanying and increasingly insistent discovery.

If I question the idea that psychoanalysis is the 'new orthodoxy' for feminists, it is at least partly because of the strong political counterweight of this idea of femininity which appears to repudiate both these Freudian insights together.

To return to the relationship between Marxism and psychoanalysis with which I started, I think it is relevant that the most systematic attack we have had on the hierarchies and organization of the male left (*Beyond the Fragments*, Rowbotham *et al*, 1979) gives to women the privilege of the personal in a way which divests it (*has* to divest it) of psychic complexity at exactly this level of the conflicts and discontinuities of psychic life. Like many feminists, the slogan 'the person is political' has been central to my own political development; just as I see the question of sexuality, as a political issue which *exceeds* the province of Marxism ('economic', 'ideological' or whatever) as one of the most important defining characteristics of feminism itself. But the dialogue between feminism and psychoanalysis, which is for me the arena in which the full complexity of that 'personal' and that 'sexuality' can be grasped, constantly seems to fail.

In this article, I have not answered all the criticisms of psychoanalysis. It is certainly the case that psychoanalysis does not give us a blueprint for political action, nor allow us to deduce political conservatism and radicalism directly from the vicissitudes of psychic experience. Nor does the concept of the unconscious sit comfortably with the necessary attempt by feminism to claim a new sureness of identity for women, or with the idea of always conscious and deliberate political decision-making and control (psychoanalysis is *not* a voluntarism, Sayers, 1982). But its challenge to the concept of psychic identity is important for feminism in that it allows into the political arena problems of subjectivity (subjectivity *as* a problem) which tend to be suppressed from other forms of political debate. It may also help us to open up the space between different notions of political identity – between the idea of a political identity for feminism (what women require) and that of a feminine identity for women (what women are or should be), especially given the problems constantly encountered by the latter and by the sometimes too easy celebration of an identity amongst women which glosses over the differences between us.

Psychoanalysis finally remains one of the few places in our culture where our experience of femininity can be spoken as a problem that is something other than the problem which the protests of women are posing for an increasingly conservative political world. I would argue that this is one of the reasons why it has not been released into the public domain. The fact that psychoanalysis cannot be assimilated directly into a political programme as such does not mean, therefore, that it should be discarded, and thrown back into the outer reaches of a culture which has never yet been fully able to heed its voice.

■ Notes

This article is reproduced from *Sexuality in the Field of Vision* (Verso, 1986) by permission of the publisher.

1   Where two dates are given, the first is to the original date of publication; page references are to the more easily available editions (e.g. English translations, collections of articles, where possible).
2   For more detailed discussion of the relative assimilation of Kleinianism through social work in relation to children in this country (especially through the Tavistock Clinic in London) see Rustin (1982: 85 and n). As Rustin points out, the state is willing to fund psychoanalysis where it is a question of helping children to adapt, but less so when it is a case of encouraging adults to remember.
3   References to Freud are to the *Standard Edition* and to the Pelican edition where available (in italics).

ISSUES AROUND

LESBIANISM

The Dyke, the Feminist and the Devil

Wendy Clark

This article was written within the context of considerable debate in both the women's movement and the lesbian community. It came at a time in which the lesbian identity I knew appeared to be in some danger of being absorbed by new, stringent requirements for a correct lesbian and feminist identity and self-image. The issues remain unresolved and the continuing debates around various forms of sexual practice (for example, SM issues) contain the same ingredients of sex, pleasure, desire and identity.

While the concept of 'difference' is crucial for all women it is not experienced in the same way by all of us and is not a concept that sits easily within feminist politics. The movement for women's liberation has been premised on translating differences into similarities and on the basis of similarity pushing for a wide variety of changes. As a consequence, any differences within our ranks become either those that must be conformed with (that is, similarities) or they stay as differences, uncomfortable and problematic. I feel the differences should remain, as they are a strength for the women's movement that need to be acknowledged and worked with rather than assimilated into a whole that gives them no recognition or meaning.

Once upon a time a Dyke was on her way to a bar when she met a woman. This woman called herself a Feminist. The Dyke was very taken with this woman. They appeared to have a lot in common. Much of what the Feminist said made sense to the Dyke at that time. The Feminist introduced her to her feminist friends, consciousness-raising, feminist ideas and *Spare Rib*. At last, thought the Dyke, she'd found a place where she could feel herself and not have to hide anything. The Dyke developed into a feminist, politically she was moving fast. But she was still a dyke and she had strong desires and lustful feelings for the Feminist. One day when she was out walking in the woods she told the Feminist how she felt towards her. The Feminist was not shocked or horrified, she smiled serenely and explained to the Dyke that she did not know her well enough for a committed sexual relationship. She also explained she was not into objectifying sexual experiences and besides she wasn't sure she reciprocated the feelings. She explained that her oppression as a woman and her experiences with men had left deep scars. At the end of the walk she reassured the Dyke that she was a 'woman-identified woman' and she did truly love her. It was just that sex was such an emotionally charged area. The Dyke was very miserable but she understood, the Devil was perverse and had tainted all sexual activities to the point that women now had to question those very activities. All her CR groups and her lesbian support group had been saying the very same things. They were right. So why then did she feel sad and confused? Perhaps she wasn't struggling enough, not cleansing the distasteful from her thoughts or fighting hard those awful devilish fantasies. She worked hard at her new project to become a feminist dyke. She saw, she talked and listened to (even occasionally slept with) other feminist dykes. But after some time the Dyke still felt sad and confused and by now she was also quite fed-up. She still fancied the Feminist even though it was not the correct thing. Disillusionment was creeping into the Dyke's feelings and thoughts, there was even some cynicism. She felt that she had moved and was no longer the Dyke she had been on that first day she'd met the Feminist. But it did seem to her, though, that the Feminist hadn't moved as much in her direction. The Feminist and the new feminist dykes were moving somewhere else, somewhere where the fight against the Devil counted for more and the Dyke for less. One day while drinking a pint at the annual *Spare Rib* bop she told the Feminist her doubts and fears. This time the Feminist was shocked and horrified. What was the Dyke about? Where was her feminism, her outrage, her sense of oppression, her sisterhood? The Dyke

knew she had all of these, they were still there, but they had a
different form from the Feminist's feelings. The Dyke felt in
danger of losing her self, her identity, her 'dykeness'. It was a
sad occasion. The Feminist cajoled, argued, shouted, pleaded
and cried. The Dyke felt lost and upset. The short walk to the
bar had turned out to be long and involved. She knew that she
wasn't the same Dyke that had set out that day and she was
glad of that. If only the Devil hadn't got in the way. The Dyke
left the Feminist and wandered out into the street. Perhaps the
bar was still there???[1]

Sex has been the thing of which feminists have rightly been most wary,
since sexuality is the key area in the management and control of
women's oppression. But something has happened to this concern and
a reasonable mistrust is in danger of becoming a 'form of
erotophobia'. 'Anti-sexist' is turning into 'anti-sex'. A recent article in
the *Village Voice* was entitled 'Lust Horizons? Is the Women's
Movement Pro-Sex?';[2] while in this country the sex issue of *Heresies*[3]
is sold from under the counter at Sisterwrite, the London feminist
bookstore. Something is happening! Is it that sex is now something
which the feminist movement can only sell or buy in brown paper bags
because it is so tainted? Are we becoming the dirty mac brigade of the
eighties?

The realm of the sexual has always been in the forefront of our
practice and analysis. But it is an area riddled with contradictions
which we are only just beginning to grasp. Our practice and analysis
have also been circumscribed by the wider ideological concerns of the
women's liberation movement. This has meant that we have discussed
sex and sexuality largely in terms of relationships, gender
construction, sexism, femininity-masculinity, division of labour and
such like. Consequently we have not found it easy to focus on sex or
on other central elements of sex like desire, lust, physical response,
fantasy, eroticism or masochism. We are caught in our own feminist
rhetoric and our sexual activities and behaviours are measured against
this rhetoric. They are found to be wanting if as feminists we do not
follow the new 'straight' road.

To make an attempt to examine some of the questions raised for me
in 'The Dyke, the Feminist and the Devil' is extremely problematic,
and in saying that I am *not* trying to dodge the issues. There is no
subject on which feminists will wax more eloquent than sex and
sexuality but there is also no subject on which we hold more opposed,
stubborn and opinionated views. Despite years of endless discussions
we do not have any coherent agreement among ourselves. We are as

divided and dogmatic about the subjects as those outside the movement. The problem facing us is a diversity of sexual constructions and practices. The contradictory elements contained in that diversity have produced a confusion which dogs our footsteps now just as it did ten or eleven years ago. We claim to ourselves the ability to talk openly about sexuality and its construction but this stands uneasily beside our difficulties in examining such things as emotion, eroticism or desire in sex.

The debate up to now has concentrated understandably on the oppressive nature of sexual and social relations between male and female. We have discovered a society constructed along patriarchal lines which has imposed severely rigid strictures on the development of our sexual selves. Having identified the structures of patriarchal sex there has been an attempt to redefine our feminist sexuality around the concept of a 'woman-defined woman' who is working to develop mechanisms to resist compulsory heterosexuality. As a result of this practice various things have happened to the way some experiences of our sex and sexuality have been defined. The meanings constructed by us from our pre-feminist experiences have been questioned and then often dismissed. Whole areas of our lives including motherhood, monogamy, heterosexual activity, self-image and even bras have been subject to such scrutiny that they have barely been able to continue to exist in feminist practice. The questioning is fair enough and it must continue. What is distinctly unhelpful, and lesbianism is a particular case of this, is the dismissal of much that is vital to our self definition and existence. The result is that feminism has never been able properly to get to grips with certain glaring problems. Heterosexual feminists are faced time and again with the fact that given all the feminism that exists, the damning critiques of men and male behaviour, they are still attracted sexually to men. And lesbian feminists, like myself, still do not see men as 'the enemy' and continue to define ourselves primarily through an erotic and sexual attraction to women. Yet in the new feminism of the eighties views such as these and contradictions such as these may not be acceptable – like the Dyke, we may not be trying hard enough!

■ Lesbianism and the women's liberation movement

No woman is intentionally socialized by society to be a lesbian, indeed the opposite is true. But I and many thousands of women call ourselves lesbian and consider it to be one of, if not the prime factor, in our personal identity construction processes. How then do I order and interpret myself and the society I live in and what kind of lesbian identity have I assumed? How is it that lesbians can have positive self identities when so much presents a negative view of our sexual orientation? Lesbianism, like any other sexual practice, has always existed within our society. Society has neither condoned it nor has it totally suppressed it. What has been done though is to construct the category and circumscribe the meanings and limits within which lesbianism (as homosexuality in men) was permitted existence and toleration.[4] However the regulation of lesbian behaviour has never been as enshrined in the law as male homosexual behaviour has been and continues to be so, even today. But both were recognized by the growing medical and psychological professions of the late nineteenth century and early twentieth century which did their utmost to create a category of a homosexual person, predominantly male, but with reference to women from time to time. And the public face of lesbianism produced by both these professions was overwhelmingly negative.

> Homosexual women have a well-marked tendency toward male habits and mode of dress. They smoke, drink ... cut their hair short ... dispense with feminine underwear ... sometimes a growth of hair about the upper lip and chin is noticed ... Of all forms of sexual perversions [of women] ... [it] is the most widely diffused at the present day ... The subject is an unpleasant one to discuss ... such a woman is outside the social pale ... A confirmed tribadist is a most dangerous member of society ... [who] is usually irresponsible, hysterical and often mentally deranged ... The whole subject is repugnant in the extreme to the normally minded individual ... Unhappily the physician is not able to do much towards effecting a cure ... He can at all events point out the dangers ... and purposely draw a lurid picture of ... and awaken a feeling of disgust ... enforced seclusion may be the only answer ...[5]

We are familiar with accounts such as the one above and we are well aware that such views have now passed into the 'common sense' mythology of our society and as such are still dragged out to explain, attack or excuse lesbianism. It is as part of an attempt to counter such images and explanations that lesbians have, through the gay movement and the women's liberation movement, tried to construct an alternative and positive view of lesbianism. New meanings have appeared and the 'definition' of lesbianism has become 'definitions' and we now have a more attractive and certainly less sordid picture of lesbianism. What happened to the definition of lesbianism and more importantly for me and others, what happened to the lesbianism with which we identified and from which we created our sexual selves? The women's liberation movement has taken lesbianism and joined it to itself in theory and practice so that in some explanations the justification for lesbianism was feminism and vice versa. In the first flush of our enthusiasm for feminism we tended to invalidate or at the very least heavily criticize our history and construction. As the debate around sex and sexuality and sexual practice comes up again in the women's liberation movement I find that I have come to accept that I have not ordered my world through 'rage against men'. In certain crucial areas my view of and construction of my own lesbianism is quite different from that of many women who came to it through feminism.

The statement 'feminism is the theory, lesbianism is the practice' has a righteous ring which reminds me of the rigid moral biologism of early medical practitioners. The process of comprehending lesbianism and its meaning cannot be reduced to slogans of scientific phraseology. The process of constructing yourself primarily from sexual and erotic experiences or desires is not the same as constructing a woman-identified lesbian woman. Some women do argue that there is intrinsically little difference. For me there is a difference and that has been obscured by the women's liberation movement. My criticism of men does not equal lesbianism. My desires and my sexual practice are not predicated on a dislike of men and my lesbian identity is not to be equated with an anti-male stance. Women who feel they are lesbians have a right to call themselves lesbians but what is in contention is the way they 'explain' their lesbianism and the way new explanations have subverted previous experience.

It's like this, said the Feminist and her friends, the personal is political, right? Well, I suppose so said the Dyke not sure if she ought to voice her view that they just didn't follow like bread and cheese and women had to work to connect them. The others went on. Therefore, lesbianism is a political act. Heterosexuality has just been imposed on women by men, it's a form of sex which is no good to women, it can cause harm and even kill women. The Dyke shuddered. But lesbianism is free from that; no penetration, no harm to women. Lesbianism is women's power, it's a rejection of sex with men, it's the model for our new society. All the Dyke could do after that was agree but she knew she wasn't completely happy about it.

We all know that the way 'the Feminist and her friends' explained it is not exactly what is said, nor is it a true account, since the current explanations of lesbianism encompass quite complicated and at times extremely persuasive theorizing. But in spite of denials it is often viewed in the way described above. There exists an explanation of my sexual identity and practice which is based on a critique of heterosexuality. It posits lesbianism as a new model, and it develops a picture of lesbian love as a revolutionary alternative to the dangerous and violent hetero sex. This seems at its root to reinforce the view of men and male sexuality as expressed in repression models and women as expressed in romantic models. Lesbianism is as a result almost becoming a compulsory new orientation for feminists.

■ Who is the Dyke?

Lesbian identity is indeed determined by the dominant views of female sexuality as they have been constructed over the years. The social constrictions placed on lesbians were dictated by the general attitude to women and their sexuality. When the lesbian was being constructed as a 'social' category rather than just a particular form of sexual behaviour, it is interesting to note that she had to conform to certain male attributes as 'women' just did not behave that way (did not behave sexually that is). The lesbian was a pseudo-male preying on and seducing unsuspecting, sexually naive young women. It was unheard of that a woman might have an autonomous sexuality. Nor was it seen as possible for her to construct herself a sexual identity apart from that already assigned to her via her maternal instincts, natural passivity, reproductive role and social position. Consequently it was assumed that the lesbian ghetto was as those outside it had made it – a sordid nasty place where predatory pseudo-male women preyed on weak, submissive, confused women. All the women who inhabited this world were of course said to be consumed with a most terrible guilt, shame and desperation. But recent studies and my own re-examination of my history indicate that the construction of a woman's lesbianism in the society at large did not necessarily fit this stereotype.[6] Within the subculture, meaning was often different. This was not a totally alternative meaning but it was enough to help women to feel reasonably positive about themselves, to engage in relationships, and to continue to be lesbian. However, a veil of secrecy existed then, even as now. The severe segregation of the lesbian world from the wider social world has not helped lesbians today to look as closely at their own history and subculture as perhaps they ought. Not everything was perfect in the lesbian world and many women hated the whole scene but it also gave a security and support to many. The feminist co-option of lesbianism has created a kind of fashion to decry the old days, the role playing and secrecy of the ghetto. It is not easy to go against this and try to re-examine the places, the activities and meanings of our own history. Nor is it any answer to claim that all the rediscovered woman to woman friendships that are being unearthed were lesbian relationships. There are two assumptions that need to be examined and challenged. Firstly that lesbian subculture was experienced in the ways defined by the dominant culture outside it and secondly that lesbianism is synonymous with feminism. It *is* possible to separate oneself from the identity imposed by the society that has created the category. This applies not only to sexual subcultures but to all subcultures that are identified and categorized by society at large (or experts in particular). When one's identity is secret and stigmatized it takes on a particular and vital significance to the participants. Most of our identities take shape through 'normal' social interactions with others so that the intimacy of our sexual identity does not always dog our everyday lives. *If* however there is a part of yourself that is hidden; *if* that hidden part *appears* to have been defined by others not privy to it; *if* that part of yourself is in direct and immediate opposition to the social and cultural mores of society, *then* the question of identity and self becomes much more important if not all-consuming. And what is significant for us is that the 'secret' alternative way of viewing yourself may *not necessarily* relate or correspond all the way to its 'proper' definition. It cannot be entirely true that lesbianism today is intrinsically better than lesbianism before the women's liberation movement. In the past there was some degree of transformation of the negative images given, into different and possibly positive meaning.

What she might have been doing when she did it

The dichotomy between the outside image and the internal meaning allows the lesbian, if she wishes, to move a considerable way in the direction of a positive self-identity as a lesbian (which is not the same as a feminist). Because it is not possible to construct something new out of nothing the alternative meaning comes through manipulation of the given construction and categories. The given meanings are in a sense stood on their heads, in that we are redefining the images towards a meaning more acceptable to the individuals within the category. The next step is to have that in some measure accepted by society into the general common-sense mythology of the category.

It is my contention that as far as lesbianism is concerned feminists may well have allowed rhetorical and theoretical stances to influence their view of lesbian practice and activity. *As an example*, consider the terms 'active/passive' and the synonymous linking with the given roles of 'butch and fem'. Because a certain core of lesbian self-identity does have to do with sexual activity between women (or the possibility thereof) then some examination of actual sex practice needs to take place. By means of a crude assumption the passive/active of heterosexual sex is passed on to lesbian sex. Whereas in heterosexual sex, because of the present influence of social relations between women and men and the history of those relations, active = taking = men, while passive = receiving = women, in lesbian sexual practice the reality of active/passive can be experienced differently. In lesbian sex the active is the one *giving* pleasure to the other as well as possibly obtaining pleasure from the act as well. Even the passive is in a way active. Having pleasure can be an active thing, even though its heterosexual meaning is not that. Because of the way the active partner has always been seen as the man our feminist use and meaning of active/passive has been severely restricted to embody a critique of sex where the man uses the woman for his own pleasurable ends. But in lesbian sex (except for extreme role-playing behaviour) the basic actions of the active and passive are different and therefore, within lesbian practice, the meaning is also different. Hence it is incorrect to take the meanings of active/passive in a heterosexual sense and just apply them as if they were the same to a sexual practice which is quite different. Power relations to do with sex itself are not the same as the power relations of heterosexuality and the power is experienced differently in lesbian relations than in male/female relations. The power relations between two women are not the same as those between men and women and this helps to construct an alternative meaning.

■ The Dyke's new tie

If active and passive can be seen differently what then of the role play which is so linked in our minds with the stereotypes of active and passive. The role play of sexual stereotypes is seen as the visible proof that after all lesbian sex is really just a substitute for 'the real thing'. On top of that a feminist distaste for any sexual stereotyping behaviour in women and men has spilled over into attitudes towards lesbianism. Therefore not only was a particular presentation of one's self condemned but it was also equated with equivalent heterosexual sexual practices. Re-examining history, thinking about myself and reading certain recent articles has convinced me that it is time to look more closely at our blanket condemnation of role play behaviour amongst lesbians.

> The Dyke had a very clear recollection of her first striped tie. It had taken a lot of agonizing to get up the courage to wear it openly and not just in front of the mirror at home. She knew what it would mean when others saw her in it. That's why it had been so hard to do. But she was obsessed with it; brown with a thin blue stripe. It looked superb with the waistcoat from the jumble sale. The afternoon she stepped out into the street with her tie on, the Dyke felt terrific. Somehow it was all coming together and as she hit the streets a wide smile broke out on her face.

Sexual visibility in the sense of assertion of one's sexuality and sexual needs was something that was allowed only to men. If a woman wished visibly to assert her sexual needs the only model was the male one. Although adopting trousers and short hair did not mean you were a man, there was no sexual model for lesbians offered, only stereotypes. There was no mode or way of dressing differently. The use of male clothing by women in itself expressed a contradiction and so became an act of defiance challenging the narrowness of the traditional sex stereotypes which could not encompass lesbianism.[7] And as it is put in *Lesbian Woman*:

> If you look like every other woman on the street how in the world are you going to find other lesbians, or, more to the point, how are they going to find you? (Martin and Lyon, 1972)

Lesbians discovered long ago what many women now realize: that trousers and shirts are more comfortable than nylons and tight skirts. Those who also transferred in a wholesale fashion the behaviour of male chauvinism and total sex roles were always in the minority and it is correct to criticize them if their behaviour was also 'male'.

Are we who now wear ties, waistcoats, trousers and boots (along with the models in *Cosmopolitan* and *Vogue*) making the same statement as the women who walked around similarly attired some years ago? The significance of clothing depends on historical context and it is not right to assume that our present unisex clothing has the same function now as it did for dykes of another period. The obscuring of these alternative meanings is not therefore only to be laid at the door of a homophobic society, but is also due to well-meaning feminist idealism.

■ Feminism and lesbianism. Or why it took the Dyke so long to get to the bar

I feel the relationship of the women's liberation movement to lesbianism has moved considerably from the tentative early encounters to an almost wholesale appropriation, and it makes me feel uneasy. Before looking at this it is important to make the point that although in this article I am concerned primarily with lesbianism, heterosexual feminists have not had an entirely creditable role in the present state of relations between feminism and lesbianism. Many heterosexual feminists have colluded with the way lesbianism and feminism have come to mean one and the same thing. Feminists have found themselves unable to rebut adequately the view that to engage in heterosexuality and therefore heterosexual sex was to co-operate with the oppression of women and this has made them feel guilty. Conveniently so too, as there was something obviously 'wrong' with being turned on by men. They are now the new deviants while lesbian feminists were in the vanguard of feminism.

However I feel that the sexual act alone cannot define the political meaning of a relationship. Just as my physical act of making love with another woman does not put me in the vanguard of feminism so the act of heterosexual sex does not make you an oppressor of other women. But the inability of feminists to respond to the lesbian 'takeover' has also made it difficult for lesbians like myself to respond. Not only has feminism used lesbianism as a way of avoiding examination of the practice of heterosexuality, but it has also misunderstood lesbianism itself.

The women's liberation movement has contributed to a construction of lesbianism as an ideal practice which is free of the worst excesses of the patriarchal heterosexual social system. Yet lesbianism cannot be free of it, as it is a category created by that very system. The feminist redefinition has deliberately played down the sexual side of lesbianism as there has been an understandable reaction against what was seen as a sexual definition of lesbianism solely as a particular form of sexual activity between women. (And a revolting one at that, we were told.) Consequently the specificity of lesbianism has been exchanged for an all-embracing 'woman-identified woman' and woman power perspective. This perspective makes me uneasy because it comes from a negative source: the rejection of men. Because of the way lesbians construct themselves, a lesbian identity cannot be based solely on a rejection of men. Lesbian identity will be established in the first instance out of a sense of difference and awareness that the norm round you is not your norm. Part of that sense is related to emotional and sexual feelings towards other women. An attempt will be made to define the feelings and give them some meaning in order to make the sense of difference valid. Internally the identity is assumed gradually as the category fits and because the woman does not reject the category of lesbian then a redefinition of meaning can take place for some of the aspects of the category – a move away from a stereotyped understanding of lesbianism. The final steps are taken in the act of sex with another woman, although I recognize there are lesbians who have not had sexual relationships with women but certainly still define themselves as lesbians. The ultimate statement about identity is the important action of 'coming out'; first to one's self – accepting and recognizing one's self as lesbian – and then communicating one's lesbianism to a wider community. Because some feminists have found it possible to have a lesbian practice without the primary identity construction having taken place, the major identity for them is actually 'feminist lesbian' and not lesbian.

Debate around sexuality has been predetermined by the sexual revolution of the sixties and the feminist equation of heterosexuality and male violence. The problem with the sexual revolution was not the liberation of sex and sexual matters but that it was not coupled with an attack on sexism. The sexual liberation movement was not the movement that feminists or women wanted; to separate sex from reproduction did not hit at social relations or their oppressive nature. The reaction of many feminists now to the sixties has been to place the sexual liberation movement firmly within male sexual demands and male supremacy. While there is a lot of truth in this I also remember that from that very movement sprang firstly gay liberation and then feminism. It also did much to contribute to women's sexual demands within relationships as well as the general conception of women's sexual needs in society at large.

The assumed link between heterosexuality and male violence has led to condemnation of all male sexual activity whether heterosexual or homosexual. The result is that feminist lesbians can now advocate lesbianism for all women as 'lesbian women put women first, and women-identified heterosexual women put men first'. A particular category, lesbian, is now being indiscriminately applied to women and feminists, partly because of lack of any other word to describe close relations between women, and partly because of a re-interpretation of women who did not share the lesbian culture. Consequently a unique, complicated, radical world is sliding into the shadows. Both feminism and lesbianism lose as a result. Lesbianism has lost its autonomy, sexual radicalism and cultural identity, while feminism is in danger of becoming no more than a critique of male behaviour. It must be acknowledged that feminism has had an important effect on lesbianism, has enabled lesbians to understand themselves in a new light and has opened the gates to allies they never had before. But lesbianism is not just feminism and the road to change is not to replace the dimly understood category of heterosexuality by the equally misunderstood category of lesbianism.

■ Conclusion – the Dyke goes home to look in the mirror

I have been arguing for the importance of re-examining, as lesbians, some of our long-held cherished views. At no point is there any implication that the dingy, sordid squalor that did, and still does characterize some lesbian practices, can be glossed over. But we need to look at our lesbian culture and history to see if it is as we thought when we embraced feminism.

If lesbians continue to allow the category 'lesbian' to be the same as 'woman', then we deny ourselves and allow only a continuing existence as another social category with different and distinctly gendered limits. Feminism's remarkable ability to accommodate difference has extended even to sexual orientation so that that too has become its property. We discovered painfully that we could not unproblematically graft socialism, Marxism or psychoanalysis on to feminism. The same may well be true of lesbianism. The women's liberation movement will continue to be the dominant context for lesbianism and we will continue to be a major presence in the movement. But the lesbian struggle for self-definition and autonomy has been in process for a long time. If we want further to strengthen and develop this self-definition and autonomy we have to circumvent this present impasse in which lesbianism finds itself engulfed by feminism. The geography of both countries is complicated and unique, and the boundaries overlap only in places.

> The Dyke stopped outside the bar. She stood alone in the middle of the road. Sounds came from the bar on one side, and on the other the Feminist stood watching her from outside the disco. It was even snowing that night and the Dyke was feeling pretty miserable as she stood still and cold.
>
> She knew she was a Dyke. She also knew she was a feminist. Sometimes she was even a feminist dyke. She had a place in both worlds. So why was she standing there upset and crying? The Dyke turned up the collar of her jacket, pulled her cap down over her eyes and trundled off to the place she knew she could feel O.K. in. Home was just a short walk away.

■ Notes

The ideas here are not my exclusive property and owe much to discussions with women over the years. In particular, thanks to all the women from the Social Policy Group; and especially to Margaret and Carole.

1 Original story (part of) by me.
2 *Village Voice*, 17-23 June 1981. See also English, Hollibaugh and Rubin in this volume.
3 See *Heresies* (1981).
4 For further amplification, see Weeks (1981), particularly chapter 6.
5 *Sex Problems in Women*, A.C. Maglan (1922). Tribadism: mutual masturbation or, if one woman has a sufficiently enlarged clitoris, the introducing of this organ into the vagina of the other. Lesbianism: lingual excitations of the vulva. (It is interesting that at this time, 1922, lesbianism was just one form of sexual 'perversion' in women; was it not yet a category? When did it become the general term for woman-to-woman sex?)

6   Articles: *Sex Heresies*, The Butch-Fem Relationships; *Frontiers*, Lesbian History Issue Vol. 4, No. 7; Barbara Ponse (1978).
7   See Martin and Lyon (1972).

Becoming Visible: Black Lesbian Discussions

Carmen, Gail, Neena and Tamara

■ Coming out and the joys of visibility

I've been really excited about this, but I've also been worried.

Carmen: There's two sides to my worry really, one is to do with being known by the state. You know, the drastic way things are going in this country, names in print are prime targets because of the threat our words make. It could also affect our freedom of travel into different countries. On the other hand, there's the way that names in print get taken up by the media, they like to pin mass movements onto a few individual 'heroes' or leaders. It's a totally false representation. Of course, they can still get to you, but it's a little bit harder, just one more layer.

Tamara: *I* think it is different for Black women – the whole notion of coming out – than it is for white women. One is made to feel guilty if you don't come out. At one time in the gay movement there was this pressure that 'You've not really come out till you've come out to your family' and I find that really oppressive. I feel that doesn't hold in the same way for us because often we don't want to take the risk of total rejection by our families who we might rely on for lots of different kinds of strength and support.

Neena: The myth that Black families or people are more homophobic than whites should really be demolished, because what is obvious is that the security links we need with our families/communities are stronger.

Gail: The family! The family is very contradictory for us. There are emotional involvements, there are ties, the roots that it represents for us all as individuals in a fundamentally racist/sexist society. That's why Black people may decide not to come out as lesbians or gay for fear of being rejected by a group of people whom you not only love but who represent a real source of security, of foundation. That's a choice that has to be respected as a political choice, not just an individual one. But we also have to recognize that not coming out does exact a terrible toll, or can do, in the sense of living this huge personal/political lie. I was terrified to tell my mother, who in fact told me in the end, and who came to accept and love me for that. In fact just before she died last year she spoke very honestly to me and my lover of the time and said how upset she would be if we broke up. That was very important to me. But I must say that before it was all in the open, and I was living closely with my family and my husband, I found it intolerable that they didn't know this important thing about me, especially because I felt *so good* about having become a lesbian at last. Now I feel that coming out can be very liberating, a feeling of release. But I don't believe in that old GLF idea that every gay man and lesbian should immediately come out in every situation – that doesn't deal with reality, nor is it a very good way of supporting others who can't come out.

C: It definitely is what we should be working towards. But there's also the threat of our own Black communities as well. I feel that these guys are quite willing to come and burn your house down.

T: I still don't feel sure about using my name … On the one hand I really want to use it and be who I am and be identified. My greatest fear is total rejection from my family, who I really am close to.

N: Yes, I can understand that fear and I may well have experienced it myself if I had come out at home, in India. But being here, so far away from family, it does become marginally easier. But it does pose problems if I were to return to India to live …

T: It's good for women to see that there are others with similar fears. I think it is a real dilemma because the more of us that come out the stronger we are going to be, and the more other women are going to feel that they are able to come out, because we are creating that kind of a situation where it is possible.

C: This very discussion makes a point about lesbian oppression. Either way, there are going to be four Black lesbians talking about our lives in this publication!

G: Yes! It never stops being difficult ... There may be a period say twenty years later when you are confronted again with the difficulty of coming out. If any of us go and live at home [countries of origin] what is going to happen? In all seriousness? It is important for people to know that coming out is liberating in an individual sense, but it is also very much a process that you have to go through all the time.

T: I remember the very first time I came out publicly was at the OWAAD [Organization of Women of African and Asian Descent] conference in 1981, when there was that big uproar about Black lesbians demanding an autonomous space for a workshop. I remember standing in the lunch queue when this woman I vaguely knew asked me quite loudly which workshop I had been to. I just froze inside and said what am I going to do? Am I going to lie? Or am I going to tell her? And I said 'Oh the Black lesbian workshop' before even thinking about it. Afterwards it was a real sense of 'well, I've said it and felt good about it' but it was frightening. She looked at me blank and then turned away, there was no other response.

N: I found that experience at the conference really painful ... It was a process that all of us had to go through, lesbian or not, their fears, our anxieties, and our insistence that our demands be met. I felt we were exposed in a terrible way. I felt so disappointed that we were under attack, in a sense, at this conference where we should have experienced a feeling of togetherness ... We were up at the top on this gallery where everyone could look up at us and there was such a feeling of hostility coming towards us ...

G: The whole of the Saturday night I remember that I felt bad because I had split with other lesbians at that conference. I split over the closed workshop because I felt it went against the grain of what OWAAD had been about and because I felt it let a lot of people off the hook. A bit like whites not having to deal with racism if they 'let' us have our own workshops. I felt angry for lots of reasons. I felt angry at my group, angry at OWAAD past and present organizers, angry at other lesbians for not allowing me to say what I wanted to say without being hostile to me … at myself for not articulating clearly what I meant to say. The only time I felt solidarity with other lesbians was over the fact that they and I declared our sexuality and therefore made ourselves vulnerable, and that in a way is one of the most important lessons of feminism, that politics and vulnerability are not mutually exclusive. There were lots of other women there who would not even say they were bisexual but who we all knew were sleeping with each other.

C: I was one of those!

G: I didn't know you were. I was angry at those women even more because this was the time to say there are lots and lots of Black women who are activists and lesbians and there is a range of political opinion over these questions among us. I suppose I just felt that whatever position you took on the workshop the time had come to declare yourself, even though I know that is a very difficult thing, especially because many women acted like complete voyeurs.

But the whole issue of our relationship to heterosexual women and differences between us was an important issue that was missing and that opportunity in a way has not come back again. It's not that it won't, it *will*.

T: Despite all these horrible things happening, for me, in a lot of ways, being able to have that Black lesbian workshop was the beginning of something important, personally and politically, because that was the beginning of the Black Lesbian Group [BLG] that Neena and I were involved in. It played an important part for me and gave me the confidence and support of other lesbians to be able to come out in ways that I'd not been able to before and be much stronger in myself about my own lesbianism.

At the conference, despite the tensions, Black lesbians still forced and created a situation where we did meet, and when we turned up in the room where we were meeting it was really good to see so many women walking in. For the first five minutes we all looked at each other, sharing a real high because there were so many of us, forty of us, there.

N: Also I knew there were several others who did come up to those of us who had identified ourselves and whispered 'thank you' … just because we had been there.

C: I was one of the women who didn't stand up and declare my bisexuality. But it all depends where you are at the time. I've been heterosexual and anti-lesbian; I've been bisexual; now I'm a lesbian and coming out strong. Opening your mouth at a conference is a harrowing enough experience. But for me at the time I did speak out and argued for the closed workshop for Black lesbians on the principle of independent organization, which after all is what a Black women's conference is all about. But I also felt, yeah, I want to discuss those things too. It was about where did we fit in. There was a definite disrespect for bisexual women. But I guess it was up to us to make our space, in some ways.

N: Another point is that at the conference there were so few visible Asian lesbians. I know a dozen Asian lesbians in this country and that's very few, but then I think that five years ago I only knew one other so now it is twelve times better! I know many more Afro-Caribbean lesbians and what bothers me is that I wish there were more Asian women able to come out.

T: In the past year, when I've heard about all these other Asian lesbians, it has been really good to hear about more Asian women coming out. I know of quite a few young Asian women who are fifteen or sixteen living at home and wanting to explore their sexuality, some of them know that they are lesbians, some of them are already having a relationship with their best friends but are frightened about what to do about it. It is nice to know that there are *young* Asian women who are coming out or who are lesbians.

N: I used to feel the gap more strongly in the Black Lesbian Group where there were only four of us out of thirty.

G: You said that you wish there were more Asian women who were able to come out, but come out in what? We only know the people who move about in certain circles, although I understand what you mean because I had this same feeling about two years ago when more lesbians of African descent became visible. But I also feel a joy and strength at seeing any Black and Third World women coming out because they all help to shatter the myth that lesbianism is a 'white thing'. It's also important that we don't forget that there are lots of other Black lesbians we will never meet but we know are there – and that's one of the joys of visibility – it's not just about seeing it's also about 'knowing'!

N: Did you see *Eastern Eye* recently? The presenter, and I never thought I would hear this, said '*Our* gays are having a hard time out there', but again, this was gay men and didn't include us. Overall I suppose the tone was quite sympathetic. I never thought they would discuss the issue in the first place, and then I was surprised that they weren't being anti-gay. It's silly but I found myself being put in a position of having to be grateful ...

T: That's about being recognized within our own community and that's really important.

■ Working/challenging racism

G: I felt excited about doing this tonight because I thought it would help me sort out a problem about coming out at work. There are a lot of white lesbians who ask me to join in some of their activities, but I feel very unsure about it, because there are also a lot of Black people with whom I have to work directly, in an atmosphere of political tension, about how to challenge racism there. So I don't want to be more alienated from the Black people but I feel there is no way at all I can begin to discuss this with the white lesbians. In a way just having said this to you makes me feel better and stronger about dealing with it, and I know I'll feel good when I do eventually come out to the Black people, especially those whom I respect politically. I suppose it's just an example of what I was saying earlier about coming out never ending! Ah well. [Since then I have begun the process of coming out to some of the people and it wasn't too painful.]

T: In a way for me, working in a feminist project, the problems of challenging racism are there all the time, even though I am out as a lesbian. I think it is a real problem when white feminists set up projects without including Black women at the start because they set the terms. So when individual Black women go to work with them it is always on their terms and within their frameworks. I have found the battle to change their structures so that we and our work is not marginal or token, really exhausting. It also makes me resentful because I might try and integrate an anti-racist perspective within the work situation and it might seem to work for a few days or weeks, then again it's back to normal. Unless white feminists who are genuine about change begin to internalize anti-racist ways of behaving and an anti-racist consciousness, and I don't mean just by adopting the right rhetoric, I am increasingly sceptical about wasting my energies on educating them.

N: Yes, you're right. I see in various publications the number of advertisements from white women's projects, urging Black and working-class women to apply for jobs. And I have strong suspicions sometimes about these because, for one, it might suggest that Black women are being employed in great numbers, and that is just not true. It disguises the realities for the vast numbers of Black women who are being made redundant, unable to get employment, facing the cuts, etc. And secondly I think that it can be dangerously tokenistic. I mean, why are they suddenly doing it now? Why did they not do this earlier? Okay, I know they are having to respond to really strong pressure from us about racism, and being included in projects, etc., but it can backfire. Merely employing Black women to make up the numbers, as it were, is no guarantee that there is a real change of politics or political direction in the white women's commitment to taking up issues of racism, imperialism, class issues, etc. It's ironic really, there they are, falling over backwards to employ Black women, and sometimes those Black sisters are having a really hard time and are being forced to make the choice to leave ...

G: Yes – definitely, and what is frightening is that often white women don't even realize this.

C: Definitely so, and these groups are also pressured by their funding bodies to employ Black and working-class women. What you say is so true about being forced to leave in the end. I'm fast coming to the conclusion that I am totally unemployable. At the moment the only practical choice for being employed to work with Black women has been within white feminist organizations. A refuge for two years, and now a women's centre. The isolation you feel as the one, or lately two, Black workers is incredible. Even if there are Black women on the support group, which itself is rare, the white women cannot understand that our whole experience has been different. Our perceptions of the state, of other community organizations, of white women, are through the experience of racism. It's not just a case of adding the word to the long list of oppressions that us 'right on women' are 'uniting' to fight together. Both our priorities and the compromises we are prepared to make are therefore different. Also our willingness or ability to deal with unnecessary bureaucracy.

T: I also think that the fact we are seeing more jobs being advertised by white feminist projects encouraging Black women to apply is really suspicious. There are many Black women being rung up to join management committees at the last minute, by white feminists, because it looks good when applying for funds, particularly to the GLC women's committee, where priority is supposed to be given to Black and 'ethnic' minority women. (Some of us know otherwise.) I find it really disgusting because we are just included superficially and once they've got their funding, Black women are either slowly eased out or leave anyway, because the structures they have to work with, even in so-called feminist or left collectives, are inherently racist. And it's all about getting us in there on their own terms and even though they don't recognize that and some of them might genuinely believe that they are open to us, they are unwilling to change so that more Black women get access to the resources they have. Ultimately I don't feel that there is any change happening. I feel pessimistic because on that fundamental level of giving up power, there is a reluctance to do so.

N: That depends on, as you were saying earlier, the terms that have been set. I work with Black and white women, but I feel that the situation there is different, and that's because the project was started by Black women/women of colour. That was important because we had a long period in which we were able to discuss what *we* wanted. Then, as white women started joining us, we were strong in our aims, and I would like to think that those white women still with us have shown commitment to politically understanding many issues. But more important for me is that I am working with Black lesbians and the variety of politics and origins of the Black women in the group is always stimulating. I know I have learnt more in the past three years there than for a long time previously. It's understood that priority is given to our issues.

T: I am also much more concerned about putting energies into creating our own work situations and our own structures. Like, for instance, Carmen and I are involved in setting up a Black women's publishing co-operative. This comes directly out of our experience of being excluded and/or being made invisible by white feminist publishers, as much as our commitment to seeing Black women taking control and creating our own media and means of communication.

■ White women's movement scene

T: What I find disturbing is that very often in the white lesbian scene there is a sense in which Black women are made to feel that they have to prove their lesbianism. A lot of it is to do with the ways in which we organize as Black women and as lesbians. For some of us, our sexuality doesn't mean that we have the 'luxury' of organizing as lesbian separatists, nor do I particularly believe in doing so. So while my sexuality is a part of me, it's not the only thing. My race and class are equally important and this has an implication for me in the way I organize, or want to organize, politically. If you don't have the same politics as some white lesbians and are seen to be politically involved with Black men, then they somehow patronize you and think you haven't quite made it yet. And they believe themselves to be at a much higher stage of consciousness because according to them they are woman identified whereas you are still male identified.

I remember having several experiences of being harangued and pressurized by a few white women who called themselves revolutionary feminists, when I was part of a Black mixed group and doing anti-racist work. They would say things like 'Wouldn't it be better for you to spend your energy working with white women around their racism and gain some ground of sisterhood than to be politically working with Black men?'

At another time, at a meeting when there were some Irish women from the Relatives Action Committee who had come to speak from Belfast, one of these revolutionary feminists said to them 'Have you ever considered the fact that it might be in your interests as women to have the British troops there until such time as all of you as *women* have organized yourselves because the Republican movement is so male dominated.' That was in 1977. I'm sure that some of these women have had to change their views, but some have got worse. The implications of their politics are so totally reactionary that I felt quite strongly that I had nothing in common with them, even though they are lesbians, and I had much more in common with the Irish sisters who had an anti-imperialist perspective.

N: Here's another example ... I'll never forget reading an article, again by a revolutionary feminist, which implied that perhaps it was not such a bad move really that Asian men were not being allowed into this country, because 'we' did not want more men in this country and 'we' should be fighting arranged marriages anyway. At the time a lot of us were making a noise about the immigration laws, etc. and I was so angry that such a reactionary position was being published in a feminist newsletter. That certainly made me stay away from revolutionary feminism, and made me cling more fiercely to what I believe is my brand of radical feminism. I don't want them to define it,

I don't see why they should because it only alienates more of us away. I think there are useful things to be found in radical feminist theory – I believe that of most radical theories. They are worth investigating, discussing – you can get something out of them to suit your own situation. Recently, *Trouble and Strife*, a radical feminist magazine, declared in its first editorial that they could not find any Black radical feminist (in their terms) to join their group ... I think that is outrageous ... they did not bother to explain why, or challenge their own definitions, or allow for other definitions ...

T: That's a new trend, because a lot of books are being published and they say this is only going to be dealing with white women's experience because we are not in a position to deal with Black women's 'experiences'. It's a cop-out, absolving themselves from the responsibility of what they are saying. Possession of definitions is so crucial because they have been defining the terms forever and that's why it is so important for us to get together and create our own definitions.

G: Yes I think we should be – in fact we are – in the business of making our own definitions. But making the terms our own is also about defining the content of those definitions. This is is why I feel that our challenge to the assumption that feminism is the exclusive property of white British women includes a challenge as to the *content* of feminism. We are saying feminism is also ours but we define what that means – we are defining our Black Feminism. And this has its roots in the Black Power Movement, in the Women's Liberation Movement and in the struggles against imperialism and for national liberation. It is essentially about the simultaneity of class exploitation and race and sex oppression and that is in no way about getting a fair share of an unequal system. We can redefine the same terms and fundamentally alter them because our starting point is so different. And what's so potentially revolutionary about it is that our definitions, so long as they are based in and extend their roots, are not colour bound, because white sisters involved in the struggle for National Liberation can understand us and unite with us. The obvious example being Irish sisters.

T: I totally agree. I think that, as you say, because our starting point is different, and because as Black women, we are up against so many different systems of oppression and exploitation, our political analysis and practice has the potential to be all-embracing as well as the most threatening. What I mean is that, if, as we do, examine our histories of dispersal around the world, and look at why and how we come to be living here and at our collective and individual past and present experiences, we are forced to see the links between all these systems and develop a global perspective.

G: Separatist political strategies are always simplistic and I believe essentially reactionary. The example Neena just gave is a supreme illustration of that. This is one of the reasons why I could never define myself as a radical/revolutionary feminist. I do, though, respect the fact that Black women who define themselves so are in the business of challenging racism amongst radical feminists.

■ About relationships with white women

N: I know some women who are so insistent that Black lesbians must not have relationships with white lesbians and if you do, that it was sleeping with the enemy. I did find that excessive because I could see and still can see *lots of other enemies around* ...

C: I can't imagine me having a sexual relationship with a white woman, but that's my conclusion at the moment. There is too much clubbing each other over the head between Black women for whatever reason. There are so many reasons why we are who we are at a particular time. We need to give each other more space and respect. It happens all the time in meetings, there's a line and whoever says it the heaviest gets to win.

G: Again it comes down to separatist politics being facile. But I do feel that if we are going to argue that there is no hard and fast rule about whom we have relationships with, then we have to take the responsibility for that position and support sisters in relationships with white women. Unfortunately I do not see an awful lot of that sort of support.

C: We definitely do have to talk about differences but it is the way that we do it. If you start off with this 'I think what you're doing is a load of shit and I disrespect you because of it' then where can the discussion go from there? Nowhere. We can learn from each other in so many ways, like sharing experiences rather than saying 'This is what is politically correct.'

T: I don't think anyone should make hard and fast rules about whether you have relationships with white women or not. Although I personally wouldn't any more, because when I have in the past it's been at a cost. It's been unequal, not just in terms of sex but also class. I also felt forced to make personal and political compromises. I couldn't always afford to jeopardize what little I had, and challenge white women's racism, because if I did that then I would be even more isolated. But the thing is that at that time I didn't have much choice; many sisters still don't. Because I didn't know many other Black lesbians, there was nothing like the networks we are developing now amongst ourselves ...

N: But people do make hard and fast rules.

C: But then I don't think we should have hard and fast rules about relationships with men either.

N: I do see a difference between sleeping with men, whatever men. With a woman you would not get the power relation based on sex lines, of course, other power relations based on race and class are still there, but heterosexuality is an oppressive institution for women.

C: I remember thinking along those lines once but I don't anymore. It seems like a hierarchy of oppression, of sexual oppression being more devastating than others, which I don't agree with although it is very fundamental. I'm not about to have sexual relationships with men, but it's still not a hard and fast rule. It's more that what counts is whether they're gonna respect you or not, and treat you in a way that is equal. So until they can do that I'm not going to, but then that goes for white women as well.

T: It would be good to go on to talk about the development of a Black lesbian feminist perspective, particularly in terms of how it can inform political organizing, our different experiences of working with heterosexual Black feminists, Black male activists, and also discuss the possibilities of making alliances with white women, mixed groups etc ...

C: Becoming lesbians within the local Black women's group I was in wasn't easy. It became more and more tense and difficult because it seemed as though the Caribbean women were more questioning in this direction than the Asian women. But Afro-Asian unity wasn't really the issue, as two of the Asian women were very supportive, one of whom is now a lesbian herself.

It seemed such a contradiction, you would be in a Black feminist group and then outside of that you live your life with men. What we were putting up with from men seems incredible now. Some of us felt we should talk about it in the group, but others felt that to be completely out of order. That that area was their personal life and had nothing to do with politics. But it reached such a height for me and one of the other West Indian women. We read this pamphlet 'Love Your Enemy' – a discussion between many different kinds of lesbian and heterosexual feminists – which we'd never seen the likes of before.

It was Christmas two years ago, and we settled down with this book, and talked through every argument and personal experience for four days. By the end of it we couldn't bring any reasons forward for continuing relationships with men and that was it. But we felt very isolated because in that part of London, we didn't know any other Black lesbians at all. We did hear about the Black lesbian group, but just as we were deciding to get involved it packed up. Although there were white lesbians involved in the local refuge where I was employed for two years the isolation from Black lesbians was too much and we ...

N: Did Southall Black Sisters not change after that?

C: I feel that the group still needs to take us more seriously as lesbian feminists.

G: When I first joined the Brixton group I was terrified because I knew that I, at some time, would have to make it clear that I was a lesbian, even though I didn't push for that [i.e. a politics of sexuality] to become a focus of its politics. I was also a bit scared about saying that I was involved in the Women's Liberation Movement – though on that issue I was just being paranoid – accepting stereotypes of Black women's organizations. My stereotypes were also challenged by the fact that most of the other lesbians or bisexuals hadn't had anything to do with the Women's Liberation Movement, but had their roots in the Black movement (if anywhere). That taught me a lot about the invisibility of lesbians in the Black community and about the lack of space that the Women's Liberation Movement provided for Black lesbians.

But it has been incredibly hard because the group has been so rabidly homophobic, though I feel there's been such a lot of movement. Now it is easy to get a discussion about lesbians/- lesbianism within the group and I feel the atmosphere is much more supportive to lesbians.

In the past we had the problem that Carmen talked of – that of some people not wanting to talk about sexual love and practice. Ironically I have been one of those at times, and I feel now that a lot of that had to do with not feeling strong enough to get into detailed discussions about sexuality because I'd be isolated in talking about being a lesbian. Though I must say that people have commented on how closed I am and inaccessible, so that they have felt unable to raise it with me. But in a way that's been the problem that I would have had to make myself vulnerable in what felt like isolation.

I've also found it much easier to have one-to-one discussions about lesbians/lesbianism, its political importance etc. with some of the heterosexual women. This has been because these were often women who had some notion of political accountability and had the politics to want to ask questions about all social relationships and constructions. Consequently it's been amongst these women, who were often examining their own relationships with men, that I've seen the most changes. And the group has changed a hell of a lot, and that's meant that we've all grown together. It's not been easy and it certainly isn't over, but it seems that we've learnt that we must put all of our feminism into action and discuss the political importance and limitations of questioning heterosexuality, lesbianism and the whole area of the construction of sexuality.

T: What sometimes concerns me is the gap between our political development as Black feminists and/or lesbians and our male 'comrades'. I feel that we are moving forward all the time but they seem to be standing still or getting worse, in some cases. One of the challenges of Black feminism to the Black movement is that we have and are creating intrinsic links between our personal political practice and wider political concerns, and knocking down some people's assumption that sexual preference is just about being interested in an alternative lifestyle. I wonder if they will ever accept Black lesbians as political activists and not dismiss our sexuality as 'lifestyle politics'.

G: For me it's been more a case of relegating my lesbianism to my private life, as though it's nothing to do with my overall political perspective. That of course allows them not to think about the oppression of Black lesbians and gays. But it's not that I'm not taken seriously or dismissed outright, in fact I'm often chastized for not being involved in certain things because I've something to offer. It's more a case of selecting parts of my politics that 'fit'. A selective dismissal if you like and sometimes I find that harder to deal with.

T: What I've found is that when you work with Black men politically and they know you are having a relationship with a woman, they think it's something you do in your spare time. Before, I didn't allow my sexuality to come in, in any way, into how I was working politically, because I didn't have the confidence to do it. As long as I worked within the framework that was laid down by them it was all right, and if I brought in any kind of serious discussion about feminism or lesbianism as part of my political perspective, then it wasn't acceptable.

I didn't always have the courage to do it either. I know I too have compartmentalized my politics in the past because it's often been the only way I could cope. It's also because it's only now that I am beginning to be able to integrate the various aspects of my politics and feel confident about being more upfront, but it's still an ongoing and difficult process, really. But when your sexuality does inform your general political perspective, how do you make those connexions you made in your head more concrete?

C: You can't do it on your own. What the mixed groups have got to realize is that they have got particular structures, particular oppressive ways of working, apart from the issues that they don't see as important. It is not till there is space with Black women and especially Black lesbians, that you start to see that we have so much in common – a particular perspective and ways of organizing. Mixed organizations have got to learn, but they won't until there is a general movement of Black women enforcing those changes.

G: One of the difficulties I find concerns the points of tension between Black lesbians and Black heterosexual feminists. Sometimes I feel more angry at them than the men, especially in social situations where their behaviour can be very unfeminist in my view, and extremely exclusive, and that serves to isolate us or dismiss our personal practice. Of course, I sometimes feel quite disgusted at the way lesbians behave in social situations but that doesn't have the same effect of excluding us. So for me sometimes the same questions are raised by both heterosexual feminists and male comrades.

C: Yes, maybe the same questions, but how to deal with them is completely different if it's men or women.

G: Yes, maybe different, but the same questions. How you resolve them, the way in which you tackle them, will be different, and anyway, because we are working on a more daily level with women, there is more space to resolve them. But I just feel it is important that we state that there are points of tension between us as feminists.

T: In a way just thinking about that, many Black heterosexual feminists do feel really more threatened than the men do because it is about acknowledging the potential in themselves, and it's that fear they have about themselves.

N: Yes, it's about their friend who was heterosexual last year and *this* year ...! (Laugh).

T: And more of them are coming out. Some of them can't deal with it and because from their own experiences and development, the logical conclusion of what they are feeling and doing is to have sexual relationships with Black women, it's that jump and so many of them are frightened.

G: I think that particularly when they learn that what they are doing is not just spending time with other Black women but growing to love other Black women, and stopping competing with them. I'm sure that is what happened with me in a way, and I clearly see it happening with the women I work with. And you almost sit there smugly smiling to yourself thinking I wonder when it will be ... It's not just the working together, but it's all these other things. Ultimately that has to force the changes on all the Black organizations. When it's one or two women they know they can isolate you and say 'Oh no this is crap politics.' When you are doing that work, and you are still involved with Black struggle, and there are more and more of you that are coming out but are still involved, and often leading the way of the struggle, not in a sense that it is always written down but you know that is what is happening in practice, that forces changes. Sometimes there are minor ones, not very overt, but like the fact that they will ask opinions on issues. I see that as part of the movement forward. And that is not overtly about them beginning to say that questions of sexual construction are something that should be taken on board, as social constructs. But they can't write you off any more and say that you are just nothing. A few groups can continue to ignore and attack you, but this would always be the case because there will always be real political disagreements.

C: There is so much violence among the men that it really puts me off thinking that I can begin to start talking about where I am. Also those that are not dealing with direct violence against us, just the structures of the way they organize. Just to get yourself heard you have to become like them which I am not prepared to do. There are only certain people who will get listened to, of a certain type. There isn't a thing about making space for everyone to speak. Things like that are definitely coming out of feminist organizing. I mean it's got to be broken down but I just don't think it's going to happen until there is a general movement of Black feminists rather than individuals within the mixed organizations.

T: Rather than being on the defensive in those situations, and going to them and saying or feeling that it's us who have to make those moves about forging alliances or working on general political issues, the initiative has got to come from them ... I feel that we have done that enough either as individual Black women activists or as small groups. They have got to make the moves because they have to recognize that there is a force here that they have to reckon with, and that Black women are not just into their 'ghetto' politics, of looking at just their issues, issues about being women, but also involved in a whole lot of other things. They should be coming to us and saying we would like you to work with us on this particular campaign, etc. I don't think the initiative has yet come from any of these organizations, it's always been from women's organizations because we recognized the necessity of being involved in wider political issues as they are directly linked to our specific situations as individual women.

G: For me though, from my political perspective, it is important to maintain links with mixed organizations in the Black community. Anyway, I don't see the Black movement – and we are part of that – as a monolith, as one homogeneous thing. I think there are sections of it in which there have been progressive developments on the question of women, whilst others have regressed. But I also see this as having followed the development and strengthening of autonomous Black feminist organizing. Definitely as the Brixton group has got stronger in its feminism and less willing to compromise, we have forced some movement on the part of mixed organizations we work with. It's not that all is wonderful and we ourselves are not clear on all the implications. But the fact that we have developed our feminism but still maintained links for me illustrates the importance of not writing off comrades and allies.

C: But it's really a question of priorities, isn't it? Because we have only got so much energy. I am very interested to hear what is happening with the mixed Black organizations and how they are developing, but I am not prepared to put my energies there at the moment. It would have to be really different before I started doing that. I think there is definitely enough work to do with Black women. We have to respect each other's choices.

N: I suppose I want them to start thinking we are valuable to them, and our ways of organizing and our ways of being, and all that we are saying, is going to be valuable to them. I have not had a political history of organizing with men, and it would be in 'crisis' situations that I would consider temporary alliances. I want us to be working with women, for women, because if we don't, who will?

T: Gail, what you were saying that the Black movement is not homogeneous and that there are different sections within it ... We have had different kinds of experiences from the Brixton group which has been around a long time – it's established, it's got 'status' – for individual women who have been around the same kind of political arena, but have not got the same kind of reputation and support to fall back on, it's been different. I think that it's those women, and groups that have formed more recently, who have had the negative experiences with Black male activists, which has made them say that they don't want to struggle with the brothers, because the brothers are not really our brothers anyway, and because of the kind of shit they've been giving us. Which is not to say that they have necessarily written off the possibility of ever working politically with men in the future.

G: I just want to clarify. I am not saying that changing mixed organizations in a direct way is a major focus of our energy. What we *are* saying is that we work with mixed political organizations with whom we have a general empathy, as a way of winning them to feminism. In fact the reverse has happened. As we have become stronger, more confident and clearly defined as a Black feminist group, so we said we are *not* going to subsume all our work to you, and that's really important. And what's been important about that is that whilst these groups may have felt that we've made wrong decisions – and don't forget that includes the women in those organizations too – they have still been prepared to work with us. Maybe the fact that the group has been around for ten years and has some base in Brixton and Stockwell has something to do with it. But I think the most important point has been maintaining a political perspective which told us that while we develop our feminism, we mustn't do that at the sacrifice of other struggles. It's been about being around, trying to get feminism taken on board as of relevance to all the Black community, and about making alliances. And all that has stemmed from our socialism as much as our feminism.

C: Some Black women and Black women's groups are able to work with mixed Black organizations because of having a socialist-feminist line. There can be this agreement over – yes, women are oppressed, yes, there has to be women's liberation – because capitalism is the root cause of all oppression, class, race and sex. We can therefore unite on that basis. But I feel we are often being tolerated, you know, because the responsibility is taken off men, off their sexism, and put on to capitalism. It means that a socialist-feminist could be comfortable in a way that I couldn't, because although I am not saying that all men are responsible for all the shit, I think they have got a definite responsibility. When it's pointed out to them they find it hard to accept.

G: But in order to understand that, in order to understand any social relationships, we have to see what the dominant form of exploitation is, in terms of the way that actual things are produced and the way that all that is reproduced, and to see how the oppression of women fits into that (and the way that reproduction itself is reproduced). So that if then when you say that, you can't say that patriarchy precedes anything if patriarchy means the oppression of women, because these forces act on each other, and change each other even at the same time as they entrench each other. So having said that, that is the framework in which we would try and understand the situation of Black women and Black people and homophobia and the oppression of gay men and lesbians within that ... They are aspects of a whole.

C: We're getting into some heavy things. (Laughter.)

G: But that's because you said what you said, and I can't say to you 'No we don't see capitalism as the source of women's oppression' because it's not simple like that.

C: But even hearing what you said I disagree ...

G: Yes, you may do ...

C: It's going on to another level.

T: I would say that a socialist analysis is very much part of my political practice. But while I believe class relations are important, I also want to stress that race and gender shape class as much as the other way round. What I think the Women's Liberation Movement and the Black Power movement has done is challenge the traditional left's heavy emphasis on class as a unitary category. I sometimes think that the hostility many feminists feel towards the word socialist is justified and that's because of the way in which the white left organizations, usually male dominated, have appropriated the term and given it their own specific connotations, depending on their particular sectarian tendency. To me, being a socialist is very much about having a vision of a future society and what and how change is going to come about. I often think it's a vision many of us share despite using different labels to define ourselves.

C: There is no sort of definite category of this equals this, we're all somewhere in and around and somewhere in between. But I just know that that is the direction I've been in and moved away from since becoming a lesbian and so there is a direct connexion. That's why I call myself a Black lesbian feminist, because my lesbianism is not just about who I sleep with or just about anti-heterosexism as an institution, it's also about an understanding of all the oppressions that we face. I don't agree that you start from this place of production and that the relations involved in production can be seen as dominant.

G: That's what I was trying to say we did not do. In brief, we are talking about production and reproduction, but that production itself is reproduced and it is a location in which oppression reproduces itself, manifests itself. Why I can't call myself a 'lesbian feminist' is because to me it is a whole concept that says you subsume everything to patriarchy.

C: It depends on what patriarchy means ...

G: It depends on what capitalism means ...

(Laughter)

T: Fighting patriarchal oppression, the power men have over women, is very much intrinsic to my understanding of socialism, and is very much on my political agenda. At the moment that's what I am putting a lot of my political energies into fighting and organizing against, particularly within our communities. Incest, rape and violence are common experiences for many of us and to me organizing against these forms of oppression is as important as organizing against state racism, factory closures and unfair work conditions, etc. All this brings me back to what I was trying to say before about our definitions of feminism, which inevitably must extend beyond colour, gender, class, sexuality as single factors; rather our concern is to create a synthesis ... I don't think, though, that it's always very useful to operate within definitions because they are and can be dangerous blocks to being open to hearing what other sisters are saying ...

N: I define myself as a radical feminist if I have to define myself. But I can see from the conversation we are having now that sometimes those definitions are quite useless. I also consider myself a socialist, definitely, I have for a very long time, but again, like Carmen, I do not call myself a socialist-feminist because for me that means taking certain very definite positions, for example, being a Marxist feminist or adopting a certain kind of theoretical base from which we then work outwards or fit your feminism into. And for me radical feminism has been about *asking questions about power*, and who has the power in a given situation. And why I feel it is quite broad based is because I feel the method of that sort of questioning politics can be applied to any situation: imperialism, racism, sexism. Who has the power? Who benefits from a particular situation? Who is going to profit from oppression? And then learning from the answers which you see and which you can apply to your own experiences. I think going back to your own experience of your life, and what has happened in it, for me the most useful way of learning and growing politically rather than reading a book, getting a theory, trying to understand it (which is also sometimes difficult because it is very often written in a language which is not accessible to you), and then trying to fit your life to it. I'd rather do it the other way round, talk about our own experiences and learn from what we share between us, from what has happened to us, what is happening to us, as a method of leading to change as a result of that.

G: What do you mean you are a socialist?

N: That means I would like to see an end to systems of exploitation and oppression based on class, race, imperialism, sex, other power structures. I would define myself as a Black lesbian feminist who is also a socialist and an anti-imperialist. Take socialist theories and practices – it's very evident that historical, cultural and political circumstances have determined particular *kinds* of socialism. Similarly, I feel we should be able to adapt feminist theories. They are not the prerogative of the west and should not be allowed to be. We should define our feminism as Black women, Black lesbians. And then again, there are a wide range of differences between us (I always think these are necessary and healthy!) depending on where we are coming from ...

G: Why doesn't radical feminism or Black radical feminism include that?

N: For me they do, for me it is part of that. That's why I said that the method is quite important. I can apply to different situations not just my situation as a woman, or me as a Black woman, or as a worker ... Does that make sense?

C: Yes.

N: That is why I do not find it useful when people make a distinction between socialist-feminist on one hand and radical feminist on the other, as if they are two opposing forces. For me there's been more of a difference in method, and because you have a difference of method, you have a difference in identification of root cause – saying that yes, men as men have power over women as women. For me this is as true as saying that capitalists as capitalists, wherever they are in the world, have power over the workers as workers. There are different power systems operating. I won't accept that capitalism is the root cause of oppression of all types the world over. I won't accept that a man who rapes his wife or daughter has necessarily got anything to do with the capitalist system existing in this country, or, if a Third World country, the country that colonized him. To me that is male power over a woman. And men do exercise that power.

G: I think that it is wrong to assume that people who define themselves as Marxist-feminists would say that 'Oh that is because of capitalism.' Okay, say the situation for Black women at home where there is feudalism of some sort, it's about how all those things in a difficult situation intermesh with the systems of exploitation, which is probably more accurate on a world scale. All of the philosophies that have informed their political development – like Black Power, women's liberation, class, or systems of exploitation – all of them are about questioning, about how you understand the situation. The point of difficulty is how you answer the questions ... I can't begin to answer any of the questions without understanding how oppression relates to the systems of exploitation, and how they are reproduced. Which is why it is not just about production in the workplace, it's about production and reproduction, not just biologically, but how the whole thing gets turned over time and again in the process of change and continuity. If I don't understand that, I don't see any way out, because I won't see where the points of contradiction are or where the weaknesses are and where the dialectic is and where the imminent change is.

■ Strengthening our love and building alliances

T: Okay, so while we have our differing yet similar political perspectives, it seems to me that we have to begin to think about the dilemmas we are often faced with in terms of political organizing ... I mean, we all only have limited energies and often it's a problem deciding how, and who you organize with, how you create alliances with other groups and struggles from a position of strength, how you incorporate your overall political perspectives into the day-to-day organizing you are faced with ...

C: We were discussing this at home recently and ended up drawing this diagram and picturing what we are facing. If you imagine oppression coming down on the Black woman – so you've got racism, sexism, anti-lesbianism and class through the different state institutions, and individuals. You've got Black women at the bottom, then there's a two-way process of struggle for us. There's coming together as Black women in our independent organizations, and that's crucial because that's the only way to find out what our priorities are and strengthen our core. Then from this strong centre we go back out taking our understandings and demands into the movements for socialism, Black liberation, women's liberation and gay liberation. So we're going back to the places we've left but from a position of unshakeable strength and resistance to all the old shit we used to get.

T: Recently, I've been inspired to think about all these things by reading some of the Black feminist literature from the States, where they are having discussions about integrating Black feminist lesbian perspectives into an overall discussion about strategies and political organizing.

What Bearnice Reagon and Barbara Smith in *Home Girls* [see

Smith, 1983] are saying about building alliances is really important and so crucial.

G: But making alliances in that way isn't just necessarily going into those movements where you'd be a minority ... for example, talking about Afro-American women doing things with other Third World women in the States, where maybe they may not be the majority in terms of numbers but where the traditions that they're bringing are dominant. In the *Home Girls* book[1] the last chapter by Bearnice Reagon is so good because there she's saying making alliances isn't just about not subsuming and never letting go of your struggle. It's saying in certain situations you will listen to other people's perspectives and that can be so within the Black women's movement, or over difference between radical and feminist separatists, or whatever we define ourselves as. But particularly in the States, and to some extent with us in the African-Asian split – I don't know if we've called it a split – then it's about us listening to what Asian women have got to say for example about the practical problems raised by organizing all under one umbrella of Black because that was a concrete aspect of OWAAD and that was about not allowing others to subsume. That's maybe one of the major political questions that perhaps we're just beginning to learn, because we've always been having to say 'but what about us?' Sometimes we say it so much that we can't say 'just listen now a minute'. Personally that's what I'm saying about listening to other people. I still feel very opposed to separatist politics but listen to what other people are saying as a movement or as a social force. We have to do that within our own ranks and that also means listening to heterosexual Black women who've oppressed us and continue to do so – serious ones I mean. People who are saying 'yes we've learnt and we must listen now', but listening to what their fears, anxieties or questions are as well.

C: It's difficult at the moment because most of us have been concentrating on Black women, those we work with. But the way it's going worldwide, and in this country, something really drastic is just around the corner and if we don't do something quick, not just in our Black women's groups, but if there's some massive rebellion then it's just going to be too late.

T: So what does that mean in terms of our organizing as Black women or Black lesbians specifically?

C: Theoretically it'd mean putting some energy into, on the one hand, building this strong centre and, on the other hand, taking it out as far and as wide as we can. But that's theoretically.

T: But practically we are so stretched as individual activists. Often it seems like a drop in the ocean, but when you're absolutely tired out, not having the time, yet knowing that there ought to be all these other things happening too, that's a frustrating part of it like the Police Bill's coming up, which is crucial for us as Black women, people, lesbians, all those.

N: I think we have the potential in us to be the most radical because all those forces have fashioned us: being women/Black/working class/lesbians/anti-imperialist/coming from Third World countries, so your consciousness has been made up of surviving many oppressions, that when you start rebelling your consciousness is necessarily going to expand to take in all these factors. You get exhausted because all these issues affect us, you can't choose one and dump the others. So many white women, white lesbians or white socialist feminists/radical feminists can pick and drop issues. That can't be the same with us because we've got to face these head on, because whether you like it or not it's going to face *us* at some time or the other. And we should allow for contradictions, for prioritizing different issues at different times depending on what's going on for us. At the moment I'm quite a visible lesbian in the circles I mix in. At home I could keep it relatively quiet because my priority might in fact be to do something about poverty. It annoys me that making this space for us is not allowed to happen. Sometimes you can only fire little bullets at little things ...

C: We're facing everything, but there's still more that I think the white women have started to look at more than we have – like disability, motherhood.

N: But there are material reasons why white women have organized around that much more than they have around racism, for example. I've not come across white women who have spent time talking about racism or thinking about it or organizing around it.

T: I think we are getting trapped by labels and definitions and what I can see is a hell of a lot of similarities.

C: But that might come out. I think that is quite positive, because it is something that has raged through the Black women's movement. For anyone that brings up one of these words there's another that goes ooohhhhhhh, when really I don't see any reason for it to be like that.

T: Being a socialist for me is not so much being informed by the Euro-American traditions of socialism but much more about the creative forms of organizing and resistance found in some of the Third World countries, where there has been a revolution or there is a national liberation struggle. Okay, I'm not saying they are perfect, but in some places they have actually created their own definitions and methods of socialism informed as much by their cultural traditions as by the economic conditions, well beyond anything Marx had envisaged, or had the imagination for ... That's another long debate, for another time ...

N: I've actually found it very useful to read Black lesbian literature from the USA.

T: I have as well, I've gained a lot of strength from it. I feel it's also given me confidence to come out and begin to talk about those things here.

C: It's also given us the inspiration and energy to set up our own Black women's publishing co-op. We want our voices to be heard as well. Because you also feel frustrated that it is always coming from the USA and you want to hear what British Black women are saying. This is a really crucial thing to do.

N: Also the things I've read about lesbians surviving in the Third World I've found that sometimes much more pertinent to myself, and a source of strength. I don't know other lesbians who have lived in India and who are in England now. Sometimes this can be isolating for me as there are differences between those of us who have grown up and lived in Third World countries, and those that haven't. But I do know other sisters – the woman I work with, for example, comes from Chile – and we have strong links between us because of the places we come from and where we find ourselves now.

T: I read the thing about lesbians in India and that gave me quite a buzz because you never see that at all and also reading the story in *Manushi* about lesbians in ancient India. There have been references to lesbians in the past ... and reading those accounts and picking them out about back home and what is going on ...

C: I am waiting to hear it from the Caribbean and African countries.

N: Diane from New York showed the Black Lesbian Group some interesting slides about West Africa; they are the results of her research on evidence of lesbianism and female bonding. That was fascinating, she was finding out all these things that nobody had found out before and nobody knew existed which had been ignored or passed over, and she was finding out and giving it a name, which I thought was really important to call it something, and not just let it pass by as 'women friends' when it was obviously more than that.

T: The *Manushi* story was written in the style of an old folk tale and it was about two lesbians ... It is a lovely story, and very intrinsic to Indian culture because of all the reference points it makes. It's not something that came from outside, but it is part of our culture. It affirms this thing you might have always known, that there has always been lesbianism in our cultures, and you begin to get some information and oblique historical references to, for example, women's kingdoms in India in the past ...

N: I have a book of Indian women poets, given to me by a lesbian from India, and that contains assertions of love between women. It's good to find out all these things in your own culture.

Let's end on an encouraging note ...

(Laughter.)

C: We've said a lot of it in other ways.

G: On a personal level, as a feeling type thing, just actually saying in connexion with my feminism and my Marxism ... that all of those things together, when I *feel* all of those things together, when I'm feeling really good about myself, I feel yes that is what you are. And then when you are able to put that into practice and raise that issue at that important meeting or conference, and there was an embodiment of your Marxism and feminism and your lesbianism ... especially if that is in a Black situation, that is when I feel really good about it. It sums up what it means to me because it is about being whole I suppose. I can't take away any of those three.

N: I feel for me it has been one of the most positive choices I have made for myself. I feel strong about it.

T: Yes, I feel exactly the same about the choice of being a lesbian. It is one of the most positive things I've done. I've never ever been really happier, even when I have been lonely, or isolated, or having a terrible time with some woman or whatever. It will still be totally different from having a terrible time from when I was heterosexual. It's totally different having made that choice. I feel really lucky that I've had that space and that I had the opportunity of being in an environment where

I could have made that choice. I can never ever think of going back on it. I have found a part of myself. There is never going to be anything that is going to change that and in that way I feel really good about that. When people talk about being oppressed as lesbians I feel that is nothing to do with me, and how I feel about it, but everything to do with society and what other people say and their negative feelings about us ... How because of their heterosexism and homophobia ... that creates situations for us where we have to live in fear. That's what I find oppressive, not being able to go down the road in the same way as heterosexual people, having to be really careful in certain situations, etc.

N: I suppose it's the oppression of not having male approval, 'The strong man by the side', of being alone.

C: And not being a nuclear family.

N: Yes.

C: With housing and jobs.

G: But I used to feel dreadful. Remember, last week I was telling you about how I felt I always knew I was a lesbian ... and I think I *like* women, not in a flirtatious way. Like I feel about Black people – yes I like Black people, and that is the irony about oppression. Because oppression is real, it is systematic, it is institutional, and yet you can feel so good, and strong ...

C: Because, for me, becoming a lesbian was about a liberation for me, as a woman, although I've been through different periods and I've felt real liberation at realizing what it means to be Black, or what it means to be working class. Those are processes of liberation for me. Lesbianism is definitely about women's liberation, or my liberation as a woman ... and it is just a feeling of freedom really. In the midst of hell it is still there.

N: It is a feeling of having control over at least one aspect of your life, when you are still fighting for control over so many others. At least on an individual level with collective support you are able to make that choice. Something I feel we haven't touched on is lesbian motherhood ...

G: And housing, being told you are insane, or need therapy/-psychiatry – the whole thing in this country, particularly if you make a proclamation about feeling good about your Blackness or lesbianism.

N: So ... something must be wrong in their eyes!

G: Like the whole threat about your children being taken away from you, or the feeling that you somehow should not have children, the internalized stuff. Not only because of the threat that they might be taken away from you, but you partially believe that perhaps they do need a nuclear family ... That is an aspect of oppression, i.e. having children ... Like all the stuff about being alienated from your parents, community, when you need the support of your family, community. Like the stuff at adolescence, when the cut-off point becomes a whole realm of sensuality, or when eroticism is cut off from you. I didn't think that at the time, but I think that is what happened to me. If I could have come out when I wanted to I could have been happy all these many years. (Laughter.)

N: Well I hope that now we are here we can provide some sort of short cut to other sisters who are lesbians or about to come out. I would like to encourage other Black women, here, everywhere, to come out, to demand respect for our choices, to tell others we are here, and make ourselves visible.

■ Note

1   See Barbara Smith (1983).

As an Asian lesbian I have been extremely privileged in participating in the production of this crucial work. I have learnt so much and gained so much strength from reading all the articles I typed.
Thank You, In Black Sisterhood, *R.S.*

'Everybody's Views Were Just Broadened': A Girls' Project and Some Responses to Lesbianism

Mica Nava

This article is about the impact of a feminist 'girls' project' on the personal consciousness and sexual behaviour of a group of (mainly) working-class girls – and hence upon the community in which they lived. Part I was originally commissioned for inclusion in a book aimed specifically at a young female readership but was excluded from it at the last moment, on the grounds apparently that I, as the author, was not a youth worker or a lesbian (see correspondence in Feminist Review *No. 13, 1983). The article was eventually published in* Feminist Review *No.10 in 1982 with a new section – Part II – which brought the story up to date and addressed some of the criticisms that had been levelled against the original part.*

I doubt whether such a relatively modest theoretical-political contribution would prove as contentious today. This is partly because feminism in the second half of the eighties is less marked by a moral pursuit of correct positions than it used to be. There are also other reasons. One is the proliferation over the last eight years of youth work with girls and of written commentaries on it; another is that young lesbians have increased both their networks of support and their visibility,[1] so single articles assume a lower profile. In addition, channels of communication with girls and young women have over recent years been augmented and diversified. Apart from the successful initiatives of municipal socialism (like those promoted by the GLC, ILEA, for example), there has been since the seventies an enormous increase in the exposure of feminist issues upon the pages of commercial magazines for young women like Cosmopolitan *and* Just Seventeen *(see also Winship, 1985). Although these developments may not always be consciously identified as feminist, either by their sponsors or consumers ('I'm not a feminist, but ...'), they address the very core of the woman question and represent a far greater dissemination and popularization of* feminisms – *among young men as well as among young women* – *than existed at the time this article was written.*

■ Part I[2]

It's nice to get it out into the open and talk about lesbianism to girls of our own age – because you just don't normally.

These friends are really open-minded, they've made me think about things. If you'd have talked to me about lesbians before I started going around with this lot, I'd have said, 'How disgusting' and all that. But now it don't bother me. They're just like other people, aren't they? They should just get on with it if they want to.

If I went in and told my mum I was pregnant she'd most probably thank the stars above her, you know, like: 'She's all right after all'.

These are some of the comments made by girls who attended a 'girls' project' in a London youth centre in the Spring of 1979. Many issues which were of interest to the girls were raised during the course of the project. Lesbianism was one of these, and is the one which will be focused upon in this article. But it is useful first of all to present some general information about the project, its objectives, and about the girls who attended it.

This particular project was organized by a group of local teachers, youth and community workers and parents (all of whom were women) and consisted of ten evening sessions. It was designed for girls only, in order to provide them with the opportunity for thinking about subjects which were of special concern to them (as girls) and were rarely covered by the school curriculum or normal youth centre activities. Films, plays and improvisation were used to examine such topics as: girls at school; families; health; work opportunities; relationships. The sessions included discussion and practical workshops, simple electrical and plumbing skills were demonstrated and girls were encouraged to participate in the music evening. Overall, the project was intended to familiarize girls with some of the basic questions raised by feminism; but importantly it was also intended to create a time when girls could meet on their own, develop a sense of solidarity with each other and enjoy themselves.

Between eighty and a hundred girls came to at least one evening session. About thirty attended on a regular basis. These ranged in age from thirteen to seventeen and came from a number of different schools; some were middle class, others working class. At the organizing stages it was expected that many girls would attend the project without becoming conscious of its connexion with ideas developed in the women's movement. In fact it emerged that most of the girls were aware of the feminist orientation but were not deterred by it. All of them, to a greater or lesser extent, were already challenging conventional ideas about the sort of behaviour which is considered appropriate for girls. In interviews afterwards many girls told me that what they had valued most about the project was the discovery that other girls felt the same way about various aspects of their lives. They said their ideas had been clarified, they had found the sessions fun, made new friends (age differences between girls were considered insignificant) and learned some new skills. In addition the girls had become more sensitive to the ways in which their problems were often the same as those of adult women.

Thus there were many effects of the project, which during a short space of time had covered a broad range of issues of relevance to girls. For the purpose of this article, however, I want to concentrate on the dimension of lesbianism, as I have already mentioned. The subject of homosexuality was first raised in a play performed at the project, and then discussed by the girls. This session continued to have reverberations for a long time afterwards; in the interviews I discovered that not only had it made the girls think differently, but in some cases it had substantially changed their lives. This is the reason I have chosen to focus on it. I shall first sketch out the background to the relevant session of the project, and then look at what the girls themselves had to say about their responses to it.

All societies define the boundaries of acceptable behaviour for men and women; within these, certain types of behaviour are approved, others merely tolerated. In our culture, lesbianism falls outside the boundary of what constitutes tolerable behaviour for women; it is taboo. Homosexual women have been forced to conceal the fact, or alternatively, have been obliged to suffer extreme disapproval. Most have chosen to hide it. With the rise of the women's movement in the late sixties, behaviour that was previously taken for granted was questioned. It was pointed out that there was nothing 'natural' about sex roles and the sexual division of labour (they varied from one culture to another), and that existing arrangements tended to benefit men. The 'naturalness' of sexual preferences and prohibitions was also called into question.

This is the kind of analysis which, in a very general way, underpins one of the plays shown at the project. The performance of *Is Dennis Really a Menace* by Beryl and the Perils,[3] was the trigger for the initial discussion on homosexuality among the girls. The play is harsh, and very funny indeed. Through naive cartoon characterization and presentation, the authors/performers introduce subjects which are normally unspoken in public situations. They look in particular at the different ways boys and girls (and men and women) feel about and act out their sexuality. The play is controversial as well as funny, but the girls considered it one of the highlights of the project and enjoyed it very much. The discussion after the performance lasted well past the time the sessions usually ended.

> *Lisa*:[4] At first the play made me a bit embarrassed, but after a while it was all right. It was acting things in front of you that made it different. When you talk about it with your mates, it's not the same.

As the discussion continued it emerged that many of the girls were made uncomfortable by a relatively small section of the play about lesbians: between jokes, a serious but fleeting (two seconds at most) kiss had occurred between two of the women. Here is part of the discussion that followed the performance:

> *Lisa*: I'll be honest, right. The bit that really embarrassed me was the bit about homosexuality. I don't know why. It's not a subject that I talk about at home, or even with my mates. You sort of shun away from it.
> *Jill*: Yes, you pass by it. You get to talk about everything else, but you just pass that by.
> *Lisa*: I feel a bit of a hypocrite though sometimes. I've seen girls kissing each other on the street and that, you know, and when

you talk about it with a group of mates, you think, yes, why shouldn't they, if that's the way they feel. But if you're walking along and see something like that, you sort of turn round and say, 'Ooh, isn't it horrible, how can they do it!' It makes you feel a bit of a hypocrite. You've got to have a lot of guts to say your point of view. I think every girl knows that every other girl wants to say something about homosexuality, but they all know that each one is going to be embarrassed, and they don't want to be the first to bring it up.

Not much more was said about homosexuality on that occasion. The girls continued to talk for another hour about the way in which boys are under pressure to act tough, about how some boys discussed girls in sexual terms, about relationships, fears of the dark and rape, and so on.

About three months later I talked to Ruth and Eva about the project and about that evening. Ruth was seventeen, Eva was fourteen, both their mothers are feminists so they were already familiar with some of the issues that were raised. They had very vivid memories of their responses to the play.

> *Ruth*: That was the best session for me. The discussion was really good.
> *Eva*: It answered a lot of questions, I don't know what they were, but it answered them. I knew that if the boys would give me half a chance, I'd relate better to them than I did before.
> *Ruth*: It gave me a kind of strength. It was saying, 'Everyone thinks like that, you're not alone in the world.'

Their response to the lesbian content of the play was more ambivalent:

> *Ruth*: I noticed that everyone was scared. It's not so much thinking about it in yourself, it's 'What are they thinking, the person sitting next to me, how do I react so that I don't embarrass myself?' Everyone is so aware of each other.

For boys and girls there is a constant process of checking out in order to assess the status of particular ideas and ways of behaving among their friends.

Eva talked about what she thought about the play.

> *Eva*: I must admit that when I first saw it I began to get a little defensive. I'd never seen anything like that before. When they

talked about lesbians, I didn't know what I felt – I think I felt a little defensive. But when we started talking about it in the discussion afterwards, it was a lot better. Everyone was talking about it, they didn't feel so shy anymore.

Ruth: I think it's very heavy, that play. When the woman was discussing it with the psychiatrist, that was really good. When the psychiatrist said, 'If you could take a pill to make you straight, would you take it?' And she said back to her 'Well if you could take a pill to make you gay, would you take it?' I loved that. That brought a lot about lesbians out into the open. But when the two started kissing, I think it was very frightening. I mean even me; I'm around lesbians all the time, because lots of my mum's friends are, and I see them kissing all the time. But those two, standing there in front of everybody, having people actually meant to be watching them, it was *very* strange ... so if I felt like that I can imagine how the others felt ...

For Ruth, the acting exposed aspects of her private life to the judgement of the other girls. She felt personally threatened. But she was right to suppose that the anxieties were greater for the others.

Lesbianism continues to be a very taboo subject, particularly the overt defiant lesbianism represented in *Is Dennis Really a Menace*. Having it talked about in the play made many of the girls feel uneasy, but having it acted out, seeing two women kiss (even if ever so fleetingly) was worse (and not comparable to moments in the play when the women performers portrayed men, and acted out sexual situations with other women which depicted heterosexuality and were therefore unproblematic). But the very fact of watching the play and discussing it afterwards seemed to break down some of the taboos and ease the situation. As Eva said, 'When it did come out, it made me feel a lot better inside.' Tentatively the girls were beginning to ask themselves why sexual relations between women (and as a consequence, the exclusion of men from the sexuality of women) should pose such problems and be such a forbidden topic. As a subject for discussion the standing of lesbianism had shifted slightly, it had ceased to be unmentionable.

At about the same time, I interviewed Lisa and her friends. For them the impact of that evening at the project was far greater than it was for Ruth and Eva. 'We talked all the way home, talk, talk, talk,' they said. Lisa was fifteen, the group of girls she hung around with were Jo, also fifteen; Carol, sixteen; and Maria, seventeen. There were some others in the group who had not attended the project. All of these girls and their families had known each other for many years, they lived on a housing estate in part of the borough which was reputed to be a tough working-class area. Most of the girls' evenings were spent at their local youth club, or sitting on the wall outside it. They looked and dressed like other girls from the working-class areas in their part of London, but in other respects they were not so typical. This was partly because of their very good relationship with the youth leader at the club, Jenny, who had a lot of confidence in the girls and encouraged them to do things they would have otherwise been unlikely to do.

> *Carol*: Jenny doesn't act as though we're a bit thick, she talks to us as if we're people. She doesn't talk down to us. That's how she gets us to do things.

Although many of the young people who went to the youth centre were in non-academic CSE streams, Jenny had convinced them to do 'O' level maths and other exam subjects at the centre after school. The girls had made films and videos with her using professional equipment; she had involved them in the administration of the centre and encouraged them to sit on the Borough Youth Committee. Quite often she talked to them about feminist and socialist ideas, and it was through her that they had heard about the girls' project. Altogether Jenny was a very important influence in their lives.

> *Carol*: It was mainly through Jenny that we thought about anything at all really. But it developed more at the project. I really liked it there, because it made everybody think more, just about the things you do every day. Everybody got talking ...

Later Carol said:

> Jenny has talked to us about feminism, but she's never really said much about lesbians.
> *Jo*: Nobody ever does. It's just not talked about. At school in sex lessons it's always a man and a woman ... 'And when you go out with a boy, this'll happen and that'll happen', and things like that. What if you don't go out with a boy? What happens then?
> *Carol*: I was just *hoping* and *hoping* it would come up at the project ... I thought it would.

The discussion after the performance of *Is Dennis Really a Menace* at the project, during which the subject of lesbianism had been raised very briefly and in very general terms, had enabled Carol to talk about her own feelings to her closest friends for the first time.

> *Carol*: It was after that session that I could first tell the others about me, because I knew then what their reactions would be, a bit. I've known I was a lesbian since I was twelve or thirteen, I used to write it in my diary, but I didn't know what to do ... I never told anybody till after the project.

The girls described the walk home on the evening when Carol told them.

> *Lisa*: We was together when she told us, walking along ... I was looking at her ... because we knew Carol was before she told us.
> *Maria*: We just sort of guessed it.
> *Lisa*: I was thinking to myself, is Carol going to turn round and say, 'Well, so am I'?
> *Maria*: We tried to get her to talk about it ... Then she told us.
> *Carol*: They just ignored it at first, didn't make any comment on it ... it wasn't till the next night, when we was a little bit drunk, that they all started talking about it ... There was Maria, Lisa, Jo, Sophie, Gill, Karen ...
> *Maria*: That night was funny, because you see it was all so new to us, right. Because you think, ooh, lesbians, yuk, funny kind of people, homosexuals. But then, someone you've known since you were about that high and grown up with, well you think, mmmm, no, there's nothing wrong with them, there's nothing different with them, you know ... First it was twenty questions: What's it like? We used to be a bit, what did she call it? Patronizing, she called us. That annoyed us first of all, but we were, when you think about it now, we were being patronizing, saying, 'We're good, we've accepted it.' Whereas we shouldn't have been like that, we should have said, 'So? So what? All right, you're gay, that's it.' We shouldn't have thought to ourselves, we're really good and that. Because we were so close we could talk about a lot of things a lot more.

The seven girls spent the evening exploring the meaning of Carol's disclosure. The next step was to decide what to do about it.

> *Carol*: After I told all my friends, I wrote off to a sort of gay group, Parents' Enquiry,[5] but that wasn't much good. They kept

telling me there was nothing to worry about. I wasn't worried anyway really. I've never thought I was disgusting or anything like that. So then I went to Grapevine,[6] to the gay teenage group.
Jo: We had to drag you up there, didn't we?
Carol: I was so scared, I wouldn't go by myself.
Jo: The group's mixed, you meet once a week and talk.
Maria: You don't have to be gay to go there, we went along with Carol. But that one bloke gave me an awful look the other day, I don't think he liked me because I'm straight. But it's not right for him to have prejudice against me, whereas I haven't got any against him.
Carol: It was all blokes there practically.

Carol didn't feel that she and the homosexual boys had much in common.

Carol: So then I started going to the discos. I met Elaine because she put an ad in *Gay News*, just to start writing. You lot didn't know that, did you? That was the first time I bought *Gay News*. Then we met, and we liked each other sort of straight away, it was good it was. I've been going out with her for five months now, I hadn't been out with anybody before. We used to go out a lot to discos, because my mother wouldn't let Elaine in the house at all – not even for half an hour.

There are very few places where gay women can go and feel comfortable.

Carol: We really only like going to the discos because you don't have to worry about everybody looking at you and coming up to you. Even in a gay pub, it's full of blokes and weirdos sitting there staring at you. I hate it.
Jo: When Carol told us she was gay, we started going to places with her, to the gay discos.
Maria: She said to us one night, 'Why don't you come up? They're not going to jump on you.'
Lisa: To tell you the truth, honestly, when I walked in there I was shitting myself, I really was, I thought everyone was going to be staring at me. I didn't want people to think that because I went up there I was a lesbian.

But it turned out to be comfortable for women who are not lesbians too.

> *Maria*: We used to just go up there. I got to like it. It was the atmosphere that's completely different from what you get in a straight disco – when you get the boys down that end and the girls down that end, with about three people dancing in the middle and that's it. And you sit there. And you're afraid to get up and dance by yourself in case the boys start laughing ... this is really different. They do come on and that down there, but you don't care because that's a woman, and that's it, you could face a woman and it wouldn't bother you. I mean, if they started anything, you wouldn't be afraid to argue back.
> *Lisa*: Whereas with a bloke, you'd think, bloody hell ...
> *Maria*: Because they'd always get back to you in some way or another; blokes get violent with you.
> *Jo*: Since I've been going down there I haven't seen a single fight. Go to a disco around here and it's guaranteed there's going to be a fight that night.

Things started to change for Jo as well.

> *Jo*: When we started to go to discos with Carol, I used to sit there and think: my God, I'm really enjoying myself, and I shouldn't be because I'm straight, I should be out there with all the boys, and that. For about two weeks my mind was really confused, I didn't know what I was going to do. Then I thought: there's only one way I'm going to find out. I can't go through life thinking: I'm straight, I'm straight, when I've got a little thing in the back of my mind saying, 'No, you're not really'. So I just tried it. And here I am. I'm still alive.

> (*Laughter from all the girls.*)

> *Lisa*: And you ain't got pink spots on your face or nothing.
> *Jo*: I caught the measles through it.

The girl Jo met at the disco was Christine whom she had first met at the project. Christine was seventeen and was on a Youth Opportunities Programme Placement with a cabinet maker. When I talked to Jo, she and Christine had been together for three months.

> *Jo*: One night up at the disco, I met two of my teachers. I couldn't believe it. And because I'm always bunking off, they said, 'Perhaps we're going to see a bit more of you now.' At first when I saw them, I tried to hide. I said, 'Cor, look, there's my teacher', and I went straight to the toilet. I didn't think: they're here for the same reason as me, they're lesbians too. I just thought: ooh, what have I done!

It often seems to be quite difficult for girls to realize that older women have the same experiences as themselves. This is one of the ideas that the project helped to break down; it was recognized that age is not always a significant difference.

All Jo's friends, including Carol, were very surprised when Jo started going out with Christine, because she had always gone out with boys before (whereas Carol had never felt that she was heterosexual). It is possible that because lesbianism was no longer quite so taboo, Jo's expression of it was to some extent a gesture of solidarity with Carol, a confirmation of their group friendship as well as an exploration of her own sexuality. In addition it could be interpreted as a kind of resistance to the acute sexism of the local male culture.

Maria and Lisa firmly defined themselves as 'straight', but they both agreed with Jo about the boys in the neighbourhood:

> The boys around here have got to be such big hard men, they really are enough to turn you off. Especially when they're all together, then they feel they've got the right to act tough.

When confronted by aspects of the boys' culture that they disliked and wanted to challenge, Maria and Lisa, as heterosexuals, were not prepared to consider the strategy of resistance that Jo had opted for. In their relationships with boys, they had to cope with quite profound contradictions; they wanted to go out with them, but most of the ones they knew they had little respect for.

> *Maria*: *Sometimes* some of them have good ideas: when one of them actually does say something intelligent, you can't believe it.

Jenny, the youth worker, told me that in her experience, the boys rarely explored their own private lives and found it almost impossible to talk to each other about personal matters. While they were in the club, they were also less likely to discuss issues of general social and political interest than the girls.

Lisa: There's one of them, he's really clever, he knows a lot. But he's National Front. I think to myself: what a fucking waste, you've got those brains, but you're stupid. All he wants is to be one of the boys, work at the post office, get someone pregnant, marry them.

Maria: When we argue with them and get the better of them, they don't like it.

Lisa: Sometimes they just use violence, like chuck things at us in the street.

Maria and Lisa and the other girls down at the club had often had negative and frustrating experiences with the boys. This probably contributed to the sympathy and sensitivity they were able to feel towards Jo and Carol.

Lisa talked about how many people seemed to think that if a woman was a lesbian she was going to make advances to all other women and behave in a sexually aggressive way.

Lisa: I've got this teacher who said, 'Beware of lesbians, they follow you down the street.' She was talking a lot of bullshit. I mean just because someone's a lesbian, it doesn't make them a different person, right. It doesn't stop us being mates. I mean, if Jo or Carol come up to my house and I'm wearing my knickers and bra, I don't think they're going to start ripping them off or something, I don't think I've got to cover myself up.

Maria: Where I work, people think like that too. They are very ignorant of the facts of being gay.

Lisa: Personally, I think there's a lot less risk of a lesbian attacking you than what there is of a bloke.

But although Lisa was quite emphatic in her statements of support during her conversations with me, Jo and Carol felt that in fact she was still very ambivalent; most of the time she seemed to accept them, but sometimes she didn't. Perhaps this was because Lisa was still in the process of making up her mind about a lot of new things. She hadn't been part of the group as long as the others, and her parents were far more strict. So coming to terms with lesbianism wasn't all straightforward. It wasn't consistently easy for any of the girls down at the club to accept the changes.

Jo: I went down to the club one night and said, 'I don't go out with Christine no more', and they were all so pleased: 'I knew Jo would go back out with boys again', and things like that. And I just sat there. Because really I *was* still going out with Christine. And I told them. And they all got embarrassed and laughed it off.

Carol: That really showed what they were thinking though, because if they were so pleased that she was going back out with a bloke, that shows that they're not all that keen on her being a lesbian in the first place.

Carol's interpretation may well have been correct. Under the circumstances it's not difficult to understand why the girls down at the club reacted in the way they did: supporting Jo and Carol was not easy, it involved them in many confrontations. The hostility towards lesbianism from most people in the community was considerable. In Carol's experience men seemed particularly threatened and angered (although some were prepared to defend them as the following incident shows).

Carol: Elaine and me went to this straight party. We'd kept separate most of the night because we didn't want to start any trouble. We were standing in the hall and Elaine put her arms around me, and we just hugged, and then we split apart. Then this man came over and said, 'Are you two lezzies?' And we said 'Yes.' And he said to me, 'I'm going to put your head through that brick wall.' A great big fat pig he was. Then this bloke leapt up and said, 'Oh, she's with me, it's all right.' But we had to go. They asked us to leave.

It is worth noting that the man who protected Carol did so by denying her lesbianism. The kind of aggression shown by the first man at the party was not uncommon.

Carol: It's nearly always blokes who come up and start taking the piss and threatening to kick your head in and that. I've never had a woman come up to me and say, 'You make me feel sick.'

Jo talked about some of the initial reactions of the boys around the club.

Jo: When some of the boys found out I was a lesbian, for two days running we had eggs on our heads. Everywhere we went it was, 'Hello Jo, fucking dirty lezzie', things like that.

Carol: Practically every time I walked past, if I was on my own or with Elaine, they went, 'Oh there goes the lezzie.' It's only one boy now, Reg, he's the worst one, he just keeps kicking me and poking me. Not hard, but it's just so aggravating. The first time they saw me with Elaine they said, 'Oh, you're not a lesbian are you?' And I said, 'Yes.' They said, 'We don't believe you, you'll have to kiss her.' They wanted a show, so we just ignored them.

Jo: One day me and Christine was kissing at the bus stop, we didn't realize some of the boys were there. And they goes, 'Oh my God, they are!' they walked off really disgusted. Scared them off. So next time they come near us and we don't want them, all we have to do is to start kissing.

Carol: They're pathetic, they go on about cucumbers and things like that, because they can't imagine it in any other way.

Carol laughed at the boys' assumption that sex necessarily included penetration and at their ignorance of the different ways in which women experience sexual pleasure. 'Sex between women is much more equal,' she said.

In spite of the opposition they encountered, the girls no longer attempted to deny their lesbianism. The exception to this is that Jo refused to tell her mother. Jo's mother Ann, and Carol's mother Margaret, had been best friends since their children were babies, both had been separated from their husbands for many years. They were very upset when they discovered that Carol was gay.

Jo: They took it really badly. They thought it was wrong. Carol's mum was really frantic.

Carol: I told her in the end, because she half knew. She had a mad fit to begin with. She was going to take me to see a psychiatrist. She went down to the GP to get a letter, and he told her, 'It's no good taking her somewhere unless she wants to change.' But as I don't, she changed her mind. She still has the odd fit though; the first time I wanted to stay out all night, she came up and got me and battered me up in the car. She's all right now, but she doesn't talk about it. Ever since that first day when she sat down and talked to me for a while, asked me some questions, since then she's just ignored it.

Carol felt that Jo's mother, Ann, was more understanding than her own. Jo said that was because Carol wasn't Ann's daughter.

Carol: Her mum was good, she was talking to me, being more kind than my mum. It was pretty amazing really. One day I was just sitting there, and she started asking me what women do when they're in bed. I never expected her to ask that, it was just because she's never known and she wanted to know. I was really stunned. It was really good, just talking about it *properly* ... but she did say she thought once I'd slept with Elaine I'd go off it. Pathetic that was! As though I'd go off it after that. (*Laugh.*)

In the months that have passed since Carol first told her mother and started going out with Elaine, things have begun to change, people have become more accepting.

Carol: I'm getting so used to being able to say it and talk about it to my friends. Practically everybody who knows me knows now. I don't have to watch what I say any more.

For a long time Jo wouldn't tell her mother although Carol thought she should, because Ann knew anyway.

Carol: Jo's mum said, 'Is Jo?' I didn't know what to say because Jo doesn't want me to tell her, so I said 'No.' But Ann wouldn't go mad, I know, she told me.

But in the end Jo did talk to her mother about it, and Ann later told Jenny, the youth worker, that she had felt much closer to Jo ever since. Carol's mother isn't so upset about it any more either.

Carol: She knows what we're doing when I stay out, she doesn't like it very much, but she accepts it now. I don't stay out very often. I suppose I can't expect her to let Elaine stay the night, she wouldn't let me if it was a boy, not in the house. But she does let Elaine come up in the evenings now, so we don't go out so much.

The boys down at the club are changing too.

Carol: Most of the time they're all right now, just every now and again when they get bored, they start taking the piss.

Robert was one of the boys who had thrown eggs at Jo and Christine.

Jo: When Robert was on his own he was fine really, he used to come up and say, 'Hello Jo, how are you?' But after the eggs thing, I used to look at him as if I didn't know him. That got him really annoyed, so then when he was with his gang he got even worse ... but he's come to since. He's eighteen now, I think they must get better when they get older. The other day, me and Sophie was sitting on the wall and he came over. We just ignored him. Then he said, 'I don't go around with the others any more.' So we said 'Why not?' And he started pouring it all out. He sat there and tried to have a serious talk with us, he said he realized how silly he'd been, and if we wanted to go with girls, we should go with girls. Things like that. He said he was fed up of going around with silly little kids. Then he actually *apologized*! We couldn't get over it. We just sat there and looked happy ... so I say hello to him now.

Jo added that she thought the other boys had quietened down now too, they all seemed to be getting used to it.

So through having the courage to persist in publicly expressing their sexual preferences (which was possible partly because of the sensitive support they had received from their friends and a few adults, and partly because of their contact with feminist ideas), Carol and Jo had in a very short space of time managed to alter the way other people in their community thought about lesbianism. It had been accommodated, transformed from being a taboo into being a relatively commonplace topic of discussion, not approved of, but tolerated.

A substantial hurdle that remained was the assertion of Carol and Jo's homosexuality in the context of work and school. Both recognized that this would be much more difficult, because they wouldn't be able to rely on long-standing friendships which could act as a foundation for the restructuring of ideas about lesbianism in the way that they had been able to do in their community. Carol had just started her first job.

> *Carol*: I don't know what's going to happen at work. Everybody round here knows now, but I'm going to have to go through the whole thing again. It was different with that lot, because I knew them. I'll tell them at work eventually I should think, because they're bound to start asking things like, 'What did you do at the weekend?' And I'm not going to lie to them, I'm not going to make up a boyfriend or anything like that ... You know, in spite of everything, I've never really thought: Oh I wish I wasn't. I don't know why it's never bothered me. The way I've been brought up you'd think it would. But it just never did.

We know very little about how girls of any class are brought up, behave and think. Youth studies have confined themselves almost exclusively to boys, and clearly a lot more work is necessary. There has been almost no consideration of the specific ways in which girls are regulated, either by parents in the family or by boys in youth clubs and on the streets.[7] It is quite probable that the confidence, courage and perception shown in the face of a very difficult situation by the girls I have written about is not typical. All the same I believe that these girls represent a growing number who refuse to consent to prevailing ideas about how they ought to think and behave, not only in the field of sexuality but in relation to all areas of their lives. An examination of what is not typical is worthwhile not just because it is interesting in itself, but also because it helps us understand the nature and processes of what *is* typical. In this case it can, for example, lead us to challenge the claim that 'femininity' is deeply embedded in the culture and that change occurs only very slowly. The second and related point which I think emerges from the experiences of these girls is that small interventions (like youth work and girls' projects) can have quite extensive repercussions. There is a ripple effect; though exactly how this works and why it takes place at some times and not at others is difficult to know.

Before concluding I want again to emphasize that in this section I have chosen to deal with one aspect only of these repercussions. In the interviews with the girls they talked at length about their families, schools, work, boyfriends, books and their future. Finally I would like to draw attention to the general assumption that feminist ideas have most pertinence for and impact on middle-class women. It is clear from the expressions of the working-class girls who attended the project that they have been as affected as girls from middle-class homes. As Lisa said, 'When it comes to things like this, no matter what background you come from, most of us feel the same.'

■ Part II

These interviews with Carol, Jo, Maria and Lisa took place in the summer of 1979; Part I of this article was written at the beginning of 1980 and can stand on its own as a discrete entity. Because publication was delayed, I decided two years later to return to some of the girls for further interviews, and to write Part II as a rather lengthy postscript, thus transforming the original piece of work into what is in effect a kind of longitudinal study. This has allowed me not only to document some of the changes in the lives and thoughts of the girls which have occurred over the two years, but also to re-examine certain points made in the initial article, and raise new ones.

The material in Part II is based mainly on interviews with Maria and Carol, each on their own, during the summer of 1981. In the course of the interviews I showed them the article I had written and told them that I intended to write a postscript which I would also show them on completion. I have included as well information gathered from conversations with Jenny which took place at different points during the interim period. In my description and analysis of these most recent events, I have attempted to maintain a continuity of approach and style; however since the intended readership is no longer the same as it was for the original article, I have also raised certain questions at a slightly more theoretical level.

I shall start off by returning to the proposition made in Part I which was deduced from what the girls themselves said in 1979. This was that small interventions like youth work and girls' projects could have quite extensive repercussions, and that lesbianism had ceased to be taboo and had become in some ways tolerated within the community in which the girls lived. This kind of claim, in order to be fully substantiated, requires widespread interviewing and observation within the community. Since this was not possible, I decided that the most fruitful approach was to ask the girls and Jenny for their opinion on the matter. Maria's response was emphatic:

> People's views did change a lot. Everybody's views were just broadened.

She talked about how she and many of her friends could no longer take heterosexuality for granted.

> *Maria*: Since Jo and Carol, I've never thought of anybody as 'straight'. You shouldn't assume that anyone is just heterosexual.

When Maria said she was convinced that the views of all those involved had broadened as a result of the discussions and confrontations triggered by Carol's and Jo's lesbianism, she was perhaps referring principally to the people of her own age who attended the youth centre; from her account it appears that these were mainly girls, though she also made a specific reference to a boy whom she felt had changed. The overall impression that emerges is that the greatest and most painless changes took place among the girls' own (female) contemporaries. However, Maria also talked about the conversations she had had with Carol's and Jo's mothers and with the women at the local shop where she used to have a Saturday job, and told me that she felt that their opinions had altered too.

When I asked Jenny how she felt about the assertion that there had been a slight shift in attitudes among the people of the community in which the youth centre was located, she agreed with it, and in her answer referred mainly to the adults. She was very close to several of the mothers in the neighbourhood, among them Jo's and Carol's. Most people in the area had lived there a long time and knew each other well, and Jenny felt that in the period after Jo and Carol told people they were gay, there were a number of serious discussions about homosexuality among them. Many of the women came to terms with it, she claimed, though not always easily. On one occasion they even defended it. About a year after Carol and Jo had started having lesbian relationships, Carol's mother, Margaret, gave a birthday party for one of Carol's younger sisters and asked Jo to help out. One of the children who went to the party was the young daughter of a man named Reg who used to live on the estate and had known Jo's and Carol's families for many years. When Reg discovered, shortly after the party, that Jo had been present at it, that (as Carol put it) 'this "disgusting" lesbian had been near his daughter,' he went back to Carol's house, and although Jo and Carol and their mothers tried to reason with him, he could only shout. He threatened to beat the girls up and come back with his mates to burn the house down. Jenny told me that many of the women on the estate rallied angrily to the defence of the girls over this and vowed never to talk to Reg again. She interpreted the event as evidence of Margaret's and Ann's greater tolerance towards lesbianism, and since it was Ann (Jo's mother) who told her about the incident, she was obviously in a good position to make this kind of assessment. Carol, however, was a little more sceptical: 'It's true they were great at the time, that they were really angry, but I think they were defending us more as their children than as lesbians.'

It is impossible to establish the precise nature of either Ann's or Margaret's motives on this occasion, or of their more general responses to Jo and Carol's lesbianism, because in the case of both women, their feelings about their daughters' sexuality was affected by a number of disparate factors. There certainly is evidence to indicate that Margaret has changed a great deal since her first panicky attempt to get Carol to see a psychiatrist and her initial point-blank refusal to have Elaine in the house. Margaret had been brought up as a Catholic, and the reservations she continued to have seemed a great deal to do with her anxieties about all unsanctioned expressions of sexuality. For her, homosexuality was included in this category. Carol described to me how Margaret eventually made the decision to allow Elaine to stay over in her daughter's bed.

Carol: I thought she'd never do it. But one night nearly two years ago, it was my seventeenth birthday and Elaine was there, my mum said, 'Come on, I'll take you to the pub.' So we went to the pub and got really pissed, and my mum was telling Elaine all about me when I was a baby. Then I said, 'Well, Elaine's got to go now, to get her last train,' and Mum said, 'Oh, no, it's OK, she can stay, but she can't stay in your bed.' All right. But she did, we just collapsed we were so pissed. But then Mum said, 'Well OK, Elaine can stay at weekends, silly her going all the way home. But she'll have to stay in your bed and you can sleep with me.' And I said, 'OK.' It seemed reasonable enough, I just thought I'll work it up from there. But when it came to it – the first Friday – I couldn't stand it, it was worse than her going home because at least then she was twelve miles away, but being fifteen foot down the corridor, I couldn't stand it. So I said to my mum, 'I'm going in there to sleep with her.' And she said, 'If you do that, Elaine can never stay again.' So I said, 'What is it you mind?' And she said, 'Well, it's not right, is it, sex in your mother's home.' So I said, 'What did you do with Bill (the bloke she used to live with) when he used to stay? You slept with him, you didn't just cuddle him and go to sleep.' And she said, 'Ah, I knew you'd throw that back in my face.' Because she felt really guilty that she'd had a man living there. Well, then I started getting a bit bold and said, 'You just don't like sex very much, you think it should be done when you're married. But we're not going to get married, are we?' I think she didn't really like sex, because she thought it shouldn't be done in your mother's house, because it wasn't 'decent'. I kept saying, 'Why, why, why is it wrong?' And she just said, 'Well you're not supposed to, it's not decent.' And I said, 'Of course it's decent, people do it all the time.' So we talked about it for about three hours. All night. About her attitudes to it and why I couldn't sleep there. I mean it's bloody stupid that she doesn't let my sister's boyfriend stay over either.

In the end, she just cried, and she said, 'Go on, go in there, go on, go in there,' in a really martyred tone. And I said, 'All right then Mum,' and just went in there. And after all that, Elaine was asleep! But it was really good, I'm glad that I talked to Mum like that. We were just talking for hours and hours. After that she let Elaine stay at the weekends.

Different factors influenced Jo's mother, Ann. Her feelings about her daughter's lesbianism were complicated by the fact that Jo's relationship with Christine was often unhappy.

> *Carol*: Initially Ann was upset because Christine was a woman, but I think she would have come to terms with it in the end. But because Christine hurt Jo so much, that's what put her completely off the idea. I mean Jo was really hurt by the whole affair. It was horrible to see it and not be able to do anything about it.

It is important to point out here that Christine was not interviewed and in all likelihood would have had a quite different version of these events. In spite of this, I feel Maria's and Carol's opinions must be documented because it was clear that they considered the nature of the particular relationship to be one of the most significant developments of the past two years. Both of them had a lot to say about it.

> *Carol*: It was incredible; before, Jo was always bubbly and lively, but for the two years she was with Christine she never made one friend, because Christine was so bloody jealous.
> *Maria*: Christine was really messing her about with other girls. Jo found out that it wasn't all nice, she found out all the grotty bits – that women can be just as bad as blokes at times.
> *Carol*: I think Christine was the nearest Jo could have got to a bloke, in her attitudes to women. You can't just assume that every lesbian is also a feminist, or thinks of women in any different way from how a man would. And you know, I think that Jo and I both just assumed that at the beginning.

This appears to be a harsh criticism of Christine. It must not be forgotten that Jo was prepared to engage in the relationship for two years, and that almost certainly there were positive factors in it for her to which Carol and Maria did not refer, or perhaps chose not to see. To them, as well as to Ann, it was the negative aspects which appeared paramount. They told me that at one point Jo was so miserable about Christine she took an overdose of sleeping pills and alcohol and had to go to hospital.

> *Maria*: That drove Ann really mad. She didn't want Christine ever to come to the house. If Christine had even attempted to knock on the door Ann would have smashed her one.

It seems pretty clear that Ann's feelings about lesbianism were coloured by the particular relationship Jo was involved in. Carol insisted that Ann's hostility didn't necessarily imply hostility towards lesbianism in general. She mentioned again how moved she had been when, right at the beginning, Ann had talked to her seriously about lesbian sex; and although she wasn't convinced that at the time of the burning threats Ann and Margaret had defended Jo and herself as lesbians rather than as daughters, all the same she maintained that significant changes had taken place in the attitudes of their mothers and of other people – it was not that anybody approved, but people had become more tolerant and 'were forced to think more, mainly'.

In this respect, Carol agreed with the points about change made in Part I of this article and understood that these claims were quite modest. In addition both Maria and Carol told me that there was no question that the trigger for the interrogation and declaration of lesbianism among the girls of the group was the performance of *Is Dennis Really a Menace* at the girls' project, and the discussion which followed it.

> *Carol*: God knows when I would have told them otherwise.

There is also no doubt in their minds that Jenny has had a tremendous influence on their lives. Carol said: 'It was Jenny who made us realize there were alternatives.' Jenny was both supportive and encouraging.

> *Carol*: She pushed us into going to the project in the first place.
> *Maria*: She got it into our minds that if you're a woman, don't let them look down to you. You've got your rights. I was thinking about that the other day – we really used to have some rows with people. Since we've stopped coming to the youth centre so much – because everyone has split up – our views have changed. We're not all into it as much as we used to be. It's not women, women, women, all the time. At one time I was a fanatic. Now, it's give a little and take a little. I still read *Spare Rib*, though not all the time. But on the subject of lesbianism my views haven't changed.

Thus, the girls – now young women – had (predictably) made a number of transitions in their lives since the summer of 1979. In some respects the events which had taken place two years earlier continued to have repercussions and a direct influence on the way they thought and behaved. In other respects the effects had been modified by new experiences.

Maria, Carol, Jo, Lisa and their other friends from the club were no longer as close to each other as they had been that summer.

> *Carol*: Since then we've all drifted a bit. That was the closest we ever got, it was really intense.

Both Carol and Maria said that reading through this article aroused very vivid memories in them. With hindsight Maria was able to analyse what underlay one aspect of the confusion and excitement that she and several of her friends had felt when they started to consider the idea, in response to Carol's and particularly Jo's experiences, that sexuality was not fixed.

> *Maria*: It was really confusing, because every single one of us – we didn't admit it at the time, not till months or a year later – but everyone of us had sat down and actually thought, could I ever be gay?

For some of the group the assumption that sexual preferences are immutable continues to be questioned, as can be seen from Maria's and Carol's descriptions of the general developments in their own and in Jo's and Lisa's lives over the last two years. Maria, now nineteen and the oldest of the group, had just spent two years training to be a hairdresser. She told me she had really enjoyed it, and was now looking for work. For about a year, she had been going out with a man she had met at college.

> *Maria*: We've had our rocky patches now and then. At one time I said, 'Yes, this is the bloke for me', and I lost all my ideas and interests. It was really weird, I was becoming the girl I didn't want to become. You know what I mean? Like I was looking up to him for everything, letting him decide where to go ... But now I'm getting my ideas back again, and I'm starting to think on my own. And I still think that there could be the possibility that one day I could have a relationship with a woman. I don't know. Just see what happens. I don't think I'd not want to have it, I'd like to experience it. But just at the minute I'm quite happy as I am.

Lisa had left school at Easter and was working in a large office.

> *Maria*: She really enjoys it, she's really good at her work. She's been going out with a bloke called Dave for about two months. If you spoke to Lisa now, I don't know what she'd say, but I

think she'd say, 'Well, I'm definitely straight, and that's it', because she's getting on so well with Dave.

Jo (now seventeen) had just got a job in a restaurant. When her relationship with Christine finally ended she started going out with Mike, the boy she had been going out with when she first met Christine. A few months ago she had a miscarriage, and now she and Mike are trying for a baby again.

> *Maria*: I used to go round and talk to Jo's mum. Once she said, 'Do you think Jo will change back?' And I said, 'Well, I don't know, I don't know.' I mean Carol, she always will be gay, but with Jo I always had this strange feeling that she'd get back with Mike. When her mum first heard she was pregnant, it was another shock to her. Her mum hasn't stopped having these shocks with Jo. Every time I go over there she says, 'She's doing my brain in again.' But I think she's quite pleased.

Maria talked about the changes in Jo.

> *Maria*: It's like she's never been gay, just like she's been with him all the time. She rang me up one day to tell me. I knew she hadn't been getting on well with Christine. She rings up and goes, 'I didn't realize it then, but I realize it now, it was just a phase that I was going through.' She goes, 'I regret it now' I said, 'Well you shouldn't regret it' ... I think she's happy enough now.

Jo wouldn't come with Carol when we arranged to do the interview. Carol said caustically, 'Pretty obvious why she won't.' Although she didn't say so, I think that one of the reasons she was so angry with Christine for hurting Jo was because it had meant that as a consequence she had lost Jo's companionship – she felt more isolated. Carol said that she and Jo still got on well, but that they rarely saw each other any more because they went out to different places.

> *Carol*: She sees one of my younger sisters down at the pub. The thing is that because Jo was with Christine and got so hurt, she won't even consider having a relationship with a woman again. Never. It's completely out of the question now, because of Christine. She won't even come for a drink with me somewhere where there might be gay women. She just won't. Well, she says one day when she's drunk, she might.

This clearly reluctant concession to Carol, seems to indicate that although Jo now appears firmly and defensively heterosexual, she has not totally denied the significance in her life of sexual relationships and friendships with lesbians. It is also worth noting that Jo's actual relationship with Christine, which I described when I discussed her mother's response to it, was quite different from what she had anticipated it would be. My interpretation two years ago (see p.255, in Part I) in which I suggested that Jo's lesbianism was in some measure a resistance to the sexism of the local male culture, has turned out to be far too simple. Jo was obviously not able to jettison totally the pervasive assumptions about gender roles within relationships – about passivity and activity – any more than Christine was. In fact paradoxically Jo and Christine seemed more tied to them in the context of their lesbian relationship, at least at a visible level, than Jo appeared to be in her relationship with Mike. One could speculate that Jo's pregnancy represented cast-iron evidence of her femininity and so freed her to be less passive in other respects than she was while she was with Christine.

> *Maria*: Being with Christine calmed Jo down. In that relationship, Christine was the more domineering one. Before, Jo would always say what she wanted to say, and she's like she used to be now.

Carol is working for a bank, she has been there two years and has been promoted, but she finds the work boring. She would like to do something more challenging, though she is not yet sure what. Her colleagues at work know that she is a lesbian and a feminist and seem accepting, and her relationship with them is quite good in spite of not having much in common. They have elected her as their Union representative because they know that she is prepared to argue for what she believes in. Carol is still going out with Elaine. It has been two and a half years now and they continue to get on very well with each other, although about a year ago they broke up for about three months.

> *Carol*: I wasn't glad at the time, but I'm glad now, because when I met Elaine ... I met her straight away, and I often thought what would it be like to just go out on my own and meet people. It was terrible when it happened, but after a month or so, even though I was sorry not to see her, I was glad, because it gave me

the opportunity to make friends of my own and not just friends of hers.

Carol talked about the effect that Jo going out with Mike again had had on her own mother.

> *Carol*: Up until that happened my mum had thought well, right, this is the way she is, and just accepted it. But as soon as Jo started going out with Mike again, it was like, will it happen to you?

Then she added:

> I'm not saying it won't, but it's not very likely in the near future anyway.

She was aware that for most of the people who know her this would come as a surprise and that compared with two years earlier it indicated a change in her feelings.

> *Carol*: I was thinking that I'd changed when I read the article. But it was early days then, wasn't it? I was preaching, I was very enthusiastic about everything. I think I'm gay now. But I'm not going to say that in twenty years time I'd never have any relationship with a man. It seems unlikely, but I'm not ruling it out. That would be rather a stupid thing to do I think.

So what other points are to be drawn from these new conversations? In this section I want to consider some methodological issues which emerge from the particular nature of my relationship with the girls and, at a more general level, from the dilemmas of feminist research. Secondly I want to look more specifically at the way in which the impact of feminism on the girls has combined with the more general process of maturation and the influence of significant adults to produce certain effects. Finally I intend to examine some of the ways in which the new material ties in with the conclusions arrived at in the first part of this article.

First however, I want briefly to refer to the terminological issue which has political and theoretical ramifications. Interest in working with younger women and girls and recruiting them into the women's movement is a relatively recent phenomenon, as is theoretical interest in generational distinctions. Feminism of the early seventies was concerned principally with women in the family and in the workplace. Although there was concern about sexist educational materials[8] and a few relatively isolated attempts were made at presenting feminist issues to adolescents,[9] it is only since the late 1970s that we have seen a general shift of concern towards younger women and girls, in the form of youth work directed specifically at girls, conferences and newsletters for workers with girls,[10] journals set up by girls, anti-sexist programmes in schools etc. And it is out of this section of the movement that the problem of terminology has arisen: are females under eighteen years of age 'girls' or 'young women'? For some of the women (young and older) involved in these activities, it seems as inappropriate and derogatory to call these people 'girls' as it has been to call adult women 'girls' for those in the mainstream of the movement.[11] Yet, as is obvious from my article, it seems to me useful and indeed necessary to maintain at times a conventional distinction between adults and younger people. It is true that this form not only describes but in some measure reinforces generational differences and power relations, while simultaneously minimizing the significance of gender as a unifying principle. But the implications of doing away altogether with the conceptual categories of 'boys' and 'girls' would be I think to obscure the specificity of the social construction of youth and childhood – the distinct oppression and denial of independence to which young people are subject in all spheres. Thus I have retained the use of 'girls' to describe the young females in this article, particularly in the discussion of the periods during which they are still at school and economically dependent; though in doing so I am certainly not denying the importance, especially for political organization, of the similarity of the subordination and interests which exists between women and girls.[12]

Next I want to discuss two related methodological issues. These are: first, the nature of my relationship with Carol, Jo, Maria and Lisa; and secondly, the questions raised by feminist research of this kind. My relationship with the girls was in the first instance superficial. I met them every Thursday evening over a period of ten weeks (they all attended practically every session) and chatted to them no more often than to any of the other girls, though in a sense the contact was special in that they knew I was a good friend of Jenny's. When, a couple of months later, I went to interview them to find out their impressions of the project, Jo, Lisa, and Maria chose to talk to me together. (Carol was not at the club that evening.) The interview, which lasted two and a half hours, was far more animated and wide-ranging as well as longer than any I had had with other girls from the project; and it became clear later, as I read over the transcript of what was said on that evening, that they were working up to the point where they could tell me about this pretty momentous occurrence in their lives. I was the first adult they had confided in, and they were both excited and remarkably forthright. That summer I had one further very long interview with Jo and Carol. So our initial hours of contact were very limited, and I do not pretend in anyway to have been a very significant figure in their lives. On the other hand, precisely because I was relatively remote from their everyday world, yet also one of the organizers of the project and a friend of Jenny's, I was perhaps ideally placed to be the one to listen to their story. And of course I was not neutral as I listened, my position was a partisan one. Although I didn't say very much, it must have been clear that I was full of respect for their courage, for their clarity and subtlety of thought, for the support they offered to each other, and for the way in which they challenged in general what girls are supposed to do and say. It is quite possible therefore that my response and my situation placed me into the category of supportive adult (along with Jenny) and so in some small way affected the mode in which their subsequent lives were lived out.

This phenomenon, in which the researcher affects the outcome of the research in which she is involved, is of course not unique; however it remains important to acknowledge it. Ann Oakley (Oakley, 1981:58), in her article 'Interviewing Women', has referred to:

> the mythology of 'hygienic' research with its accompanying mystification of the researcher and the researched as objective instruments of data production ...

and urges that this:

> be replaced by the recognition that personal involvement is more than dangerous bias – it is the condition under which people come to know each other and to admit others into their lives.

'Intimacy', she argues, is not possible without 'reciprocity'; that is to say that the interviewing process must offer some personal satisfaction to the interviewees. This is both in order that, as feminist research, it be effective and valuable so that it facilitates the making visible of women's experiences and thus makes a contribution to the sociology of women; and, as importantly, in order that it be politically justifiable so that interviewees do not consider themselves exploited as a source of data, but on the contrary feel that the intervention has been positive both in relation to their own lives and the lives of others in their situation.

With these criteria in mind therefore, I want to refer to the comments made by Maria and Carol on the text of Part I. Both said they thought it accurate, really interesting, and were pleased it was going to be published. Carol was enthusiastic about the idea of writing a postscript; she said that she and her friends were amazed that anyone should consider that what they had to say was important enough to write about. On an earlier occasion Jo had said that she saw no reason to change her and her friends' names for the article (though on this I decided to override her judgement). When Maria told me how much she liked the article she added that she thought most people of her age would understand it. At the end of my last interview with her, having explained to her the hazards of this kind of research for feminists, I asked her whether she felt she had been 'used' at all.

> *Maria*: No, no, not at all, I feel sort of – you know – sort of proud in a way. I was in a really bad low all day today, I've cheered up a lot now.

At this point in the concluding section I want to examine the specific forms that the young women's ideas and behaviour have taken as a consequence of their association with feminism. Of course in this article I have barely referred to areas like work and politics; but in the realm of sexuality and maturation, feminism has combined with a more general adolescent rebellion to produce certain kinds of outcomes in the lives of these girls. Their refusal to concede to orthodox processes of sexual categorization – that is to say their refusal to accept that sexuality must be heterosexual or indeed fixed – has, it seems to me, two components. On the one hand, this refusal is linked to a generational resistance to the status of youth, which in its specifically gendered form is likely to be expressed in the arena of sexuality (rather than, say, street crime) and can include pregnancy and motherhood as a means of subverting parental and school authority. This is certainly not to suggest that all adolescent expressions of sexuality are of this kind, but rather, that the adoption of an 'adult' form of sexual behaviour is probably the most common strategy employed by girls in their confrontation with the social constraints of adolescence. But this strategy is limited by its failure to challenge the subordination of femininity; its paradoxical nature lies in the fact that it frees girls to some extent from the regulation of adults while simultaneously reinforcing their (highly probable) regulation by the boys with whom they have sexual relationships. And it is precisely this contradictory quagmire that the girls I interviewed were helped to negotiate because of their contact with feminist ideas. Through their refusal to consent to heterosexuality as the only valid form of sexual expression, they were able, as young women, to engage in *both* rebellious *and* autonomous behaviour.

But in addition, and this is the other component, because the girls' refusal to consent to orthodox processes of sexual categorization derived (in part) from an understanding of feminist principles, they were also able to make sense of Jo's unfortunate relationship with Christine; they felt that Christine was not a feminist, she behaved like most of the men they knew. Feminist principles however, as is well known, are not uniform, and it looks as though Jo's experience with Christine was one of the events which contributed towards the shift that can be detected in the young women's attitudes over the two years. I am not suggesting that they were conscious that these moves within the spectrum of feminist politics and theory were being made. All the same I think there is evidence of a rejection of an essentialist position, which identifies all women as essentially wonderful, to one which recognizes that some women, even if they are lesbians, are not; and therefore to a position in which the social nature and fluidity of gender construction are implicitly understood. And perhaps it follows that if not all women are wonderful, some men might be. It is this phenomenon which helps to explain the most striking feature to emerge from the second round of conversations: Maria, Carol and Jo have made it clear that for them sexual preferences are not fixed; neither heterosexuality nor homosexuality are assumed.

Finally I want to return to one of the dominant themes of both Part I and Part II of the article. After examining the content of the second round of interviews I believe that justifiable grounds continue to exist for arguing that certain changes took place as an indirect consequence of: the influence and support of a feminist youth worker; the discussions and implicit support of women workers and other girls engendered at a girls' project which ran for ten weeks only. Although these changes, mediated by the actions of the girls, are complex and contradictory, I think they cannot be denied. To do so seems to me to be taking on board the conceptual approach adhered to by certain sectors of the left in which the state and ideology, defined in both capitalist and patriarchal terms, are perceived as so monolithic that no inroads can be made.[13] Yet we are all aware that over the last twelve years the women's movement and the ideas that the movement has generated have had a very substantial impact. But we have grown accustomed to assuming that this impact has been confined mainly to middle-class university-educated women, that is to say, to those who have articulated that impact and been politically involved in the mainstream of the movement. However it is quite possible that participation in the movement is no indicator at all of its influence. And perhaps the description of the events in these girls' lives constitutes an exemplar of how the process operates.

■ Notes

Many people contributed to this piece of work in different ways. I particularly want to acknowledge my indebtedness to Sue Crockford, Ann, Anna, Antonella, Jamie, Hermine, Rebecca, the organizing group of the girls' project, and Beryl and the Perils, without whom there would have been nothing to write. Thanks also to Clara Connelly, Angela McRobbie, Suzy Oboler and Diana Leonard for their support and comments.

1 See, for example, *Veronica 4 Rose*, a film about young lesbians by Melanie Chait, shown on Channel 4 in 1984 and available for hire from Cinema of Women, 27 Clerkenwell Close, London EC1R OAT; tel. 01-251 4978. See also *Framed Youth*, a documentary by the Lesbian and Gay Youth Video Project, winner of the 1984 Grierson Award and distributed by The Other Cinema, 79 Wardour Street, London W1V 3TH; tel. 01 734 8508.

2 Part 1 of this article was not originally written with a *Feminist Review* audience in mind. It was intended to be part of a reader directed primarily at young women in the age group of those I interviewed.

3 A video of the play has been made and is available from the National Association of Youth Clubs, PO Box 1, Blackburn House, Nuneaton, Warwickshire CV11 4DS.

4 The real names of the people quoted in this article have been changed.

5 A group of people who have organized on the basis of being the parents of homosexuals.

6 An advisory centre for young people in north London which deals with personal and sexual problems. For a while, Grapevine's premises were being used by the Gay Teenage Group for their meetings. For further information about the group, now called Lesbian and Gay Teenage Group, tel. 01-263 5932.

7 These points have been expanded in my article in *Schooling and Culture* (Nava, 1981).

8 See, for example, Northern Women's Education Study Group (1972).

9 For example, the Women's Theatre Group worked primarily in schools and youth clubs from 1974. One of their plays of that period, *My Mother Says I Never Should*, was published in 1980.

10 The National Association of Youth Clubs (NAYC) publish a newsletter called *Working With Girls*, available from 70 St Nicholas Circle, Leicester.

11 An issue of *Girls Line* advertises a 'feminist drama workshop for young women aged nine to twelve'. For another interesting example of shifts in language use since the late 1960s, see *Shrew* (1970), the journal of the Women's Liberation Workshop, in which feminist demonstrators are called 'girls' by other feminists.

12 For a longer discussion of the relative significance of gender and generational distinctions, see Nava (1981).

13 For example, see Althusser's reference to the radical teacher as a kind of ineffectual hero (1971).

A note of interest to end up with: I worked on this article on and off for over a year and a half, and it was only as I was typing up the final clean copy that I realized the two fictional names I had given the mothers in the story were virtually those of my own mother, Anna Margareta!

Upsetting an Applecart: Difference, Desire and Lesbian Sadomasochism

Susan Ardill and Sue O'Sullivan

We've been asked to write an updated introduction for our article two months before it actually hits the streets in the Summer 1986 issue of Feminist Review. *So at this point we're in a bit of a vacuum, wondering what sort of reaction it will eventually get.*

The moment we handed over our article, bid it goodbye after struggling to get it written, we were struck by all the things we'd left out, didn't explain properly or express strongly enough. Perhaps this was more than just the usual pre-publication nerves. In a letter to us a friend, Diane Hamer, wrote: 'If I have any criticisms of the article, it would be that it feels slightly unbalanced – maybe it too quickly shifts from the particular to the general and back. This is partly due to the SM debate itself. It has always been a short cut to a whole host of issues, but that isn't immediately obvious to those who weren't actually involved in the debate, so SM takes on this appearance of being "everything and nothing".'

We agree with her, and think that the actual contradiction within the way SM is taken up as an issue was reproduced in the way we wrote the article. Thus there is an unresolved tension between general theoretical exploration and the chronological story. Details from both had to be sacrificed (including many spicy anecdotes). So we're left with the feeling that we didn't capture it all, or as we wanted.

We're curious about the reception our article will get. We're not immune to the climate of not talking openly for fear of ridicule or excommunication. But we have to reiterate that talking about sadomasochism hasn't turned us into fiends, and at one level it's bemusing constantly to come up against horror and incomprehension.

We also want to make clear that we do not want our criticisms of some aspects of lesbian feminism to be used by heterosexual feminists, or non-feminists, to shore themselves up. Too often recently, in newspapers and magazines, we have seen self-congratulatory articles by straight women, criticizing 'separatists' for rigidity and moralism. Along with many other lesbian writers, we've tried to be open about our sexuality and our subculture. We've seen very little besides defensiveness from heterosexual feminists about their own sexual practices.

This is by no means a definitive article about the issues raised by sadomasochism; we haven't even attempted a thorough investigation of those issues, for instance around racism, public and private behaviour, fashion. Instead it is an article about one political struggle. We had to seize the time to write just about that, with all its contradictions and omissions. We hope it will be read as a working article ... from a struggle in progress.

This article is about an ideological and political set-to over defining, discussing and organizing around sexuality as lesbians in the mid-eighties in Britain.

We were both involved in the battle at the London Lesbian and Gay Centre (LLGC) over whether SM (sadomasochism) groups should be able to meet there. This battle went on for almost six months in 1985 – explosively, at times viciously. It was not just confined to the centre. Battlelines were drawn in many lesbian groups, women's centres, even bars and discos. The consequences linger today.

We want to talk about the different feminist politics which informed the groups engaged in the tactics and open fights which went on over the months. We want critically to examine SM and its lesbian feminist manifestations. We want to discuss politics which arise out of and around our sexual practice.

Although this was ostensibly a political struggle over a sexual practice, sex remained the silent item on the agenda.

It seems to us that in the London Women's Liberation Movement (WLM) there is often a chasm between discussions about the 'politics of sexuality' and discussions about what our actual different sexual practices are. Over and over, workshops at conferences, even whole conferences, bill themselves as being about sexuality, only to turn into talk shops about the things which *determine* sexuality, or how frightening it is actually to talk about sex. Evocative words are thrown around, like 'pleasure', 'danger', 'lust', 'romance', but as often as not, on the day, it's other words which apply, like distance, analysis, evasion – and above all, frustration, confusion and boredom.

Sexuality is for both of us a political and a personal concept and fact. Intriguing, jagged, hurting, sunlight and shadows, movement and moment. Recalled alone and recalling together. But the divide remains as we attempt to bridge it. That's the skirmish which we, two socialist-feminist lesbian friends, are having to go through to get this article out.

We approach our sexuality to capture it. But is it ever steady enough to capture? To haul into the political arena? Can we break through the reactions of our feminist sisters, lovers and friends? Their disapproval or feigned boredom makes us falter, blush and backtrack. Is talking about sex political? Can politics encompass sex? Is feminism a dour tendency? Do feminists do peculiars things in secret? Do we tend to come unstuck in sex? Do we get stuck up about sex? Is secret sexy? Does any of it matter in cold, cruel light?

Here *we* are, with daring words to start yet knowing another page will be quite ordinary. But that's it: how to talk about sex – boring, passionate, regular, surprising, absent – and how it intersects with different women's daily lives as Black or white women, as workers, as people in relationships, with or without children, as feminists meeting all the oppressions and hierarchies of this society. Because it *does* matter – though it matters differently in different historical moments, in different geographical areas. The literature of oppressed people so often contains the dreams which sexuality seems to offer, intertwined with their struggles to do with class, with race and imperialism, and with gender roles.

The movements for gay, lesbian and women's liberation have offered a way to understand, change or enhance those dreams. Or, rather, they have increasingly offered many *different ways*.

■ Shattering reality

This article is being written at a time of depression and lack of confidence in feminist and left-wing politics. The reality of fragmentation and the development of a politics around the autonomy of 'new' political constituencies – women, Black people, gay men, lesbians, old people, disabled people – has thrown up its own theoretical discussion around 'difference'.

From the beginning of the women's liberation movement in the west, when differences were sheltered (and hidden) under the benign umbrella of sisterhood, we moved to the situation of the early 1980s when 'differences' pulled down the umbrella and claimed sisterhood as an autonomous state for their own group. A multitude of identities defined lives, loyalties and political correctness, as the totalizing world view feminism offered to some, mainly white, women cracked open. Conflict became the keynote.

This article is about one such conflict – one which was crucially concerned with differences *between* lesbians. It struck both of us that while recognition for the oppression of different 'other' groups of people constantly came up during this struggle, in fact our political opponents had a basic difficulty in acknowledging that within our own shared identity of lesbianism, other women could drastically differ from them in attitude or practice. We wanted to take apart this apparent contradiction, wondering if it could offer us any insights into the roots of the bitterness of the conflict, or give us any help in creating the alliances or coalitions we must make to affect radical change.

▓ Hello. What's your name?

What we felt happened with the increasing dominance of 'identity' as the organizing factor of so many feminist activities and discussions is that 'naming' and 'claiming' came to be invested with a peculiar moral authority. Just to *name* yourself as part of a given group is to *claim* a moral backing for your words and actions.

Where does this sort of 'naming' get its power? Why have certain words become icons? In the LLGC battle, for example, speeches by women who were opposing SM often began with a declaration of identity: for example, 'I am a lesbian mother and I think ...' In this context the words 'lesbian mother' are meant to convey a specific moral weight, not just that of personal experience. What was being invoked was a particular feminist ideology. We cannot *name* this ideology. It's not a simple political tendency, but an amalgam of various strands of feminist politics. As we see it, there are two key ingredients: an analysis of the world as made up of a fixed hierarchy of oppressions (or a select collection of oppressions) around gender, sexuality, race and ethnicity, age and ability; and notions of the 'authenticity' of subjective experience – experience which can be understood only with reference to the hierarchy. So, to say, 'I am a lesbian mother' within this mode of politics during the LLGC struggle was to allude to a whole set of oppressions as a way of validating the speaker's current political position. (A number of other things were going on too, but here we want to get to the root of the tone of self-righteousness we often heard.) Within these politics, there's little room for distinguishing between politics and those who speak them, little space for such things as evaluation of strategies or criticism, or making mistakes.

Somehow, the radical power of uncovering by describing, creating language for experiences that have previously gone unarticulated, just becomes labelling, slotting things neatly into place. In this value system 'naming' and 'experience' are privileged – but there is little room for movement once the words are out. To speak experiences, to claim identities, is to be tied into positions, and everything is assumed to follow on from them. A lesbian mother, then, will automatically have certain positions on men, women, money ... sex.

The inherent problem with taking subjective experience as the main key to political action is that people have differing experiences. Not only that, they may also interpret the same experience in differing ways. The solution of some feminists, be they revolutionary feminists, cultural feminists or socialist-feminists, is to fall back on their own particular hierarchy model; those more towards the bottom bear more of the weight so our/their experiences must speak more 'truthfully' of oppression. In this context, any clash, whether between groups or individuals, becomes a matter of rank determining righteousness. While this hierarchy model has developed partly as a response to difference, and conflict, it doesn't do particularly well with diversity or contradiction. It too easily lends itself to a politics of 'truth'. Taken to extremes, if there are divisions within the same 'rank' or group, suppression becomes necessary, so as to protect the 'official' version's claim to define and describe the oppression.

These basic premises, with their reliance on the truth of the hierarchy or the sacrosanct nature of a collection of oppressions, and the claiming of identities, have increasingly become an implicit part of much feminist politics. They act as the framework, the supports, for political positions around the different issues.

Feminists' ideas about lesbianism have formed and changed over time. In the last few years one ideology of lesbian feminism became dominant and claimed feminism for itself. This ideology operates within the framework we have just outlined. 'Anger', 'identity', 'experience' have become the hallowed passwords among large numbers of lesbian feminists.

Imagine their consternation, then, if another group of lesbians pops up – who are *angry* and who want to *identify* around a different *experience* and *interpretation* of it. But this interpretation, in the realm of sexuality (that most subjectively experienced area), upsets the whole previous applecart of lesbian feminist assumptions about who lesbians are. It is this fundamental clash which forms the basis of the entanglements over SM, and because it's a struggle over definitions and the power to define, now at the crux of some political positions, emotions ran high. Unravelling the tangles at the roots of the bitterness that fuelled the LLGC SM debate has been emotionally fraught for us as participants, and difficult to do. But ultimately that unravelling exposes many of the underpinnings of the various politics involved. It presents possibilities for stating differences and divisions while working to change and challenge exploiting power. And, in the course of the struggle at the LLGC, it's just possible there started a fracture which could impede the ascendancy of a brand of lesbian feminist politics which has been prevalent in this country for long enough.

■ The premise of the premises

The London Lesbian and Gay Centre is the result of certain possibilities meeting certain perceived needs. It would not exist in the form it does today without the politics which the radical Labour GLC embraced and propagated. It wouldn't exist as it does now if a particular cross-section of gay men and lesbians hadn't come together with an understanding of all this and with a vision of a centre.

The centre, an old four-storey building, almost across from London's Farringdon tube, opened unofficially and unfinished in late December 1984. The plans were for stylish and well-appointed premises which would meet the needs of a wide variety of London's gay and lesbian population. Included were the inevitable disco/bar/theatre space, a café and kitchen, another bar, a bookshop run by Gays the Word, a creche, a large lounge and meeting room for lesbians, a media resource floor, various centre offices and a number of spaces for rent to gay and lesbian projects and enterprises.

By the time of the 'official' opening in March 1985 the centre was being booked for meeting space by a number of different groups. The co-opted management committee (MC) had already discussed the issues which would soon break out into bitter fighting between users or potential users of the centre. Wendy Clark, one of the co-opted MC members, told us, 'We knew from the women's movement what some of the issues would be and that sometimes clashed with some of the views that the men held.'[1]

Bisexuality, paedophilia, sadomasochism, transsexuality, dress codes – all came up in the MC discussions about who could or should be welcomed into the centre. At the same time the MC, an all-white group of men and women, discussed making the centre accessible to more Black and working-class gay men and lesbians.

Wendy Clark maintains that the majority of the women on the MC were antagonistic to the SM groups who wanted to hold meetings in the centre, and in particular they were not keen about the men. Yet the centre's ideological underpinning was a liberal tolerance which incorporated the 'wide diversity of the gay community'. This contradiction was not fully faced, until it hit them in the face.

■ Zoning in on the centre

It was in this context that the first stirrings of a more public debate about SM and the centre occurred. Different eddies and currents, already swirling elsewhere in the WLM, settled on the centre with histories already in the process of gelling, with scuffles recorded and bad guys and good guys named. A coalition of lesbian feminists saw that the centre was (unenthusiastically) giving a place for SM groups to meet. Already they had managed to trounce the possibility of any of this ugly business happening at A Woman's Place (the central London women's centre) or of SM being discussed in the central London women's newsletter. Letters arrived at the centre from these women demanding that SM groups be forthwith excluded. They declared with their usual confidence that they represented *the* lesbian feminist position on the subject.

By the time the centre opened officially, the 'debate' was underway, particularly within the weekly meetings of lesbians who were trying to co-ordinate events in the lesbian-only lounge and work out the relationship that space had to the rest of the centre.

It was not a new debate – only the instance and place made a difference. Political positions over the SM issue by no means followed a clear-cut path. But certain trends could be discerned.

■ Sexuality and feminism

In the mid-70s lesbianism and/or separatism were first presented within the women's liberation movement as possibilities for all women to take up as part of their political struggle. For many feminists the printing of the CLIT statement from the USA in issue after issue of the London Women's Liberation Workshop newsletter was shocking, frightening and led to the first significant withdrawal of women from under the umbrella of sisterhood. (We're aware that many, particularly Black and working-class women never got under it in the first place.) In the CLIT statement all heterosexual women were named as untrustworthy dupes at best, or, at worst, as active collaborators with the enemy. Given that, the only feminist choice was withdrawal from men and bonding with women.

In London there was no sustained political rebuttal of CLIT – only the outraged cries of wounded and angry heterosexual feminists. In this instance, heterosexuality was attacked on moral/political grounds and the response was moral/personal outrage. No one spoke directly about sex; there was no ongoing discussion about desire or sexuality. But, after this, the earlier possibilities for heterosexual feminists to explore their relations with men didn't exist in the same way. Being a heterosexual feminist, even an angry-with-men one, was not enough any more.

However, from then until the emergence of revolutionary feminism, and in particular the Leeds revolutionary feminist writing on political lesbianism in 1979, heterosexuality was still the assumed sexual identity of most, if not all, women in most feminist circles. Lesbians had certainly made their presence known inside the WLM, but often they still had to assert their presence in order to avoid being incorporated back into the assumed heterosexuality of all women. This was true even on *Spare Rib*, a magazine of women's liberation. Continued sorties against that assumption were made by lesbians and/or separatists. Often the basis of the criticism was confused. In some cases it veered towards biological determinism, as in the then-infamous 'boy children' debate in London, where the presence of the boys of feminists at women's centres created a furore. In other instances the argument tended to be couched in terms of lesbianism's 'natural' subversive and revolutionary character in relation to the patriarchy.

Revolutionary feminism, as distinct from radical feminism or socialist-feminism, is the forerunner of a particular English feminist politics which six years later ended up fighting SM at the LLGC in the garb of Lesbians Against Sadomasochism (LASM). LASM had links, through particular women and, more importantly, through its political opposition to SM, with the early political lesbianism of the Leeds revolutionary feminists, and with the anti-porn politics of Women Against Violence Against Women (WAVAW): 'Porn's the Theory, Rape's the Practice.' But other lesbian feminist political positions were also present in the anti-SM grouping.

Radical feminists, even if in relationships with men, tended to say that they rejected male sexuality as it is now, totally. But on *Spare Rib* magazine, the early years produced confident articles on sexuality; articles which were going to teach women how to have orgasms, how to demand what they wanted from men. By the late 70s that confidence had gone.

Spare Rib spent much of 1980 tearing itself apart over the issue of sexuality. The collective was split over whether a submitted article claiming that lesbians had silenced heterosexuals in the women's movement was anti-lesbian and, secondly, whether *Spare Rib* should print it. The lesbians and heterosexuals on *Spare Rib* (all white women at that time) differed over the article and the lesbians differed among themselves. However, the 'naming' and 'claiming' tone was set by those lesbians on the collective who felt that the article was anti-lesbian and that they suffered as a result of it. Because they suffered, their position had to hold sway. The other lesbians, who either did not think the article was anti-lesbian or who felt that the best way to deal with anti-lesbianism among feminists was to bring it out in the open, air it, confront it and struggle with it, did not count. They didn't display the requisite pain. The *expression* of anti-lesbianism in whatever form, from whoever, became the *oppression* of lesbians, full stop. The article was not printed and the collective went on in a confused, moralistic and contradictory way to confront and be confronted by racism, Zionism and anti-semitism.

■ What's that you're grappling with?

The rise of revolutionary feminism in the late 1970s claimed a certain place for sexuality on the feminist agenda – firmly in the centre. Men's sexuality was the key problem, but in a different way from the view of many radical feminists. In revolutionary feminism, male sexuality was, for the foreseeable future, irredeemable. Feminists' struggle was *against* male sexuality, not *with* it; they mobilized against it in WAVAW and anti-pornography groups. Woman's sexuality was the key to both her oppression and liberation.

Suddenly everyone was grappling with compulsory heterosexuality and political lesbianism, separatism, non-monogamy, lesbian lifestyle, lesbianism as the practice of feminism. Where was socialist-feminism in all this? Despite the brief existence of Lesbian Left, the terrain around lesbianism seems to have been left wide open for revolutionary and radical feminism to claim as their own. In the late 70s and early 80s, heterosexual socialist-feminists, confronted with the growing divisions in the autonomous women's movement, not the least of which were accusations of consorting with the enemy, dropped out in droves. And they made a beeline for the mixed organizations of the left – trade unions, the Labour Party, campaigning groups – leaving those socialist-feminist lesbians who remained socially and/or politically active in the grassroots of the WLM not a little isolated in the face of the now dominant assumptions about lesbianism and feminism.

It is ironic that while many of the best-known socialist-feminist intellectuals are lesbians, over the years socialist-feminism has come to be associated with heterosexuality. It has concentrated on analysing desire in the abstract and has had virtually nothing to say about lesbianism. It has made no significant political intervention in the ongoing messy debates about sexuality, heterosexuality and lesbianism. This is a schematic view, of course, but one which we think accurately describes the relative power (or lack thereof) of socialist-feminism *vis-à-vis* radical/revolutionary feminism in speaking to lesbians about the experience and the politics of sexuality.

■ Tipping the cart

So, 'woman-identified' ruled OK. Then *Sex Heresies* came along, published in the spring of 1981. This issue of an American feminist periodical was an attempt to combat the latent feminist assumptions about how we, hets or dykes, 'should' express sexuality. With a paucity of feminist writings around on sex, and after a few years of *The Joy Of Lesbian Sex* and others of that ilk, it was definitely exciting. And shocking to some – with articles on butch-femme relationships, sadomasochism, masturbation and celibacy, prostitution, fag hags and feminist erotica. Whatever else, *Sex Heresies* signalled a move to put the erotic back into sex. Whereas the British revolutionary feminists appeared to see sex as a pleasant possibility between women who had withdrawn from men, *Sex Heresies* underlined the deep and confusing currents of desire between women.

In the USA *Sex Heresies* seems to have been the first salvo in a battle over sexuality which has been intense, overt and wide-ranging. A loose coalition of sexual radicals (who include lesbians, heterosexual feminists and gay men) has sprung up, stringing together the unrespectable issues, like paedophilia, SM, promiscuity, willing to dissect, bring into the open and mostly defend all the variations of sexual pleasure and desire. All of these overlapping issues have had specific ramifications amongst lesbians – but, in the lesbian feminist subculture, SM has become the peg from which all the others have been hung. And it was the SM debate which turned up among lesbians in Britain.

■ SM's shifty meanings

Why do we keep naming it 'the SM debate'? One of the most difficult aspects of this ideological struggle around sexuality has been sifting through a quagmire of shifting definitions. A simple description of SM might be the sexual dramatization of acting-out of power relations, with its own history of codes and meanings, of ritual and paraphernalia. But is SM a clearly delineated physical practice which only a certain percentage of lesbians will ever be into? Is it therefore of limited relevance to most lesbians? Or is SM the crystallization of the most vital components of *all* erotic tension: teasing, titillation, compulsion and denial, control and struggle, pleasure and pain. Alternatively it could just be that, in the vacuum of lesbians speaking and writing about sex, the language of sexual excitement used in, for example, *Coming to Power: Writings and Graphics on Lesbian SM*, resonates with a great many women who are not, technically speaking, into SM (SAMOIS, 1981).

Debates specifically around lesbian SM *have* taken place in the context of a general challenge to feminist sexual orthodoxy. SMers indeed have aligned themselves with other self-defined 'sexual outlaws' – prostitutes, butch and femme lesbians, bisexuals. Several things seem to have been happening at once, and at times it's hard to keep a grasp on exactly what it is at any given moment.

SM lesbians have been engaged in a struggle to 'come out SM', to be open and proud of their sexual practices. Because of the negative connotations of sadism and masochism (linked to actual torture,

cruelty and emotional suffering), and the hegemony of political lesbianism, they have been come down on – hard – by large sections of lesbian
feminists. Other lesbians, including many socialist lesbians like ourselves have acted in defence of SM dykes around issues of censorship
and exclusion. This defence has necessarily broadened into an intense
struggle over definitions of feminism and lesbianism, the rights and
wrongs of lesbian sexual practice, desires and fantasies in general.

In participating in these struggles, we've become aware of the
absence of language that can deal with different lesbian sexualities. To
some extent, SMers have captured the market of sexual description. But
it's plainly no use dividing all lesbians (as some SMers do) into SM and
vanilla dykes. During the last year we've been dismissed as liberals
(from both sides) because we've appeared to be just tolerantly defending
the rights of others. However, we don't disavow our own interest or
involvement in some aspects of SM. We do think, though, that a
socialist-feminist critique of SM as a political theory and pleasure as a
supposedly neutral playground is needed.

In Britain, the struggle around lesbian sexuality has been muted and
spasmodic, though accompanied by often violently intense reactions.
This struggle to retrieve eroticism in the face of, among other things, the
political desexualization of lesbianism, has been characterized here by
an almost complete absence of talking or writing about sex. A magazine
like the explicit Californian *On Our Backs* seems unthinkable in
London. Even the sexual liberationists, in discussions about 'Pleasure
and Danger' in the avant-garde *Square Peg* (No. 10, 1985), resort to
allusions to 'tops' and 'bottoms' and various interpersonal dynamics.
Having bought their under-the-counter (yes – from Sisterwrite in
London) copies of *Coming to Power*, lesbians might make either covert
references to their 'favourite article', or disdainful jokes. The possibility
of having, for example, a frank and public discussion on the lesbian
gang 'rape' fantasy ('Girl Gang' by Crystal Bailey) seems out of the
question in London – and yet one of us has been in on a discussion on
that, and many others like it, in Australia. We're forced to fall back on
the suspicion that sex itself *is* relatively more hidden in British society,
and that goes for the women's movement too.

■ Reactions

The reaction against *Sex Heresies* and all it stood for was well under
way by late 1981. Articles in the internally published *Revolutionary
and Radical Feminist Newsletter* posed a dichotomy between sexual

liberation and women's liberation reminiscent of the early 70s – only this time it was some forms of lesbianism, not just heterosexuality, that were under attack. Revolutionary feminists and some radical feminists sought to set the terms of the discussion: political lesbianism (lesbianism as a political strategy for fighting male power) was such a central tenet of their politics that any challenge to the orthodoxy of lesbian sex was a challenge to the entirety of their feminism. Anyone mounting such a challenge was not a 'true' feminist.

But the sexual pleasure brigade continued to make inroads, in books, conferences, discussions. By late 1982 articles in the *Revolutionary and Radical Feminist Newsletter* had to take some of the issues on board, though still with a completely hardline rejection of SM. They were obviously worried that talk of sexual fantasy, masochistic feelings and erotic pleasure was ringing a few bells among lesbians. They felt the 'SM lobby' was capitalizing on the silence of its opponents, so their strategy became one of talking about sexuality. They wanted to demonstrate that most lesbian feminists had perfectly reasonable non-oppressive sex lives (and thus didn't need SM). They acknowledged that many women had masochistic (even sadistic) fantasies. However, if feminists were 'afflicted' with the 'internalization of the male (hetero) sexual model', change was possible and *necessary* for feminism.

With this strategy in mind, revolutionary feminists organized the Lesbian Sex Conference in London in April 1983. However, although they planned it and wrote all the pre-distributed papers, the conference ended up having a non-specific atmosphere. Attended by hundreds of women, with workshop titles ranging from 'Lesbians and Fashion' to 'Monogamy' to 'Heterosexism', there was a general air of waiting to see what would happen. With no organized speakers in workshops, and no plenary session, complete pot luck determined any individual's experience of the weekend (see Egerton, 1983). There was the odd rumour of disagreement from the SM workshops, and there were conflicts involving the felt exclusion of some working-class women and the physical exclusion of women with disabilities. But in general nothing much seemed to happen. If there were few open discussions about sex, neither was revolutionary feminism much in evidence. It was a diffuse and defused occasion.

In the following two years, questions of sex and sexuality went slightly out of focus, as struggles and eruptions, especially around racism and anti-semitism, took centre stage in the WLM. The 'sex' debate had been, in Britain, primarily conducted between two (or more) camps of white women, with individual contributions by some Black lesbian feminists (Bellos, 1984). This, we think, is unlike in the USA where the concerns and theories around sex of Black women and women of colour had a strong voice among the pro-pleasure groupings, though not without hard criticism of the racist elements of much white theory. Here, the increasingly organized and powerful presence of Black lesbians has had a gradual impact on the terms of reference of the SM debate. Some Black lesbians have made it clear they don't want anti-racist rhetoric used in an opportunistic way to bolster up *either* side of the debate, particularly as it has remained a white-dominated discussion. Racism in sexuality remains largely unacknowledged on the white lesbian political agenda.

■ It's getting closer

On to the next round of skirmishes. During the winter of 1983-84, the *London Women's Liberation Newsletter* refused to carry a notice about a meeting called by SM Dykes to discuss sadomasochism. The few individuals (including members of a lesbian sexuality discussion group we were in) who raised voices in protest at the censorship were shot down in a barrage of abuse and condemnation.

At the 1984 Lesbian Strength March the storm in a teacup blew up again when SM Dykes appeared with a provocative banner (lesbian symbol intertwined in chains). Newsletter writers raged at the shame and horror of it all. SM Dykes, having been silenced, kept silent in feminist circles.

Less than a year later, the LLGC opened its doors and the anti-SM lesbians were busily writing letters to the MC protesting about any SM presence there. A few of these women started to attend the weekly meetings of the Lesbian Co-ordinating Committee, set up as an open voluntary group to plan and organize the lesbian-only space. Instead the meetings (in which we took part) spent a lot of time skirmishing, fighting, going over and over the subjects of SM, lesbian identity, political acceptability and the role of the centre. No one talked about SM *sex* or whether anyone should do it. We were talking about the presence of small groups of women and men who might use the centre for meetings on the same basis as many other lesbian or gay groups. No one defended the 'right' of any fascist or racist group to meet at the centre, no matter how 'well' they might behave. In fact the centre's constitution clearly excluded any such groups from meeting in it. The argument remained one about definitions of SM, and the supposed behaviour of SMers.

Because no one really believed SMers were going to do 'it' in the centre, the focus was on their presence – how they looked became all-important. The practice of lesbian SM was, on both sides of the debate, described with dualistic pairings of words: power and submission; pleasure and pain; dominance and subordination; passive and active; top and bottom. Alongside these went the apparel and (optional!) accessories: whips, chains, dog collars, caps, leather, studs, handcuffs. The 'look' (often indistinguishable from punk) became overloaded with meaning, and as threatening as the acts themselves. The question of women who might take part in SM sex without dressing the part was never dealt with. An extreme image was set up to be knocked down.

SM acts were, in the eyes of LASM women, irredeemably connected to heterosexuality. As most heterosexuality was considered violence to women, the added ritualization in SM sex made it more horrific and dangerous. In lesbian SM the fact that the oppressor (man) wasn't actually doing it made it even more reprehensible.

The Leeds Revolutionary Feminist Group had written their paper 'Political Lesbianism: The Case Against Heterosexuality' in 1979. In it they said '... it is specifically through sexuality that the fundamental oppression, that of men over women, is maintained' (Leeds Revolutionary Feminist Group, 1981). The Leeds group stated it very directly. In 1979 they wrote as if class, race and disability didn't exist, even if they were heavily criticized for this at the time. Now the same revolutionary feminist analysis came shored up with the opportunistic use of race, class, anti-semitism and disability. In a sense these become the stage props of the central drama which, for them, is still the determining division between men and women. But this is our interpretation and lies beneath the surface of the politics we are describing. The debate over lesbian SM was carried out by using their hierarchies of oppression, their collections of 'most oppressed', and attaching them to the practice of SM sex – thereby 'proving' how dangerous, disgusting and politically incorrect SM is. SM Dykes became the walking repositories of racism, fascism and male violence.

■ Mixing it up

It seems, in retrospect, no coincidence that this long-running drama in lesbian feminist circles finally came to a head in a mixed centre, though at first glance it might seem strange that women whose political position tends towards separatism even bothered to care about what would go on there. After years of separation, the LLGC marked an auspicious attempt for lesbians and gays to bridge the gap. A whole generation of lesbian feminists had gained their political experience in women-only centres and groups. It may have been a shock, even an affront to some that an attractive, well-equipped centre was opening outside of their assumed sole claim to lesbian politics.

Lesbian SM, and SM Dykes themselves, had been fairly easily squeezed out of the increasingly prescriptive feminist channels of organization and communication. (Long gone are the days when a feminist cabaret act could call itself the Sadista Sisters and get away with it!) But owing to the different historical development of gay liberation politics, a mixed gay centre potentially offered them a home. Confirmation to its opponents, perhaps, that SM *is* an essentially 'male' practice, and that the struggle against it is part and parcel of the larger feminist struggle.

At most points during this struggle, LASM's main argument was against the contamination of lesbianism *and* the centre with a violent 'male' ideology. At other times it seemed that some anti-SM women were in complete opposition to any alliances or solidarity with (gay) men at all, and that was really the basis for their involvement at the LLGC. It was when this fundamentally destruction-minded position seemed to be gaining the upper hand that some of the group of women we were working with gave ourselves the somewhat dull title of Lesbian Feminists for the Centre.

Not that our support for the centre, or for working with men, was unproblematic, but then, we had entered into it anticipating that. When the SM debate came along, the primary aspect for us two was the struggle over ideologies of sexuality and lesbianism. The playing out of antagonisms between lesbians in front of men obviously posed difficulties. We had to be very wary of colluding with the view of feminists as spoilsport puritans perpetrated by some gay men (and women). One of us was disturbed by the anti-feminist tone of some statements at the first meeting of the Sexual Fringe (a coalition of women and men who defined themselves as sexual radicals). On the other hand, we would have liked to know how to protest openly at some lesbian behaviour towards men at the mass meetings, without swelling male egos. Too often we found ourselves silent, loyalties and politics pulling us all ways at once. Our main concern was to focus on the other lesbians involved, and to mobilize more lesbians to get involved. So, throughout the struggle we organized in an autonomous group of women. We wanted to keep distinct from the centre, and from men, in order to engage fully with the LASM women within a feminist framework. But at no time did we consider the presence of men as incidental, or something we'd rather have done without. When it became apparent that we'd struck, and were up against, a deep anti-coalition vein within feminism, our commitment to this mixed centre clarified. It became, then, partly also a struggle to maintain the right to political optimism; to retain a sense of the possibilities for new things which the centre stood for.

■ Putting the extraordinary into EGM

In April 1985, the first extraordinary general meeting (EGM) was held at the newly opened LLGC. Most women and men came thinking that they were there to discuss and resolve the issue of SM at the centre. The management committee, after its initial acceptance of SM groups meeting at the centre, had reversed that decision. After receiving letters and protests from LASM women and their supporters, they changed their minds. Wendy Clark says, 'So we took an interim decision that as a group they couldn't meet until there had been an open meeting or the first general meeting of the centre members and ask them to decide.' In fact SM groups took legal advice, consulted the constitution and called the first EGM.

It was a packed, tense meeting. Nothing was resolved. For constitutional reasons we were unable to take a vote on the proposed ban. For us the tension arose from our own silence and inability to support SM groups meeting in the centre in the face of the emotive presence of LASM women and their supporters, some of whom had never set foot in the centre before. Immediately after some angry scenes, *lesbians* were invited upstairs to a meeting in the lesbian meeting room. When some of us went our presence was challenged because we were 'pro-SM'. By this point feminism and lesbianism were claimed as LASM's own.

LASM's reports of the meeting were outraged. In newsletters and on the grapevine came news of a meeting packed out by SM men and women dressed in fascist gear who, by displaying continuous misogyny and hatred of children, oppressed the LASM women. The act of opposing their demand for exclusion of SM groups was, they claimed, an SM act in itself. (As far as dress goes, some strange outfits were worn, some leather and a few studded collars and leather caps. We saw no fascist gear.) The North London Lesbian Mothers Group, supporters of LASM, produced a leaflet for the EGM which illustrates some of their politics. 'For those of you who claim to oppose censorship of any kind, ask yourselves if you would allow a group calling itself "Gay Fascists" to organize in the Centre. There have to be *limits* in order to *prevent oppression* of all kinds' (our emphasis).

Here is the usual equation of SM with fascism. But we are interested in other aspects of the quote. So – oppression of all kinds can be prevented by imposing limits! Well, unfortunately oppression is not the product of 'no limits'. It comes, in however devious a route, from particular social systems and from particular sets of relationships which are part and parcel of those social, economic and cultural systems. To propose setting 'limits' as if that could take care of oppression and exploitation in our society is a travesty of the sort of changes we need to go through in order to transform anything. Our criticism of the lesbian mothers' leaflet is on this basis, not about whether or not 'limits' are sometimes necessary or a good thing.

The static moralism of this political position is ripe for reformism too. It's been noted often enough how many socialist-feminists have been drawn into municipal socialism and the Labour Party. What has not been noticed at all is the number of revolutionary feminists and those influenced by them now working in the same institutions, usually around women's issues. It would be interesting to trace out the reception their politics are getting in the Labour Party, and the influence they are having.

■ An extraordinary repeat

After the April EGM many centre users became more organized. Spurred on by LASM's tactics at the first EGM and ashamed of our inertia around that event, Lesbians for the Centre began to meet independently to formulate a proposal for the next EGM (on 9 June at Conway Hall) and to discuss how we should go about trying to engage with LASM in order to defeat it. Our politics were diverse; we were not a group of SMers, nor were we all socialist-feminists. We lacked a common theoretical base, but shared general agreement in practice about the centre. We knew that LASM would propose an outright ban on SM groups, and that the Sexual Fringe wanted a completely 'anything goes' situation. We wanted to defend strongly the rights of the SM groups, while raising questions about what *could* be problems in such a centre in terms of dress and behaviour.

■ Stuck in dilemmas

This led us into hours of debate over a dress code. Our proposal reflected the compromises we all made. Tagged on to the end is the one dress ban we all agreed on (the swastika, in the west a symbol of fascism past *and* present) and the one we compromised on: that no one should be led around the centre on a leash or chain. (Yes, we know it sounds ridiculous.)

No one in our group questioned that certain clothing or equipment evoked images of reaction and oppression. What we divided over was whether some styles or equipment – handcuffs, for instance – were in themselves symbols of oppression and therefore in themselves racist, fascist or anti-semitic. The two of us agreed that meanings of objects are socially and culturally constructed. That did not mean that certain dress or behaviour could not be contested or even banned, but it should be on the basis of political discussion about the relationships between people in the centre and between the centre and the outside. Our motion said:

> The LLGC is a centre for a wide variety of lesbians and gay men who have different political perspectives. We are committed to an outreach programme to actively encourage the participation of black and ethnic minority lesbians and gay men, disabled lesbians and gay men, and younger gay people. In order to ensure participation, the centre holds a firm policy of anti-fascism, anti-racism, anti-sexism, and an opposition to anti-semitism and aggressive behaviour. The centre is closed to any group that advocates fascism, racism, anti-semitism, or sexism as any part of their stated aims or philosophy.
>
> Lesbians and gay men have a diverse range of 'sexualities'. We advocate no *one* sexuality for lesbians and gay men, understanding that sexuality is very complex, but we do recognize that the centre should be a place for constructive discussion around all aspects of our sexuality.
>
> Certain symbols and actions will not be permitted in the centre, namely the wearing and displaying of swastikas, and the leading around of individuals by means of chains or leads.

Of course this was seen as the very life blood of liberalism by LASM. Our aim neither to identify with a simplistic pro-SM stance which absolved anyone of critically looking at *that* sexual practice nor to dismiss the fears of LASM was not particularly appreciated by anyone.

In any case the second EGM was beset by similar constitutional problems as the first, and the few motions or proposals discussed could be voted on only in order to ascertain the sense of the meeting. A large group of LASM women and their supporters demanded and got separate votes for men and women, obviously in order to *prove* the connexion between 'male values' and pro-SM politics. Finally, at the end of the day, about one-third of the women present and three-fifths of the men voted to allow SM groups to meet in the centre.

The meeting was as acrimonious as the first, at times disintegrating into shouting matches. When a small group of women (about twelve of us) who sat together on one side of the hall raised our hands to oppose a ban, women on the other side of the room, LASM supporters, stood up to stare at us. The divide by the aisle was as literal as the divide between our politics.

■ Gathering forces

All during the spring other groups had been meeting and politicking around the centre. The Sexual Fringe included SM lesbians and men as well as bisexuals, transsexuals and celibates. They saw themselves romantically as sexual outlaws, wherein the very fact of 'difference' put them in the same political position. They produced several leaflets which took on what they called prescriptive feminism.

When LASM put out a leaflet headed 'What Is This Big Fuss About Sado-Masochism?' it sparked off a number of responses. The LASM leaflet itself is interesting. Its pompous question-and-answer format compares very closely with the Leeds Revolutionary Feminist paper of 1979 on political lesbianism. There, the same irritating, moralist question-and-answer format places the authors in the superior, vanguardist position of explaining it all to backward children. For instance:

> *Q*: But we don't do penetration, my boyfriend and me.
> *A*: If you engage in any form of sexual activity with a man you are reinforcing his class power.
> *Q*: But I like fucking.
> *A*: Giving up fucking for a feminist is about taking your politics seriously.
> *Q*: Are all lesbian feminists political lesbians?

A: No. Some women who are lesbians and feminists work closely with men in the male left (either in their groups or in women's caucuses within them), or provide mouthpieces within the women's liberation movement for men's ideas even when non-aligned.

The 1986 LASM leaflet, 'What is This Big Fuss ...' includes 'answers' too:

S/Ms often wear clothes expressing real power, pain and humiliation, eg Nazi style caps, dog collars, chains. This is racist, anti-semitic, and offensive to all oppressed people.

A pathetic questioner goes on to ask:

Q: But isn't Lesbian and Gay Liberation about freedom, not more limitations?
A: Total freedom is the freedom of the powerful to oppress – do you condone racism, anti-semitism, heterosexism?
Q: But I like wearing long spiked belts and dog collars – and I'm not into S/M.
A: So what. If you don't care that others see them as racist, anti-semitic etc then you are being racist, anti-semitic, fascist.

In that leaflet and in another called 'Sado-Masochism – the Reality', which was produced after the second EGM in June, SM takes on vast meaning: 'Remember that SM was a significant part of the "decadent" social scene in 1930s Berlin – part of the political climate of the day. People acclimatized to SM brutality would have failed to notice the threat of the "real Nazis" approaching.' Not only is SM equated with racism, fascism and anti-semitism, but it also appears now to have allowed the rise of fascism in Germany! A view of 'decadent homosexuality' which is uncomfortably similar to the Moral Right's. The leaflet goes on to say: 'Similarly, we are all brought up to have racist feelings, otherwise the institution of racism could not survive.' These are the sentiments which fuel much of the racism and heterosexism awareness training industry: it is feelings which allow the institutions to survive.

The Sexual Fringe members responded to these lectures with some wit and precision, though their libertarian outlook sometimes weakened their insights. However, one of their leaflets which appeared before the second EGM was more sophisticated and responded to

LASM's equation of SM and fascism. In 'Who Are the Real Fascists?' they say:

> To label SM fascist is to trivialize the real fight against fascism. To throw the word fascism about with no reference to what it means is to make the real fight more difficult. To use people's sexual revulsion as a scare tactic against sexual freedom is a real insult to fascism's victims.

In an unpublished letter to *Feminist Review* last summer, four women members of the Sexual Fringe wrote:

> We feel that the women's movement has become more concerned with constructing and policing its own categories of sexual identity than with attempting to understand the complex and often contradictory construction of women's sexuality in a male-dominated, capitalist society.

All of these positions and arguments circulated in the weeks leading up to the second EGM and afterwards before the Lesbian Strength March and the July AGM. The LASM women were furious and disgusted when they lost. The fallout was heavy. Various lesbian groups had to decide what to do after the defeat. Some decided not to hold any meetings at the centre – fair enough. But at least two or three groups wrote letters to the GLC claiming that the centre was racist, fascist and excluded lesbians. They wanted the GLC to chop its financial support. A few LASM supporters inside the GLC even attempted to represent LASM's position on SM and the centre as the one and only true feminist one. It's quite a turn-up when lesbian feminists, some of whom advocate withdrawal from men on an individual sexual basis as a political stance, run to a male-dominated bureaucracy to denounce other lesbians and gay men. All that was quite shocking and indicative of the bankruptcy of their politics.

In the weeks leading up to the Lesbian Strength and Gay Pride March in June and before the AGM at the end of July, leaflets attacking the centre were distributed at women's venues, clubs and discos. Immediately before Lesbian Strength March, when the centre served as a meeting point and the evening celebrations were in the lesbian lounge, a warning was handed out to women in London: 'Warning. Do not go to the London Lesbian and Gay Centre unless you are prepared to be in an environment that is rife with fascists, racists, misogynists and sadomasochists.' It offered an alternative social event after the march at Tindlemanor, a women's centre.

Hundreds of women ignored this, and a fantastic evening followed. The centre was claimed as a place for many of London's lesbians.

■ Opening up the space to explore

So what were the consequences of all this fighting? The centre doesn't appear to have been overrun with whips and chains – at times it's a positively tame place to be. A large number of lesbian feminists undoubtedly stay away. But many others do come. Most significantly, for us, a politics founded on an apocalyptic vision of what would happen if SM groups merely met at the LLGC has been publicly defeated and proven wrong. We definitely get a sense that LASM's ideology has suffered quite a big dent, and that some space has opened up for more discussion about lesbian sexuality. For, if anything, this debate showed that we are hardly at the beginning of being able to talk about it.

SM literature has said much about sexual daring, openness and excitement. It has said a lot to verify our own experiences, to incite us to further fantasies and possibilities. It has brought into the open naked desires. But it hasn't said much about situations where desire is absent or fantasies won't come; much less about, for example, the mundanities of a fetish-less long-term relationship.

We don't want to fall into the trap of posing these as opposites of each other (cruising v monogamy!). We're not saying that SM Dykes are responsible for articulating all sexual possibilities. The struggle around the rights of SMers has made space for more writing about sex – some great, some awful – though there's still far too little of the good stuff about. However, we do think that the Sexual Fringe (not an SM group, but from within the same political stream), during the LLGC struggle, *failed to acknowledge* that 'vanilla' sex can be exciting or that sexuality can be problematic (and not just because of 'repression'). By default, their position seemed to amount to one of 'uninhibited pursuit of the sexual high' – which leaves a lot to be desired!

Ultimately the Sexual Fringe's libertarianism ended up glorifying a kind of individualism. They romanticized categories of 'deviant' sexual practice – if you can't claim one of their identities, well, frankly, you're boring.

Boring equals vanilla sex, which is what? For lesbian SMers and for us, the ritual of the sexual interchange is very important. But for us an SM interchange can be as much about finding pleasure in the unplanned holding down of one lover by the other. 'The way we think about sex fashions the way we live it' (Weeks, 1985). Our own political position on SM is that we are all on a continuum. (We refuse the label liberal over this — stuff it.) Is the thrill of deliberate touch on muscle, a pressure on shoulders, done with a sense of dominance, accepted with a sense of submission, any less exciting than tying someone up? We suspect most of our sex lives and sexual histories are very uneven: cuddly sex, bondage, kisses and affection, one-night stands, dressing up — any of these can be what we crave or pursue at any given time.

We should make it clear that, issue by issue, we would line up with the Sexual Fringe in defence and support of a radical sexual politics and practice. The question of desire is crucial to our understanding of sexuality. Where we disagree is over the context for those politics.

The centre's 'Fringe' and the SM groups saw their rebellion against society's 'norms' and, further, against the 'norms' of what constitutes 'acceptable' sexual practice according to certain groups of lesbians, as a radical act with political significance. In denying that playing out society's power roles in bed had any causal connexion to the continuance or development of such relationships in the big wide world, they tended to exclude any discussion about the ways in which sexual relations *are* related to the rest of our lives. For instance, around housing, work, family — as well as state institutions. Lesbian SM literature suggests that organizing around oppositional sexual difference constitutes not just a political practice but a whole political perspective. It's here that SMers come unstuck. By failing to situate themselves as within particular subcultures, linked to certain lifestyle requirements, they inflate their sexual politics with a universality it almost certainly does not have.

The most absurd extension of the SM political position is the implication that if we all played out our SM fantasies in bed, the world would be a better place. The connecting line between this mode of thinking and the LASM one is striking, even if they draw the opposite conclusions.

LASM women claim that they have no real interest in the acts of SM sex except as they represent and become all of the pain, horror and degradation of women, Black people, Jewish people, mothers, disabled people, and so on. Unlike the SMers who deny any harmful reality of sexism, fascism and racism in SM sex roles or rituals, LASM goes to the opposite extreme and claims that things like tying up, spanking, whipping, and wearing collars or belts with studs are in themselves violence against all the oppressed peoples of the world.

LASM say they 'do not consent to being terrorized by the presence of the symbols of brutality, which are *just* as threatening as the presence of the real thing' (our emphasis). They deny any possibility of consensual agreement or equality in SM sex, just as the political lesbians do to women in 'ordinary' heterosexual sex. In an unquestioning SM view, we can choose our stage and role. In LASM's view we are acted *upon*; we are permanent victims (or bearers of oppression) except when we refuse the acts, deny the feelings which make us victims. We are implicated in our own victim status if we refuse to do that. This is where morality makes its entrance. (It's a remarkably religious scenario.)

Neither of these views sees the world in movement, in tension, dialectically. Still, is any of this SM debate/struggle really important enough to go on about? Why do we care so much?

■ Taking a stand

Sexuality in Britain in the 1980s sits uneasily in the political domain, with other matters such as class despair, racist attacks and economic depression demanding feminist attention. They demand our attention too, but we don't want to loosen our claim to the sexual as political and as important to our everyday lives. The thoroughgoing heterosexism of this society makes the struggle around sexuality an especially crucial one for us as lesbians.

Both of us live out our lives at least partially within the lesbian subcultures – socially and politically. We have no intention of quitting that world, and every intention of standing our ground there as lesbian feminists. As lesbians we have chosen to criticize the words and actions of other lesbians, we hope in a way consistent with our politics. A LASM leaflet said about *us*:

> SM Dykes have in fact never spoken up at any of these meetings, leaving the shouting to SM Gays and a group of 'liberal' women – none of whom are interested in defending any 'minority groups' other than the so-called 'sexual fringe' groups. The 'rights' of SMs, paedophiles and transsexuals are given priority over the right of women who are Black/Jewish/Irish/of Colour/disabled – and all other women who are threatened by male violence and are therefore excluded from the centre.

That leaflet exemplifies the sort of intimidatory tactic which has fuelled our anger during this struggle. We think this sort of tactic has serious implications for lesbians and for feminism. We know of many individual lesbians who have taken up the LASM position on the centre because it was presented so heavily as the 'correct line'. This represents a wider trend. Doubts, ambiguities, confusions are shoved under the carpet under this sort of pressure. The mere expression of dissenting ideas has become synonymous with endorsing oppression. There is no room in the LASM view for struggle, for admitting that we all can harbour reactionary ideas at the same time that we hold on to progressive ones.

Exploring complexities within the framework of the need for socialist-feminist change is a way of understanding where we are now – alone, together, in different groups. As lesbians, we do not want to be restrictively told what we are, or should be. As women, we do not want to be presented with a feminism predicated on a false portrayal of ourselves. That will not take us anywhere.

■ To sum up, then

The fight between feminists about SM groups meeting at the LLGC represented a lot more than that. It was the location, for a brief and tumultuous time, of a battle around particular feminist politics. It was ostensibly about sexuality and yet sexuality was hardly mentioned in detail. For us it was largely a political struggle between different groups of lesbians. We don't believe for a moment that many of the LASM women gave two hoots about the centre. In that way it was a symbolic occasion for the anti-SM women and, even though we were very involved in the centre, for us too.

History, in the short and long term, while open to analysis, has a messy daily life. It's a sad if not unsurprising irony that a socialist understanding, one which could help explain at least some of the reasons behind the exploiting divisions between particular groups of people, has not 'fitted' in a lasting way with the development of the women's liberation movement here. All through the 1970s the voices of excluded, ignored or patronized women sang angrily, accusingly about class, about race, about sexuality. Yet the practice of the white-dominated women's movement, with a large and vital socialist-feminist presence in it, was unable to answer those voices.

Whether this says more about British socialist history, contesting Marxist analyses of the 1970s, or about women's attempts to merge socialism and feminism, is open to debate. In any case, by the late 70s and early 80s those different voices finally resonated in many of the organizations, structures and publications of feminism. 'Difference', so long acknowledged but not dealt with, came home to roost, at the same time that socialist confidence in affecting social change was waning. It was then that the whole reality of unequal power relations between feminists and in the world was taken on board by an increasingly dispersed WLM. In some instances, the resulting lessons and achievements offer exciting possibilities for really radical change. But, for some, 'difference' became *in itself* an explanation, an organizing method, a static and moralistic world view. The anxieties about differences between women provided fertile ground for the rise of a simplistic politics within lesbian feminism which grasped for the seemingly easy answer of 'authentic experience'.

The possibility socialist-feminism had of pushing forward a historical and dialectical analysis of difference between feminists and women in general which could produce a politics that could move, embrace, challenge yet forgive, had been overtaken by a rigid feminist politics which elevated some differences to the basic underpinning of political organization. What any one individual 'makes' of what she undeniably feels is open to many possibilities. The 'truthfulness' of the experience of the individual is not what we would question. Nor the reality of conditions which give rise to the experience. But the fact that there is no one unifying response to sexism, to racism, to class exploitation, to heterosexism, forces us to examine the *place* that individual experience should hold in the development of theory and practice.

The contradictory responses of people to their particular oppression and/or situations alerts us to the often contradictory and complicated intertwining of the forces which course through the body politic. Far from making us throw up our hands in despair, we believe feminists can use that reality to develop an analysis and practice which takes into account the messiness of real life, the hopes, fears, angers and acquiescences.

The 'things which divide us' are as hard to discern as a sliver of glass and as huge as a boulder. The individual experience, however subjective, is an engagement with a force with a half life of its own and another half owned by other social forces. Racism exists. Sexism exists. Class exploitation exists. Imperialism exists. But each tangles with the other, feeds from or subtracts, adds to or bloats up another.

The way we 'feel' or experience any of these forces, either directly or indirectly, either one or the other or all, cannot be claimed as the only authentic one. In the first place that totally individualizes the effects of social forces. The social construction of an individual neither means 'free will' nor victim status. And secondly it removes individual constructions of feeling or experience from the impact of historical, economic and cultural forces. Thirdly, it proposes that there is a straight, short line from experience, to consciousness, to understanding and, finally, to political action.

What we feel as women from a thousand different realities, as oppressed and oppressor, actor and object, is a vital *part* of what goes into our political analysis as feminists. Often it is the key to our political awareness, or our awakening. But we don't base our understanding of women's continuing oppression and exploitation on it. No white person can claim to define a Black person's experience, nor a man a woman's, nor a heterosexual a homosexual's. Any of us must be able to develop politics which make us sensitive and open to learning from the experience of others *and* provide us with the tools and a framework for critically assessing theoretical analyses and daily political life.

It is the absence of discerning, exciting and accessible feminist and left political theory and practice at this particular point which makes it so difficult to stand up against the politics of experience or 'identity' politics. It's one of the elements which has swept through so many of the bitter eruptions in British feminist politics during the past five years in particular. It's what we falteringly and finally tried to come to grips with at the London Lesbian and Gay Centre.

■ Notes

Thanks to *Feminist Review* members for helpful notes and reactions. We would both like to thank the women with whom we worked politically during this debate. As well, Susan would like to thank Penny, Gerri, Anne and Paula for comments on the article, and Norie and Kim for thought-provoking discussions about sexual politics while writing it. Sue would like to thank Ruthie, Jill and Diane for long discussions on sexual politics over the years.

1 From a very helpful interview we did with Wendy Clark in September 1985.

PORNOGRAPHY AND
REPRESENTATION

Sexual Violence and
Sexuality

Rosalind Coward

Pornography looks like becoming as contentious an issue within the women's movement in Britain as it has been in America. It is unlikely that any feminist would condone the form in which pornography is consumed, or the culture which surrounds it and to which it contributes. But some feminists, including myself, feel uneasy about the general implications for sexual and feminist politics that arise from some current feminist campaigns against pornography. This article is a reflection, in parts speculative, on exactly what we mean by pornography and on how it relates to our society in general. The article is informed by a political commitment to increased exploration of sexual desire and identity, since I think that this is a crucial element in both criticizing existing forms of sexual behaviour and developing new forms.

> *'Pornography is the theory; rape is the practice'*
> *'Pornography is violence against women'*

Two slogans from the women's movement: two assertions arising from the increasing concern within feminism about the prevalence of pornography and male violence.[1] The argument behind these slogans is that apparently disparate sexual practices – on the one hand representations of sex and on the other violent sexual assaults – are connected. Pornography is part of a spectrum of male behaviour which exhibits its most blatant form in literal physical violence against women. These practices are all instances of the workings of male power and, if we take Andrea Dworkin's ideas as representative here, then these instances of male power have as their effect the control of women (Dworkin, 1981). Phenomena like rape, the sexual harassment of women at work and on the streets, sexual and violent assault on women, the sexual abuse of children by older men (especially fathers), are all seen as instances of the exercise of male power. And the representations of women circulated in pornography are seen as equivalent instruments in the control of women. The effect of the form taken by male sexuality is a literal, and frequently brutal, control of women, hence the suggestion that the representation of women found in pornography is the theoretical expression of the same physical violence found in rape.

Such arguments are completely explicit about what is at stake in sexual relations in our society; it is the forcible control of women, whose sexuality, fertility, productive capacity have been 'stolen' by men to enforce their dominance and control. The prime instrument in this is 'heterosexism', the compulsory imposition of heterosexuality, by which women as a subordinate class are bound to the master class by the powerful bond of sexual relations and sexual desire.

These arguments take us a lot further along a particular route than feminist sexual politics has previously travelled. They amount to a direct onslaught on sexual practices in our society. Criticism of, and attack on, sexual behaviour has always been a crucial part of feminist politics. How to understand and challenge degrading images, sexist language, forms of sexual behaviour, have formed a crucial element in most women's involvement with feminism. But these have now been politically prioritized in a very particular way. And this radically changes previous investigations and challenges to the forms of sexual relations and behaviour in our society. There are several reasons why these political priorities have met with resistance among some feminists.

This resistance springs from the fact that aggressive male sexuality has been specified as the main political problem confronting feminism. One reason for opposing this is that it leads to a very reductive sort of politics. It becomes virtually impossible to formulate strategy either at a local or national level for confronting issues such as wages, work conditions, or for changes in various social policies. All these questions are seen through the lens of the one issue of male sexuality. The second reason, and the one this article is concerned with, is that the designation of aggressive male sexuality as the main problem has other implications.

First, it implies that male sexuality is in fact almost always violent.

Therefore *any* expression of male sexuality will be a problem. It follows from this that any woman engaging in sexual relations with men is wilfully or unconsciously sustaining the structures of male domination. A further implication has been that, given that male sexuality is a problem, any sexual display or representation of sex which gives men sexual pleasure is also a problem. And consequent upon that has been the argument that representations which give sexual pleasure to women, in the same way that they appear to give pleasure to men, should also be resisted. This appears to reverse the previous commitment, in feminist sexual politics, to the positive assertion of women's active and independent sexual needs, whether they be with men or women. It appears to assert that women's 'true' knowledge of their sexuality can only be worked through outside the dominant structures of our society; if need be, there will have to be a withdrawal from public exploration of our sexual needs in order to prevent male manipulation.

If, as most of us would, we acknowledge that there is a very real problem about 'masculinity', and many aspects of masculine behaviour, why should some of us find ourselves in the anomalous position of feeling critical of these particular arguments? I want to deal with this dilemma specifically in relation to pornography, but I believe that the same questions apply to a number of issues in sexual politics at the moment. Is it true that because sexual violence exists at *one* end of the spectrum this means that male sexuality is *always* a problem? Is it true that *any* public representation of sex is *only* for male sexuality and therefore male domination? Is it true that pornography is about violence against women or *necessarily* sustains violence against women? If we are to express any reservations about these propositions, what is it that we object to in pornography and, above all, what can we do about it? Should pornography be banned or are there more progressive ways to deal with the degrading images which so often characterize pornography?

There are three factors which should be foregrounded in thinking about pornography. One is that there are very few clearly agreed definitions of what pornography is and in particular, how it differs from 'erotic' images of naked bodies in general. Given this, there is an obvious need to specify how images produce meanings. Another is that when we talk about intervening in anything to do with sexuality, sexual practice and sexual activity, we are not talking about a society where men and women are lined up in clear and obvious opposition to each other on every single issue. We are talking about intervening in a society where sexuality has historically been regulated by the state and by legal and social policies. It follows from this that however we explain theoretically the emergence of the state, it is dangerous to ignore the specific ways in which the state operates in this society and how this affects what is strategically possible, feasible or indeed desirable. Finally, we have to recognize that positions on pornography are now well staked out in terms of either 'liberalism' or 'censorship' and ask whether we can escape from this way of posing the issue.

■ Pornography: A regime of representations

Pornography is a regime of representations of sex. By this I mean that pornography is not generally an act but representations – writings, films, photos, videos. These show bodies (usually naked) in a sexualized way, or people involved in the sex act, according to certain conventions which mean they are interpreted as pornographic by society.

When I use the term representation, I deliberately use a term which could apply equally to language and to visual images, even though I want to concentrate on pornography in photography. I use the term representation because I think that language and visual images construct their meanings in identical ways and that we can usefully advance our understanding of the meanings in visual images through an initial consideration of how 'meanings' are produced in language. In the first place there is no intrinsic meaning in language. Words do not have a fixed and constant referent (their meaning) which exists out there and which we can embody by using language as a tool. We can see this in several ways; first there is no universal human language; even so-called onomatopoeic words (where the sound echoes the sense) differ from language to language. Moreover the same word can change its meaning in different contexts, depending on different elements such as place in the sentence, emphasis, dialect. 'I long for grace' in a religious context has a quite different meaning from 'I long for Grace' in a more secular situation. Recent adverts have exploited this aspect of language, playing on the fact that puns are produced by the multiple meanings of words: 'Less congestion on the tubes this winter', 'Watch sales escalate' ... and so on. The same words of a sentence can also be rearranged to produce different meanings, demonstrating again that there is no intrinsic meaning to terms. It is this which is exploited in anagrams and crosswords, the requirement being to reassemble the terms into a new series with different meanings.

These aspects of language are to do with the nature of language. Language is made up of a relatively limited number of terms (called phonemes) which, combined in numerous different ways, have the capacity to produce an almost infinite number of words and concepts.

There is a commonsense view that visual representations like film and photography show what is *really* happening, that they show reality just as it is. But the visual meanings of photography are produced in just the same ways as meanings in linguistic statements. Their meanings arise from *how various elements are combined*, how the picture is framed, what lighting it is given, what is connoted by dress and expression, *the way these elements are articulated together*. The meaning of one object can be completely changed by the addition of a caption, the juxtaposition of another object (montage), by cropping the photo in various ways. In other words, just like language, there is no intrinsic meaning in a visual image; the meaning of an image is decided by the way it is articulated, how the various elements are combined together (Figs 1 and 2).

Figs 1 & 2:
'We'll back Ed says Chelsea manager.' 'Well backed to win Gold Cup.'
Two headlines using the same terms, 'We'll back Ed', to produce different meanings. In just the same way, Fig 1 is relatively ambiguous. It could be a depressed/nostalgic/lonely woman. The complete picture, Fig 2, shows how the addition of another element, the British Rail sign, determines the overall meaning.

Figs 3 & 4
The overall meaning is determined by the combination of elements. Fig 3 shows a positive image of women. In the overall picture this is contained, though not suppressed by the reference to men.

But having said that visual images do not reflect reality, nor do they have any intrinsic meaning, it should also be clear from the argument that they cannot be considered as innocent either. It's just as common to meet the opinion that visual images are 'innocent of meanings' as it is to hear that they represent things 'the way they are'. It is commonly suggested that you can't talk about the meanings of photographs, films and TV in the same way as you talk about what is meant by a particular statement. Visual images are constantly exempted from scrutiny; either they are 'real' or they are just 'aesthetically pleasing'. This is a particularly sinister view given that our culture is so bombarded by visual messages (and most of these require that we understand them clearly). It exempts us from the necessity of understanding precisely how visual images have very definite meanings, which is something we must understand if we want to advance beyond saying this or that image is offensive without saying how and why.

In beginning to analyse how meanings are produced for photos, an initial point to be made is that there is always a potential 'polyphany' in representations. Various elements in an image can be ambiguous, and suggest very personal chains of association. It is this which tends to condition the fact that images rarely appear alone in our culture; they are almost invariably pinned down by some linguistic caption

LES HOMMES PEUVENT ALLER SE RHABILLER

which fixes the meaning in an irreversible direction (Figs 3 and 4). Where there is a regime like pornography, which is basically selling the expectation of a particular kind of pleasure in the image, the ambiguity of visual message is reduced to a minimum: the codes are familiar and repetitive, they are contextualized by very distinct kinds of writing. The meaning of a photo is also given by its contexts and uses. We would find it acceptable that Fig 5 should be shown, but would balk if a snapshot of a naked adolescent girl was passed proudly across the dinner table.

These brief comments on visual representations can be summarized by saying that the pleasures, interests and meanings conveyed by photographic images are decided not only by contexts and the conventions which they presuppose (thus the family snapshot assumes that infantile nakedness is not sexual nor is it open to sexual interests in the viewers) but also by how the terms of the photo are arranged, and what this arrangement connotes, what chains of ideas we have to mobilize for the photo to be intelligible (Fig 6).

This approach suggests a certain understanding of pornography. It suggests that there is no intrinsic 'meaning' in a representation of sex or nakedness; the meanings are decided by the particular photo and the codes mobilized to make that photo intelligible. What is a problem is the *particular regimes of meaning surrounding specific practices of*

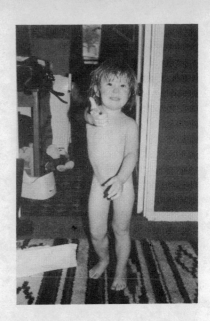

Fig 5
The acceptable face of female
nakedness.

representation. To pose our understanding of pornography in this way is useful since it allows us to develop our argument about 'sexist representations' beyond the bounds of what is conventionally designated pornographic.

What, then, are the specific codes at play in pornography? What is this 'regime of representations'? What if anything is objectionable to feminists about these practices?

Definitions of pornography are notoriously difficult. This is because what is designated pornographic is not fixed. The boundaries are constantly shifting; there is a ceaseless quest to find yet more bizarre practices (or specialisms), as the boundary of what is acceptable extends. The contemporary pornographic industry depends on this distinction between acceptable and 'unacceptable' – distinctions which have been embodied in legal recommendations.[2] Even if pornography is widely available at corner shops or is shown (as it apparently increasingly is) at businessmen's lunches, it still thrives on its suggestion of being illicit or 'naughty'. Our society constantly encourages this distinction between what would offend 'a reasonable person' and what is best kept for 'private' or adult viewing. The distinction is interesting because it amounts to a distinction between all-male company and the heterosexual couple, or the family (the

Fig 6
The image of the two women on the left is open to a number of possible readings. The portrait on the right and the linguistic caption, however, require that we read it in a particular way: as women leered at on the street. Whether we like the meaning or not, the arrangement of items in the image requires that we share the codes which make it intelligible.

What does a young man's fancy turn to in Spring?

Elida in Terylene

TERYLENE

dominant ideological form in which 'mixed' company is usually thought). Video catalogues advertise their products as 'not for family viewing', whereas television (except for its 'adult' films) is geared to the idea of mixed company. The distinction corresponds to other divisions in our society. The idea of the respectable woman within the family or the heterosexual couple who would accept a 'reasonable' amount of explicit sex but no more is on one side. On the other is the 'goer', the women who would participate in pornography, would be available for anything which a man could fantasize, and who is represented as actively enjoying this.

This then is the first (and necessary) defining feature of pornography, an industry that thrives on its designation as illicit. Secondly, it is an industry that sells an expectation of pleasure in images. It has this in common with films, where the viewer purchases a certain expectation of pleasure from images. In pornography, this

Fig 7
It is not representations of
women's bodies that is in
and of itself a problem.

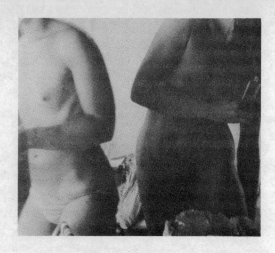

expectation of pleasure is the expectation of arousal. And it is here that many of the problems reside, since male sexual arousal is a problem for women in the forms it is currently expressed. In our society, sexual connexion is often constructed through men taking the initiative and women responding with choice or preference. This is not quite as simplistic as it sounds, for of course women have active sexual aims, but there does seem to be a general ideological construct that one of the preconditions of female desire is that we are desired. Men on the other hand seem frequently to feel that to establish sexual connexion is a matter of pursuing, initiating, harassing or forcing. It is in this sense that it is correct to talk of rape as at one end of the spectrum of sexual behaviour. In a society where women's sexuality is supposed to exist as a stimulant and response to men's predatory sexuality, then rape is clearly a logical extension and this is why there has been such leniency in the treatment of rapists.

But is it only the fact that pornography aims at eliciting sexual arousal that makes pornography a problem? Or is it the representations themselves which are part of the problem? I don't object in principle to representations either of naked women or of sex (Fig 7). In some instances these images seem inoffensive, though for the most part the contexts and meanings with which sex and women's bodies are invested reactivate sexist connotations. Were it possible to imagine these images outside the context of the texts and the massively male-dominated forms of consumption I would not find them objectionable. It is necessary to make this hypothetical point in order to stress that were the *content* to change, and were we to find new codes of representation, it would not be sex or bodies that is the problem. On the other hand, many of the images are of brutalization, and represent women in postures inviting not sexual intercourse but also forms of violence. It is easy to specify our objections to these images where women are shown in positions actively enjoying and submitting to male brutality. It is relatively easy to argue that such images do contribute to a climate where men's sexual needs are seen as depersonalized and aggressive; where women are shown complicit in this expression of male needs. It is also relatively easy to object to the texts which frequently surround such images. Again they frequently emphasize the violent element within sex and show women complicit in forms of male brutality (though it should also be noted that the 'fantasies' also dwell on women's brutalization of men).

What is much more difficult is formulating our precise objections to the codes which dominate the much more routine images of women that pervade pornography. If you are not prepared to dismiss 'erotic' images as in and of themselves problematic in this society, then the

Fig 8
The way pornography suggests female availability and presents a woman's body as sexualized is not confined to pornography.

specification of sexist meanings in images becomes an urgent task. Additional urgency is lent to this by the fact that the codes which characterize pornography are by no means confined there. The direct look of the woman to the viewer, who identifies with the position of the camera, for example, pervades not only fashion magazines and advertising images but is also characteristic of 'portrait' photography and is emulated in the upmarket snapshot.[3] Certain postures – again dominant in pornography – appear indissolubly linked in the ideologies of 'good photography' with representations of women. A woman caught in the middle of peeling off her t-shirt or jersey, her arms suggestively above her head, is common (see Fig 8). All are images which have become a short-hand for 'sexuality' in photographic canons much broader than pornography.

Then there are the codes of submission and fragmentation. I want to think about these in some detail both because it would be useful to specify how they work and also because they may show the root of some of the extreme anger which pornography provokes in women.

Firstly, fragmentation. This is a tendency to concentrate on areas of a woman's body in an extremely fetishistic way: bottoms, breasts, genitals or legs. This tendency to fragmentation is not confined to pornography. It characterizes advertising images, where this fragmentation coincides with the proliferation of sexualized areas of the body, requiring work and therefore commodities. Some women say that they object to this characteristic fragmentation because it does not show 'the whole personality' (which has also been a reason for objecting to depersonalized erotic images). I am not convinced by arguments that the sexual response should only be provoked by 'the whole person', and I have yet to hear a convincing argument as to why it is wrong to gain pleasure from representations of bodies or even 'snatches' of representations of bodies. Anyway, in viewing pictures which we might find pleasurable, it is often a detail on which we might focus; a certain expression in the eyes, the nape of the neck, the way a hand rests on a part of the body (Fig 9). There's no guarantee that in confining a sexual response to the whole personality we will perceive this personality as it really is and not according to our projections, nor that we will necessarily do, or be done, less harm in a sexual encounter. Not to mention the fact that desire might be killed stone dead by the whole personality. Nevertheless there are some very disturbing aspects of the photographic fragmentation that dominates images of women generally. This is because the fetishistic form of photography – quite apart from the somewhat unhealthy obsession

Gold lurex sweater dress, £46 99

Miss Selfridge

Fig 9
It is often a detail on which
we might focus: a certain
expression in the eyes, the
nape of the neck, the way a
hand rests on a part of the
body.

with bits of the body – overlays the 'death effect of photography' (Fig
10). Photography has a particular claim to being realistic; it claims to
have been witness. What you are seeing really happened and it looked
like this. It is a form of witness, however, that in being present and
held in the hand is also evocative of absence. What is shown is not
there, but absent. What can be possessed in the hand is only an image,
a presence strongly reminding you of absence and death. It has been
suggested that perhaps this is why we can be fascinated by images of
ourselves and our families, the obsessive collecting of the family
album, an endless representation of presence to cover the fear of
absence. The form which fragmented photography of women's bodies
has taken has been built in a most unfortunate way. It uses codes that
evoke death not just by the photographic effect, but by the particular
posture, style, arrangement of 'the body'.

This leads on to the question of the code of submission, which is
similarly problematic. This is the dominant code by which female
sexual pleasure is represented. Women's pleasure is represented as

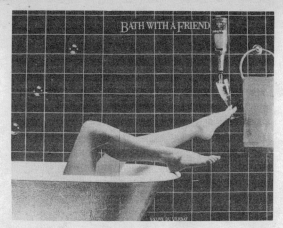

Fig 10

All around there are images of bits of bodies, bits separated from bodies, or arranged in such a way that the rest of the body must be contorted or dead.

'The surgeon cuts and all at once there leaps a mighty blood ... The scalpel sings ... The flesh splits open with its own kind of moan. It is like the penetration of a rape.' From *Mortal Lessons: Notes on the Art of Surgery* by Richard Selzer.

'Sir Michael said that Sutcliffe carried with him in his car a hacksaw blade, a hammer and a knife'. *Daily Telegraph*, May 1981.

simultaneously languid and turbulent, the combination of orgasm and passionate death. The explicit association with death which is frequently seen is extremely disturbing; women are shown in passionate submission, their posture evoking at best romantic deaths, at worst sexual murders (Fig 11). This, overlaid on the potentiality of photography unconsciously to suggest death, creates a regime of disturbing and erotic photographs. Not only do they reinforce ideologies of sexuality as female submission to male force, but they also powerfully recirculate the connexion between sexuality and death which is so cruelly played out in our society.

It can be seen from this argument that the regimes of meaning which are characteristic of pornography are by no means confined there. Certain things are characteristic of pornography, particularly the way it is predominantly consumed by male viewers and is therefore predominantly geared to male arousal. In such a context, the repeated images of female availability reinforce ideologies that female sexuality is a response, albeit an active one, to depersonalized male needs. What is more, the constant contextualization of these images in allusions to violence clearly sustains damaging associations between

Fig 11
The representation of female sexual
pleasure: submission and the ultimate
passivity, death.

male violence and sexual pleasure. No studies have proved
conclusively that there is a direct link between representations and
imitative acts of violence.[4] What can be demonstrated, however, is
that images reactivate or put into circulation definite meanings. And
the meanings that feminists find problematic in the images themselves
are by no means confined to pornography. The codes of
fragmentation, submission and availability are ubiquitous.

This is a primary reason why I think that pornography as such is
the wrong object of attack. Unless we refine our ways of talking about
sexist codes in general, how they operate and produce their meanings,
and why they are offensive, we run the risk of constantly being
misunderstood. Bodies like the Advertising Standards Authority view
feminist criticisms as prudish, a spin-off of the anti-porn stance. Our
descriptions of 'sexist', 'offensive' and 'degrading' remain curiously
underdeveloped. And because of this, criticism of sexist codes in films,
photography, in advertising and so on also run the risk of being
swamped by the anti-pornography positions. These anti-porn
positions assert that if it resembles pornography, it can be designated
pornography; anything that has explicit sex in it (since that is
pornography's speciality) is liable also to fall under that term.

But I also think that pornography is the wrong object of attack for
other reasons. One is that attacking pornography as merely the

embodiment of male sexual needs is a way of confirming the ideologies which the industry and images in pornography already set up. Pornography is massively used and consumed by men who appear to have no reservations about consuming these images in groups. On occasions where pornography has been passed around women's groups, many women have said that they were simultaneously embarrassed to be confronted with these images but also, on some occasions, aroused. A typical response to these 'confessions' is that, of course we are aroused by these images because this is how our society constructs sexuality; we, however, have a responsibility to confront these structures, to look at them *and put them aside*.

I am not at all sure that our contradictory responses can be dealt with in such a pre-emptive way. For example it is by no means clear to me that we have advanced very far in our understanding of the relationship between fantasy and act, between desire and sex, between the representations and the acts. Since the first flush of 'sexual liberation' feminists have come a long way in understanding that sexual relations, desire and sexual activity are also part of the problem of women's subordination; there has consequently been a dismissal of earlier positions which seemed to argue that part of women's liberation would be to get as much sex as possible. But this understanding need not lead to a position of putting public representation of sex aside until it is safe. It could be argued that women can be controlled through their sexuality, precisely because the definitions have been in the hands of men – that women have been split between those for whom sex is not so important but for whom love is all important, and those who actively participate in all the degrading things that men want. Arguing that women should put aside the degrading fantasies that seem to surround pornography seems yet again to put women in a position of being 'above' sex; women value sex only as part of a meaningful relationship. It seems to pre-empt any proper consideration of sexuality; whether sexual desire is dependent on secure and meaningful relationships or whether it is separate. It pre-empts any analysis of where our attractions and needs come from.

I remain sceptical as to whether the main problem in sexual relations is male brutality. Male violence is a real social problem.

But to state that male violence exists and that it is both condoned by our society and makes up an integral part of sexual relations does not exhaust what there is to say about sexual relations even, dare I say it, with men. There seems to me to be everything to be said and understood about sexuality. Indeed an argument could be made that one strategy towards women developing more power would be the exploration of sexual identities. It might well be just as subversive to the modes in which sexuality is currently organized if women could break the indissoluble link between sexuality and commitment. This kind of over-investment in one person is just as likely to cause suffering and it seems to me that nothing gets answered by setting up alternative versions of the same kind of sentimental commitment which has always characterized romantic stereotypes.

These then are two reasons for wondering whether we can simply regard pornography as an area of representation that is exclusively about male sexual needs and which should therefore be put aside. But there are further, perhaps more pressing, reasons to reformulate campaigns against sexist representations. I don't think that feminism can afford to get caught up in the major political positions which have hegemonized our thinking about pornography; that is, the liberal, 'anything goes so long as it's in private, without offence to "reasonable" people' or the pro-familial, right-wing, anti-sex position. Neither of these political positions has anything in common with feminism and we only do our cause harm to get caught up with either of these positions. Liberalism on the one hand suggests that each individual has the right to do what he/she wants; it refuses to see that individuals, in an unequal society, are the representatives of power groups. Thus nothing can be done against racism or sexism if the law persists in dealing with individual rights rather than the social harm done to 'minority groups' by the existence of racism or sexism. For this reason I am very far from advocating that nothing should be done about sexist representations. There should be laws controlling the incitement to sexual and racial hatred. But because most feminists recognize the need for some intervention does not mean that we have to join forces with the right-wing, law and order, clean-up-the-smut league. And if we concentrate on pornography, there is no way in which we can avoid this. The political terrain surrounding pornography is already carved up with hard and fast positions: are you for intervention in sex or are you against it? This should not be a feminist question. Clearly we are in the business of challenging attitudes and practices but we must surely distinguish our position from a right-wing prescriptive sexual morality?

Our strategy towards pornography might be more productively thought about in relation to anti-sexist legislation. I think this for several reasons. One is precisely that I do not think pornography is exclusively 'sexist' in its images and that the truly offensive codes in pornography are also to be found pervading other representational practices like advertising, television programmes, photography in general and so on. Secondly, if anti-sexist legislation could only be thought of in feminist terms and not in 'puritan' terms, we would be forced to formulate some wording about 'degrading to women' or 'against the dignity of women' which could encompass scenes of violence against women which are not specifically sexual (such as terror films). There are of course a number of dangers in making any call for legislation; the problem of who implements the law and to what end it is put is no less of a problem for anti-sexist legislation than it is for anti-pornography legislation. But two qualifications could be made. One is that a call for anti-sexist legislation could be treated as a propaganda exercise; it would be a victory for feminist critiques of representations and behaviour, whereas to raise the issue in terms of pornography makes it easy for our position to be overwhelmed by right-wing ideologies. It would mean we had to refine our discussions of what is sexist. Secondly, it is a call for legislation which insists on the necessity of socialism for feminism. However neglectful socialism has been of feminism, and it has been, we can neglect alliances only at our peril. Campaigns against male behaviour and certain sexual practices presumably hope to have some effect. No one is naive enough to think that this effect might be simply a change of attitude. Even changes of attitude have to be backed up by changes in legal statutes and practices and in social policies. If we are really hoping for such change, it would be incredible if we neglected a struggle for increasingly democratic participation and left implementation of policies to the groups who already have power and have not been concerned with feminist objectives in the past.

It will be clear from this argument that I am interested in a strategy which does not pre-empt explorations of sexuality, sexual desire and identity within the movement. I think an anti-pornography stance is not very useful because it assumes we all know what pornography is. It assumes that erotic images contribute to a culture where male arousal necessarily results in violence; the feminist critique of 'sexism' disappears under the question of pro or anti sex, which has already decided the discussion around pornography. If we are going to get any further in both specifying what sexism is, and also positively exploring new forms of sexual identity, then we can't afford to regard these questions as closed.

■ Notes

This is a version of a paper first given at the Communist University of London in July 1981. Since then these ideas have been discussed with the Socialist Feminist Social Policy Group: Fran Bennett, Wendy Clark, Margaret Page, Maria Black, Sue Lawrence, Rosa Heys and Ann Wickham. I am also extremely indebted to discussions with Eva Eberhardt, Wendy Clark and Margaret Page in the context of preparation for a workshop on sexuality and social policy.

1 In Britain these slogans are closely associated with Women Against Violence Against Women.
2 Recent restrictions on the display of pornography were drawn from the recommendations of the Williams Report – Report of the Committee on Obscenity and Film Censorship HMSO Nov 1979 and Cmnd 7772. The Advertising Standards Authority also refer to an unwritten code of what the person might find 'decent' or indecent. They dissuade from any legal action against images which women have found offensive on the grounds that 'reasonable' people in contemporary society do not object to a certain degree of 'explicitness'. (See report on the treatment of women in advertising, ASA report June 1980.)
3 There has been a certain amount of work on the codes which 'eroticize' images of women. Laura Mulvey's (1975) 'Visual Pleasure and Narrative Cinema' remains a crucial investigation of this process in film. At a practical level, the exhibition of photography by the Polysnappers, *Family, Fantasy, Photography*, also investigates the processes by which photography uses certain codes to give definite meanings to women.
4 This inconclusive work on effects of images of violence has mainly concentrated on studies of television, see Halloran (1970), Himmelweit (1960), and Lyle *et al* (1961).

The White Brothel:
The Literary
Exoneration of the
Pornographic

Susanne Kappeler

I originally wrote this piece as a contribution to the English Studies Group at the University of East Anglia, as part of a struggle, together with Diane DeBell, to introduce a feminist voice into the discussion of 'the literary'. D.M. Thomas's The White Hotel *seemed to me to embody the problematic of 'the literary' in stark measure, and its introduction to the group as a topic confirmed the resistance of 'the literary' to a feminist intervention. While the men of the group eventually agreed to read Andrea Dworkin,* Pornography: Men Possessing Women, *this turned the focus on to 'smut' and 'violence' and once again away from 'the literary'.*

When I submitted the article to Feminist Review, *it contained a first section attempting to link the issue of pornography in a literary work to discussions of pornography among censorship experts. However, I was asked to cut the first part which, it was felt, distracted from the analysis of the novel and its reception and seemed of minor relevance. I realized at that point that the connexions I wished to make between 'the literary' and 'pornography' could not be made in the space of an article and that I would need a full-length book to make the full argument. I have since written that book,* The Pornography of Representation *(Polity Press, 1986), in which a revised version of 'The White Brothel' has become 'Problem 7: Art and Pornography'.*

My experience of discussions of pornography since has confirmed my view that Art is probably the single most resistant area for ideological inquiry. A group of people may share the same view of conventional pornography, hold the same political position on the question of women in society and the same aspiration to equality and an end to oppression, and yet stop in awe and reverence before a work of art which is openly pornographic, oppressive of women and advocating domination – simply because it is a work of art. Art in our society enjoys a status comparable to that of religion in earlier societies, requiring an a priori belief in Art and an unshakable faith in its embodiment of the self-evident Good. As a result of this faith, works of art are apparently beyond criticism and beyond change. It is this faith I wish to challenge.

Response to D.M. Thomas's novel *The White Hotel* seems to be of two kinds only: either praise in the highest terms, or simple dismissal. In the case of the latter, there is not even any argument; what we hear therefore is mainly the former.

I myself find nothing to praise in Thomas's novel. But I do think it is worth talking about it, not only because of its wide acclaim, but because of the terms in which this praise is framed. For it is as a work of literary achievement that this novel is celebrated.

The White Hotel is an excellent example for a study of the interaction between the pornographic and the literary. For we need for our discussion not only a text classified as 'literary', but all the attendant buttressing of literary appraisal which, more than the text itself, indicates the points of defence, the points at which the literary is used to argue positively for the salvaging of the pornographic; where the presence of the literary is said to neutralize the pornographic. Bernard Williams, as a member of the Committee on Obscenity and Film Censorship, asks a French official how to define a 'film's being pornographic'. The Frenchman, dismissive of the philosopher's problem, answers:

> Everyone knows what a pornographic film is. There are no characters or plot, there is nothing but sexual activity, and it is not made by anyone that one has heard of. (Williams, 1983: 23)

Williams, thinking that he is about to catch him out, insists: 'But ... what if these criteria diverged? What if a film of nothing but sex were made by, say, Fellini?' According to the Frenchman's criteria the case is clear: the film is (would be) made by someone one *has* heard of. While the British censors may not be happy to enshrine these criteria in law, these are precisely the criteria of the literary establishment, the liberal cultural elite. Leaving aside the fact that there is extensive room for argument over 'nothing but sex' (at what point does a character cease to be a character, or sexual activity cease to be/have plot), there have been films which pose exactly this dilemma, amongst them Pasolini's *Salo* and Oshima's *Empire of the Senses*. Film censors in different countries have responded with different measures, but the cultural establishment, by and large, has firmly adhered to its tradition of recognizing, and defending, its artists. The French censors' solution is interesting: they did not banish *Salo* to the blue movie houses with a 'P' certificate, but confined it by special decree to two art houses in Paris (Williams, 1983) – where, one presumes, it met only with a 'responsible' metropolitan audience who appreciate Pasolini and was safe from abuse by the masses and the provincials.

The definition or categorization of something as 'literary' relies crucially and in the end circularly on the successful association with something else already categorized as literary. The hypothetical case of Fellini pornography and the actual instances of *Salo* and *Empire of the Senses* obligingly illustrate the point. Critics will of course expend much effort in arguing the literary qualities of the works in question; but the decision of the critic to put himself thus on the line in defending the daringly pornographic has been reached a) beforehand, and b) in the safe knowledge that Fellini, Pasolini, Oshima *means* 'literary', 'artistic', 'of quality'.

D.M. Thomas's *The White Hotel* is a similar case in point. While Thomas may not have been as assuredly known as, say, Fellini, he nonetheless already belonged to, and participated in, the domain of the literary as a poet, translator of literature and novelist. The publication of his novel by Victor Gollancz, and as a King Penguin (Penguin's answer to Picador, the specialists in the 'contemporary literary'), and its presentation to the Booker Prize and the Cheltenham Prize (1981) are all indicators of its claim to the literary. The piquancy of the case, however, rests on its obvious, 'daring' pornography. In fact, the British reception was somewhat hesitant at first, and the proper boom started only after the book's stormy success in the United States. Since then, it has been widely discussed by the media and prominently displayed and promoted by publishers and booksellers, and its rising sales figures quickly put it on to the bestseller charts. While the novel did not, in fact, win the Booker Prize competition, held before its American success (rumour has it, owing to objection from women on the panel), it is now advertised as the book that 'narrowly missed the 1981 Booker prize' (*London Magazine*, February 1982) and as 'soon to be a major film' on the back blurb of Penguin.

My argument is that it is due to the conjuncture of the pornographic with the literary that the novel enjoys such insistent acclaim, and that the arguments for its literariness 'in spite' of its pornographic qualities reveal the fundamental investment the literary has in pornography. Let me emphasize here that by pornography I do not just mean a degree of obscenity that falls beyond the mark of the censor's yardstick. A particular form of sexism, pornography is one of the most fundamental patriarchal structures in our culture, and one that is by no means simply avoided by the category of the literary. It is the gradeable and changing quality of obscenity that is deemed to be neutralized by the (universal, timeless) quality of the literary. The obscene, one might say, is a category of the dominant culture invented almost in order to protect the prevalence of pornographic structures: its appearance in its starkest (not to say most naked) form in the culture's category of pornography proper (the extreme) threatens to make visible the nature of the culture's values and sexual structures everywhere else and to show them up as in contradiction to the overt moral and political ideals. It is therefore expedient to point to a boundary – extremely difficult to establish in practice, as the obscenity trials, the Williams Report and so on show – to the one side of which lies the obscene, pornography proper, censured and disowned by law, while the other side of the boundary is thereby salvaged. I shall henceforth use 'pornography' as a feminist critical category, and not as the label for the culture's legitimated dustbin. For this I shall build on the critique of pornography already begun by other feminists.

I don't think that I need to prove the conventionally pornographic presence in *The White Hotel*, as there seems to be agreement that it is there, at least in the sections called *Don Giovanni* and *The Gastein Journal*. The literary argument runs from there, namely that it depends what Thomas 'does' with the pornographic element, what literary use he makes of it, that moves it beyond 'nothing but sex'. The expression 'nothing but sex' connotes gratuitousness. The literary provides a frame in which this element, which otherwise might appear gratuitous, can be anchored; it provides artistic purpose. Interestingly, the novel's conception follows this plot of the provision of purpose: on the acknowledgements page, Thomas states that 'Section 1 of *Don Giovanni* was first published as a self-contained poem'. *The White Hotel* was subsequently provided to accommodate it. And in an interview he is asked how he constructed the novel, in what order he did it, and did he actually write the poem first and then elaborate it? Thomas's answer is:

> Yes. And when I wrote the poem I had no idea that it was going to become a novel ... I wrote a poem called 'The Woman to Sigmund Freud', which was actually the first of the poetic pieces [i.e. *Don Giovanni*] in the novel. It was an open-ended poem, that I was quite pleased with in itself, but it didn't seem to lead anywhere ... So it was the poem first, quite independent of any idea that it fitted into a novel. (Thomas, 1982: 32-3)

In other words, the poem was gratuitous ('in itself', 'independent'). It was open-ended, it could have gone on for ever – nothing but sex, no plot. No characters either, just 'the woman', to Sigmund Freud. Thomas seems surprised that it 'fitted into a novel', unaware, apparently, that he provided a novel specifically to fit it. Let's see how he found the novel:

> It was only when I read Kuznetsov's *Babi Yar* that it clicked and I suddenly realized that the poems were, in fact, beginning a novel which would end in *Babi Yar* ... Well, that seemed to be a very exciting idea ... So, from the poem I then wrote the prose expansion, taking each part of it and re-framing it as narrative. Then it went into realism ... (Thomas, 1982: 33)

It was only when he read the account of one of history's most violent massacres, abounding in gratuitous brutality, that he saw an 'end' to which his pornographic poems could lead. He re-framed the plotless poetry in narratives. It was an 'exciting idea to work on'.

I shall now briefly show the true extent to which the acknowledged pornographic/erotic parts of the novel are pornographic in the feminist sense of the term, not that there is 'too much' sex, or sex too explicit, but *what kind of sex, what structure of sexuality, what sexual politics*. I shall then argue that Thomas's novel reflects, and invites, the pornographic structure on an extended level, and show how he, as well as one of his enraptured critics, exonerates the pornographic in the highest literary terms, exonerates it in the name of the literary.

It is above all the two parts of the novel purporting to be the 'writings' of Lisa Erdman which are overtly pornographic (in the usual sense): they are in the received mould of conventional pornographic literature, a picture of male-defined sexuality (not to mention a picture of male defined female sexual hysteria – a more refined minority genre). They are about fucking. Violence is an integral part. 'She' is the passive recipient of the fucking, suffering what is done to her and how and when it is done to her. The Penis, or its various substitutes, or the man (all paradigmatic alternatives, it seems) are the only agents in this almost plotless action:

> two, then three fingers he jammed into me ... his thrumming fingers filled me; then he rammed in again ... that night he almost burst my cunt apart ... Beneath our rug your son's right hand was jammed up to the wrist inside me ... driving like a piston in and out ... your son impaled me ... I think something inside me had been torn ... I was impaled upon a swordfish ... Then gradually it was the ice itself that cut into me ... a breast was sheared away ... the blizzard tore my womb clean out ... he came behind and rammed up into me ... he took my hand and slid my fingers up behind him there ... Your son crashed through my modesty ... my rump taking his thrust. (1981: 19-29)

Agency, as is clear from these extracts, meaning *violent* action. Apart from being the passive, receiving, suffering counterpart to this aggressive and violent action syntagm, the woman is further characterized by a lack of control even where she is, linguistically, the subject:

> I could not stop myself I was in flames from the first spreading of my thighs, no shame could make me push my dress down, thrust his hand away ... juices ran down my thighs ... I was split open by your son ... his finger jammed up right up my arsehole ... it makes me blush ... weakly I tried to push away his hand ... pulling me upon him without warning ... I couldn't sleep that night, I was so sore ... I couldn't tell which hole it was ... by the second night my breasts were bursting ... I opened up my dress, and my ache shot a gush out even before his mouth had closed upon my nipple, and I let the old kind priest ... take out the other ... I've never known my nipples grow so quickly ... my face lay buried in the pillow ... I didn't mind which one of them was in ... it was good to feel part of me was someone else, no one was selfish in the white hotel ... (1981:19-30)

Where she isn't overpowered by 'your son' (and occasionally his twin, Nature – blizzard, ice) she is overcome by involuntary bodily reactions, mostly of pain, while anything else that she might have undertaken is rendered as a failed attempt – I could not, I tried, I couldn't tell, I never knew, characterized by impotence and ignorance; the only successful 'act' being that of allowing others to do things.

The assumption of the female point of view and narrative voice does not alter the pornographic structure, the fundamental elision of the woman as subject. It is indeed one of the oldest pornographic devices to fake the female's/victim's point of view. Many pornographic books are published under a female author-pseudonym. The so-called female view point is a male construction of the passive victim in his own constructed scenario: whether 'she' resists/struggles against her violation, whether she enjoys it in involuntary physical response against her will, or whether she is infinitely available to his impositions – all available alternatives serve to enhance the pornographic pleasure. The options are strictly defined within the one imperative that it *will* happen to her, 'she' can choose an attitude. As Roland Barthes defines it with characteristic oblique strokes:

> The scream is the victim's mark; she makes herself a victim because she chooses to scream; if, under the same vexation she were to ejaculate (sic), she would cease to be a victim, would be transformed into a libertine: *to scream/to discharge*, this paradigm is the beginning of choice, i.e. Sadian meaning. (Quoted in Dworkin, 1981:94)

Note how suddenly the female, passive sufferer becomes an active responsible agent: *she makes herself* a victim because she chooses to scream; note how 'the same vexation' she is under is beyond the choice of alteration. The text is given, she can choose to mark it.

We have the whole spectrum of the victim's choices in this piece from *The White Hotel*: the resisting victim, who suffers pain from the struggle; her involuntary 'pleasure' in spite of herself – 'his thrumming fingers filled me with a great gape of wanting' (19), 'it was so sweet I screamed' (23) – to her total conversion to his intentions: 'I said, Please fuck me, please' (22). The female 'gape of wanting', the void to be filled, the great emptiness waiting for the male stuffing is another great male myth, tallying with the male obsession with the size of members and the male fear that the bigger the better.

I do not wish to reproduce Thomas's text any further, and take this as sufficient illustration of the pornographic structure, of the sexism, of the sexual politics embodied in his female character's writings. I shall now look at one critic's response to – and reproduction of – the pornographic structure. George Levine in his review of the novel in the high literary *New York Review of Books* (Levine, 1981) certainly recognizes these passages as conventionally pornographic – 'her first violent and pornographic "phantasy" is written in loose blank verse'.

He is safe in the knowledge that he will proceed to prove the novel's literary qualities – the desired remedy which salvages the pornographic from being pornography.

Looking at the larger structure of the novel, the feminist critic will find in Thomas's use of the holocaust final proof of his bad faith. It may have seemed implausible that a contemporary novelist should be unaware of the conventions of narrative and the modes of representation to the extent of thinking that he could 'speak through a woman' (Thomas, 1982:28), of believing that 'you are involving the feminine aspect of yourself in poetry' (1982:30) or that in creating a female character in his novel he would be writing 'from the point of view of a woman' (1982:30). It is inconceivable, however, that he should be so ignorant as to believe that linking sexual violence and male fantasy with the holocaust was a profound, original or artistic achievement. Nazi sadism is a stock genre of pornography, and one of the most marketable at that. Let us see what a literary man makes of this devastating conjunction.

George Levine finds *The White Hotel* 'a novel of immense ambition and virtuosity [what he 'does' with it]. With the strength of its precise and risky use of language, it moves us from the self into history ...' Whose self? Whose history? Whose 'us' does it thus move? Levine notes that the novel begins with Freud (and Jung) and 'ends somewhere beyond history'. 'Between these extremes, we follow the life of a fictional woman, Elisabeth Erdman.' Lisa Erdman, alias Anna G, is, we noted, at the centre of the pornographic experience related in the two 'writings' parts, i.e. the two pieces of acknowledged hard-core pornography, and she is at the centre of the experience of the sado-horrors of the holocaust narrative. For these narratives to be salvaged from the realm of the pornographic per se, the culture's dustbin, into the sanctuary of the literary, something major would have to be 'done' by the rest of the novel, would require audacity as well as ambition – to follow the literary argument (though in practice we know that nothing more needs to be 'done' than that it is written by someone one has heard of). Levine senses the enormity of the task: 'the audacity of Thomas's achievement can be felt most immediately in its ambition'. He obviously feels the ambition to be fulfilled, the task to be accomplished. And how does he see it accomplished? Already in terms of the novel's structure he sees Lisa Erdman's life as the mere transition between the historic self (Freud) and the 'beyond history' of the holocaust:

Freud is one of the major characters, both investigating the experience and participating in it, speaking the reticent and revelatory language of his obsessive pursuit of scientific truth.

An affinity is obviously felt between the writer/reader and this major character Freud and their joint project of 'investigating the experience' of horror, torture and sexual assault of Lisa Erdman, participating in her experience in the voyeuristic relation of the analyst/fictionalizer, participating in experience by another 'by speaking the reticent and revelatory language' of representing her as an object, the one in his obsessive pursuit of scientific truth, the other in his obsessive pursuit of the (marketable) literary. That this relationship of language, of representation, in relation to the particular 'experience' in question might be problematical, indeed is the problematic which might justify the task, seems hardly to emerge as an awareness. The author, in his only narrative intervention that might represent an attempt to salvage the audacity of his endeavour, blithely calls Lisa Erdman's experiences (and those of everyone else in the Babi Yar massacre) 'amazing experiences' (1982: 220). His awareness of the problematic of his relationship to it finds expression in the triteness of 'Nor can the living ever speak for the dead' (221). Yet speak he does.

Levine's assertion that 'neither Freud nor Babi Yar is cheapened or exploited by the fictionalizing, and [that] neither diminishes the fictional heroine, Elisabeth, who becomes a case study', is a claim which goes without any proof or evidence and seems to me to betray a pointed unease. Already, from the centre of the experience, we have moved to the priority of Freud and Babi Yar, man and history, in our quick glance to check that neither has been cheapened; the 'fictional heroine' (not even 'woman') enters as an afterthought. 'Freud is one of the major characters ... Elisabeth enters the book almost as an aside ... in a letter ... by Freud to his friend and disciple Hanns Sachs'. The critic's glance and the novel's structure in harmonious homology. There follows a quote from the letter, then Levine continues: 'the images here (which will recur throughout the book) seem almost more important than the patient'. The projects of 'Freud' (fictionalized) and of the writer/reader remain closely linked: in the one Lisa Erdman becomes a case study (no diminishment), in the other a fictional heroine of minor importance, one who, in Levine's opinion, remains a 'mystery' despite her writings. However, 'her "writings" ... alone (though they leave their author a mystery) are enough to justify the admiration this novel has already evoked from the critics'. (Remember that we set out to justify the 'writings' by the literary novel into which they were integrated.) 'Her' fantasy, represented by the dazzling 'virtuosity' and 'cleverness' of Thomas, becomes the favoured focus of this critic's obsessive pursuit of the literary, just as it does for the fictionalized Freud: 'a prose elaboration of her verse, carefully repeating images, developing them … The language of the poem and the letter ranges from the merely vulgar, or banal, to a lush, romantic intensity, with a remarkable precision of imagery. Her writing is full of dislocation and surprise; it is seductive, frightening, and beautifully alive.' It is full of pain, violence and violation: 'whatever else the book is, it is a pleasure to read'.

After a quote ending in 'I jerked and jerked until his prick released/its cool soft flood. Charred bodies hung from the trees …', Levine comments: 'Such language immediately establishes the mysterious "Anna G." as a powerful presence.' I don't know whether Levine means what he is saying here, as for once I almost agree with him. Remember that he himself said that Lisa Erdman remains a mystery despite her 'writings'. The presence of woman is not easily established through the means of representation, through the power of naming that has been men's for and in recorded history. The presence established is that of 'Anna G.', who is the construction of 'Freud', who is the construction of Thomas. The experience of Lisa Erdman is still nowhere.

But we have noticed already that Levine's interest in the novel lies elsewhere, that he reads the presented novel like the usual consumer of pornography, with the interest of the male experience to be got from it ('her' writing is 'seductive'), the woman in the piece reduced to object, means to a certain end, vehicle for his pleasure. His worry about the novel is not how the salaciousness of the pornography and the holocaust titillation might be justified; his worry is whether Thomas might stoop to discredit Freud. With a sigh of relief he observes: 'Discrediting Freud is neither a particularly interesting narrative enterprise, nor Thomas's true purpose.' 'Thomas's Freud is both vulnerable and heroic, ambivalently confirmed in his unscientific guesses, made touchingly human in his reading of the death instinct into history.' Lisa Erdman is both vulnerable and heroic, unambivalently condemned beyond the touchingly human in her experience of the death instinct manifested through Babi Yar. But Levine is immune to that side of the story. Freud has become the uncontested hero of his reading; Freud 'is a hero of the quest for a world that makes sense, and he is himself a victim'. Freud is the hero of this novel beginning with gratuitous pornographic exploitation, ending in gratuitous violence and horror laced with sexual sadism, whose plot, we understand, consists of the heroic quest for scientific truth, the vagaries of unscientific guesses, the touching vulnerability of the genius who explores 'virgin' territory of knowledge. The depth of the romantic intensity, of the emotional scope of this drama, lies in the reduction of the hero-genius to 'victim'. A most moving, stirring drama of humanity. 'Moving', incidentally, is how Levine describes Babi Yar, moving, because the intrusion by the narrator concerning the 'amazing' experiences of people like Lisa Erdman, is 'something other than a mockery of Freud's work'. The humanity of the author lies in his not mocking his fallen hero. And as this critic penetrates beneath the facts of this novel to the drama of his hero, so the hero Freud 'penetrates beneath the facts, forces the patient out from behind her firmly willed deceptions'. No change of register is needed from the pornographic to the literary (critical): penetration continues, the patient continues to be forced, forced out from behind her firmly willed masquerading as a woman, a subject, an agent. She is patient, it will be done to her; she has the choice between resisting (clinging to her firm deceptions) and welcoming it, marking the text (it is already written), with the marks of her choice: the scream of the victim or the discharge of the libertine. She does, like every pornographic victim, do both: she protests and marks the text with a footnote and a postscript (the text remains), as she literally marks and postscripts Freud's case history 'Anna G.', and she is grateful to the wise professor, her master. And the other text remains; whichever choice she makes, Sadean meaning results: it is a pleasure to read, her 'writings' alone are enough to justify the admiration this novel has already evoked. And the 'true' purpose of Thomas's novel (no, thank goodness not the denigration of Freud) emerges clearly: 'It is not simply in the ideas, in the criticism of Freud or in the dramatic confirmation of him, that this novel achieves its power and significance'. Although the ' "death instinct" is everywhere in the novel', Levine is convinced that 'the forces on the side of life [are] more powerful still' in the final balance of the work. 'In the proximity of actual death [of Freud's mother and child] to a theory that explains it, we sense the pressure of life is close as well.' In the comparatively harmless face of death that the loss of close relatives (through illness and old age) presents to the surviving observer, the proximity of a theory that explains it may well be cheering and insinuate the closeness of the forces of life. The proximity of Freud's, and more to the point, of Thomas's literary theory 'that explains it' to the multiple death and destruction in Lisa Erdman's experience is rather more chilling, and indicates the closeness and pressure of darker forces. However, Levine is fascinated with the death instinct: 'Thanatos exists in the energy of Eros, or so Freud thought. Elisabeth's fantasies provide evidence for this view, and it is true that the effectiveness of the pornography in her writing makes the inevitably accompanying fantasies of disaster the more frightening.' Pornography exists in the symbiosis of Thanatos and Eros. Elisabeth's, Thomas's, Sade's etc. fantasies provide evidence for this view. And it is true that the frightening disasters inevitably accompanying their sexual fantasies make the pornography the more effective. It is the more 'beautifully alive', the more dead the victim and sexual object.

Lisa Erdman is dead many times over. Almost killed through the sexual violations of 'Freud's son' (Thomas's fantasy), mutilated through 'Freud's' forcing her into the case study 'Anna G.', and dying a multiple death at the hands of her torturers at Babi Yar, she is buried once more by the literary reader Levine, who relegates her out of the novel, out of the plot, tossing her back at the 'hero Freud' as a toy, an object, a means of stimulation for *his* fantasies. At best, the woman, Lisa Erdman, 'the neurotic "Anna G." ', in successive stages of fictionalization at the hands of her fictionalizers, 'provides a moment of potential healing for Freud himself'. The great hero, in his untiring fantasies, is 'vulnerable and heroic' in his supremacy, 'ambivalently confirmed in his unscientific guesses' about woman, made touchingly human in his reading of the death instinct into history, in his projection of sex and violence, the pornographic axiom, into the history of humanity, the culture of mankind.

Thomas, with his 'precise and inventive prose', 'his cleverness in mixing fiction with history' which makes him join the pornographic fantasies with the atrocities of the history of Babi Yar, has become the snuff-artist of the cultural establishment: he understands that Lisa Erdman is not just the fantasized victim of his narrative, the fantasized construction of Freud's case history, but for true literary consummation has to be the real victim of authentic history. She must be a true woman and she must be truly dead to trigger the literary climax. He knows because he has one as he writes:

> Writing is also a surrogate sexual pleasure, a sublimation of the sexual instinct. And what *does* happen is that you find yourself writing something which you're enjoying sexually. Then you

> look back on it and say 'I enjoyed that, but it doesn't work in terms of the book' ... so then you have to alter it ... It was only when I read Kuznetsov's *Babi Yar* that it clicked ... So, from the poem I then wrote the prose expansion, taking each part of it and re-framing it as narrative. Then it went into realism ... (Thomas, 1982: 31-3)

Writing is a surrogate sexual pleasure. And is it surprising that this literary art is a perfect reflection, a mirror image, of the conventional male-defined sexual act, the sexual assault on the sex object:

> My editor says my novels are like explosions, and I think that's right. It (sic) may go off like a damp squib, or it may make a nice bang, but it's not going to be one of those long drawn-out ... (sic) I can't work that way. (Thomas, 1982: 36)

And as regards the mutuality of that sex act, look at what happens to his partner:

> It's ... got to have ... impact, so that the reader is left shaken by it ... – but over very quickly, or else it's just not going to interest me ... The idea of writing a five-hundred, eight-hundred page novel would be inconceivable. (Thomas, 1982: 36)

I'm quite sure.

The male literary reader, identifying with his hero Freud and his hero writer, turns on to this; responds to Thomas's realism and mistakes it for reality:

> Thomas suggests a reality at once vital and deadly, and more accessible than we – protected behind our documents and books – might care to know. (Levine, 1981: 23)

And in his enjoyment he has 'no reservations' about this great work of art, 'its strengths remain'. 'Its title suggests that life can be seen either as a matter of peace or of violence.' Perhaps it depends on your point of view. Levine, at any rate, feels at peace, feels secure and protected in the literary sanctuary.

The feminist reader, by contrast, can find no place to take up in this literary romance. Hers would be the designated place of the victim, but if the truth be known: she doesn't wish for Thomas's impact, she has no desire for his big bang (however quickly it is over). This kind of reading, pornographic reading, is 'for men only'. For she has no part in Levine's 'we': *she* finds no protection behind his ('our') documents and books, the literary is no sanctuary to her. And she has every reason to 'care to know': how easily accessible this reality is, how easily accessible she is to this reality – deadly to her, but so vital to the patriarchs, our literary men.

Anti-Porn: Soft Issue, Hard World

B. Ruby Rich

The landscape described in the following article has undergone a number of shifts and alterations since first publication in 1982. At the time that Not a Love Story *was released,* Women Against Pornography *was largely involved in picketing and demonstrations. WAP was looked upon as the feminist position on pornography, and women opposed to its anti-porn position were isolated voices in the wilderness.*

Since then, Andrea Dworkin and Catharine MacKinnon have teamed up to draft a controversial piece of legislation aimed at removing pornography, including any material deemed exploitative of women's bodies, from the realm of public consumption. They have travelled throughout the US to build support for the legislation, including the formation of a number of dubious alliances with right-leaning sectors. The legislation was passed by the City Council of Indianapolis, only to be overturned recently by a Supreme Court ruling on its unconstitutionality. Meanwhile, nearly concurrent with the Dworkin/MacKinnon legislative initiatives, the Reagan administration has been pursuing its own anti-porn campaign. Attorney General Edward Meese has led a special commission on pornography through a series of public hearings, gathering evidence and testimony on porn in preparation for the drafting of a report, recently issued, calling for new and widespread restrictions.

These trends are alarming, and would be more so if not for the emergence of a new feminist sector committed to freedom of speech and opposed to censorship, fearing that any such legislation will render our literature among its first casualties. FACT (Feminist Anti-Censorship Task Force) is a New-York-based group initially organized to combat the Dworkin/MacKinnon legal strategy and to assemble facts capable of countering the rhetoric used to fuel anti-porn hysteria.

While the politics of anti-porn, then, cannot really be said to have changed, the style and strategy of those politics are indeed different today. With the publication of literature in the US and Canada, and a vastly widened debate, my own article is no longer an individual aberration.

Why has the anti-porn movement been so popular with the dominant media? My suspicions are not benign. For one thing, in a society that has failed to distinguish between sexuality and pornography, the anti-porn movement is a perfect vehicle for lumping all feminists together into one posse, a bunch of sex cops out to handcuff the body politic's cock. The ensuing ridicule can always offset any serious statements. Second, the subject offers the chance to talk about sex – something the mainstream media are never loath to take up. Third, the anti-porn movement is probably seen, and rightly so, as profoundly ineffectual, unlikely ever to make a dent in the massive commercial-sex industry it would seek to topple. The porn companies don't have to worry about any consumer boycott by women; we're not their consumers. It is even possible that the antiporn forces get press *because* they represent no threat. *Not a Love Story* – portentously subtitled 'a motion picture about pornography' – can open at the 57th Street Playhouse in a gala premiere, emblazon the *Village Voice* and the *Times* as well with ads, boast a prestige distributor and a first-class PR firm, and even make it onto the evening news. Just in case there's any lingering doubt about its moral fibre, keep in mind that it showed at the same theatre where *Genocide* just ran.

■ Part I: The appeal

Documentary films, like fiction, have a script. The script may not be written before the shooting, as with fiction, but in that case it gets written in the editing room. *Not a Love Story* is no exception. Director Bonnie Klein, producer Dorothy Todd Henaut, and associate director and editor Anne Henderson seem to have scripted a religious parable.

In this moral tale, each character has a clearly prescribed role. Klein, who appears on-screen to supply an identification figure for the audience, plays the missionary in a heathen land. Seeking out the purveyors of porn, she is seen unearthing the sins of the world in order to combat them and save our souls. 'Blue Sky', 'Raven', and other peep-show workers and strippers all play the collective role of victim. Porn photographer Suze Randall, who photographs hard-core spreads in her studio, plays the classic madame: she who sells her own kind but probably, deep inside, is a true believer. The porn moguls interviewed are surely the forces of evil, whether represented by the sleazy panache of publisher David Wells or by the endearing just-like-your-Uncle-Henry spirit of one sex emporium manager. The male customers constitute the legions of rank sinners. A San Francisco-based group of men against male violence assumes the guise of *penitentes*; matching a sixties wire-rim style to an eighties sensitivity, they take the sins of their kind upon their shoulders and expiate them. There is, of course, a roster of saints: Susan Griffin, Kate Millett, Margaret Atwood, Kathleen Barry, and topping them all, Robin Morgan who, with husband Kenneth Pitchford and young son, presents her own version of the Holy Family. Addressing the camera with a philosophical fervour (except for the more casual Millett), the saints embody the forces of righteousness arrayed against the sinful.

The pivotal figure in the parable is Linda Lee Tracey, a stripper with a comedic 'Little Red Riding Hood' act. She performs the role of the reformed sinner, without whom no religious faith could be complete. Her redemption seals the film's theme, binds the audience to it and provides the necessary narrative closure. *Not a Love Story* opens with a series of valentines, ranging from soft-core forties-style to an up-to-date hard-core *Hustler* version, but clearly it is the Sacred Heart that takes over by the end.

Linda Lee is the real star of the film. A Montreal media personality famous for her annual 'Tits for Tots' charity-strips, she was a find for the filmmakers. It is she who accompanied director Klein on all the interview sessions, frequently asking the questions herself, challenging the hucksters, haranguing customers from a soapbox on the street. If Klein empathizes on screen, emoting outrage and concern, it is Tracey who acts, reacts and takes the risks. Just how much of a risk is made clear toward the end of the film. The audience has already been buffeted by pornographic images and film clips, appalled by the attitudes of the porn kings, overwhelmed by the statistics, and alternately inspired and outraged by what has been shown and said. As the culmination of its guided tour, the audience gets to be present at a photo session set up between porn photographer Suze Randall and our by-now heroine Linda Lee, who has decided 'to find out what it feels like to be an object'. In her willingness to embrace this risk, Linda Lee becomes the film's *dramatis persona*, the one character who is transformed, within the film, by the very experience of making the film. As if Christ had come back as a latter-day Mary Magdalene, she literally offers up her body for our, and her, salvation.

Halfway through the film, Linda Lee comments that 'it's starting to get to me at an emotional level'. She meant: *the* pornography. But I mean: the movie. *Not a Love Story* is, for me, more depressing than inspiring, more irritating than enlightening. The film hits its emotional stride early on and stays there, never straying into detours of social analysis, historical perspective or questions of representation. Klein sets the tone with her pose of womanly empathy, polite outrage and respectability. She recounts her decision to make the film after her eight-year-old daughter's exposure to porn magazines at the local bus counter. I suspect many viewers' response to the movie will rise or fall on the issue of identification with Klein. Mine fell. An aura of religiosity began to permeate the proceedings. Method and message began to blur as the film gained in momentum, upping the emotional ante into a cathartic finale.

Not a Love Story is no call to arms, but rather an exercise in show-and-tell. Gaze at the forbidden, react with your choice of anger or outrage or grief (or the male option: guilt), and leave a changed person. When Linda Lee undergoes her debasement at the lens of Suze Randall and subsequently emerges transformed and cleansed – running on the beach in the film's last frames – she is enacting a ceremony that the audience communally shares. A change in consciousness, a change of heart. Look here and weep. Post-screening goings-on, both at the New York premieres and in Canada, fortify the scenario. After-film discussions have turned the theatre into a secular confessional, eliciting testimonials, women's resolutions to confront their mates' porn collections, teenage boys swearing to forgo the porn culture that awaits them, male viewers alternately abashed or exploding in anger, etc. According to polls of the film's audiences, people are moved from seeing pornography as harmless to viewing it as harmful by the end of the film. Conversion cinema in action.

Is the appeal of the film, then, a religious one? A desire to pass through the flames, be washed in the blood of the lamb, and come out a new person? I think not. Instead, the anti-porn film is an acceptable replacement for porn itself, a kind of snuff movie for an anti-snuff crowd. In this version, outrage-against replaces pleasure-in, but the object of the preposition remains the same. Cries of outrage and averted eyes replace the former clientele's silent pleasure and inverted hats; the gaze of horror substitutes for the glaze of satiation. The question, though, is whether this outcry becomes itself a handmaiden to titillation, whether this alleged look of horror is not perhaps a most sophisticated form of voyeurism. The ad campaign reinforces the suspicion, with its prominent surgeon-general-style warning about the 'graphic subject matter' that viewers might want to avoid ... if avoidance is indeed the desired goal.

The film's own methods compound the problem. While it would be unrealistic to ask *Not a Love Story* to solve problems the political movement it addresses has so far ignored, it's reasonable to expect the film to take up those problems relevant to its own medium. A host of issues raised by pornography are applicable to cinema, ranging from voyeurism or objectification to simple questions of point of view. Instead of facing these challenges, though, the film-makers seem unquestioningly to accept and deploy traditional cinematic practices. Given their subject matter, this decision creates a subtext of contradiction throughout the film.

For example, the early scenes of strippers performing their act are shot from the audience, a traditional enough technique for a rock concert movie, but problematic here. Doesn't such a shot turn the viewer into the male customer normally occupying that vantage point? Doesn't the camera's privileged gaze, able to zoom in and out at will, further objectify the woman on stage? Worse yet is the scene shot in a club equipped with isolation-masturbation booths, wherein the women on display communicate with the male customers via a glass window and telephone, with the duration determined by a descending black-out shutter timed to the deposit of money. The cinematographer lines the camera up with this same shutter, positioning us behind the shoulder of a male customer in the booth, protected by shadows even as the woman called 'Blue Sky' is exposed to our view. The cinematographer takes this alignment with the male customer one step further by zooming in for a close-up on 'Blue Sky' – thereby presenting us with an intimate view not even available to the real-life customer. (At such moments, Klein's use of a male camera-man becomes an issue.) Why visually exploit this woman to a greater degree than her job already does? Why make the male customer our stand-in and then let him off the hook, without either visual exposure or verbal confrontation? Why not let us see what 'Blue Sky' sees? Instead, the film-maker proceeds to interview two of the women from within this same booth and from the customer's seat. Now the man has departed and we remain sophisticated consumers, out for the show *and* the facts, coyly paying money when the inevitable shutter descends.

The film-makers efface their own presence whenever the movie enters the sex emporiums. While Klein is prominent in the other interview sessions, she does not appear at all in the clubs. Furthermore, no second camera ever shows us the steady gaze of *this one* filming the scene for us, the performer's 'other' audience. True, we see the male audience – but only from the vantage point of another member of that audience. The camera is protected in its invisibility by the film-maker, just as the male customers are in turn protected in their anonymity by the camera.

This is a serious mistake, but it's a clue to the film's attitude. At no point does the camera offer a shot from the point of view of the women up on the stage. We're never permitted to share their experience while they're working – to inhabit their perspective when they're supposedly being most exploited and objectified. The result is a backfire: we remain voyeurs, and they remain objects – whether of our pity, lust, respect or shock makes little difference.

Not all the problems arise out of shooting; others occur in the editing room, particularly in the choices of sound/image combination. The key scene is Linda Lee's porn photo session with Suze Randall, whose presence overwhelms us with frequent calls for such props as 'the pussy light' and 'the pussy juice'. Although the scene has Linda Lee speaking as she starts to pose, her voice gives way to a voice-over of Susan Griffin explaining eros. Only later do we get to hear Linda Lee's comments. Why use Griffin's words when the film could have reinforced Tracey's image with her own explanation? Instead, the considerable power she wields elsewhere in the film simply evaporates.

The power of the pornography included as exhibits throughout the movie does no such evaporation act. Why does the film present us with the porn materials intact? Any number of methods could have been used either to intensify their impact or to diminish it. Some kind of manipulation of the image is standard practice in films incorporating pre-existing footage. The film-makers chose not to, with two possible results: either we're made to undergo the degradation of porn, or we're offered its traditional turn-on. Klein wants the audience to eat its cake and have it, too.

In sum, *Not a Love Story* is very much a National Film Board of Canada product: concerned, engaged, up to the minute on social questions, but slick, manipulative, avoiding all the hard questions to capture the ready success of answering the easy ones. It may have a different subject from other NFB films, but its methods are inherited. These methods have been developed for decades, and they work. If *Not a Love Story* is successful, that will be because of its emphasis on emotion, the presence of Linda Lee Tracey as a genuinely appealing star, the shock of the porn characters, and the sympathy of Bonnie Klein as our Alice in Pornoland. Not incidentally, the film offers some of the porn its audience wants to see but wouldn't be caught dead seeking out in Times Square.

Most fundamentally, though, the film's fate will signal the prospects of the anti-pornography campaign itself. The basic questions are not, finally, about *Not a Love Story* at all. They concern the past and future of anti-porn politics, the reasons for its appeal and the questions of priority it raises.

■ Part II: Displacement, confusion and what's left out

There are many unanswered questions in *Not a Love Story*, the title itself not the least of them. Assuming that pornography is not about love, what is it? The film privileges the words of Susan Griffin, who defines one of the central tenets of the anti-porn movement: pornography is different from eroticism. Kate Millett says the same thing, as have countless others. But, what is pornography and what is eroticism? One is bad, the other is good (guess which). Fixing the dividing line is rather like redlining a neighbourhood: the 'bad' neighbourhood is always the place where someone *else* lives. Porn is the same. If I like it, it's erotic; if you like it, it's pornographic. The rules don't seem much clearer than that, so the game gets murkier by the minute. Ready?

Two stories. Back in 1969, when I first started thinking about this distinction, my best friend worked as an artist's model; so, eventually, did I. She would model for painters but never for photographers, since with them you'd have no control over who saw your body. Once she broke the rule and modelled for a mutual friend, a photographer who did a series of nude photographs of her that we all loved. He had a show in a local gallery. One photograph of my friend was stolen out of the show. She went into a terrible depression. She was tormented by the image of an unknown man jerking off to her picture. Test: was that photograph erotic or pornographic?

Back in 1980, a woman I know went to spend the day with a

friend's family. Looking around the house, what should she discover but the father's personal copy of the Tee Corrine cunt colouring book. Made for the women's community, the book usually was found only in feminist bookstores. Test: is the book erotic or pornographic?

I have other friends and other stories. Surely it is not merely an *image* which is one thing or the other, but equally (if not foremost) the *imagination* that employs the image in the service of its fantasy. It is time that anti-porn activists stopped kidding themselves about the fine distinctions between eroticism and pornography. If any extra test is needed, the film offers us one in its final freeze-frame shot of a bikini-clad Linda Lee, snapped in midair, seaweed in hand. It is meant as an image of 'wholeness, sanity, life-loving-ness', according to the film-makers, but it comes out looking more like a soft-core Tampax ad. Is this image, perchance, pornographic as well?

There is no end of definitions as to what pornography is or isn't. For me, that's no longer the point. I have read the statistics, thank you, on whether porn causes violence or violence causes porn, taken part in the chicken-or-the-egg fights, steered clear of the currently chic analyses of porn in academic circles. I'm as fed up with pornography being identified as sexuality (in some circles) as with anti-pornography being identified as feminism (in other circles). The books, the articles and now the films have been rolling out. Such widespread acceptance is always a clue that the problem has moved elsewhere. Why is pornography so important, finally? Is it important enough to be consuming all our political energy as feminists? Certain it is seductive. It offers no end of discourse, arguments, connotations and denotations in which we can immerse ourselves, no end of soul searching and pavement pounding which we can enact if so moved. But whence comes its assumed political priority, and does the issue deserve it?

The film, like much Women Against Pornography campaign rhetoric, tends to identify porn both by what it is *not* (a love story) and by what it *is* at its most extreme (sadism, torture dramas). The film, like the anti-porn movement lately, emphasizes the extent to which sex-and-violence *is* the contemporary face of porn. But such a focus dodges the dilemma. If violence were the only problem, then why would the film include extensive footage of the strip shows and peep booths? If only violent sex were the object of wrath, then why would any Women Against Pornography group picket a non-violent live sex show or girlie line-up? In fact, the reliance on violence-condemnation in the rhetoric is a clue to the appeal of the anti-porn movement. Women today are terrified at the levels of violence being directed at us in society – and, to take it further, at powerless people everywhere. As one porn actress in the movie eloquently put it, we're 'the fucked'. Women are terrified at the crazy spiral of rape, assaults on abortion rights, sterilization expansion, domestic battering and anonymous bashing.

Terror is not an effective emotion, though. It paralyses. The fear of escalating violence, accompanied by the larger social backlash, has resulted not in massive political action by feminists but rather in a reaction of denial, a will *not to see* the dangers ... a desperate desire to see, instead, their disguises. Turning away from a phalanx of assaults too overwhelming to confront, the Women Against Pornography groups turn instead to its entertainment division, pornography. But whether symptom or cause, pornography presents an incomplete target for feminist attack. The campaign against pornography is a massive displacement of outrage that ought to be directed at a far wider sphere of oppression. Just as the film narrows the hunt down to sinners, villains and victims so too does the anti-pornography movement leave out too much in its quasi-religious attack on the Antichrist.

The hunt for archetypes, darkly submerged drives and other assorted ghouls of the pornography industry and the pornographic imagination has left livelier culprits out in the cold. So long as the conversion experience is the primary method, then the social, economic, historical and political determinants get short shrift. As long as they continue, of course, it is unlikely that Dorothy Henaut will get her dream – announced opening night – of seeing the porn industry up and 'wither away'.

The emphasis on violence has masked the central issue of male-female power relations which we see reflected and accentuated in pornography. Any woman is still fair game for any man in our society. Without an understanding of these power relations, no analysis of porn will get very far. It certainly won't be able to account for the prevalence of fake lesbianism as a staple of pornographic imagery (without violence). It certainly won't be able to account for the difference between straight porn and gay male porn, which lacks any debasement of women and must raise complex issues regarding sexual objectification. If an analysis of porn were to confront its basic origin in the power relations between men and women, then it would have to drop the whole eroticism-versus-pornography debate and take on a far more complex and threatening target: the institution of heterosexuality. Here, again, is a clue to the anti-porn movement's appeal for some battle-scarred feminists. Is it, perhaps, more tolerable for the woman who might attend *Not a Love Story* to come to terms with how her male lover's pornographic fantasy is oppressing her in bed than to confront, yet again, how his actual behaviour is oppressing her in the living room ... or out in the world?

Also left out of the picture are all questions of class and race, subsumed under the religious halo of good versus evil. Does it do any good, however, to view the women employed in the porn empire as victims? Linda Lee herself, in the movie, describes having gone to a Women Against Pornography demonstration in New York and feeling the other women's condescension. Or, as 'Jane Jones' told Laura Lederer in the *Take Back the Night* anthology, 'I've never had anybody from a poor or working-class background give me the "How could you have done anything like that?" question, but middle-class feminists have no consciousness about what it is like out there.' As long as the economic forces and social choices that move these women into the commercial-sex world remain invisible, they themselves will continue to be objectified, mystified and mis-understood by the very feminist theorists who, wine glass in hand or flowers nearby, claim to have all the answers. The film equally ignores questions of race, even though the porn industry, in its immense codification, has always divided the female population up into racial segments keyed to specific fetishes.

Issues of race and class, here, are particularly troubling in that they divide so clearly the film-makers from their subjects. One friend of mine, herself a Puerto Rican activist, pinpointed the cause of her outrage at the film: 'All these years, she (Klein) was never bothered by my exploitation. Now, suddenly, *she* feels exploited by *my* exploitation, and it's this feeling that really upsets her.' The film never acknowledges that there might be a difference between the physical debasement of the women who earn their living in the sex industry and the ideological debasement of all women caused by the very existence of that industry. On the contrary, the anti-pornography movement has never taken up the issue of class. If it had addressed questions of class with attention or seriousness, then it might have avoided the seeming complicity with the state (like its notorious participation in the Times Square clean-up campaign, evidenced by its acceptance of office space by the forces advancing the street-sweep) that has made so many feminists wary of the anti-porn movement's real politics. Instead, the total and very apparent isolation of the film-makers from the women who populate the various sex-establishments in their film cannot help but make the viewer uneasy. Empathy? Forget it. To put it bluntly, the anti-porn campaigners seem to view the women working in the commercial sex industry much the same way that the Moral Majority seems to view pregnant teenagers. The powerful sense of identification that has been such a keystone of feminist politics is absent; in its place is a self-righteous sense of otherness that condemns the sex workers eternally to the position of Bad Object (pending, of course, any Linda-Lee-like transsubstantiation).

Also overlooked is the aboveground face of porn, its front-parlour guise as legitimate advertising. This was the first target of WAVAW (Women Against Violence Against Women) in such actions as the attack on the Rolling Stones' infamous Black and Blue billboard. The *Hustler* cover image that made the movie audience gasp (a woman churned into a meat grinder) made its feminist debut in the early WAVAW slide shows. Such actions have faded in recent years, as debate, theory and red-light-district pressure tactics took over. *Not a Love Story* alludes to the intersection of pornography and advertising, even illustrates it at points, but never explicates the connections. The anti-porn literature does the same, condemning the continuum without analysing the linkage. Hasn't anyone heard of capitalism lately? In order to use women to sell products, in order to use pornography to sell genital arousal, there has to be an economic system that makes the use profitable. Porn is just one product in the big social supermarket. Without an analysis of consumer culture, our understanding of pornography is pathetically limited, bogged down in the undifferentiated swamp of morality and womanly purity.

Significantly in these cold war times, the different attitudes of Nazi and communist societies are not cited equally. The historical usage of pornography by the Nazis (who flooded Poland with porn at the time of the invasion to render the population ... impotent?) is mentioned by Robin Morgan in the film and has been cited by others in articles and talks. No one ever mentions (with whatever reservations) the contemporary abolition of pornography in Cuba or in Nicaragua. There, it is one part of an overall social programme; here, it must be the same if it is ever to succeed in transforming our systems of sexual exchange.

The single-issue nature of the anti-porn movement is one of its most disturbing aspects. Once the 'final solution' has been identified, there is no need to flail away at other social inequities. I'd guess that its avoidance of social context is another of anti-porn's attractions. Racism, reproductive rights, homophobia all pale beside the ultimate enemy, the pornographer. How politically convenient for a right-leaning decade. It is precisely this avoidance of context, this fetishizing of one sector or one crime, that is the distinguishing feature of life under capitalism. It is also, of course, the same fetishism and fragmentation that characterize the pornographic imagination.

■ Part III. Retro politics

How can it be that I, as a feminist, even one who objects to pornography and subscribes to many of the arguments against it, can at the same time object just as strenuously to the anti-pornography movement and to the method, style, perhaps even the goals, of *Not a Love Story*? Or that many other feminists share my objections? The answer, predictably enough, is political. It has to do with the conviction that, in the fight against pornography, what gets lost is as serious as what gets won.

Behind the banner of pornography is the displaced discourse on sexuality itself. Indeed, if the anti-porn campaign offers a safety zone within which the larger anti-feminist forces abroad in eighties America need not be viewed, it also offers a corresponding zone that excludes personal sexuality. This depersonalizing of sexuality is the common effect both of pornography and of the anti-pornography forces. It is a depersonalization that is all too apparent in the film.

Only Kate Millett speaks with ease, in her own voice, and from her own experience, lounging on the floor with one of her 'erotic drawings'. It is impossible to connect the other spokeswomen personally to the texts that they talk at us. Both Susan Griffin (with, unfortunately, nature blowing in the wind behind her head) and Kathleen Barry (framed by drapes and flowers) speak abstractly, rely on the third person, and bask in an aura of solemnity that punches all of the film's religioso buttons. When Robin Morgan hits the screen, an even greater problem appears.

It is here that we realize just how much space the film has preserved for men. Not only has its debate been framed entirely in terms of heterosexuality; not only have we been forced to watch always from the seat of a male buyer; but now we are made to accept feminist wisdom from a woman in tears, reduced to crying by the contemplation of the great pain awaiting us all, and capable of consolation only by the constant massaging of a sensitive husband (in a supporting *penitente* role) and a prematurely supportive son, who flank her on the sofa as she tells of women's suffering, boyhood's innocence and men's innate desire to do right. Isn't this going too far? Middle-class respectability, appeals to motherhood and, now, elaborate detours aimed at making men feel comfortable within the cosy sphere of the enlightened. Any minute, and the film will go all 'humanistic' before our very eyes. Men didn't used to play such a central role in the feminist movement. Nor used the women to put quite such a premium on respectability and sexual politesse.

What has happened here? It has been an unsettling evolution, this switch from a movement of self-determination that trashed billboards and attacked the legitimacy of soft-core advertising, to a movement of social determination that urges legal restrictions and social hygiene. When the anti-pornography movement traded in its guerrilla actions for the more recent route of petitioning a higher authority to enact moral codes, the political trajectory went haywire. I do not agree with those who go no further than a pious citing of the First Amendment in their pornography discussions; while the vision of free speech is a benevolent one, even at times a practicable ideal, I am cynically aware of its purchase power in this society, especially in a backlash era. While I do not, therefore, agree that WAP can simply be conflated with the Moral Majority, and that's that, I do think the notion that a feminist agenda can be legislated in our society is a naive, and ultimately dangerous, one.

Judith Walkowitz, in her essay on 'The Politics of Prostitution', traced the political ramifications of the British nineteenth-century anti-prostitution campaigns, cautioning that 'the feminists lacked the cultural and political power to reshape the world according to their own image. Although they tried to set the standards for sexual conduct, they did not control the instruments of state that would ultimately enforce these norms.' Nor do we today. Nor are feminists likely to countenance any such movement to set, let alone enforce, some notion of sexual 'norms'. This proscriptive tendency in the anti-porn movement is not offset by any counterbalancing emphasis on an alternative sexual tradition (except for the elusive eroticism). Is it a coincidence that one of the film's anti-porn demonstrators could be a stand-in for Mercedes McCambridge in *Johnny Guitar*? The anti-porn movement has a tendency to promote a premature codification of sexuality, and *Not a Love Story* may suffer for that emphasis.

Perhaps the film actually arrived just one season too late in New York. The questions of sexual norms and sexual codification exploded at the 1982 Barnard conference on 'the politics of sexuality' with a coalition of WAP and others pitted against women espousing 'politically incorrect sexualities'. The conference has trailed in its wake a series of attacks and counter-attacks, a sensationalizing of the proceedings, and one of the worst movement splits of recent times. Again, my perennial question surfaces: Why pornography? Why this debate? It seems that after a long hiatus, following Ti-Grace Atkinson's polemical assertion that 'the women's movement is not a movement for sexual liberation', feminists have come back to sexuality as an issue to discuss, argue and analyse. It is not, however, clear why this debate should focus either on pornography or on sadomasochism (the two extremes at the conference), why it should short-circuit its own momentum by immediate codification.

It's time that the women's movement got back on track. While Robin Morgan weeps on the sofa, there are worse things happening in the world. It's time to acknowledge the importance of analysing pornography, assign it a priority in the overall picture, and get on with the fight. Pornography *is* an issue of importance. It is becoming much too fashionable to 'study' pornography in academic circles to dubious effect. Unlike many of the theorists doing that work, I would agree instead with Monique Wittig in 'The Straight Mind' when she stresses that, while pornography is indeed a 'discourse', it is also for women a real source of oppression. That said, however, I would suggest that women desist from putting ourselves through the study of it. Finally, here's a proper subject for the legions of feminist men: let them undertake the analysis that can tell us why men like porn (not, piously, why this or that exceptional man does *not*), why stroke books work, how oedipal formations feed the drive, and how any of it can be changed. Would that the film had included any information from average customers, instead of stressing always the exceptional figure (Linda Lee herself, Suze Randall, etc.). And the anti-porn campaigners might begin to formulate what routes could be more effective than marching outside a porn emporium.

As for the rest of us, it is time to desist, stop indulging in false and harmful polarities, and look around. Outraged at the abuse of women in our society, there are any number of struggles that can be joined on a broad social front. Outraged at pornography's being the only available discourse on sexuality, there is a great amount of visionary and ground-breaking work to do in the creation of a multitude of alternative sexual discourses, a veritable alternative culture of sexuality, that people can turn to for sexual excitement instead of porn. It's about time we redefine our terms and move on, with the spirit of justice and visionary energy that always used to characterize feminism.

As the first mass-audience film to take up the subject of pornography, *Not a Love Story* is an important work. It opens up the issues, even if it closes them down again too soon. For the people whom the film makes think seriously, for the first time, about pornography, it is a landmark. It is fascinating to hear that the audience at a recent midweek daytime screening was all single men: is it encouraging that none of them walked out? Or discouraging that they could stay? Perhaps the film sins, for all its righteousness, in being simply too little, too late, even though it's the first of its kind.

Because it can help move the political debate on to the next stage, *Not a Love Story* deserves attention. Because it shows all too clearly the stage the debate is now in, it deserves criticism.

■ Notes

This article was first published in *Village Voice*, 20 July 1982.

The article owes its existence, in part, to the encouragement and fantastic editing of Karen Durbin, my *Village Voice* editor. In addition, the article benefited from extended conversations with Fina Bathrick, Lillian Jimenez and Sande Zeig.

Notes on Contributors

Susan Ardill came to London from Australia in 1982 after working for several years at the Sydney Rape Crisis Centre, training as a nurse and working at an abortion clinic. She worked on *Spare Rib* magazine and has recently finished work as co-editor of a community radio station in London.

Beatrix Campbell is a journalist with *City Limits*, the co-operatively owned London magazine. She was co-author with Anna Coote of *Sweet Freedom* (Picador, 1982) and wrote *Wigan Pier Revisited* (Virago, 1984), winner of the Cheltenham Prize for Literature, 1984. She is currently writing a book on Conservative Party women to be published by Virago in 1987.

Wendy Clark found *The Well of Loneliness* in a small public library in a minor town in New Zealand when she was fourteen. She read *The Female Eunuch* on the way to England in 1971 and has since been active in gay liberation, left politics and the women's movement. She has been heavily involved in the setting up of the London Lesbian and Gay Centre, and since 1982 has deviated into more mainstream activities around equal opportunities training and the role of women in management organization.

Rosalind Coward lectures in Media Studies at Reading University. Her books include *Language and Materialism* (Routledge & Kegan Paul, 1977) with John Ellis; *Patriarchal Precedents* (Routledge & Kegan Paul, 1984) and *Female Desire* (Paladin, 1984).

Celia Cowie has worked as a part-time lecturer in Social Psychology at the Polytechnic of North London and Middlesex Polytechnic. She is now in retreat from the poverty of urban life and the poverty of theory in the mid eighties with its rigorous but bleak determinism. She is currently working on possibilities for transformation, believing that there are clues in humour, metaphor and madness.

Ellen DuBois teaches History and Women's Studies at the State University of New York, Buffalo. She is the author of *Feminism and Suffrage: The Emergence of an Independent Women's Movement in America 1848-1869* and a collection of the writings of Elizabeth Cady Stanton and Susan Anthony (Shocken Press). Her current work is on political feminism in the Progressive era, especially in New York City.

Deirdre English is executive director of the US magazine *Mother Jones* and co-author with Barbara Ehrenreich of *For Her Own Good: 150 Years of the Experts' Advice to Women*, as well as numerous articles on a wide range of subjects.

Linda Gordon is a professor in the History Department of the University of Wisconsin. She is author of *Woman's Body, Woman's Right: A Social History of Birth Control* (Penguin), *America's Working Women: A Documentary History* (Random House) and *Cossack Rebellions: Social Turmoil in the Sixteenth-century Ukraine* (SUNY Press).

Susan Himmelweit teaches Economics and Women's Studies at the Open University and is currently engaged in research into attitudes to new reproductive technologies. She was a founder member of the *Feminist Review* collective.

Amber Hollibaugh is a freelance writer and associate editor of *Socialist Review*. She was a co-founder of the San Francisco Lesbian and Gay History Project.

Wendy Hollway teaches Occupational Psychology at Birkbeck College, University of London. She has completed her PhD on gender difference and identity in adult heterosexual relations.

Susanne Kappeler has taught Women's Studies at Cambridge University and for the Open University, and as part of her teaching at the university of Rabat, Morocco. She is now a lecturer in English and American Studies at the University of East Anglia, where she teaches for the Women and Writing paper. She is the author of *The Pornography of Representation* (Polity Press, 1986).

Sue Lees teaches at the Women's Studies Unit at the Polytechnic of North London. The research for her article, written with Celia Cowie, has been published as a book, *Losing Out: Sexuality and Adolescent Girls* (Hutchinson, 1986).

Toril Moi is Director of the Centre for Feminist Research in the Humanities at the University of Bergen, Norway, and was formerly lecturer in French at

Pembroke College and Lady Margaret Hall, Oxford. She is the author of *Sexual/Textual Politics: Feminist Literary Theory* (Methuen, 1985) and editor of *The Kristeva Reader* (Blackwell, 1986). When not working in Norway she lives in Oxford.

Mica Nava was a member of the group responsible for the organization of the girls' project described in her article. She is now a lecturer in the Department of Cultural Studies at North East London Polytechnic, and is a member of the *Feminist Review* collective.

Sue O'Sullivan was struck by the women's movement in 1969 and hasn't got over it. She taught at Holloway Prison, London, was a member of the *Red Rag* collective and became involved in the women's health movement before joining *Spare Rib* magazine in 1979. Since then she has worked at a variety of part-time and freelance journalist, teaching and editing jobs, including work at Sheba Feminist Publishers. She is also a member of the *Feminist Review* collective.

B. Ruby Rich is the Director of the Film Program at the New York State Council on the Arts. She writes regularly for *Village Voice* and has contributed articles on film and sexuality to such publications as *Signs, Heresies, American Film* and others. Her major review essay on female sexuality in the 1980s appeared in the Fall 1986 issue of *Feminist Studies*.

Jacqueline Rose has been involved with the women's movement since 1974. She was co-author with Juliet Mitchell and the translator of *Feminine Sexuality, Jacques Lacan and the Ecole Freudienne* (Macmillan, 1982), has written for the journal *m/f,* and is the author of *The Case of Peter Pan or The Impossibility of Children's Fiction* (Macmillan, 1984) and *Sexuality in the Field of Vision* (Verso, 1986). She teaches at Sussex University.

Gayle Rubin is the author of 'The Traffic in Women: Notes on the "Political Economy" of Sex' in R. Reiter (ed) *Toward an Anthropology of Women* (1975). She has been working in San Francisco doing anthropological fieldwork in the gay male leather community.

Elizabeth Wilson has been active in the women's movement since 1970. She teaches at the Polytechnic of North London and is the author of *Women and the Welfare State* (1977), *Only Halfway to Paradise: Women in Britain 1945-68* (1980), *Mirror Writing* (Virago, 1982), *Adorned in Dreams: Fashion and Modernity* (Virago, 1985) and *Hidden Agendas: Theory, Politics and Experience in the Women's Movement* (Tavistock, 1986), with Angela Weir.

References

ADAMS, Parveen (1979) 'A Note on the Distinction between Sexual Division and Sexual Differences' *m/f* No.3.

ADAMS, Parveen, BROWN, Beverley and COWIE, Elizabeth (1981) Editorial *m/f* Nos. 5 and 6.

ADLAM, Diane (1979) 'A Case Against Capitalist Patriarchy' *m/f* No.3.

ALEXANDER, Sally and TAYLOR, Barbara (1980) 'In Defence of Patriarchy' *New Statesman*, 1 February.

ALTHUSSER, Louis (1969, 1971) 'Freud and Lacan' in *Lenin and Philosophy and Other Essays*, London: New Left Books.

ALTHUSSER, Louis (1971) 'Ideology and Ideological State Apparatuses' in *ibid*.

ANDERSON, Perry (1964) 'The Origins of the Present Crisis', *New Left Review* No.23.

ANDERSON, Perry (1966) 'Socialism and Pseudo-Empiricism', *New Left Review* No.35.

ANDERSON, Perry (1968) 'Components of the National Culture', *New Left Review* No.50.

ARDILL, Susan and NEUMARK, Norie (1982) 'Putting Sex Back into Lesbianism', *Gay Information* No. 11.

BARRETT, Michèle (1980) *Women's Oppression Today: Problems in Marxist Feminist Analysis* London: Verso and New Left Books.

BARRETT, Michèle and McINTOSH, Mary (1982) 'Narcissism and the Family: A Critique of Lasch', *New Left Review* No.135.

BARRETT, Michèle, CAMPBELL, Beatrix, PHILLIPS, Anne, WEIR, Angela and WILSON, Elizabeth (1986) 'Feminism and Class Politics: A

Round-Table Discussion' *Feminist Review* No.23 ('Out of the Blue' – a special socialist-feminist issue).

BEARD, Mary R. (1933) *America Through Women's Eyes* New York: Macmillan.

BEECHER, Marguerite and BEECHER, Willard (1971) *The Mark of Cain: An Anatomy of Jealousy* New York.

BELDEN, Jack (1970) *China Shakes the World* New York: Monthly Review Press.

BELLOS, Linda (1984) 'For Lesbian Sex, Against Sado-Masochism' in Kanter *et al* (1984).

BERG, Barbara (1978) *The Remembered Gate: Origins of American Feminism* New York: Oxford University Press.

BERGLER, Edmund and KROGER, William (1954) *Kinsey's Myth of Female Sexuality* New York: Grune & Stratton.

BORDIN, Ruth (1981) *Woman and Temperance: The Quest for Power and Liberty 1873-1900* Philadelphia: Temple University Press.

BRAKE, Mike (1980) *Youth and Youth Culture* London: Routledge & Kegan Paul.

BROWN, Beverley (1981) 'A Feminist Interest in Pornography' *m/f* Nos. 5 and 6.

BROWN, G. and HARRIS, T. (1978) *The Social Origins of Depression* London: Tavistock Press.

BROWNE, Stella (1915) 'Sexual Variety and Variability Among Women' *British Journal for the Study of Sex Psychology*.

BROWNMILLER, Susan (1975) *Against Our Will: Men, Women and Rape* New York: Simon & Schuster.

BUHLE, Mari Jo (1981) *Women and American Socialism 1870-1920* Urbana: University of Illinois Press.

BURNHAM, John (1971) 'Medical Inspection of Prostitutes in America in the Nineteenth Century: St Louis Experiment and Its Sequel' *Bulletin of the History of Medicine* Vol.45.

BURNISTON, Steve, MORT, Frank and WEEDON, Christine (1978) 'Psychoanalysis and the Cultural Acquisition of Sexuality and Subjectivity' in WOMEN'S STUDIES GROUP, CENTRE FOR CONTEMPORARY CULTURAL STUDIES (1978).

BURSTYN, Varda (1985) ed *Women Against Censorship* Vancouver and Toronto: Douglass & McIntyre.

CAMPBELL, Beatrix (1978) 'Sweets from a Stranger' *Red Rag* No.13.

CAMPBELL, Beatrix (1981) 'Feminist Sexual Politics: Now You See It, Now You Don't' *Feminist Review* No.5 (this volume).

CAMPBELL, Beatrix (1984) *Wigan Pier Revisited: Poverty and Politics in the '80s* London: Virago Press.

CAMPBELL, Beatrix and DEER, Brian (1979) 'The Pride and the Passion' *Time Out* No. 479.

CANTOR, Milton and LAURIE, Bruce (1977) editors *Class, Sex and the Woman Worker* Westport, Connecticut: Greenwood Press.

CHANDLER, Lucinda (1888) 'Marriage Reform' in *Report of the International Council of Women* Washington D.C.: R.H. Darby.

CHESSER, Eustace (1946) *Marriage and Freedom* London: Rich & Cowan.

CHESSER, Eustace (1956) *The Sexual, Marital and Family Relationships of the English Woman* London: Hutchinson.

CHESSER, Eustace (1961) *Is Chastity Outmoded?* London: Heinemann.

CHESSER, Eustace (1966) *Love Without Fear* London: Arrow Press.

CHILD, Lydia Mary (1833) 'Appeal in Favor of that Class of Americans Called Africans' in BEARD (1933).

CHODOROW, Nancy (1978) *The Reproduction of Mothering* London: University of California Press.

CLANTON, Gordon and SMITH, Lynn G. (1977) editors *Jealousy* Englewood Cliffs, New Jersey: Prentice Hall.

CLIT (1974) 'The Second Statement' in *Off Our Backs*.

COMER, Lee (1974) *Conditions of Illusion* Leeds: Feminist Books.

CONNELLY, Mark (1980) *Response to Prostitution in the Progressive Era* Chapel Hill: University of North Carolina Press.

COOK, Blanche Weisen (1977) 'Female Support Networks and Political activism' *Crysalis* Vol.5, No.3.

COOK, Blanche Weisen (1977) 'The Historical Denial of Lesbianism' *Radical History Review* Vol.5, No.20, Spring/Summer.

COOPER, David (1963) 'Freud Revisited' *New Left Review* No.20.

COOPER, David (1965) 'Two Types of Rationality' *New Left Review* No.29.

COUSINS, Mark (1978) 'Material Arguments and Feminism' *m/f* No.2.

COWIE, Elizabeth (1978) 'Woman as Sign' *m/f* No.1.

COWIE, Celia and LEES, Susan (1981) 'On the Slagheap: The Oppression of Working Class Girls' (unpublished paper).

DAHMER, Helmut (1978) 'Sexual Economy Today' *Telos* 36.

DAVIS, Kingsley (1959) *Human Society* New York: Macmillan.

DE BEAUVOIR, Simone (1953) *The Second Sex* London: Jonathan Cape.

DEGLER, Carl (1980) *At Odds: Women and the Family in America from the Revolution to the Present* New York: Oxford University Press.

DELL, Floyd (1926) *Love in Greenwich Village* New York: George H. Doran.

DELMAR, Rosalind (1975) 'Psychoanalysis and Feminism' *Red Rag* No.8.

DIAMOND, Irene (1980) 'Pornography and Repression: A Reconsideration' in *Women, Sex and Sexuality* Chicago: University of Chicago Press.

DICKINSON, Robert and BEAM, Lura (1932) *A Thousand Marriages* London: Balliere, Tindall & Cox.

DINNERSTEIN, Dorothy (1977) *The Mermaid and the Minotaur: Sexual Arrangements and Human Malaise* New York: Harper & Row.

DORR, Rheta Childe (1924) *A Woman of Fifty* New York: Funk & Wagnalls.

DUBOIS, Ellen (1981) editor *Elizabeth Cady Stanton, Susan B. Anthony: Writings, Correspondence, Speeches* New York: Shocken.

DUGGAN, Lisa (1984) 'Censorship in the Name of Feminism' *Village Voice*, 16 October.

DUGGAN, Lisa, HUNTER, Nan and VANCE, Carol (1985) 'False Promises: Feminist Anti-Pornography Legislation in the United States' in BURSTYN (1985).

DWORKIN, Andrea (1981) *Pornography: Men Possessing Women* London: The Women's Press.

DYER, Richard, KLEINHANS, Chuck, LESAGE, Julia, WAUGH, Thomas *et al* (1985) 'The Politics of Sexual Representation' (special section) *Jump Cut* No.30.

DYHOUSE, Carol (1981) *Girls Growing Up in Late Victorian and Edwardian England* London: Routledge & Kegan Paul.

ECHOLS, Alice (1984) 'The Taming of the Id: Feminist Sexual Politics 1968-83' in VANCE (1984).

EGERTON, Jayne (1983) in *Trouble and Strife* No.1.

ELLIS, Albert (1953) 'Is the Vaginal Orgasm a Myth?' *International Journal of Sexology*.

ELLIS, Havelock (1918) 'Erotic Rights of Women' *British Journal for the Study of Psychology*.

ELLIS, Havelock (1928) *Studies in the Psychology of Sex* Philadelphia: F.A. Davis & Co.

ELLIS, John (1980) 'On Pornography' *Screen*.

ENGLISH, Deirdre (1980) 'The Politics of Porn: Can Feminists Walk the Line?' *Mother Jones* April.

EPSTEIN, Barbara Leslie (1981) *The Politics of Domesticity: Women, Evangelism and Temperance in Nineteenth Century America* Middletown: Wesleyan University Press.

FADERMAN, Lillian S. (1981) *Surpassing the Love of Men: Romantic Friendship and Love Between Women from the Renaissance to the Present* New York: William Morrow.

FANON, Frantz (1965) *The Wretched of the Earth* London: MacGibbon & Kee.

FANON, Frantz (1967) *Black Skin, White Masks* New York: Grove Press.

FARRELL, Christine (1978) *My Mother Said* London: Routledge & Kegan Paul.

FEMINIST PRACTICE (1979) 'Notes from the Tenth Year' London: In Theory Press.

FENICHEL, Otto (1945) *The Psychoanalytic Theory of Neurosis* New York: W.W. Norton.

FERNALD, M.R. *et al* (1920) *A Study of Women Delinquents In New York State* New York: Century.

FIRESTONE, Shulamith (1970, 1979) *The Dialectic of Sex* London: The Women's Press.

FISHBEIN, Leslie (1980) 'Harlot or Heroine? Changing Views of Prostitution, 1870-1920' *Historian* No.43, December.

FOUCAULT, M. (1975) editor '*I-Pierre Rivière, having slaughtered my mother, my sister and my brother* ...' Harmondsworth: Penguin.

FRANCE, Marie (1984) 'Sadomasochism and Feminism' *Feminist Review* No.11.

FREEDMAN, Estele B. (1981) *Their Sisters' Keepers: Women's Prison Reform in America 1830-1930* Ann Arbor: University of Michigan Press.

FREUD, Ernst (1961) editor *Letters of Sigmund Freud 1873-1939* London: The Hogarth Press.

FREUD, Sigmund (1892-94) 'Preface and Footnotes to Charcott's *Tuesday Lectures*', *The Standard Edition of the Complete Psychological Works of Sigmund Freud* Vol.1 London: The Hogarth Press.

FREUD, Sigmund (1893-95) 'Studies on Hysteria' *Standard Edition* Vol. II; *Pelican Freud* Vol.3.

FREUD, Sigmund (1905) 'Three Essays on the Theory of Sexuality' *Standard Edition* Vol.II; *Pelican Freud* Vol.7.

FREUD, Sigmund (1911) 'Psychoanalytic Notes on an Autobiographical Account of a Case of Paranoia (Dementia Paranoides)' *Standard Edition* Vol.XII.

FREUD, Sigmund (1915) 'A Case of Paranoia Running Counter to the Psychoanalytic Theory of the Disease' *Standard Edition* Vol.XIV.

FREUD, Sigmund (1917) 'Mourning and Melancholia' *Standard Edition* Vol.XIV.

FREUD, Sigmund (1922) 'Some Neurotic Mechanisms in Jealousy, Paranoia and Homosexuality' *Standard Edition* Vol.XVIII.

FREUD, Sigmund (1924) 'The Dissolution of the Oedipus Complex' *Standard Edition* Vol.XIX; *Pelican Freud* Vol.7.

FREUD, Sigmund (1925) 'Some Psychical Consequences of the Anatomical Distinction Between the Sexes' *Standard Edition* Vol.XIX; *Pelican Freud* Vol.7.

FREUD, Sigmund (1931) 'Female Sexuality' *Standard Edition* Vol.XXI; *Pelican Freud* Vol.7.

FREUD, Sigmund (1973) *New Introductory Lectures on Psychoanalysis* Harmondsworth: Penguin.

FREUD, Sigmund (1977) *On Sexuality* Harmondsworth: Penguin.

GESELL, Arnold L. (1906) 'Jealousy' *American Journal of Psychology* Vol.17, No.4.

GIRLSLINE (1981) A Newsletter for Girls and Young Women, Spring.

GLUECK, S. and GLUECK, E.T. (1934) *Five Hundred Delinquent Women*

New York: Knopf.

GOLDMAN, Marion S. (1981) *Gold Diggers and Silver Miners: Prostitution and Social Life on the Comstock Lode* Ann Arbor: University of Michigan Press.

GORDON, Linda (1976) *Woman's Body, Woman's Right: A Social History of Birth Control in America* New York: Penguin.

GORDON, Linda (1981) 'The Politics of Sexual Harassment' *Radical America* Vol.15, No.4.

GORHAM, Deborah (1978) ' "The Maiden Tribute of Modern Babylon" Re-examined: Child Prostitution and the Idea of Childhood in Late Victorian England' *Victorian Studies* Vol.5, No.21, Spring.

GRAMSCI, Antonio (1971) *The Prison Notebooks* London: Lawrence & Wishart.

HALL, Ruth (1978) editor *Dear Dr Stopes: Sex in the 1920s* New York: Penguin.

HALL, S. and JEFFERSON, T. (1976) editors *Resistance through Ritual* London: Hutchinson.

HALLORAN, James (1970) *The Effects of Mass Communication* Television Research Committee Working Paper No.1.

HARLEY, Sharon and TERBORG-PENN, Rosalyn (1978) *The Afro-American Woman: Struggle and Images* Port Washington: Kenniket.

HARRIS, Bertha (1982) 'Sade Cases' *Village Voice* 18 May.

HENRIQUES, J., HOLLWAY, W., URWIN, C., VENN, C. and WALKERDINE, V. (1984) *Changing the Subject: Psychology, Social Regulation and Subjectivity* London: Methuen.

HERESIES (1981) 'Sex Issue' 12, Vol.3, No.4.

HERON, Liz (1980) 'The Mystique of Motherhood' *Time Out* 21 November.

HIMMELWEIT, Hilda (1960) 'Television and Radio' *Popular Culture and Personal Responsibility* London: NUT.

HINTON, William (1966) *Fanshen: A Documentary of Revolution in a Chinese Village* New York: Monthly Review Press.

HIRSCHFIELD, Magnus (1953) *Sex in Human Relations* London: John Lane.

HIRST, Paul (1981) 'Psychoanalysis and Social Relations' *m/f* Nos. 5 and 6.

HITE, Shere (1976) *The Hite Report* New York: Macmillan.

HOLLWAY, Wendy (1984) 'Women's Power in Heterosexual Sex' *Women's Studies International Forum* No.7 Vol.1.

HORNEY, Karen (1924, 1967) 'On the Genesis of the Castration Complex in Women' *Feminine Psychology* London: Routledge & Kegan Paul.

HORNEY, Karen (1926, 1967) 'The Flight from Womanhood' *Feminine Psychology* London: Routledge & Kegan Paul.

IRIGARAY, Luce (1977) *Ce Sexe qui n'en est pas un* Paris: Editions de Minuit.

IRIGARAY, Luce (1978) 'Women's Exile: Interview with Luce Irigaray' *Ideology and Consciousness* No.1.

JAMESON, Elizabeth (1977) 'Imperfect Unions: Class and Gender in Cripple Creek, 1894-1904' in CANTOR and LAURIE (1977).

JONES, Ernest (1929) 'La jalousie' *Revue Française de Psychoanalyse* Vol.3, No.2.

JONES, Ernest (1933) 'The Phallic Phase' *International Journal of Psychoanalysis* Vol.XIV, Part 1.

KALAVROS, Philip M. (1963) *Pose and Jealousy* New York.

KANTER, Hannah, LEFANU, Sarah, SHAH, Shaila and SPEDDING, Carole (1984) editors *Sweeping Statements: Writings from the Women's Liberation Movement, 1981-83* London: The Women's Press.

KAPLAN, Cora (1979) 'Radical Feminism and Literature: Rethinking Millett's *Sexual Politics' Red Letters* No.9.

KATZ, Jonathan (1976) *Gay American History* New York: Crowell.

KINSEY, Alfred (1953) *Sexual Behaviour in the Human Female* Philadelphia and London: W.B. Saunders Co.

KLEIN, Melanie (1935) 'A Contribution to the Psychogenesis of Manic-Depressive States' in KLEIN (1975).

KLEIN, Melanie (1937) 'Love, Guilt and Reparation' in KLEIN (1975).

KLEIN, Melanie (1975) *Love, Guilt and Reparation and Other Papers, 1921-1945* London: The Hogarth Press.

KOEDT, Anne (1970) 'The Myth of the Vaginal Orgasm' *Notes from the Second Year*.

KRAFFT-EBBING (1891) 'Über Eifersuchtswahn beim Manne' *Jahrbuch fur Psychiatrie*.

LACAN, Jacques (1936, 1968) 'The Mirror Phase' *New Left Review* No.51.

LAGACHE, Daniel (1947) *La Jalousie amoreuse. Psychologie descriptive et psychoanalyse* Paris: Presses Universitaires de France. (Vol.1: *Les Etats de jalousie et le problème de la conscience morbide*; Vol.II: *La jalousie vécue*.)

LAING, R.D. (1962) 'Series and Nexus in the Family' *New Left Review* No.15.

LAING, R.D. (1964) 'What is Schizophrenia?' *New Left Review* No.28.

LAMARE, Noël (1967) *La jalousie passionelle*, Paris.

LANGFELDT, Gabriel (1961) *The Erotic Jealousy Syndrome. A Clinical Study. Acta Psychiatrica et Neurologica Scandinavica*, Supplementum 151, Vol.36.

LAPLANCHE, J. and PONTALIS, J-B (1973) *The Language of Psychoanalysis* London: The Hogarth Press.

LEACH, William (1981) *True Love and Perfect Union: Feminist Reform of Sex and Society* New York: Basic Books.

LEDERER, Laura (1982) 'An Interview with a Former Pornography Model' in *Take Back The Night* New York: Bantam Books.

LEEDS REVOLUTIONARY FEMINIST GROUP (1981) *Love Your Enemy? The Debate Between Heterosexual Feminism and Political Lesbianism* London: Onlywomen Press.

LEONARD, Diana (1980) *Sex and Generation* London: Tavistock.

LERNER, Gerda (1972) editor *Black Women in White America. A Documentary History* New York: Pantheon.

LEVINE, George (1981) 'No Reservations: *The White Hotel* by D.M. Thomas' *New York Review of Books* Vol.289, No.9.

LINDSEY, Ben (1928) *The Companionate Marriage* London: Brentano's.

LIPSCHITZ, Susan (1978) ' "The Personal is Political": The Problem of Feminist Therapy' *m/f* No.2.

LYLE, SCHRAMM and PARKER, (1961) *Television in the Lives of Our Children* London: Oxford University Press.

MacCORMACK, Carol and STRATHERN, Marilyn (1980) editors *Nature, Culture and Gender* Cambridge: Cambridge University Press.

McINTOSH, Mary (1981) 'Feminism and Sexual Policy' *Critical Social Policy* No.1.

MacLAREN, Angus (1978) *Birth Control in the Nineteenth Century* London: Croom Helm.

McROBBIE, Angela (1978) 'Working Class Girls and the Culture of Femininity' in WOMEN'S STUDIES GROUP, CENTRE FOR CONTEMPORARY CULTURAL STUDIES (1978).

McROBBIE, Angela and GARBER, Jenny (1976) 'Girls and Subcultures' in HALL and JEFFERSON (1976).

MARCHETTI, Gina, 'Readings on Women and Pornography' *Jump Cut* No.26.

MARCUSE, Herbert (1970) *Eros and Civilization* London: Sphere.

MARCUSE, M. (1950) 'Zur Psychologie der Eigersucht und der Psychopathologie ihres Fehlens' *Psyche* 3.

MARTIN, Del and LYON, Phyllis (1972) *Lesbian Women* New York: Bantam Books.

MARSH, Mary (1981) *Anarchist Women, 1870-1920* Philadelphia: Temple University Press.

MASTERS, William and JOHNSON, Virginia (1966) *Human Sexual Response* London: Churchill.

MERCK, Mandy (1981) 'Pornography' *City Limits* No.6.

MITCHELL, Juliet (1970) 'Why Freud?' *Shrew* November-December.

MITCHELL, Juliet (1974) *Psychoanalysis and Feminism* London: Allen Lane.

MITCHELL, Juliet (1980) 'On the Differences Between Men and Women' *New Society* 12 June.

MITCHELL, Juliet and ROSE, Jacqueline (1983) 'Feminine Sexuality: Interview – 1982' *m/f* No.8.

MUGGERIDGE, Malcolm (1965) 'The Sexual Revolution' *New Statesman* 2 April.

MULVEY, Laura (1975) 'Visual Pleasure and Narrative Cinema' *Screen*.

NAVA, Mica (1981) 'Girls Aren't Really a Problem: so if "youth" is not a unitary category, what are the implications for youth work?' *Schooling and Culture* No.9.

NEVERDON-MORTON, Cynthia (1978) 'The Black Women's Struggle for Equality in the South, 1895-1925' in HARLEY and TERBORG-PENN (1978).

NICHOLSON, John (1980) 'The Shrinking Stereotypes of Sex' *New Society* 18-25 December.

NORTHERN WOMEN'S EDUCATION STUDY GROUP (1972) 'Sex-role Learning: A Study of Infant Readers' in WANDOR (1972).

NORTON, Jeanette (1913) 'Women Builders of Civilization' *Women's Political World* 1 September.

OAKLEY, Ann (1981) 'Interviewing Women: A Contradiction in Terms' in ROBERTS (1981).

O'NEILL, William (1971) *Everyone Was Brave: The Rise and Fall of Feminism in America* Chicago: Quadrangle.

O'NEILL, William (1973) *Divorce in the Progressive Era* New York: Franklin Watts.

PEARSON, Michael (1972) *The Age of Consent: Victorian Prostitution and its Enemies* London: David & Charles.

PIVAR, David J. (1973) *Purity Crusade: Sexual Morality and Social Control, 1868-1900* Westport, Connecticut: Greenwood Press.

PONSE, Barbara (1978) *Identities in the Lesbian World: The Social Construction of Self* Connecticut: Greenwood Press.

RÉAGE, Pauline (1954) *The Story of O* London: The Olympia Press (1970).

REED, James (1978) *From Private Vice to Public Virtue* New York: Basic Books.

REITER, Rayna M. (1975) editor *Toward an Anthropology of Women* New York: Monthly Review Press.

RIVIÈRE, Joan (1932) 'Jealousy as a Mechanism of Defence' *International Journal* Psychoanalysis Vol.13.

ROBERTS, Helen (1981) editor *Doing Feminist Research* London: Routledge & Kegan Paul.

ROBINS, David and COHEN, Philip (1978) *Knuckle Sandwich* Harmondsworth: Penguin.

ROSEN, Ruth (1977) *The Maimie Papers* London: Virago Press.

ROSENBERG, Rosalind (1982) *Beyond Separate Spheres: Intellectual Roots of Modern Feminism* New Haven Connecticut: Yale University Press.

ROWBOTHAM, Sheila, SEGAL, Lynne and WAINWRIGHT, Hilary (1979) *Beyond the Fragments* London: Merlin Press.

RUBIN, Gayle (1975) 'The Traffic in Women' in REITER (1975).

RUSSELL, Dora (1927) *The Right to be Happy* London: Routledge & Kegan Paul.

RUSTIN, Michael (1982) 'A Socialist Consideration of Kleinian Psychoanalysis' *New Left Review* No.131.

RYAN, Mary P. (1979) 'Power of Women's Networks: A Case Study of Female Moral Reform in America' *Feminist Studies* Vol.5, No.5.

SAHLI, Nancy (1979) 'Smashing Women's Friendships Before the Fall' *Crysalis* No.8.

SANDERS, Marion K. (1973) *Dorothy Thompson: A Legend in Her Own Time* Boston: Houghton Mifflin.

SAMOIS (1981) editors *Coming to Power: Writings and Graphics on Lesbian S/M* Alyson Publications.

SAUSSURE, Ferdinand de (1915, 1974) *Course in General Linguistics* London: Fontana.

SAYERS, Janet (1982) 'Psychoanalysis and Personal Politics: A Response to Elizabeth Wilson' *Feminist Review* No.10.

SCHLOSSMAN, Steven (1977) *Love and the American Delinquent* Chicago: University of Chicago Press.

SCHMIDEBERG, Melitta (1953) 'Some Aspects of Jealousy and of Feeling Hurt' *Psychoanalytic Review* Vol.40.

SCHOFIELD, Michael (1965) *The Sexual Behaviour of Young People* London: Longman.

SCHOFIELD, Michael (1973) *The Sexual Behaviour of Young Adults* Harmondsworth: Allen Lane.

SCHWARZ, Judith (1982) *Radical Feminists of Heterodoxy: Greenwich Village 1912-1940* Lebanon New Hampshire: New Victoria Publishers.

SEARS, Hal D. (1977) *The Sex Radicals: Free Love in High Victorian America* Lawrence: The Regents Press of Kansas.

SEIDENBERG, Robert (1952) 'Jealousy: The Wish' *Psychoanalytic Review* Vol.39.

SHEPHERD, Michael (1961) 'Morbid Jealousy: Some Clinical and Social Aspects of a Psychiatric Symptom' *Journal of Mental Science* Vol.107.

SHREW (1971) journal of the Women's Liberation Workshop, January.

SIGSWORTH, E.M. and WYKE, T.J. (1972) 'A Study in Victorian Prostitution and Venereal Disease' in VICINUS (1972).

SIMMONS, Christina (1979) 'Companionate Marriage and the Lesbian Threat' *Frontiers* Vol.4, No.3.

SKLAR, Kathryn Kish (1973) *Catherine Beecher: A Study in American Domesticity* New Haven Connecticut: Yale University Press.

SMART, B. and SMART, C. (1978) editors *Women, Sexuality and Social Control* London: Routledge & Kegan Paul.

SMITH, Leslie Shacklady (1978) 'Sexist Assumptions and Female Delinquency: An Empirical Investigation' in SMART and SMART (1978).

SMITH ROSENBERG, Carol (1971) 'Beauty, the Beast and the Militant Woman: A Case Study in Sex Roles and Social Stress in Jacksonian America' *American Quarterly* Vol.5, No.23.

SMITH ROSENBERG, Carol (1975) 'The Female World of Love and Ritual: Relations Between Women in Nineteenth Century America' *Signs* Vol.5, No.1.

SMITH, Barbara (1983) editor *Home Girls, A Black Feminist Anthology* New York Kitchen Table Press.

SNITOW, Ann (1979) 'Mass Market Romance: Pornography for Women is Different' *Radical History Review* No.20.

SNITOW, Ann (1985) 'Retrenchment vs. Transformation: The Politics of the Anti-Porn Movement' in BURSTYN (1985).

SNITOW, Ann, STANSELL, Christine and THOMPSON, Sharon (1983) *Desire: The Politics of Sexuality* London: Virago Press.

SOKOLOFF, Boris (1947) *Jealousy. A Psychological Study* London: Caroll & Nicholson.

STANTON, Elizabeth C. (1860) 'Speech to the Anniversary of the American Anti-Slavery Society' in DUBOIS (1981).

STANTON, Elizabeth C. (1869) 'Speech to the McFarland-Richardson Protest Meeting' in DUBOIS (1981).

STEELE, Lisa (1982) 'Pornography and Eroticism' (an interview with Varda Burstyn) *Fuse* magazine May-June.

STOCKHAM, Alice (1897) *Karezza: Ethics of Marriage* Chicago: Alice B. Stockham.

STOEHR, Taylor (1979) *Free Love in America: A Documentary History* New York: AMS Press.

STONE, Hannah and STONE, Abraham (1952) *A Marriage Manual* London: Gollancz.

SULLOWAY, Frank J. (1979) *Freud, Biologist of the Mind* London: Burnett Books.

TAYLOR, Barbara (1983) *Eve and the New Jerusalem* London: Virago Press.

THOMAS, D.M. (1981) *The White Hotel* London: Penguin.

THOMAS, D.M. (1982) 'Different Voices' *London Magazine* Vol.21, no.11.

THOMAS, William (1923) *The Unadjusted Girl* Boston: Little, Brown.

THOMPSON, E.P. (1965) 'The Peculiarities of the English' *Socialist Register*.

VANCE, Carol (1984) editor *Pleasure and Danger: Exploring Female Sexuality* London: Routledge & Kegan Paul.

VAN DE VELDE, Thomas (1928) *Ideal Marriage* London: Heinemann.

VAUHKONEN, Kauko (1968) *On the Pathogenesis of Morbid Jealousy.* *Acta Psychiatrica Scandinavica* Supplementum No.202.

VEITH, Ilza (1965, 1970) *Hysteria, the History of a Disease* London: University of Chicago Press.

VICINUS, Martha (1972) editor *Suffer and Be Still* Bloomington: Indiana University Press.

WALKOWITZ, Judith R. (1983) 'Male Vice and Female Virtue: Feminism and the Politics of Prostitution in Nineteenth Century Britain' *History Workshop Journal* No.13; also in SNITOW, STANSELL and THOMPSON (1983).

WALKOWITZ, Judith R. (1980) *Prostitution and Victorian Society: Women, Class and the State* London: Cambridge University Press.

WANDOR, Michelene (1972) editor *The Body Politic* London: Stage 1.

WANDOR, Michelene (1980) editor *Strike While the Iron is Hot* London: Journeyman Press.

WARE, Caroline (1935) *Greenwich Village 1920-1930* Boston: Houghton Mifflin.

WEEKS, Jeffrey (1981) *Sex, Politics and Society: The Regulation of Sexuality Since 1808* London: Longmans.

WEEKS, Jeffrey (1985) *Sexuality and its Discontents: Meanings, Myths and Modern Sexuality* London: Routledge & Kegan Paul.

WELDON, Fay (1975) *Female Friends* London: William Heinemann.

WESTERMARCK, Edvard (1901) *The History of Human Marriage* London: Macmillan.

WHITING, Pat (1972) 'Female Sexuality: Its Political Implications' in WANDOR (1972).

WILLIAMS, Bernard (1983) 'Pornography and Feminism' *London Review of Books* Vol.15, No.5.

WILLIS, Ellen (1981) 'Feminism, Moralism and Pornography' in *Beginning to See the Light* New York: Knopf.

WILLIS, Paul (1977) *Learning to Labour* London: Saxon House.

WILMOTT, R. and YOUNG, M. (1976) *The Symmetrical Family* Harmondsworth: Penguin.

WILSON, Deirdre (1978) 'Sexual Codes and Conduct' in SMART and SMART (1978).

WILSON, Elizabeth (1980) *Only Halfway to Paradise* London: Tavistock.

WILSON, Elizabeth (1981) 'Psychoanalysis: Psychic Law and Order' *Feminist Review* No.8 (and this volume).

WILSON, Elizabeth (1982a) 'Psychoanalysis and Feminism, Re-opening the Case', opening seminar presentation, London.

WILSON, Elizabeth (1982b) *Mirror Writing* London: Virago Press.

WILSON, Elizabeth and WEIR, Angela (1984) 'The British Women's Movement' *New Left Review* No.148.

WIMPERIS, Virginia (1960) *The Unmarried Mother and Her Child* London: George Allen & Co.

WINSHIP, Janice (1985) ' "A Girl Needs to Get Street-wise": Magazines for the 1980s' *Feminist Review* No.21.

WITTIG, Monique (1980) 'The Straight Mind' *Feminist Issues* Vol.1, No.1.

WOLLHEIM, Richard (1971) *Freud* London: Fontana.

WOMEN'S STUDIES GROUP, CENTRE FOR CONTEMPORARY CULTURAL STUDIES (1978) *Women Take Issue* London: Hutchinson.

WOMEN'S THEATRE GROUP (1980) 'My Mother Says I Never Should' in WANDOR (1980).

WOMEN'S THERAPY CENTRE STUDY GROUP (1979) 'Letter in Reply to Susan Lipschitz' *m/f* No.3.

WOODHULL, Victoria C. (1874) *Tried as by Fire or The True and the False Socially: An Oration* New York: Woodhull & Claflin.

WRIGHT, Helena (1947) *More About the Sex Factor in Marriage* London: Williams & Northgate.

ZARETSKY, Eli (1980) 'Female Sexuality and the Catholic Confessional' *Signs* Vol.6, No.1.

ZIMAN, Edmund (1949) *Jealousy in Children. A Guide for Parents* New York.

Index

abortion, 11, 98-102
Adlam, Diane, 121
adolescent sexuality, 245-75
advertising, 9, 132, 318, 321, 324, 350
Advertising Standards Authority, 321
Africa, 241-2
aggression, jealousy and, 147-51, 152; *see also* violence against women
Algeria, 42, 45, 46, 47
Althusser, Louis, 3-4, 33, 165, 166, 175, 181, 187
anal sex, 78
Anderson, Perry, 180, 181
'Angry Women', 8
anti-semitism, 285, 295, 297, 362
Ardill, Susan, 13, *277-304*, 355
art: attitudes to, 326-7; pornography and, 357-8
Asian women, 220, 239
Atkinson, Ti-Grace, 353
Atwood, Margaret, 342
Australia, 288

Babi Yar massacre, 14, 330, 334-8

Bailey, Crystal, 288
Barnard conference (1982), 352-3
Barrett, Michèle, 173, 183, 196-7
Barry, Kathleen, 342, 351
Barthes, Roland, 332
battered women, 6, 7, 358, 359, 361
Baudelaire, Charles, 357
BBC, 56
Beam, L., 24
Beauvoir, Simone de, 23, 25, 37
Bergler, Edmund, 30
Berlin, 297
Bethnal Green, 118
Beveridge Report, 169
biologism, 12, 15, 165, 167, 206
Bird, 51-2
Birmingham, 105, 117
birth control, 25, 92, 111-12, 188
bisexuality, 162-4, 166, 219-20, 283
Black Lesbian Group (BLG), 219, 220, 241
Black lesbianism, 13, 216-44, 290
Black movement, 45, 47, 85, 225, 228-35, 237-8

'Blue Sky', 342, 344
Booker Prize, 328
Bow Marriage Education Centre, 25
Brake, Mike, 120
Bristol, 118
British Medical Association, 29
Brittain, Vera, 24
Brixton, 228, 232, 233, 234
Brown, G., 119
Browne, Stella, 24
Brownmiller, Susan, 70
Bryant, Anita, 80
Bryant, Louise, 93
Burniston, Steve, 159, 165, 168

California, 360
Campbell, Beatrix, 10, *19-39*, 355
Canada, 341, 343
capitalism, 99-102, 168, 234-5, 237, 360-1
Cardiff, 115
Caribbean, 241
Carmen, *216-44*
castration threat, 160-1
Caudwell, Christopher, 181
celibacy, 31-2
censorship, 8, 9, 327-8, 340-1
Chadwin, 127
Chance, Janet, 25
Charcot, Jean Martin, 189, 193
Cheltenham Prize, 328
Chesser, Dr Eustace, 26, 27, 29
children: lesbians and, 244; and the preoedipal mother, 140-3; sexual abuse, 7, 308
Chile, 241
China, 42, 45, 47-9
China Shakes the World, 48-9
Chodorow, Nancy, 183, 184, 197
Clark, Ramsey, 365
Clark, Wendy, 5, 12-13, *201-15*, 283, 293, 355
CLIT, 284
clitoris, 161; denial of, 25, 26; in Freud's theory of sexuality, 164-5; role of, 26-31
clothing: dress codes, 283, 295, 297; lesbian, 210-11; slags, 108-9
co-counselling, 178
codes: dress, 283, 295, 297; pornography, 14, 310-21, 323-4

coitus interruptus, 26
Coming to Power, 287, 288
Committee on Obscenity and Film Censorship, 327, 329
communism, and pornography, 350; *see also* Marxism
'companionate love', 26
consciousness-raising, 10, 33-4, 35, 39, 42, 46, 59
consent, age of, 90
Conservative Party, 9, 157
Contagious Diseases Acts, 188, 189
contraception, 25, 92, 111-12, 188
Cooper, David, 181
Corrie Abortion Bill, 11, 98, 99
Cosmopolitan, 60, 211, 246
Cousins, Mark, 121-2
Coward, Rosalind, 5, 14, *307-25*, 355
Cowie, Celia, 11, 13, *105-22*, 355
crime passionel, 147, 151
Cuba, 350

Darwin, Charles, 135, 136, 164
Davis, Kingsley, 137, 152
death: association with pornography, 319, 320; in *The White Hotel*, 336-7
DeBell, Diane, 326
delinquency, sexual, 90
Delmar, Rosalind, 173
depression, 12, 119, 141-3, 145-6
Dichter, Ernest, 54
Dickinson, R.L., 24, 29
differentiation, sexual, 11, 111, 120-2, 143-7
Dinnerstein, Dorothy, 146-7
divorce, 19th-century, 92
'double standard', 88, 90
drags, 111
dress codes, 283, 295, 297
DuBois, Ellen, 11, *82-97*, 356
Dworkin, Andrea, 8, 70, 71, 308, 326, 340, 341
Dyhouse, Carol, 188

East Anglia, University of, 326
Eastern Eye, 220-1
Eastman, Crystal, 93
Ego, 159-60, 186-7
ejaculation, premature, 26
Ellis, Albert, 30
Ellis, Havelock, 26, 27

Empire of the Senses, 328
employment, Black lesbians, 221-3
Engels, Friedrich, 166
English, Deirdre, 5, *63-81*, 356
eroticism, 34, 346-7
Evening Standard, 56

FACT (Feminist Anti-Censorship Task Force), 341
family, 174; and Black lesbianism, 216-17; family therapy, 7; nuclear, 168-9
Fanon, Frantz, 42, 44, 45, 46, 47
Fanshen, 47
fascism, 293-4, 295, 297-8, 300
Fellini, Federico, 327, 328
feminist therapy, 178
Fenichel, Otto, 144, 150-1
Fiji, 137
films: *Not A Love Story*, 340-54; pornographic, 327-8
Firestone, Shulamith, 195
First World War, 24
Flaubert, Gustave, 357
Flynn, Elizabeth Gurley, 93
Flynt, Larry, 366
foreplay, 22
fragmentation, pornography, 318-19, 321
France, 45, 89, 189, 328
free love movement, 11, 26, 91-2
Freud, Anna, 179
Freud, Sigmund, 12, 15, 158, 169, 170, 173, 180, 189; attitude to homosexuality, 172; criticism of, 185-6, 194-6; on depression, 142; feminist debate over, 177, 179, 181-2; on psychic illness, 185; theory of jealousy, 139-40, 144, 147, 151; theory of sexuality, 159-67, 178, 184-5; treatment of hysteria, 189-93; in *The White Hotel*, 330, 333, 334-7
frigidity, 22, 23-4, 26, 30
functionalism, 183

Gail, *216-44*
gay liberation, 38, 205, 213, 238
Gay Liberation Front (GLF), 217
Gay News, 253
gay pornography, 75, 76
Gays the Word, 282

gender difference, 5-6, 12, 106, 110-11, 120-2
Germany, 297, 362
Gesell, Arnold L., 135-6, 138, 148
girls' projects, 245-75
Gold Flower's Story, 48-9
Goldman, Emma, 11, 93
Gollancz, Victor, 328
Gordon, Linda, 11, *82-97*, 356
Gramsci, Antonio, 34
Grapevine, 253
Greater London Council (GLC), 9, 245, 282, 298; women's committee, 223
Griffin, Susan, 342, 345, 346, 351

Hamer, Diane, 277
harassment, sexual, 94, 308
Harlequin Romances, 73-4
Harris, T., 119
Havers, Sir Michael, 125, 128-31
Henaut, Dorothy Todd, 341, 348
Henderson, Anne, 341
Heresies, 203
Heron, Liz, 171
heterosexuality: and lesbianism, 67-70; patriarchal, 19; psychoanalysis and, 172; sexual politics, 19-23
Himmelweit, Susan, 11, *98-102*, 356
Hirschfeld, Dr Magnus, 24
history, and psychoanalysis, 187-94
Hollibaugh, Amber, 5, *63-81*, 356
Hollway, Wendy, 11, *123-33*, 356
Hollywood, 360
holocaust, 333
homosexuality, 205; and jealousy, 144, 147, 149-51; psychoanalysis and, 172; *see also* lesbianism
Horney, Karen, 185, 194, 196
hospitals, 188-9
House of Commons, 9
Hustler, 74, 76, 77, 342, 350
hysteria, 188, 189-93, 196

Id, 159-60
Ideal Home Exhibition, 42, 54-5
ILEA, 105, 245
illness, psychic, 185
immigration, 224
in-vitro fertilization, 98
incest, 6, 7, 236
Incest Survivors' groups, 6

Indecent Displays Bill, 9
India, 241, 242
Indianapolis, 8, 340
infertility, 98
International Socialists, 53-4
International Women's Day, 36
Irigaray, Luce, 150, 196
Irish Relatives Action Committee, 224
Is Dennis Really a Menace, 248-50, 251-2, 266
Islington survey, 105-22

jealousy, 12, 134-53
Jews, 362
Johnny Guitar, 352
Jones, Ernest, 184, 185, 194
Jones, Jane, 349
The Joy of Lesbian Sex, 286
Jung, C.G., 333
Just Seventeen, 246

Kaplan, Cora, 168
Kappeler, Susanne, 14, *326-39*, 356
Kinsey Report, 21, 27, 28, 29, 30
Klein, Bonnie, 341-6
Klein, Melanie, 140-3, 179, 180, 182, 185, 349
Koedt, Anne, 29
Krassner, Paul, 365
Kristevan psychoanalysis, 134
Ku Klux Klan, 26
Kuznetsov, 330, 338

Labour Party, 60, 286, 294
Lacan, Jacques, 12, 159, 165, 166, 170, 175, 181, 186-7, 193-4, 196
Lacanian psychoanalysis, 134, 172, 173
Lagache, Daniel, 148, 149, 151
Laing, R.D., 181
Lamare, Noël, 138
Langfeldt, Gabriel, 137-8
language *see* linguistics
Lasch, Christopher, 196-7
Leavis, F.R., 182
Lederer, Laura, 349
Leeds Revolutionary Feminist Group, 37, 284, 285, 291, 296
Lees, Sue, 11, 13, *105-22*, 356
legislation: anti-pornography, 8, 340; anti-sexist, 323-4
Lenin, 66
Leonard, Diana, 114-15, 119

Lesbian Co-ordinating Committee, 290
Lesbian Feminists for the Centre, 292, 294
Lesbian Left, 286
Lesbian Sex Conference (1983), 289
Lesbian Strength March (1984), 290, 298
Lesbian Women, 210
lesbianism, 4-5, 12-13; active/passive in, 209; Black lesbianism, 13, 216-44, 290; definitions, 205-6; erotica, 34; girls' projects, 245-75; and heterosexuality, 67-70; identity, 207-8, 212; political lesbianism, 289; psychoanalysis and, 12, 172; radical feminism, 36-8; role play, 210-11; sadomasochism, 5, 13, 277-304; sexual politics, 19-21, 36-8; and the women's liberation movement, 204-7, 211-13, 214
Lesbians Against Sadomasochism (LASM), 285, 291, 292-9, 300-2
Levi-Strauss, Claude, 183
Levine, George, 332-7, 338
liberalism, 323
Lindsay, Ben E., 26
linguistics, 310-11; in Lacanian psychoanalysis, 193-4; structuralism, 166
literature: pornography and, 14, 326-39; romantic, 73-4
Liverpool, 118
lock hospitals, 188-9
London, 118
London Lesbian and Gay Centre (LLGC), 13, 278, 280-3, 285, 290-91, 302, 304
London Magazine, 328
London Transport, 9
London Women's Liberation Newsletter, 290
London Women's Liberation Workshop, 284
love, 111, 112, 117
'Love Your Enemy', 228

McCambridge, Mercedes, 352
MacCulloch, Dr, 126, 127
McIntosh, Mary, 196-7
MacKinnon, Catharine, 8, 340, 341
McRobbie, Angela, 105, 111-12, 117, 120, 121, 122

madness, the 'Yorkshire Ripper' trial, 126-7
Malthusianism, 188
Manushi, 241, 242
Maoism, 36, 41, 44, 46, 53
Marcuse, Herbert, 33
Marcuse, M., 148
marriage: divorce, 92; Islington survey, 112-19; jealousy in, 136-7; 19th-century, 86, 88; rape in, 361; violence in, 114
Marx, Karl, 158, 241
Marxism, 3, 33, 66, 158, 169, 170, 180-4, 193-4, 196, 197
Masters and Johnson, 21, 30, 31, 32
masturbation, 22, 30, 72, 160
Meese, Edward, 340
Millett, Kate, 168, 342, 346, 351
Milne, Dr, 127-8, 130
Minneapolis, 8
Miss World demonstrations, 10, 42, 55-7
Mitchell, Juliet, 12, 162, 165-9, 172, 177, 178, 181-3, 195, 196
Moi, Toril, 12, *134-53*, 356-7
Moral Majority, 14, 350, 352
Moral Right, 297
Morgan, Robin, 342, 350, 351-2, 353
Morley, Eric, 56
Mort, Frank, 159, 165, 168
Mother Jones, 70
motherhood: and jealousy, 140-3, 150-1, 152; lesbian, 244; 19th-century, 86-7, 92; and the Oedipus complex, 143-4, 160-1
Muggeridge, Malcolm, 32
murder: and jealousy, 147-51; the 'Yorkshire Ripper' trial, 123- 33

narcissism, 196-7
National Film Board of Canada, 345-6
National Front, 256
National Health Service, 98
National Lawyers Guild, 80
National Organization for Women (NOW), 80
National Women's Liberation Conference (1974), 4
Nava, Mica, 13, *245-76*, 357
Nazis, 14, 297, 333, 350
Neena, *216-44*
New Left Review, 181

New York, 341, 343
New York Review of Books, 332
New York Times, 341
News of the World, 53
Nicaragua, 350
North London Lesbian Mothers Group, 293-4
Not A Love Story, 14-15, 340-54
nuclear family, 168-9

Oakley, Ann, 272
object relations theory, 183
obscenity trials, 329
Oedipus complex, 143-4, 160-1, 167, 170, 171, 175
Off Our Backs, 36
Ognall, 127-8
On Our Backs, 288
Organization of Women of African and Asian Descent (OWAAD), 218- 19, 239
orgasm, 24-32, 87-8
Oshima, 328
O'Sullivan, Sue, 3, 10, 13, *40-62*, 58, *277-304*, 357

paedophilia, 283, 287, 301
paranoia, 12, 140-3, 147, 150, 151
Parents' Enquiry, 252-3
Paris, 328
Parsons, Talcott, 168
Pasolini, Pier Paolo, 328
patriarchy, 19, 121-2, 235-6; disintegration of, 168; jealousy, 136-7, 147; psychoanalysis and, 183-5
Penguin, 328
penis: penis-envy, 3, 161-2; as symbol of power, 166, 170, 173
Penthouse, 74
permissiveness, 21, 31-2, 33
Phallus, 166, 170, 173
Phillips, Anne, 158
photography, pornography, 310, 311-14
Picador, 328
Pitchford, Kenneth, 342
Pizzey, Erin, 60-1
Poland, 350
Police Bill, 240
'political lesbianism', 19, 36-9, 289
pornography, 14, 70-5, 95; anti-porn movement, 7-9, 10, 340-1, 346-54; anti-sexist legislation, 323-4; codes

of representation, 14, 310-21, 323-4; definition, 75-8; literary, 14, 326-39; *Not A Love Story*, 14-15, 340-54; politics of, 78-81; sado-masochistic, 76, 77; *The White Hotel*, 14, 327, 328-39; and violence against women, 5, 307-9, 317, 320-1, 347-8

Poster Workshop, 50

pregnancy, 25

premature ejaculation, 26

production, 99-102

promiscuity, 107-8, 287

prostitution: 19th-century, 84-7, 89-91, 188-9, 352; the 'Yorkshire Ripper' trial, 123-33

psyche, utopianism of, 196-8

psychic illness, 185

psychoanalysis, 4, 12, 27, 157-75, 177-98; Freud's theory of sexuality, 159-67, 178; and history, 187-94; jealousy, 12, 139- 53; Juliet Mitchell's work, 165-9; and lesbianism, 12, 172; political consequences of, 169-73, 178; the unconscious, 189-96; utopianism of the psyche, 196-8

racism, 221-3, 226, 227, 236, 240, 285, 290, 295, 297, 300, 303, 323

radical feminism, 10, 22-3, 35-8, 41, 224-5, 236-7

Randall, Suze, 342-3, 345, 353

rape, 84, 94-5, 236, 316; pornography and, 5, 70-1, 308

Rape Crisis, 6

'Ravers', 342

Read, Piers Paul, 126

Reagan, Ronald, 340

Reagon, Bearnice, 238-9

Reich, Wilhelm, 33, 44, 45

religion, 19th-century, 87

reproduction, 99-102

revenge, sexual, 128-9

Revolutionary and Radical Feminist Newsletter, 288-9

revolutionary feminism, 284-6, 291, 294

Rich, B. Ruby, 14, *340-54*, 357

Rivière, Joan, 145

role play, lesbian, 210-11

Rolling Stones, 350

romantic love, 111, 112, 117

romantic novels, 73-4

Rose, Jacqueline, 12, 157, *177-98*, 357

Rubin, Gayle, 5, *63-81*, 183, 357

Russell, Bertrand, 24

Russell, Dora, 24, 25

Rustin, Michael, 182

Rytka, Helen, 128

Sadista Sisters, 292

'Sado-Masochism' – the Reality', 297

sadomasochism, 5, 13, 76, 77, 277-304

Salo, 328

Salpetrière Clinic, Paris, 189

SAMOIS, 10, 287

Sanders, Helke, 52-3

Sanger, Margaret, 11, 92, 93

Saussure, Ferdinand de, 194

Sayers, Janet, 177, 183-4, 185, 196

Scott, Norman, 31

Second World War, 168-9

separation, 22

Sex Heresies, 286-7, 288

Sexual Fringe, 292, 294, 296, 297-8, 299, 300

sexual harassment, 94, 308

sexual politics, 19-23, 32, 33-9, 40-61

sexual reform movement, 23-32

Sexual Reform Congress (1929), 25

Shaw, Bernard, 24

Short, Clare, 9

Shrew, 49-50, 53

sisterhood, 2, 4, 35, 59, 280

Sisterwrite, 203, 288

Sixth Demand, 36

slags, Islington survey, 107-12, 121, 122

slavery, Black, 85

Smith, Barbara, 238-9

Smith, Leslie Shacklady, 107

social purity movement, 11, 88-92, 94-5

socialism, 182, 234-7, 238, 324

socialist-feminism, 3, 22, 35, 41, 100, 2862, 302-3

Socialist Women, 53-4

Sokoloff, Boris, 149

Southall Black Sisters, 228, 234

Soviet Union, 48

Spare Rib, 202, 266, 284, 285

Square Peg, 288

Stanton, Elizabeth Cady, 91, 92

Stockham, Alice, 91

Stone, Abraham, 25, 27
Stone, Hannah, 25, 27
Stopes, Marie, 24, 26
Storr, Anthony, 126, 129
structural linguistics, 166
submission, pornography, 318, 319-21
suicide, 149
Sulloway, Frank, 164, 165
Sunday Times, 60
Sutcliffe, Peter, 1 11, 123-33
Sutcliffe, Sonia, 129-30, 132

Take Back the Night, 349
Tamara, *216-44*
temperance campaign, 86
Thatcher, Margaret, 157
Third World, 239, 241
Thomas, D.M., *The White Hotel*, 14, 327, 328-39
Thorpe, Jeremy, 31
The Times, 56, 58
Tindlemanor, 298
Tory Party, 9, 157
Tracey, Linda Lee, 342-3, 345, 346, 347, 349, 350, 353
transsexuals, 283, 301
Trotskyists, 41
Trouble and Strife, 225

unconscious, 12, 184, 186-7, 188, 189-96, 197
unemployment, 119
Union of Women for Liberation, 53-4
United States of America, 13, 328; attacks on prostitution, 90; Black lesbianism, 238-9, 241; CLIT statement, 284; liberation movements, 45, 47; 19th-century feminism, 90, 92; pornography, 8, 10, 307, 340-1; sadomasochism, 5, 290; *Sex Heresies*, 286-7
US Supreme Court, 340
utopianism, 11, 91, 196-8

vagina, orgasm, 27, 28-9, 30
Van de Velde, Thomas, 26-7
Vauhkonen Kauko, 138, 145, 146, 148, 149
venereal disease, 86, 89, 188
Vietnam War, 44, 45

Village Voice, 203, 341, 354
violence against women, 236; against lesbians, 257-8, 263; battered women, 6, 7; campaigns against, 5, 6-7; domestic, 86, 114; jealousy and, 147-51; pornography, 70-81, 307-9, 317, 320-1, 347-8; rape, 70-1, 94-5; the 'Yorkshire Ripper' trial, 123-33
Virgin Mary, 131-2
visual images, pornography, 310, 311-14
Vogue, 76, 211

Wages for Housework, 60, 101
Walkowitz, Judith, 188, 352
WAVPM, 76, 77
Weedon, Christine, 159, 165, 168
Weir, Angela, 177
Weldon, Fay, 150
Wells, David, 342
Westermarck, Edward, 136-7
'What Is This Big Fuss About Sado-Masochism?', 296-7
What Price Miss World?, 55-6
Whitaker, Josephine, 128, 131
White, James, 99
The White Hotel (Thomas), 14, 327, 328-39
'Who Are the Real Fascists?', 298
Why Miss World, 56-8
widows, 136-7
Willard, Frances, 90-1
Williams, Bernard, 327, 329
Williams, Shirley, 61
Willis, Paul, 107, 108, 115
Wilmott, R., 118
Wilson, Deirdre, 111
Wilson, Elizabeth, 12, 14, 31, *157-76*, 177, 185, 357
Wires, 37
Wittig, Monique, 353
Wollheim, Richard, 164, 165
Wolverhampton, 118
'The Woman-Identified Woman', 67
A Woman's Place, 283
Women Against Pornography (WAP), 76, 340, 347, 348, 349, 352-3
Women Against Violence Against Women (WAVAW), 7-8, 59, 285, 286, 350
Women's Aid, 6, 174

Women's Christian Temperance Union, 88

Women's Liberation Front, 53

Women's Liberation Movement (WLM), 36-7, 225, 228, 278-9, 283, 284, 286, 289, 303

Women's Liberation Workshop, 36, 50-6

Women's Liberation Workshop Manifesto, 50

Women's Therapy Centre, 172-3

Woodhull, Victoria, 91

World League for Sexual Reform, 24

Worthing, 118

Wright, Dr Helena, 28-9

'Yorkshire Ripper', 11, 123-33

Young, M., 118

youth culture, 120-1

youth work, 245-75

Zionism, 285